RASL

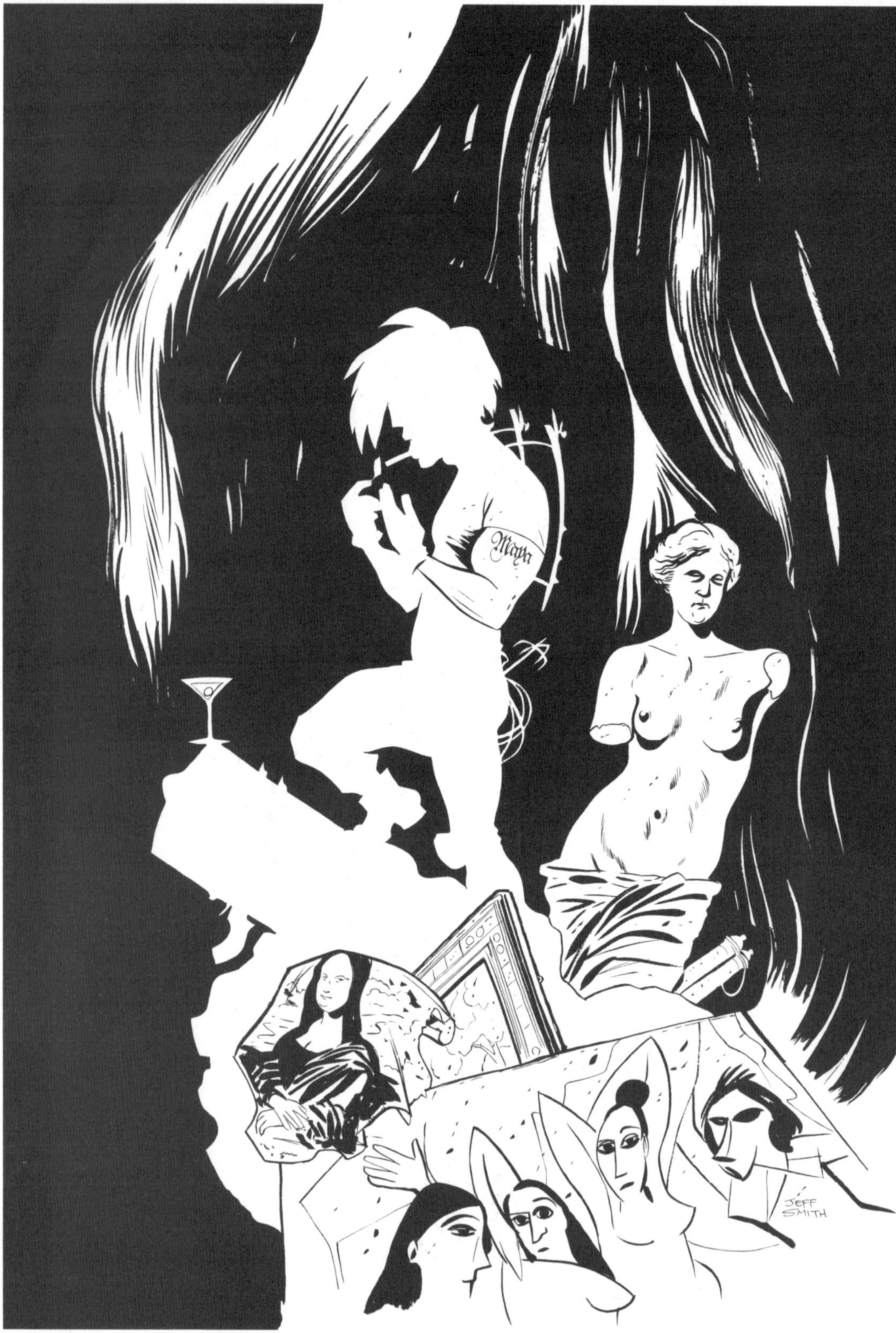
Maya
JEFF SMITH

RASL

POCKET BOOK ONE

BY
JEFF SMITH

MUSKEGO PUBLIC LIBRARY

CARTOON BOOKS
COLUMBUS, OHIO

MUSKEGO PUBLIC LIBRARY

4000203651

THIS BOOK IS DEDICATED TO
JENNIFER GWYNNE OLIVER

RASL POCKET BOOK ONE

COPYRIGHT © 2010 BY JEFF SMITH

THE CHAPTERS IN THIS BOOK WERE ORIGINALLY PUBLISHED IN THE COMIC BOOK RASL
RASL™ IS © 2010 BY JEFF SMITH.

ALL RIGHTS RESERVED. PUBLISHED BY CARTOON BOOKS.
RASL, CARTOON BOOKS, AND ASSOCIATED LOGOS ARE TRADEMARKS AND/OR REGISTERED TRADEMARKS OF JEFF SMITH

FOR CARTOON BOOKS:
COVER ART BY JEFF SMITH
PUBLISHED BY VIJAYA IYER
PRODUCTION MANAGER: KATHLEEN GLOSAN
COVER COLOR & LOGO/DESIGN BY STEVE HAMAKER
PREPRESS/DESIGN: TOM GAADT

FOR INFORMATION WRITE:
CARTOON BOOKS
P.O. BOX 16973
COLUMBUS, OH 43216

SOFTCOVER ISBN-10: 1-888963-24-7
SOFTCOVER ISBN-13: 978-1-888963-24-3

10 9 8 7 6 5 4 3 2 1

PRINTED IN CANADA

PART 1
RASL AND THE DRIFT

"Throughout space there is energy. Is this energy static or kinetic?
If static, our hopes are in vain; if kinetic – and we know it is, for certain – then it is a mere question of time
when men will succeed in attaching their machinery to the very wheelwork of nature."

-Nikola Tesla

1.
THE DRIFT

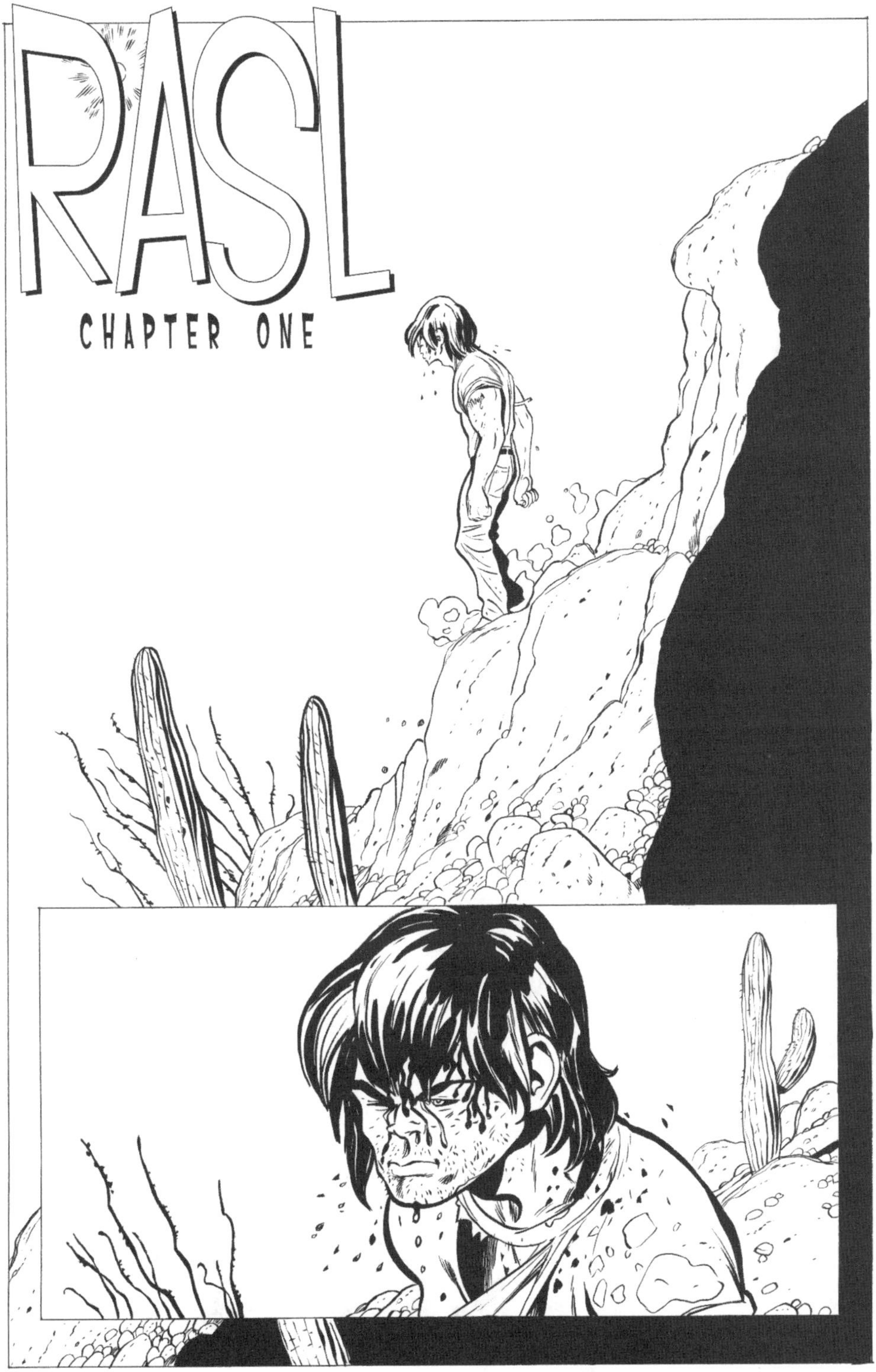
RASL
CHAPTER ONE

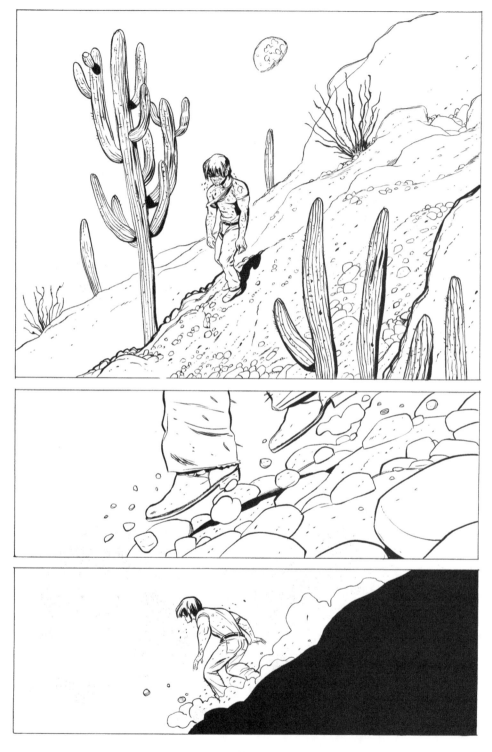

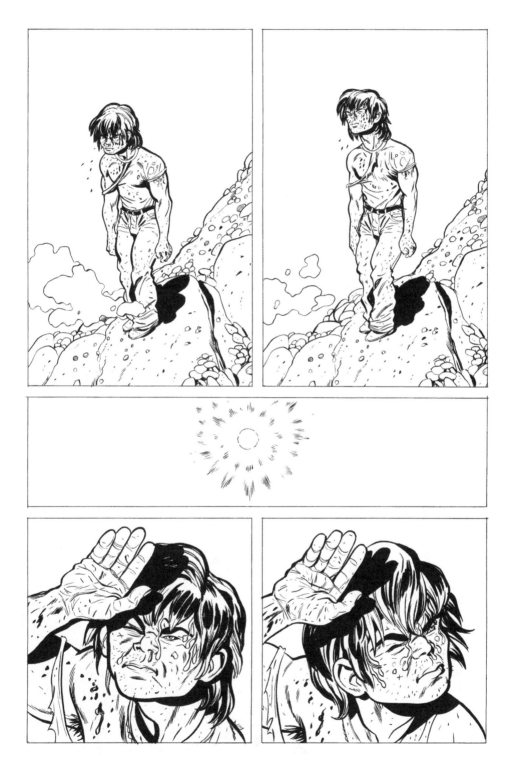

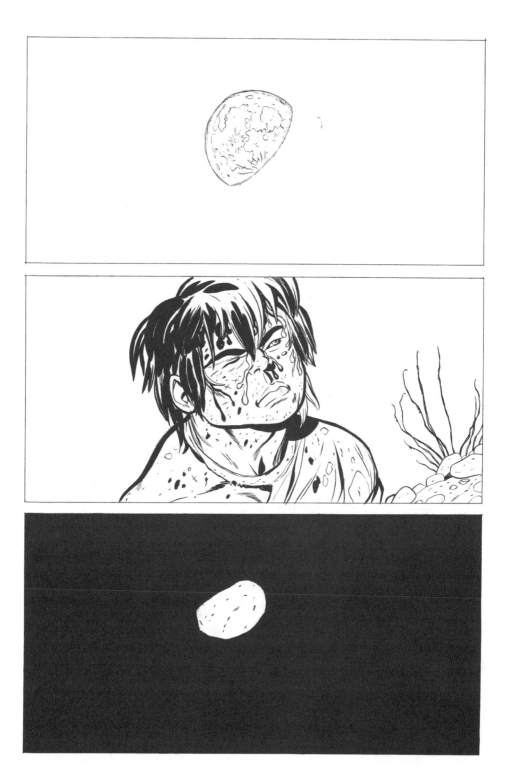

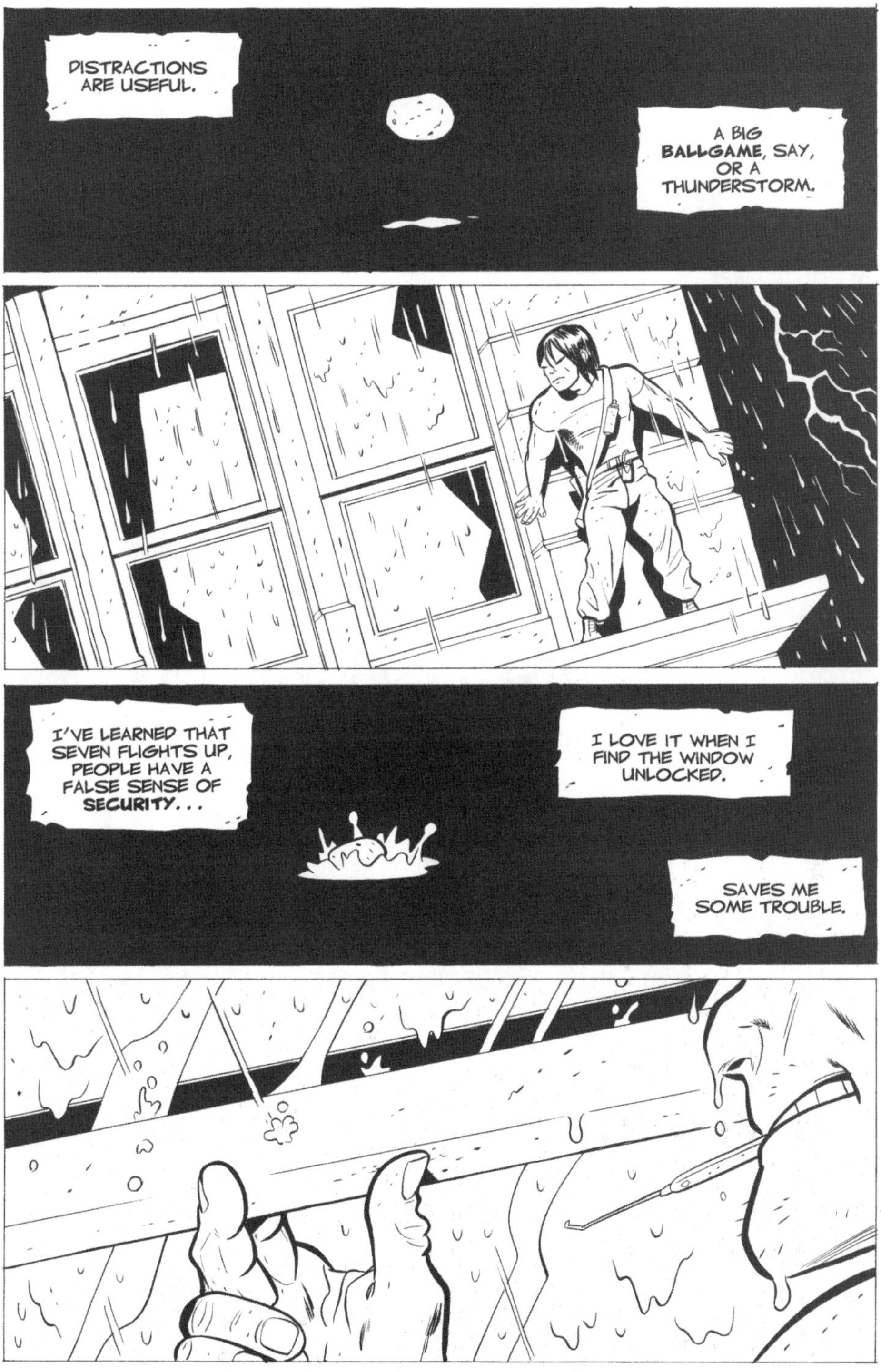
DISTRACTIONS ARE USEFUL.
A BIG **BALLGAME**, SAY, OR A THUNDERSTORM.
I'VE LEARNED THAT SEVEN FLIGHTS UP, PEOPLE HAVE A FALSE SENSE OF **SECURITY**...
I LOVE IT WHEN I FIND THE WINDOW UNLOCKED.
SAVES ME SOME TROUBLE.

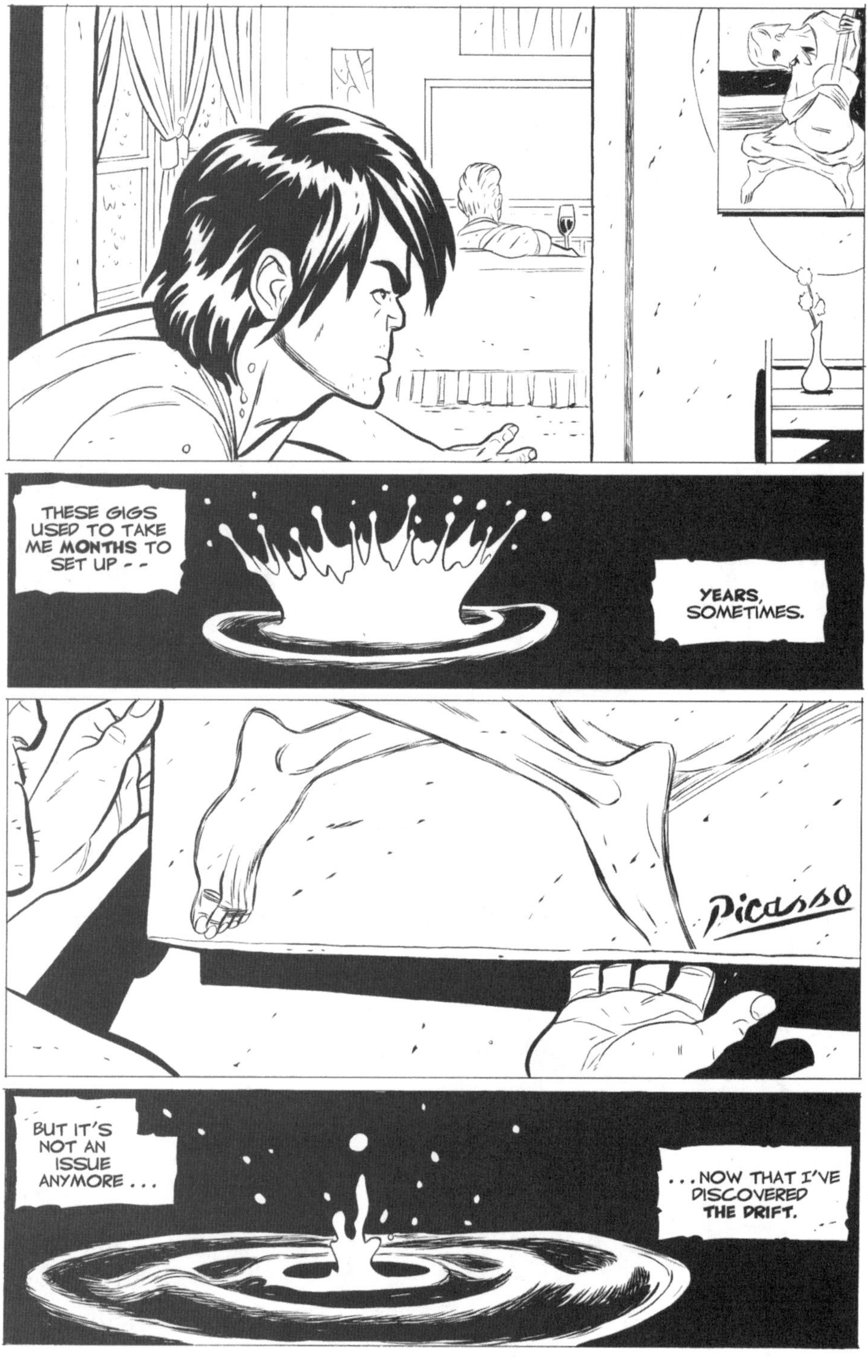
THESE GIGS USED TO TAKE ME MONTHS TO SET UP - -
YEARS, SOMETIMES.
Picasso
BUT IT'S NOT AN ISSUE ANYMORE . . .
. . . NOW THAT I'VE DISCOVERED THE DRIFT.

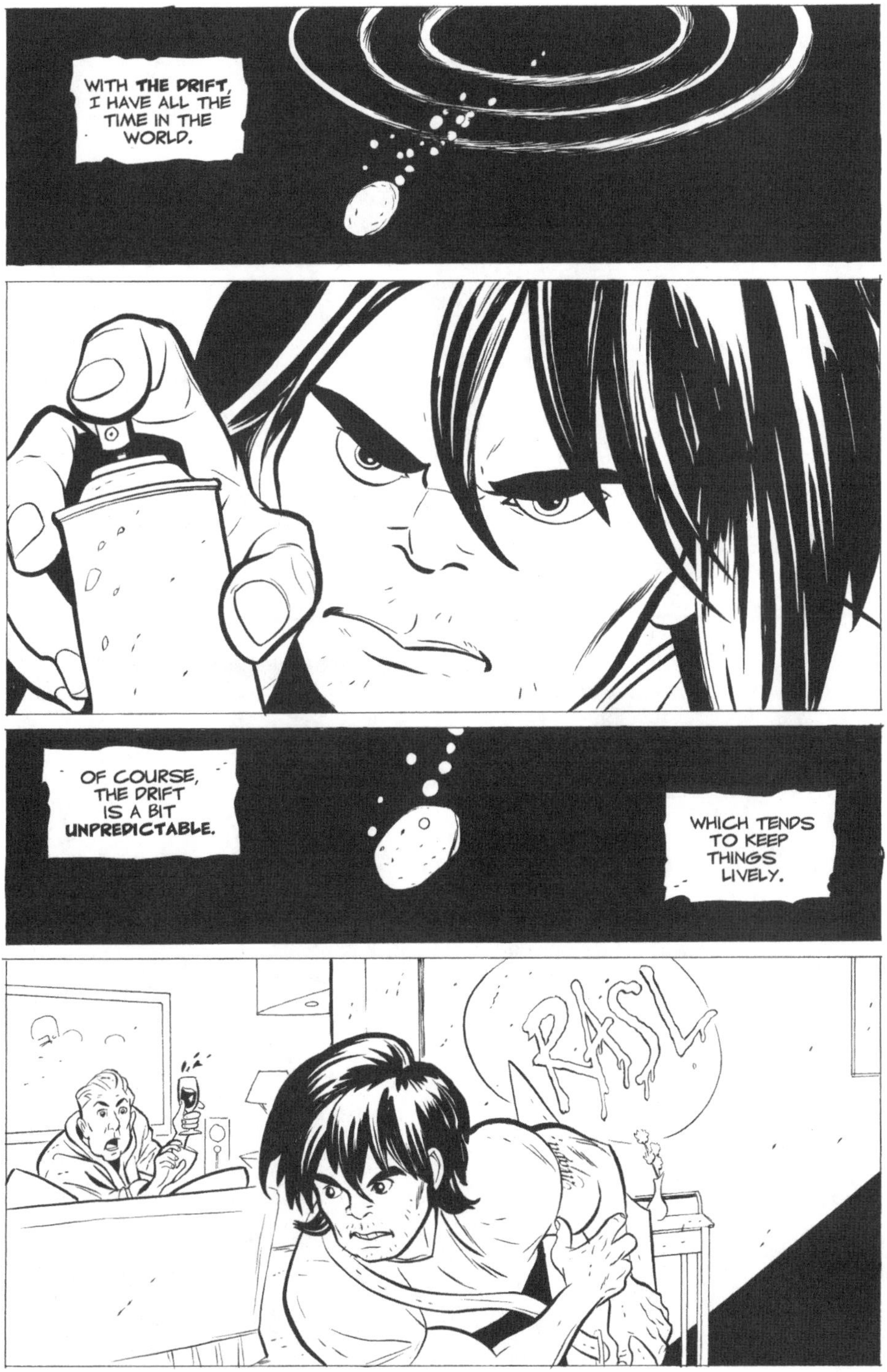
WITH THE DRIFT, I HAVE ALL THE TIME IN THE WORLD.
OF COURSE, THE DRIFT IS A BIT UNPREDICTABLE.
WHICH TENDS TO KEEP THINGS LIVELY.
RASL

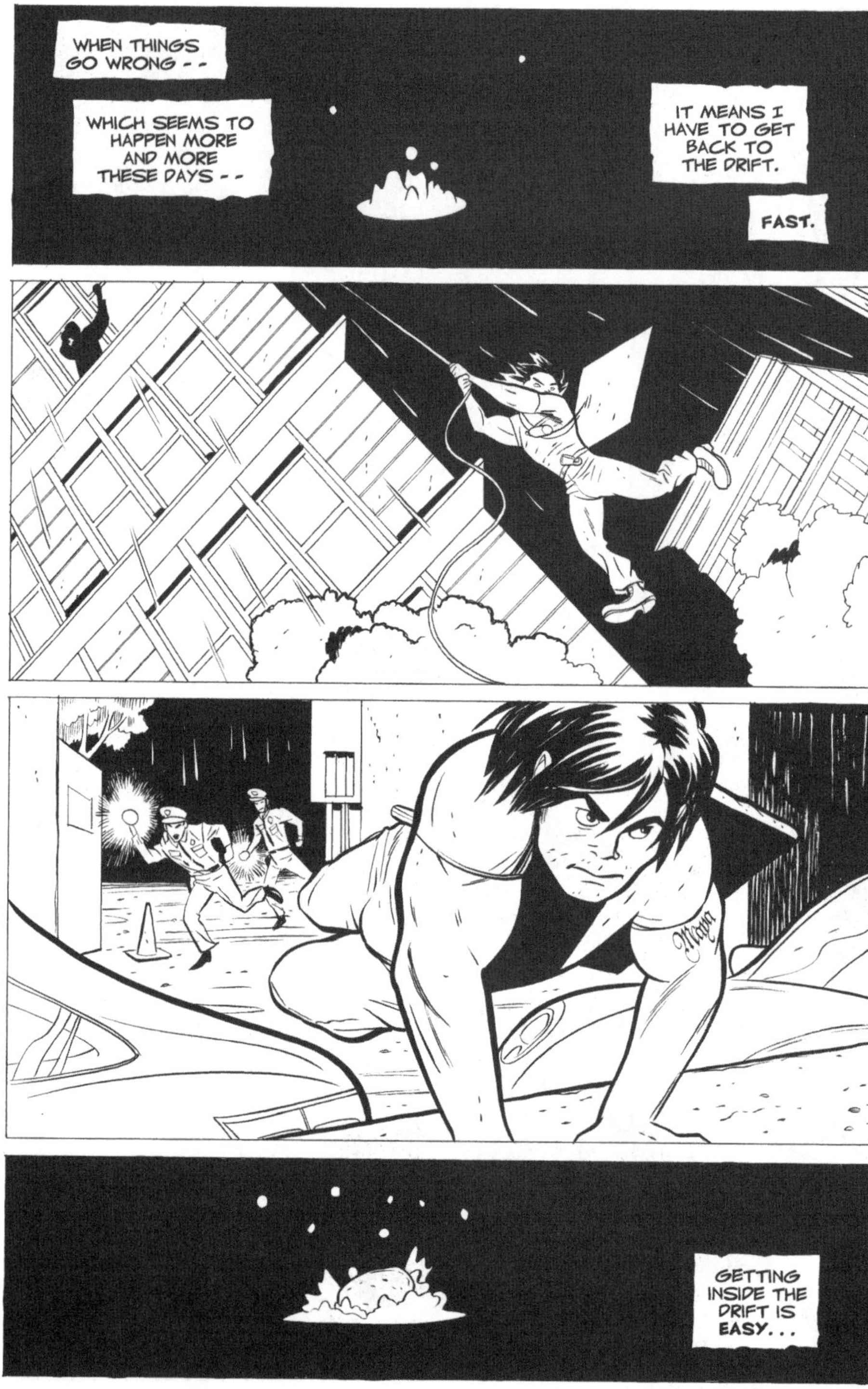
WHEN THINGS GO WRONG - -
WHICH SEEMS TO HAPPEN MORE AND MORE THESE DAYS - -
IT MEANS I HAVE TO GET BACK TO THE DRIFT.
FAST.
GETTING INSIDE THE DRIFT IS EASY...

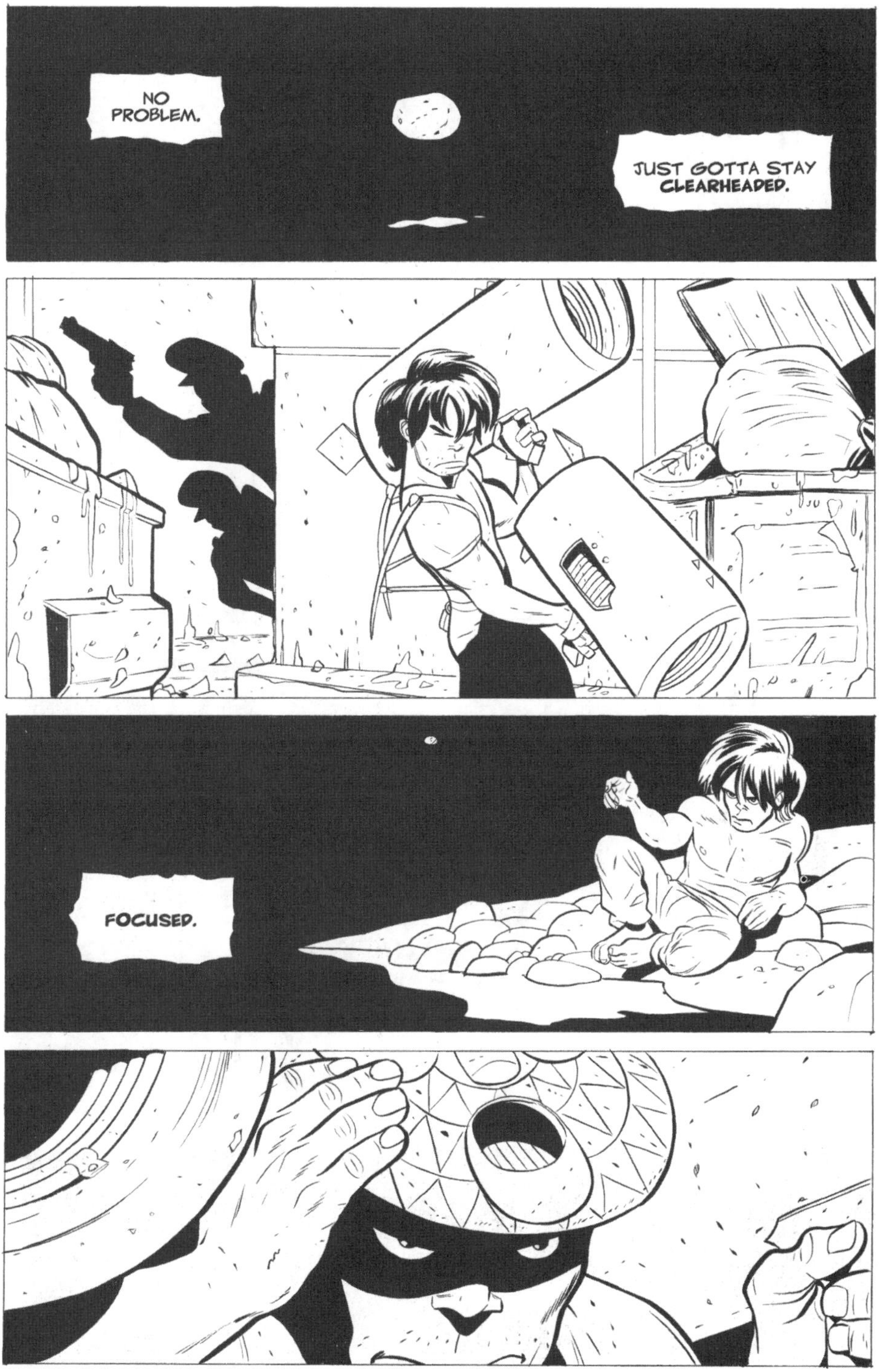
NO PROBLEM.
JUST GOTTA STAY CLEARHEADED.
FOCUSED.

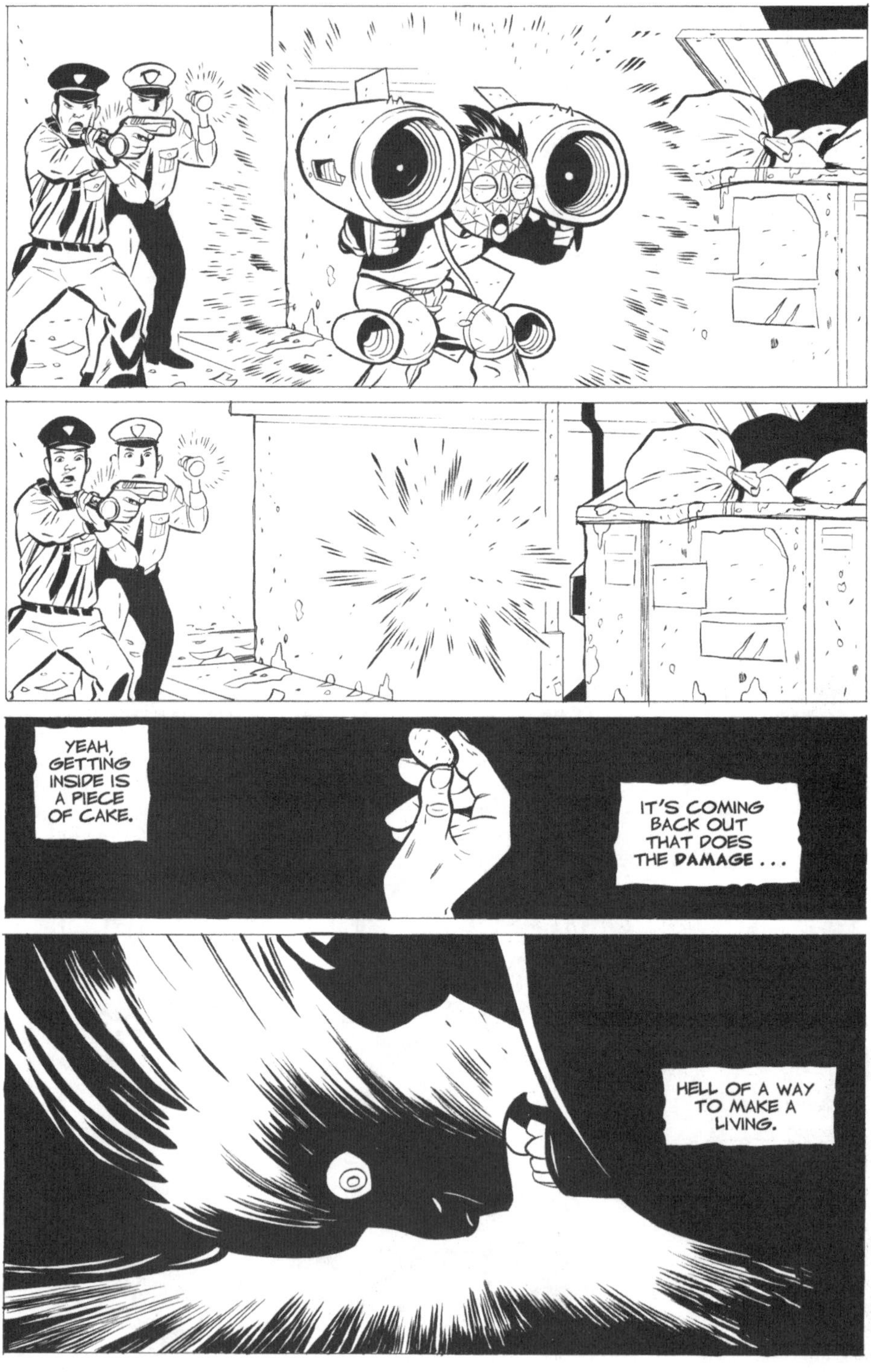
YEAH, GETTING INSIDE IS A PIECE OF CAKE.
IT'S COMING BACK OUT THAT DOES THE DAMAGE . . .
HELL OF A WAY TO MAKE A LIVING.

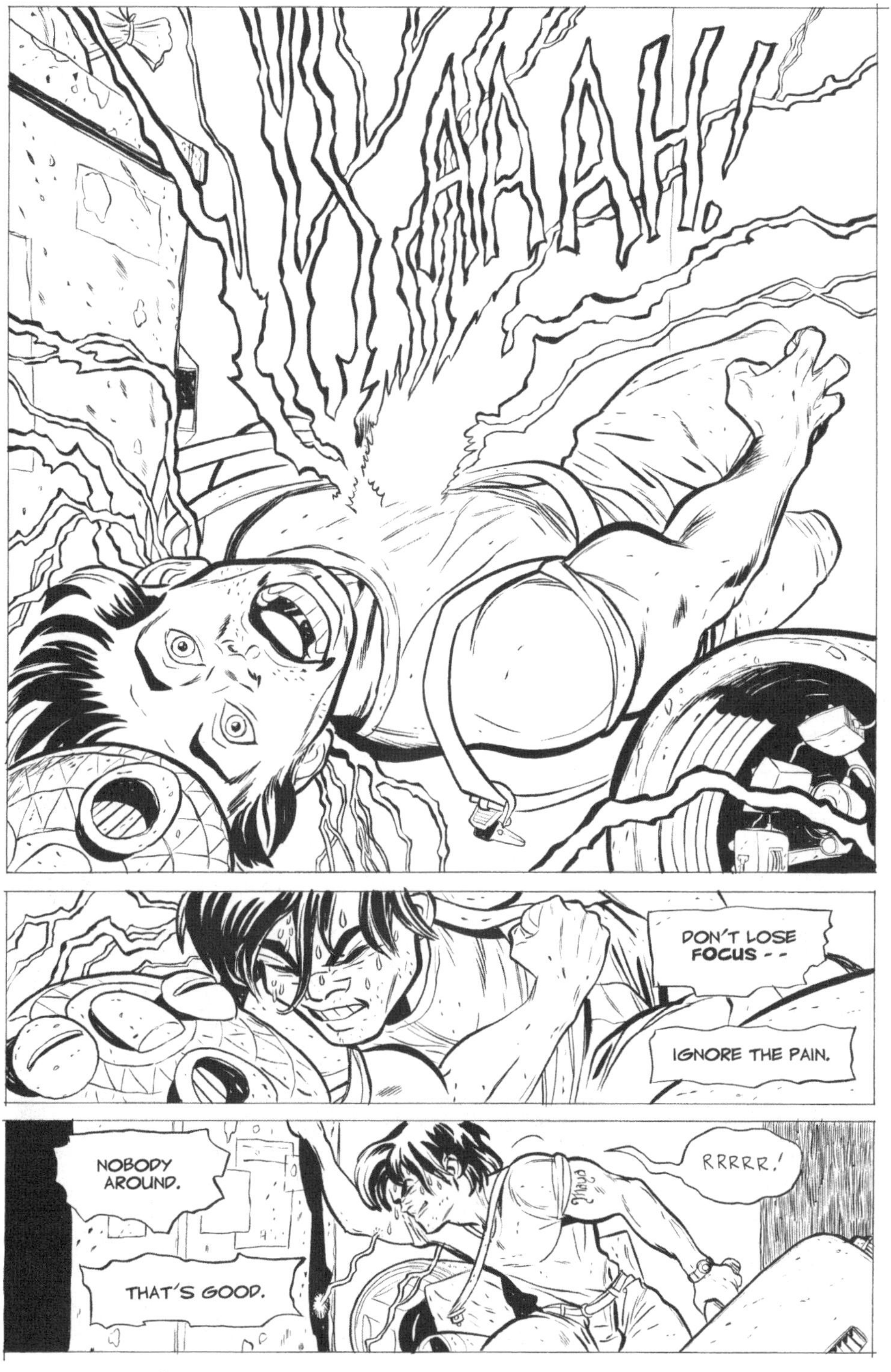
YYAAAH!
DON'T LOSE FOCUS --
IGNORE THE PAIN.
NOBODY AROUND.
THAT'S GOOD.
RRRRR!

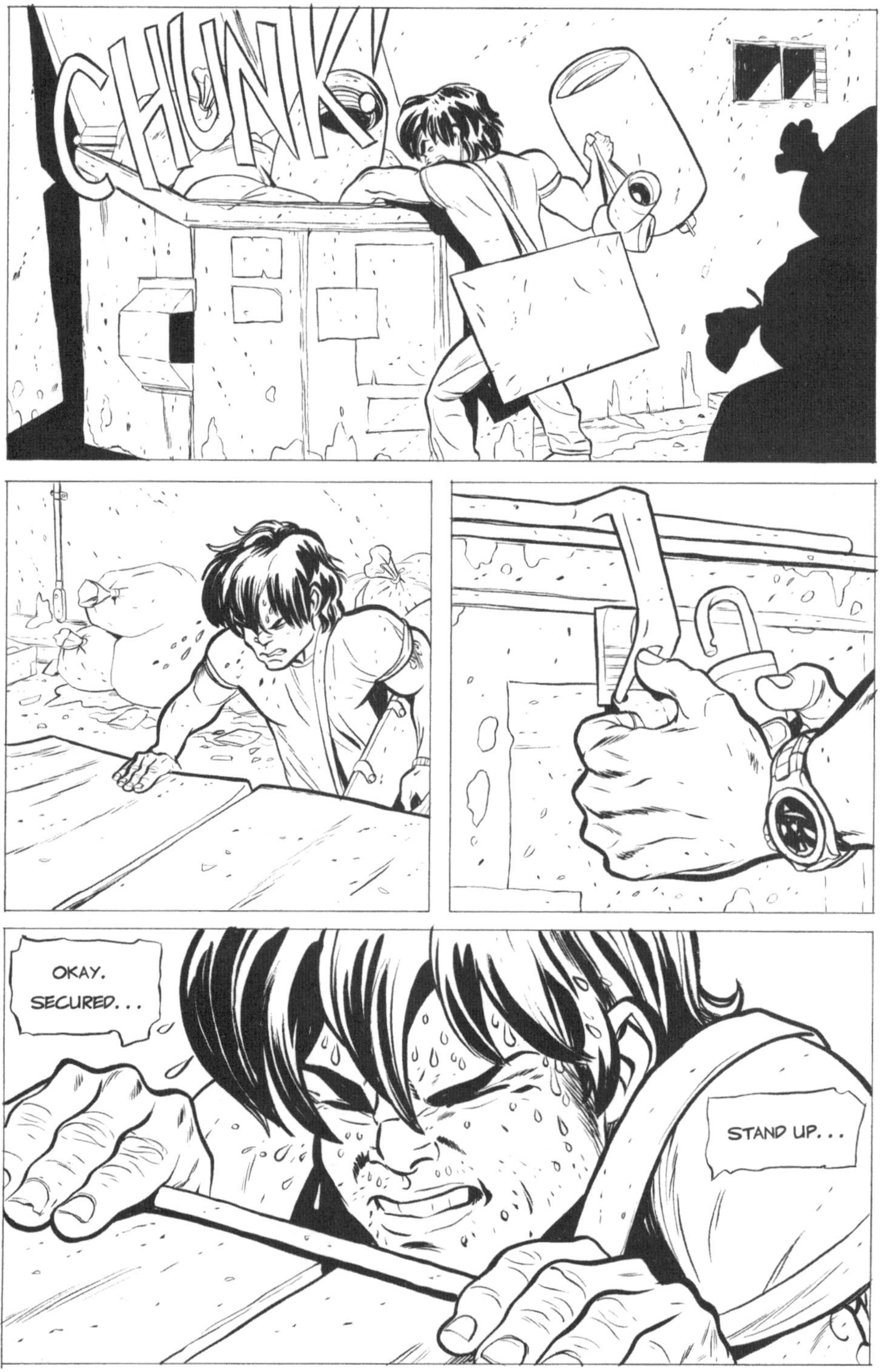
CHUNK!
OKAY. SECURED...
STAND UP...

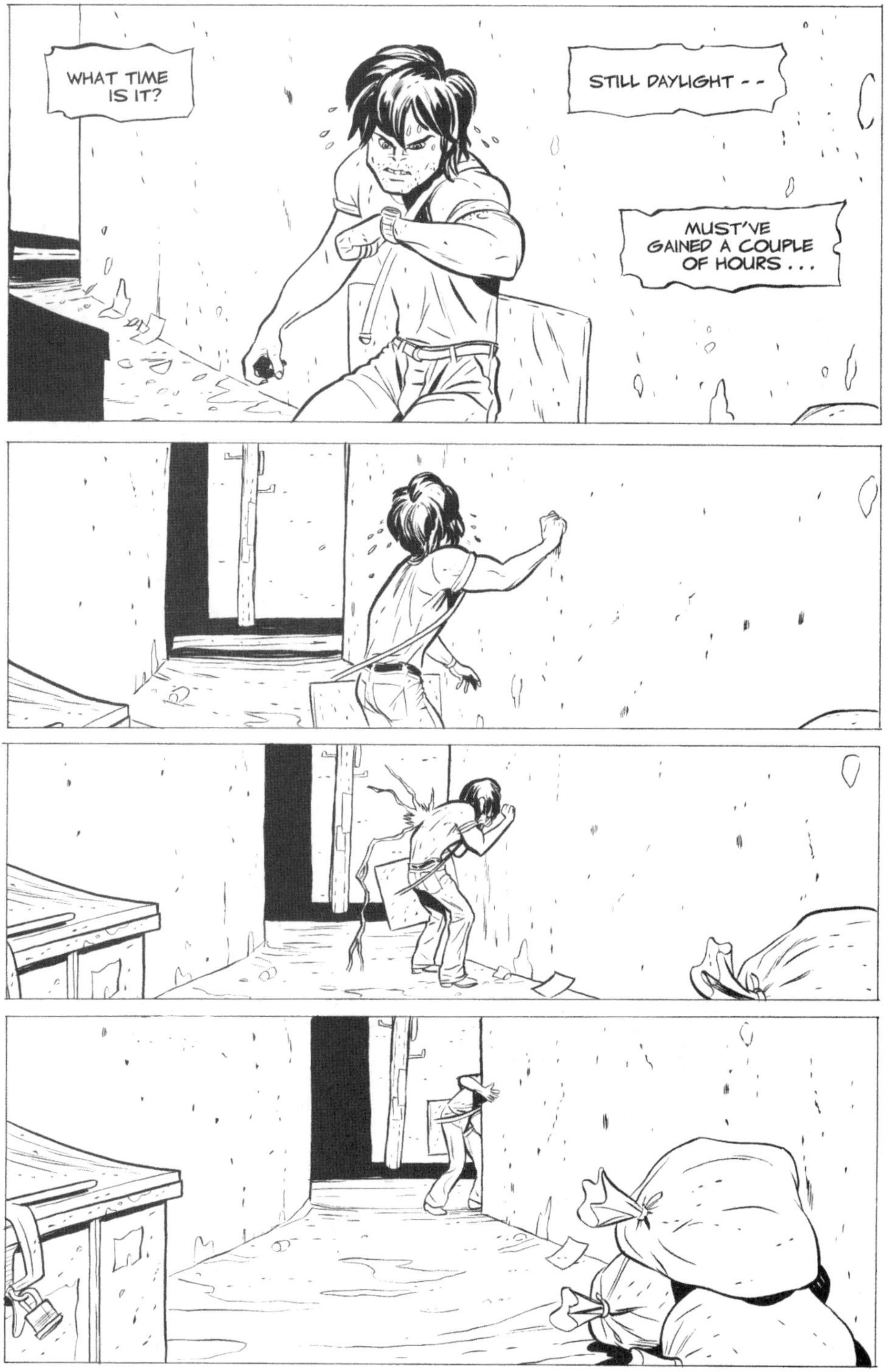
WHAT TIME IS IT?
STILL DAYLIGHT - -
MUST'VE GAINED A COUPLE OF HOURS . . .

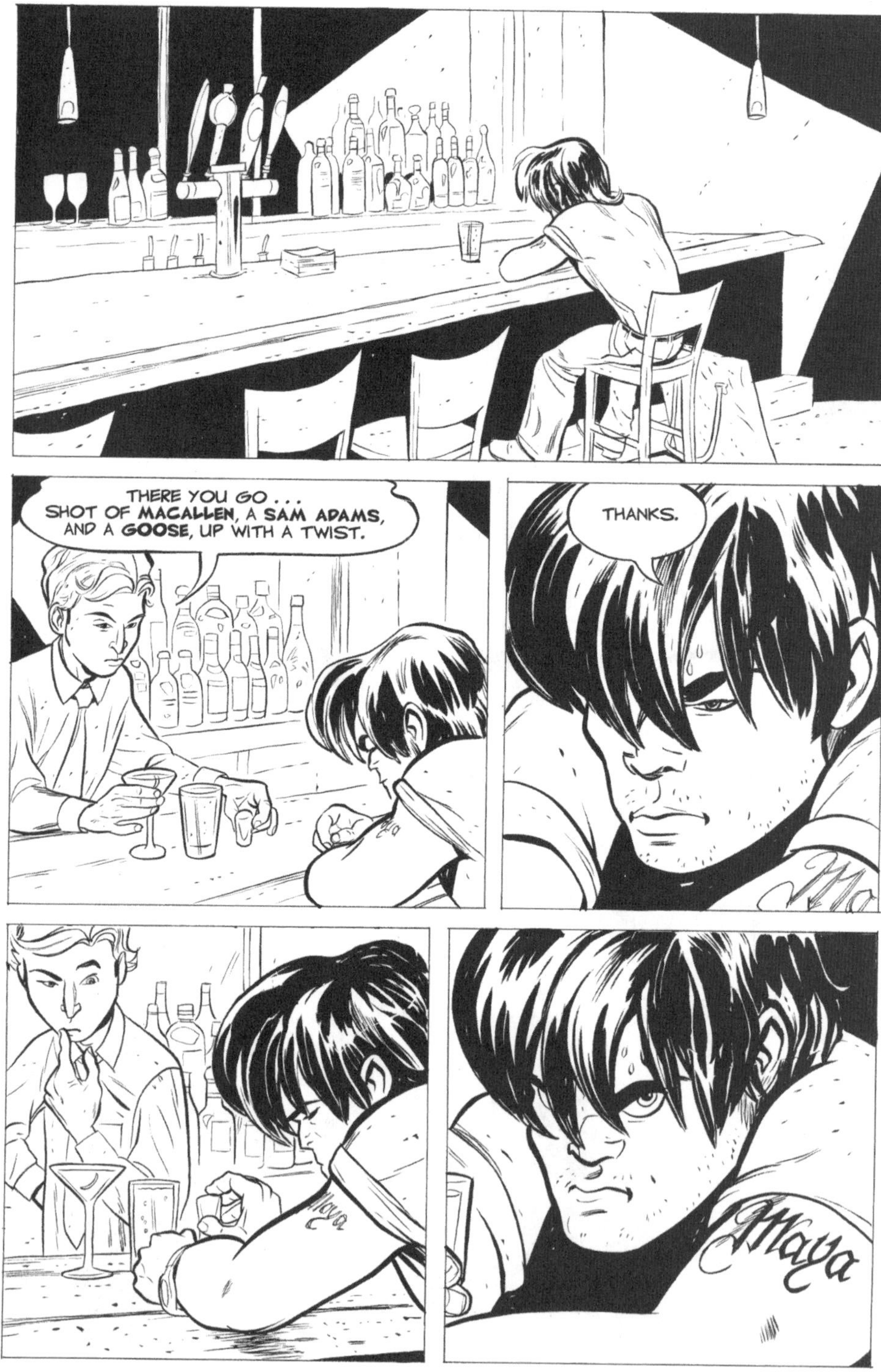
THERE YOU GO . . . SHOT OF MACALLEN, A SAM ADAMS, AND A GOOSE, UP WITH A TWIST.
THANKS.
Maya

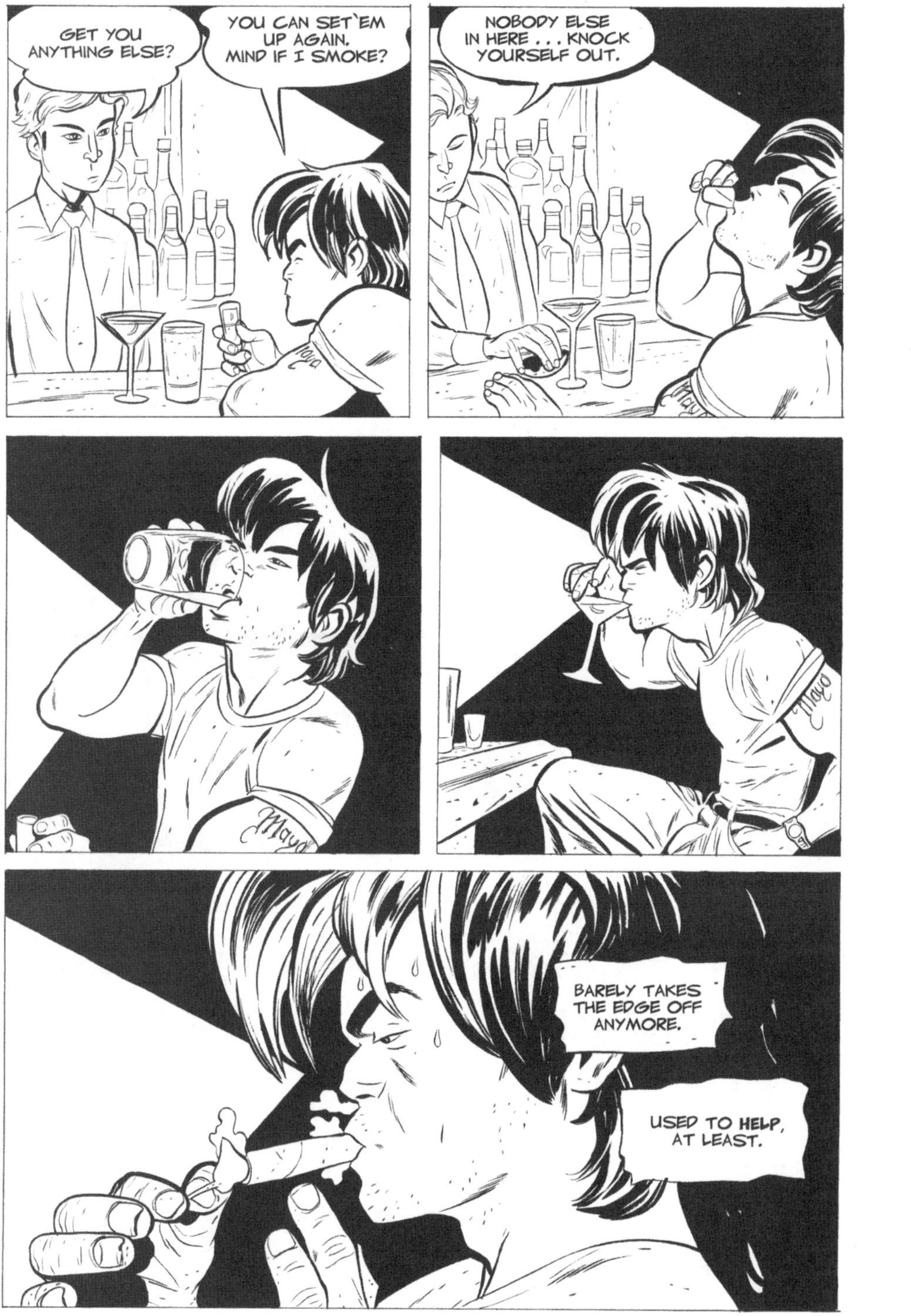
GET YOU ANYTHING ELSE?
YOU CAN SET`EM UP AGAIN. MIND IF I SMOKE?
NOBODY ELSE IN HERE . . . KNOCK YOURSELF OUT.
Maya
BARELY TAKES THE EDGE OFF ANYMORE.
USED TO HELP, AT LEAST.

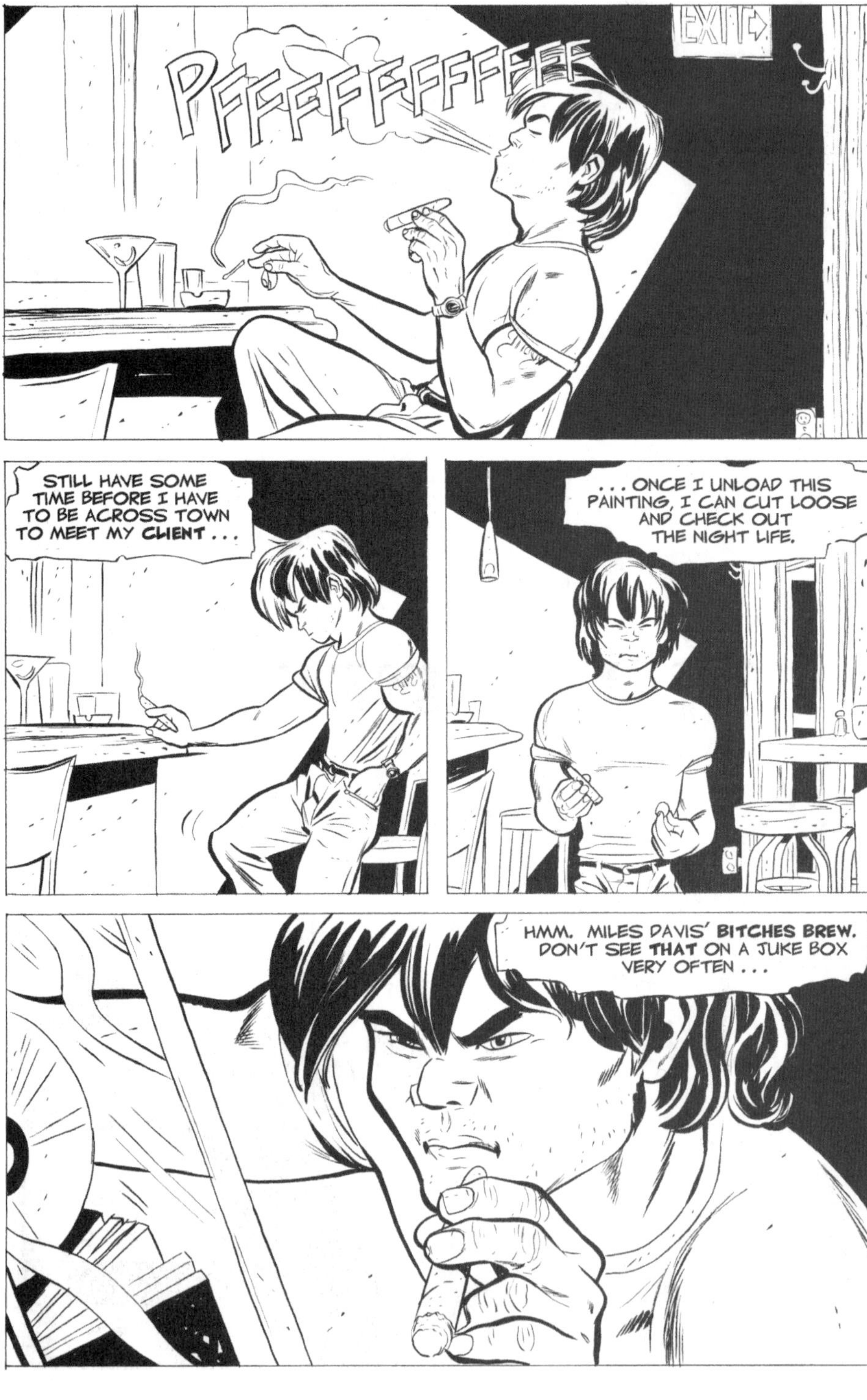
PFFFFFFFFFFFF
EXIT
STILL HAVE SOME TIME BEFORE I HAVE TO BE ACROSS TOWN TO MEET MY **CLIENT** . . .
. . . ONCE I UNLOAD THIS PAINTING, I CAN CUT LOOSE AND CHECK OUT THE NIGHT LIFE.
HMM. MILES DAVIS' **BITCHES BREW.** DON'T SEE **THAT** ON A JUKE BOX VERY OFTEN . . .

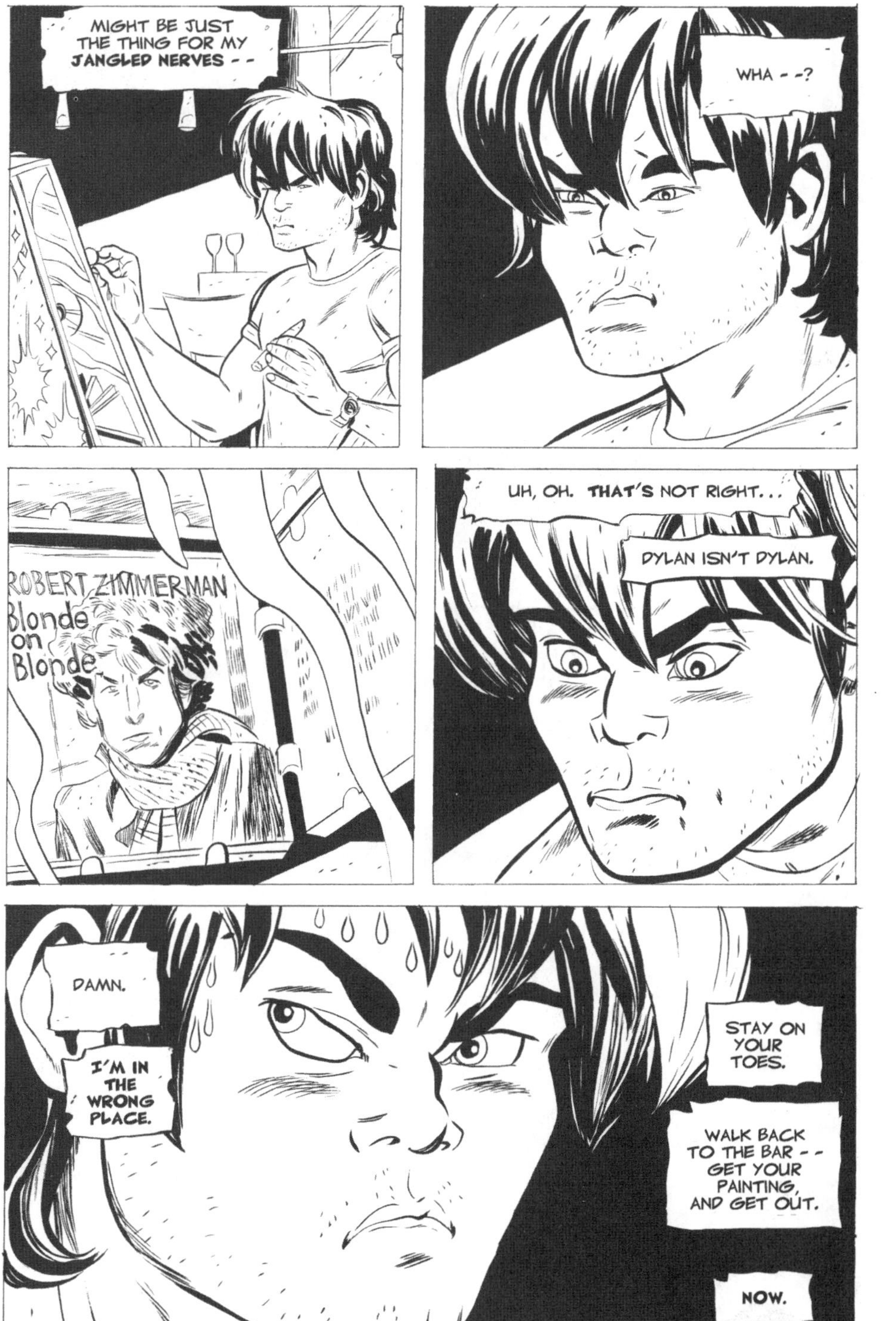
MIGHT BE JUST THE THING FOR MY JANGLED NERVES - -
WHA - -?
ROBERT ZIMMERMAN
Blonde on Blonde
UH, OH. THAT'S NOT RIGHT...
DYLAN ISN'T DYLAN.
DAMN.
I'M IN THE WRONG PLACE.
STAY ON YOUR TOES.
WALK BACK TO THE BAR - - GET YOUR PAINTING, AND GET OUT.
NOW.

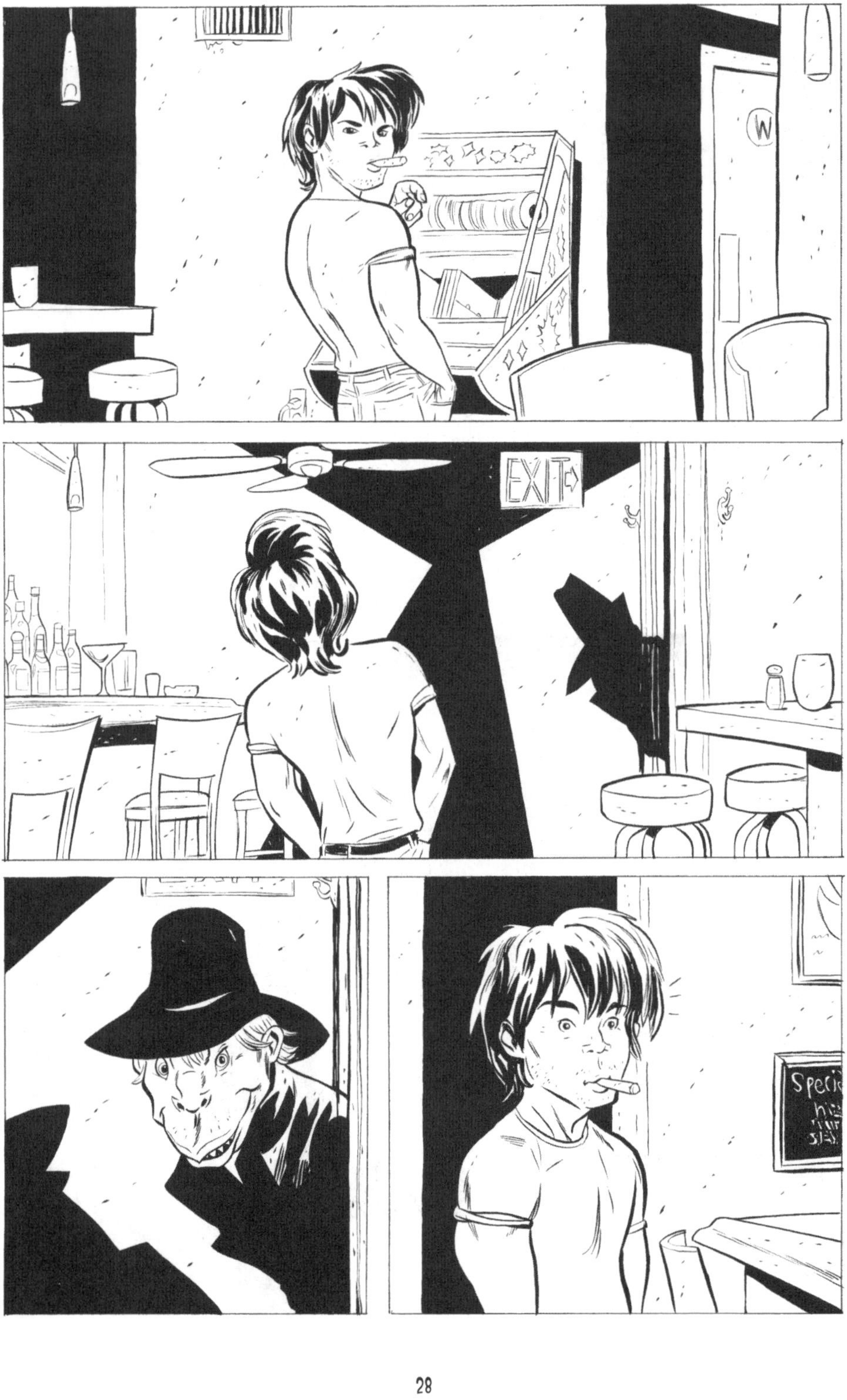
W
EXIT

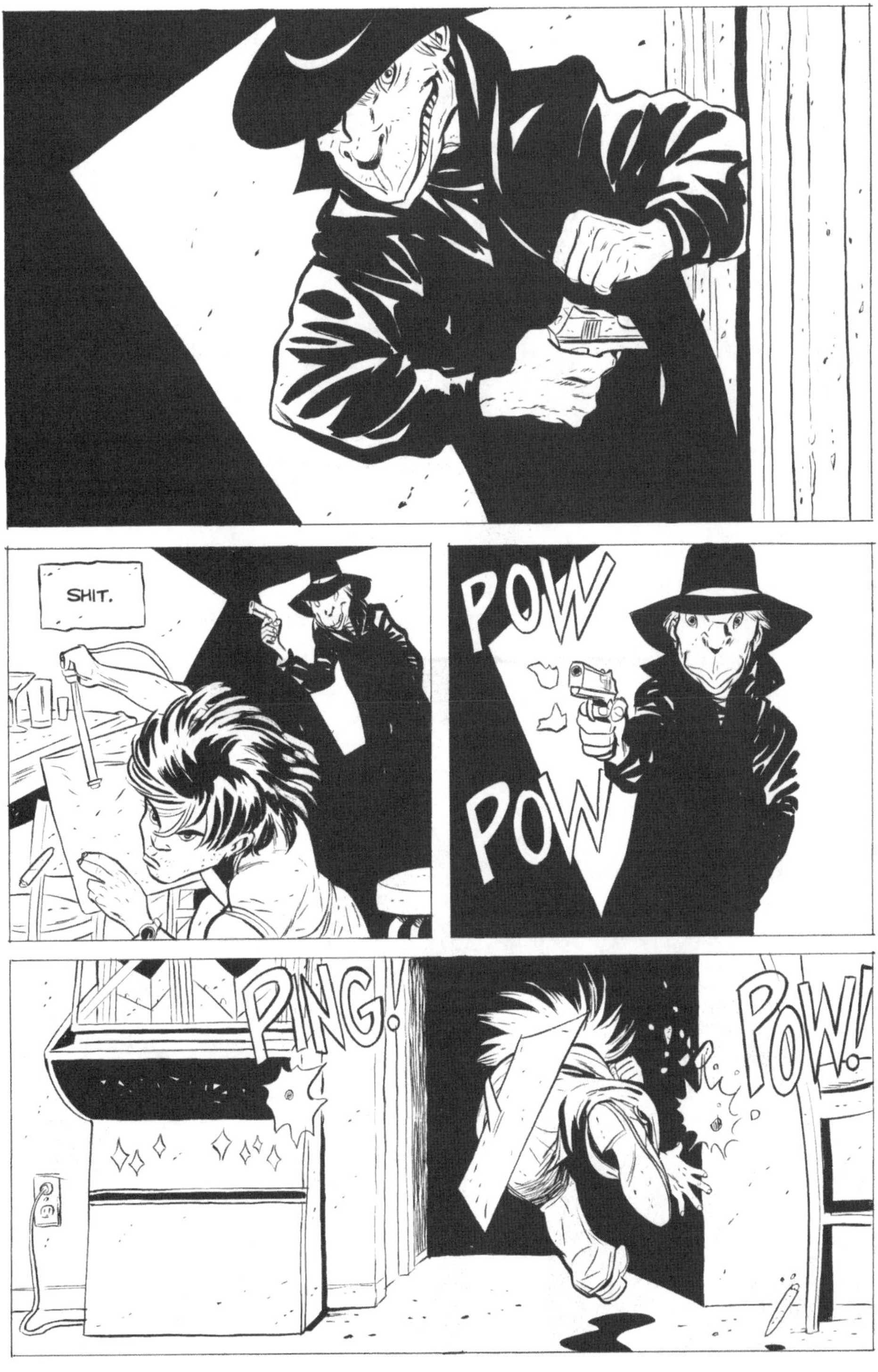
SHIT.
POW
POW
PING!
POW!

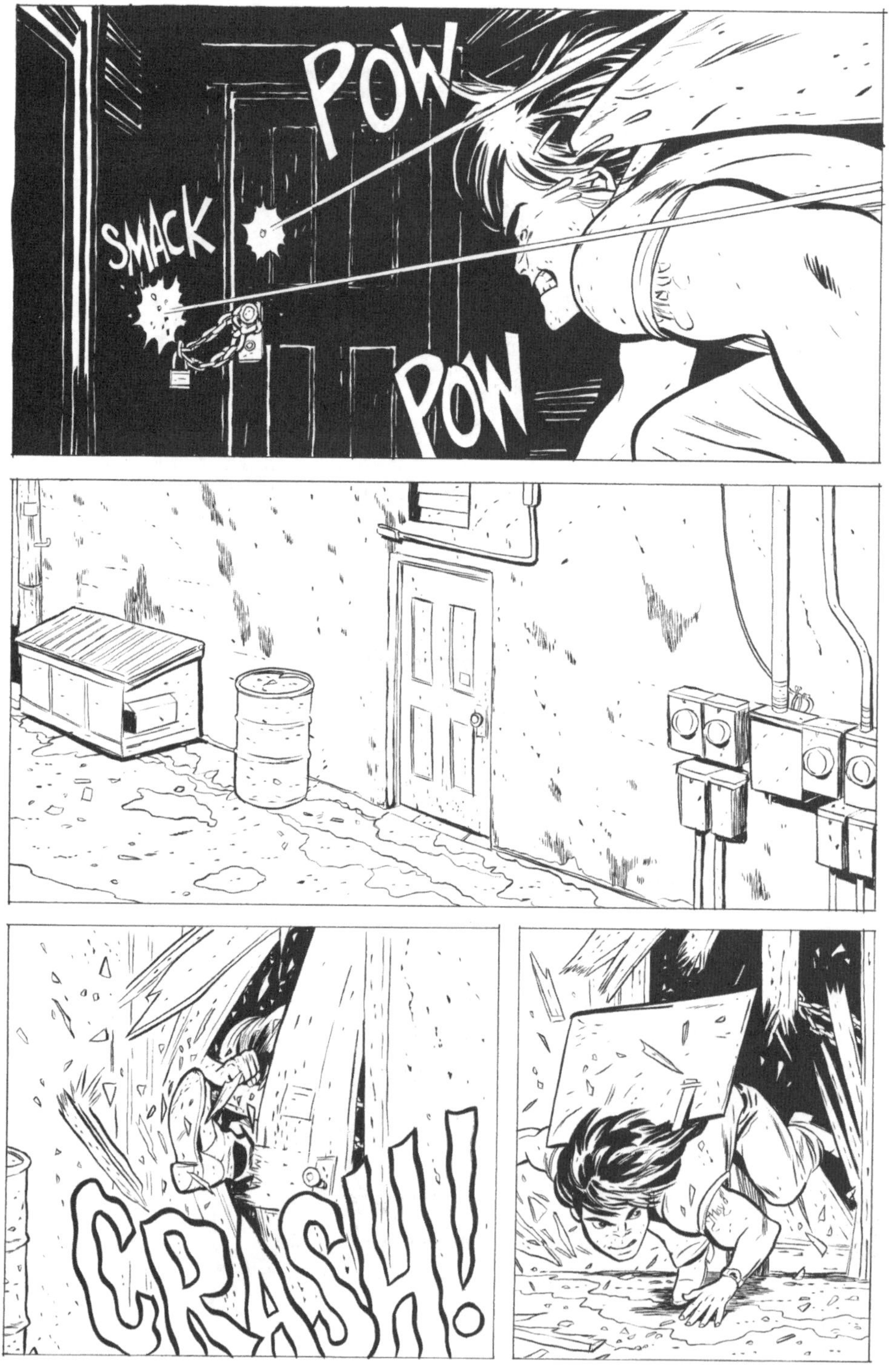
POW
SMACK
POW
CRASH!

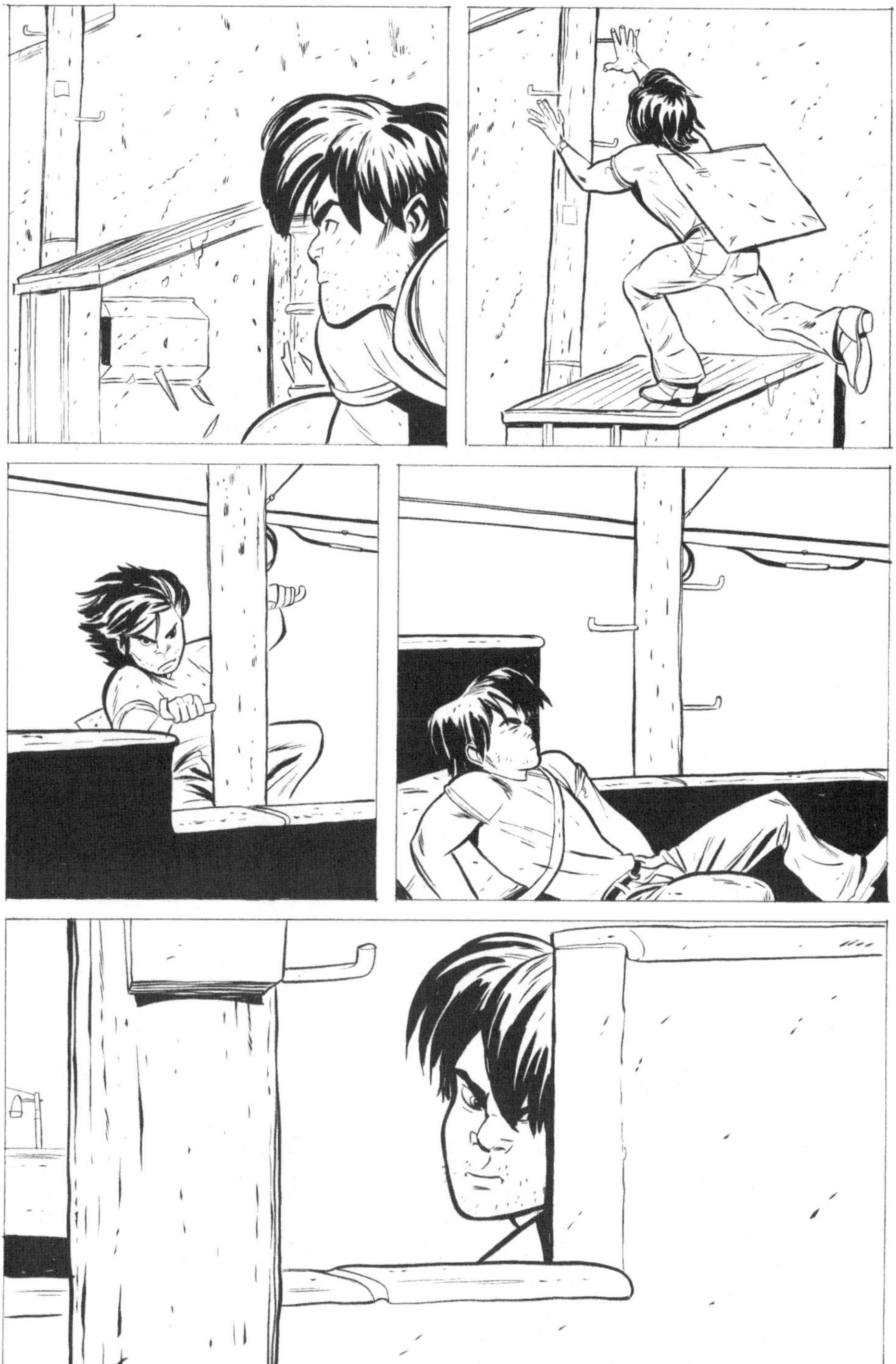

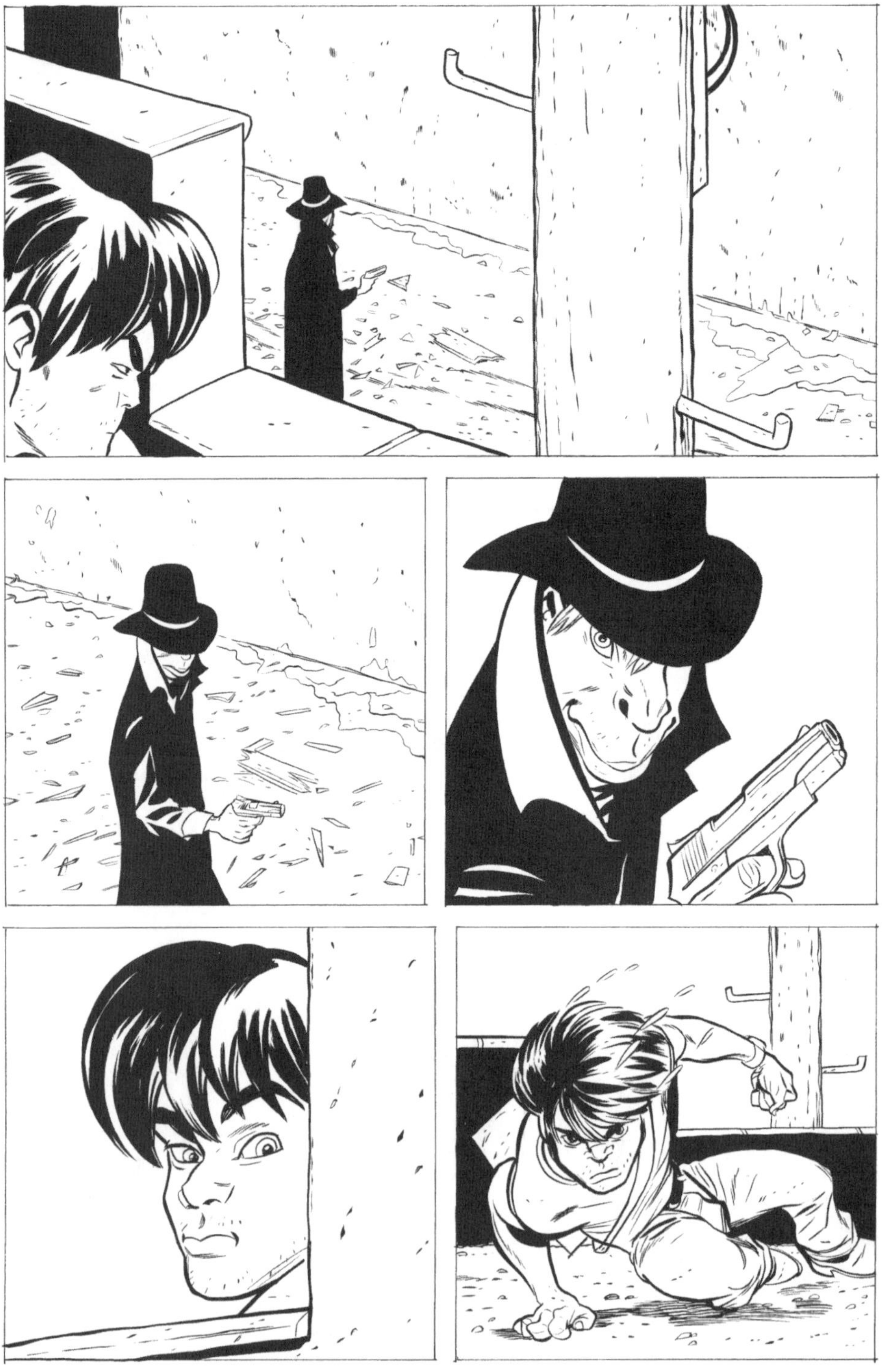

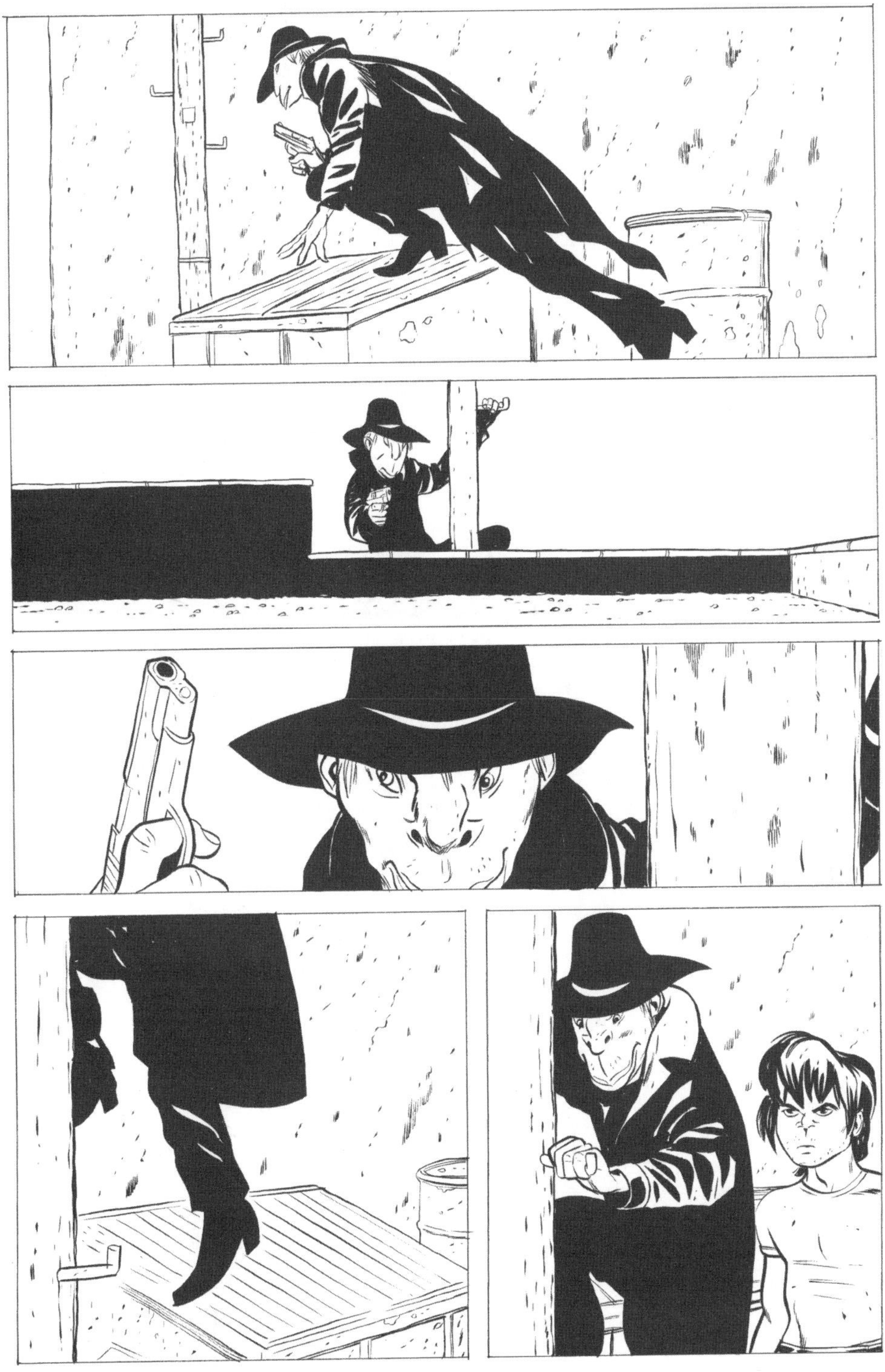

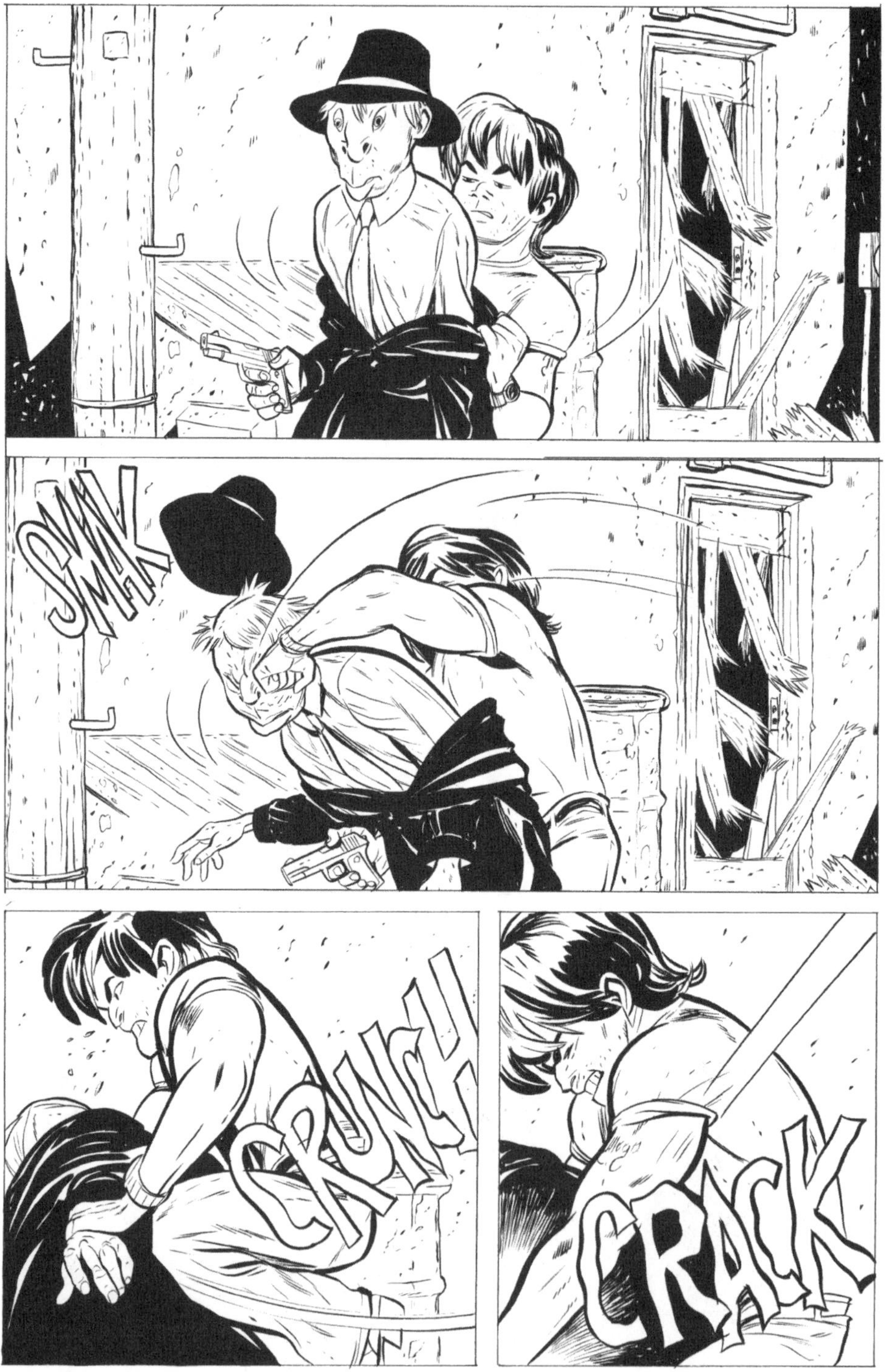
SMAK
CRUNCH
CRACK

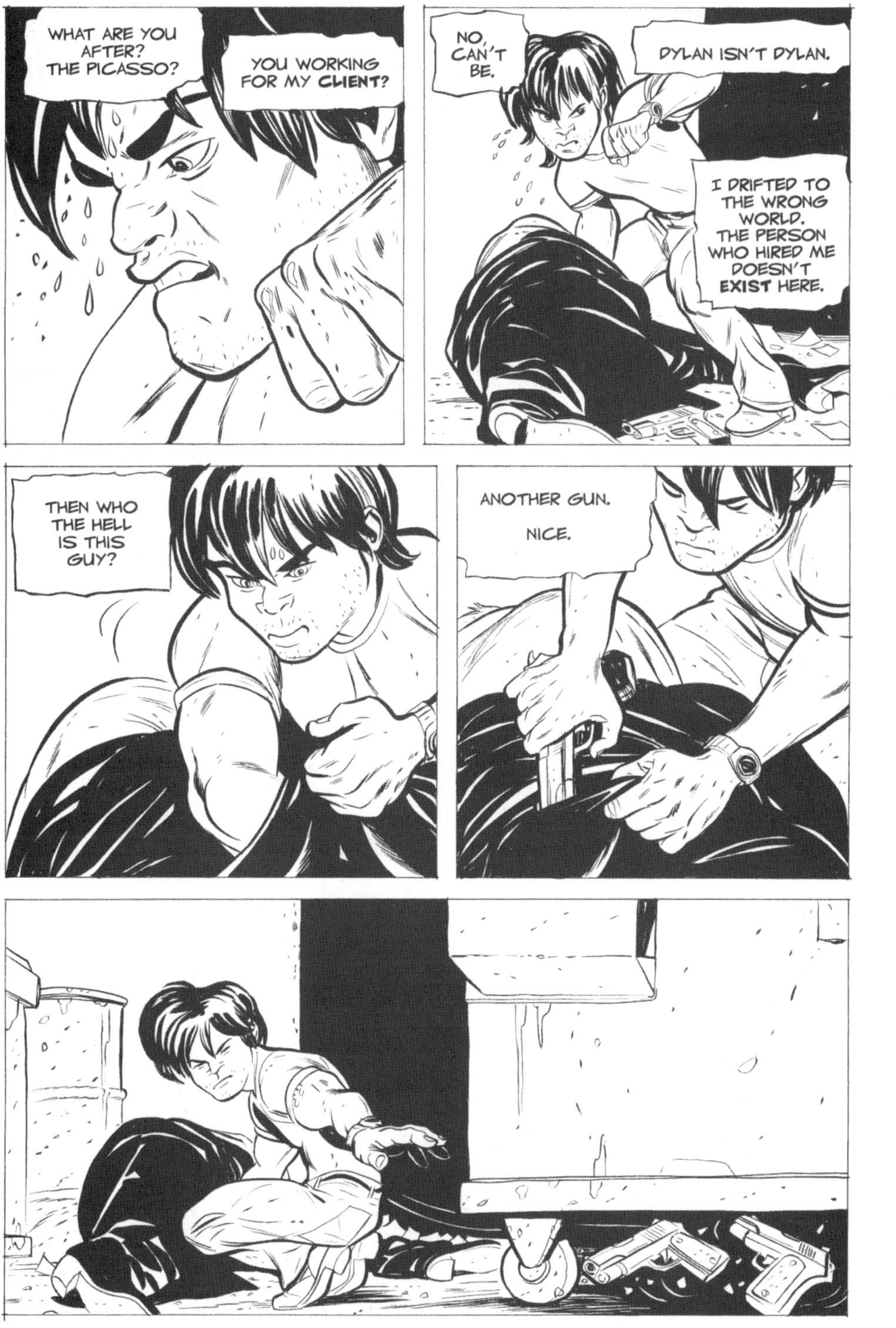
WHAT ARE YOU AFTER? THE PICASSO?
YOU WORKING FOR MY **CLIENT**?
NO, CAN'T BE.
DYLAN ISN'T DYLAN.
I DRIFTED TO THE WRONG WORLD. THE PERSON WHO HIRED ME DOESN'T **EXIST** HERE.
THEN WHO THE HELL IS THIS GUY?
ANOTHER GUN.
NICE.

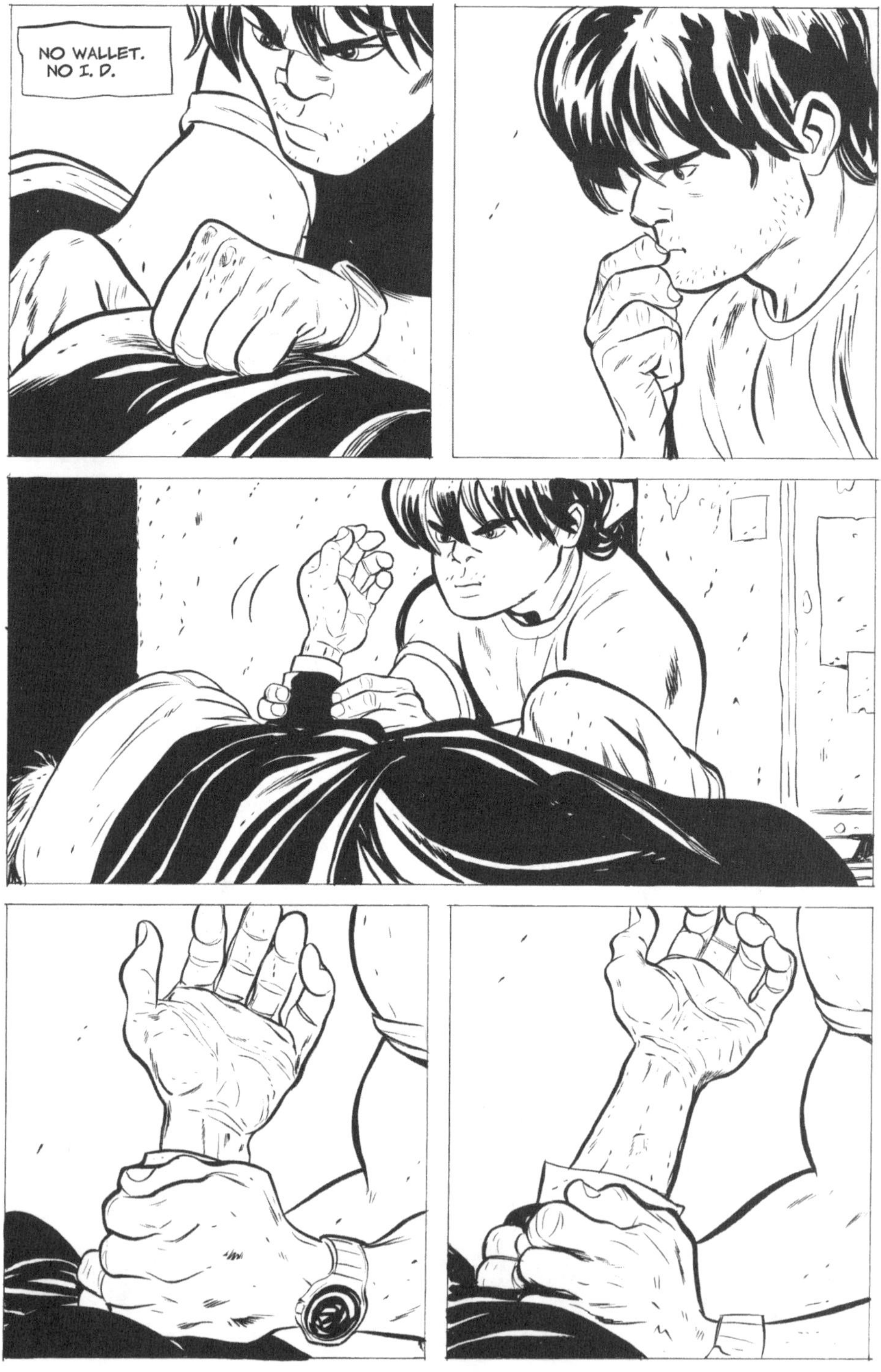
NO WALLET.
NO I. D.

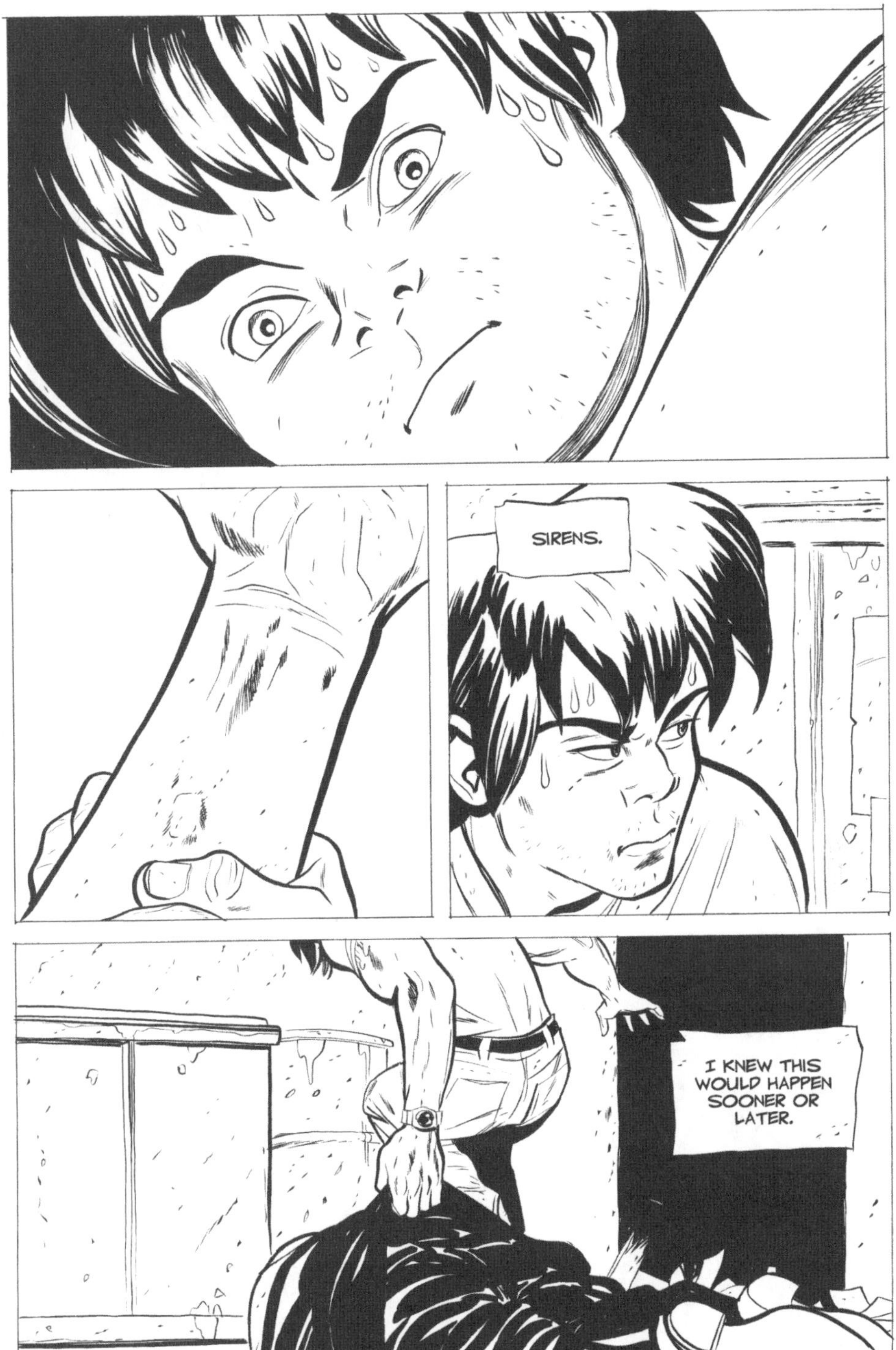
SIRENS.
I KNEW THIS WOULD HAPPEN SOONER OR LATER.

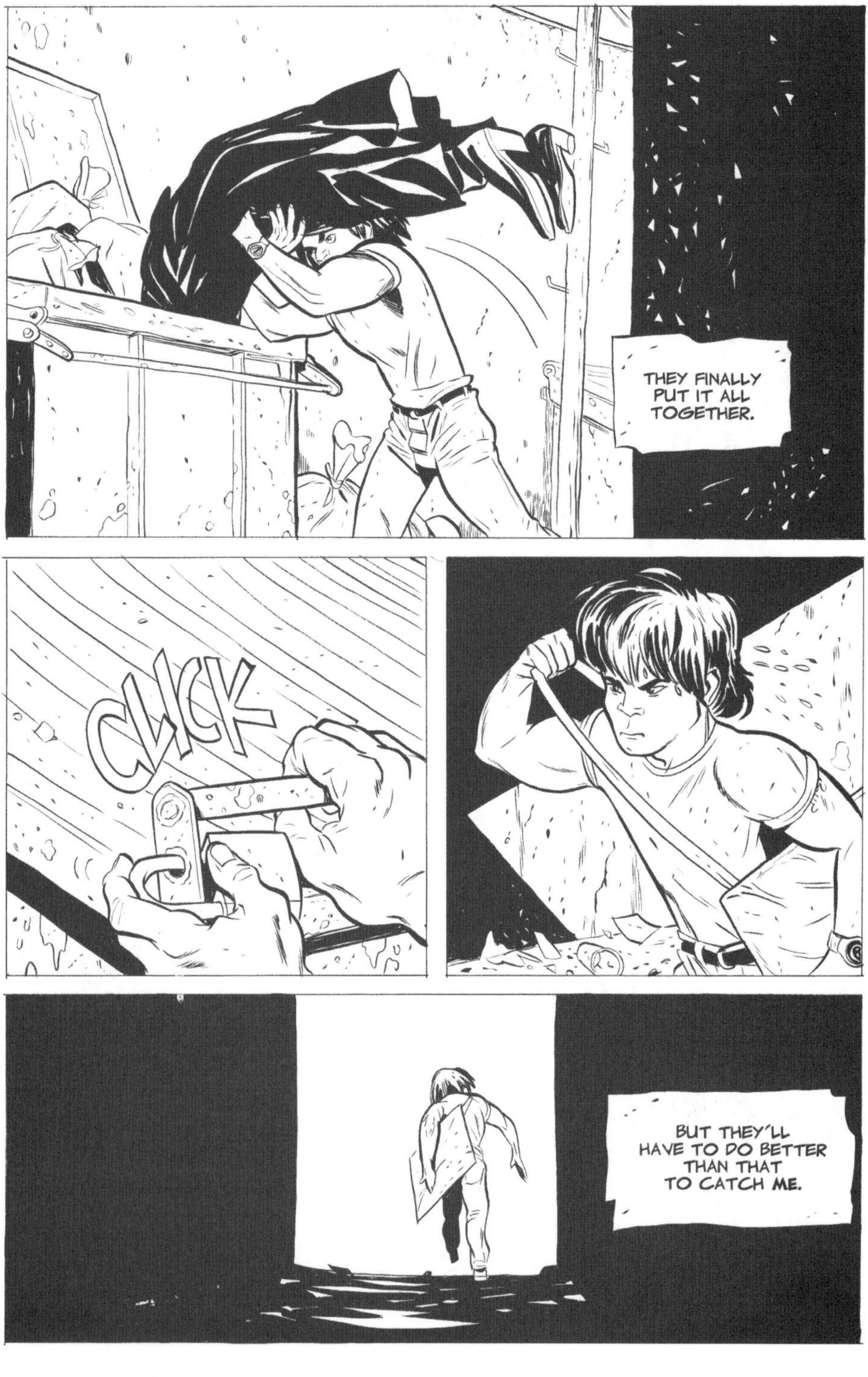
THEY FINALLY PUT IT ALL TOGETHER.
CLICK
BUT THEY'LL HAVE TO DO BETTER THAN THAT TO CATCH ME.

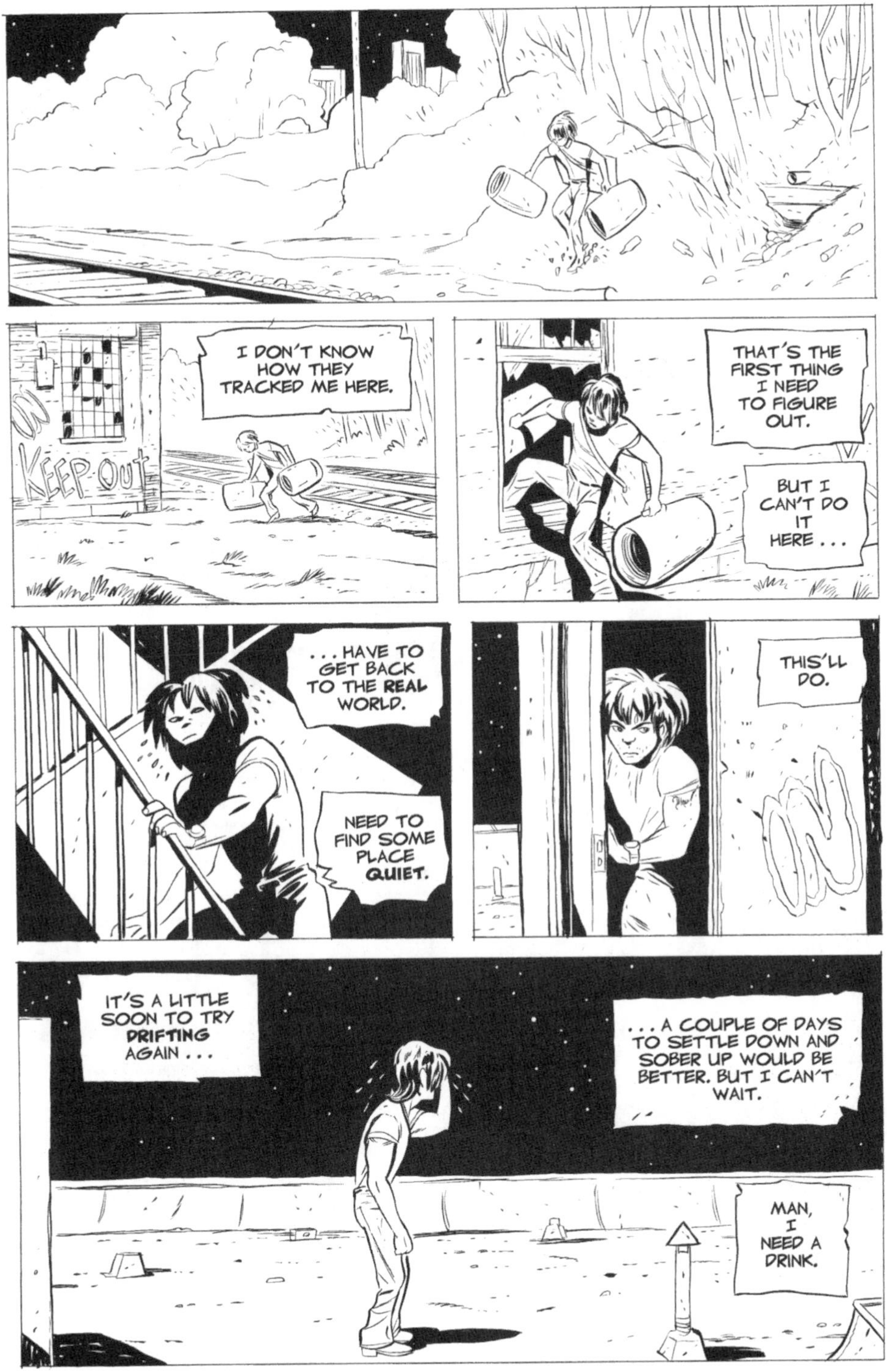
I DON'T KNOW HOW THEY TRACKED ME HERE.
KEEP OUT
THAT'S THE FIRST THING I NEED TO FIGURE OUT.
BUT I CAN'T DO IT HERE . . .
. . . HAVE TO GET BACK TO THE **REAL** WORLD.
NEED TO FIND SOME PLACE **QUIET.**
THIS'LL DO.
IT'S A LITTLE SOON TO TRY **DRIFTING** AGAIN . . .
. . . A COUPLE OF DAYS TO SETTLE DOWN AND SOBER UP WOULD BE BETTER. BUT I CAN'T WAIT.
MAN, I NEED A DRINK.

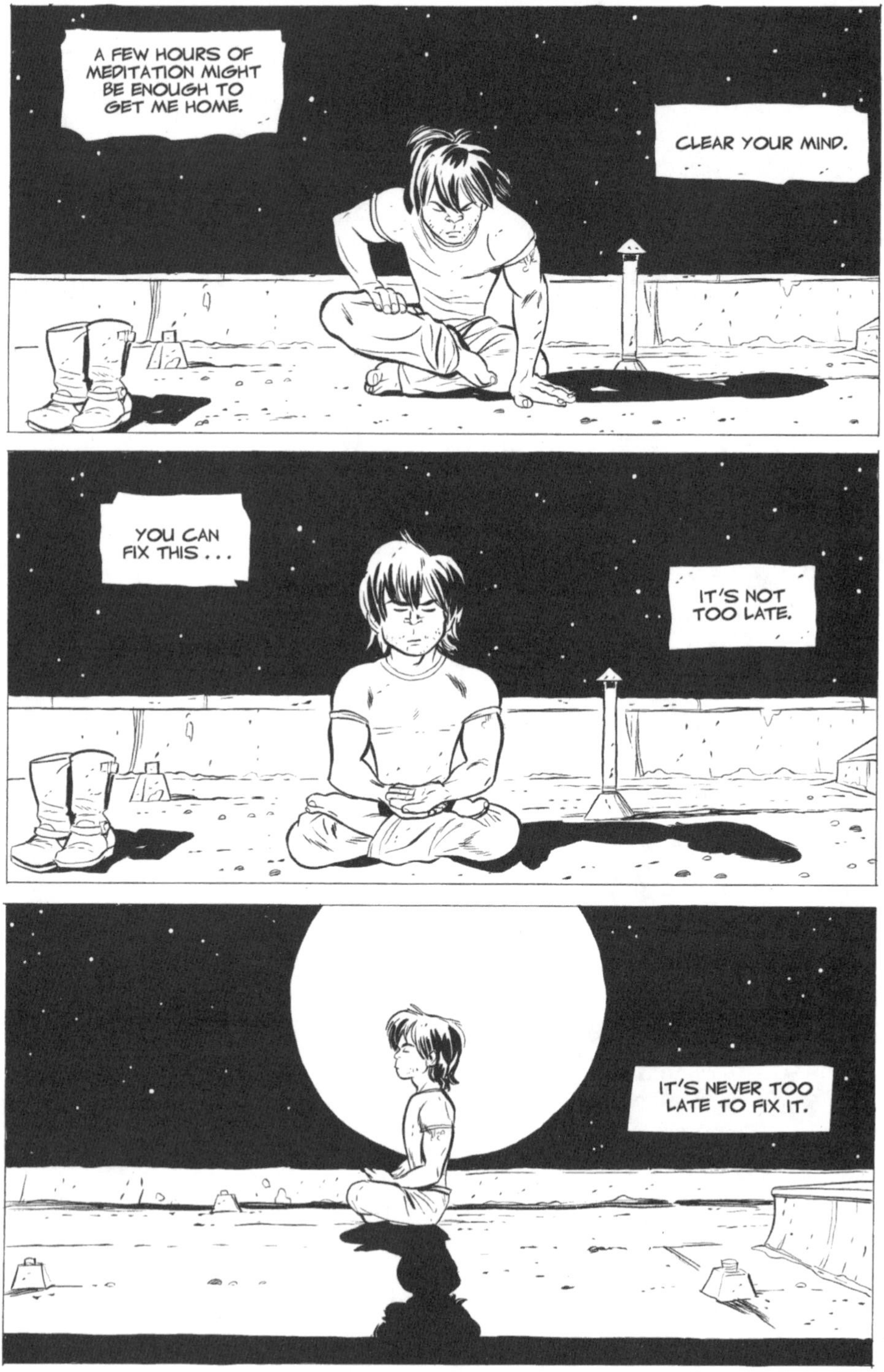
A FEW HOURS OF MEDITATION MIGHT BE ENOUGH TO GET ME HOME.
CLEAR YOUR MIND.
YOU CAN FIX THIS . . .
IT'S NOT TOO LATE.
IT'S NEVER TOO LATE TO FIX IT.

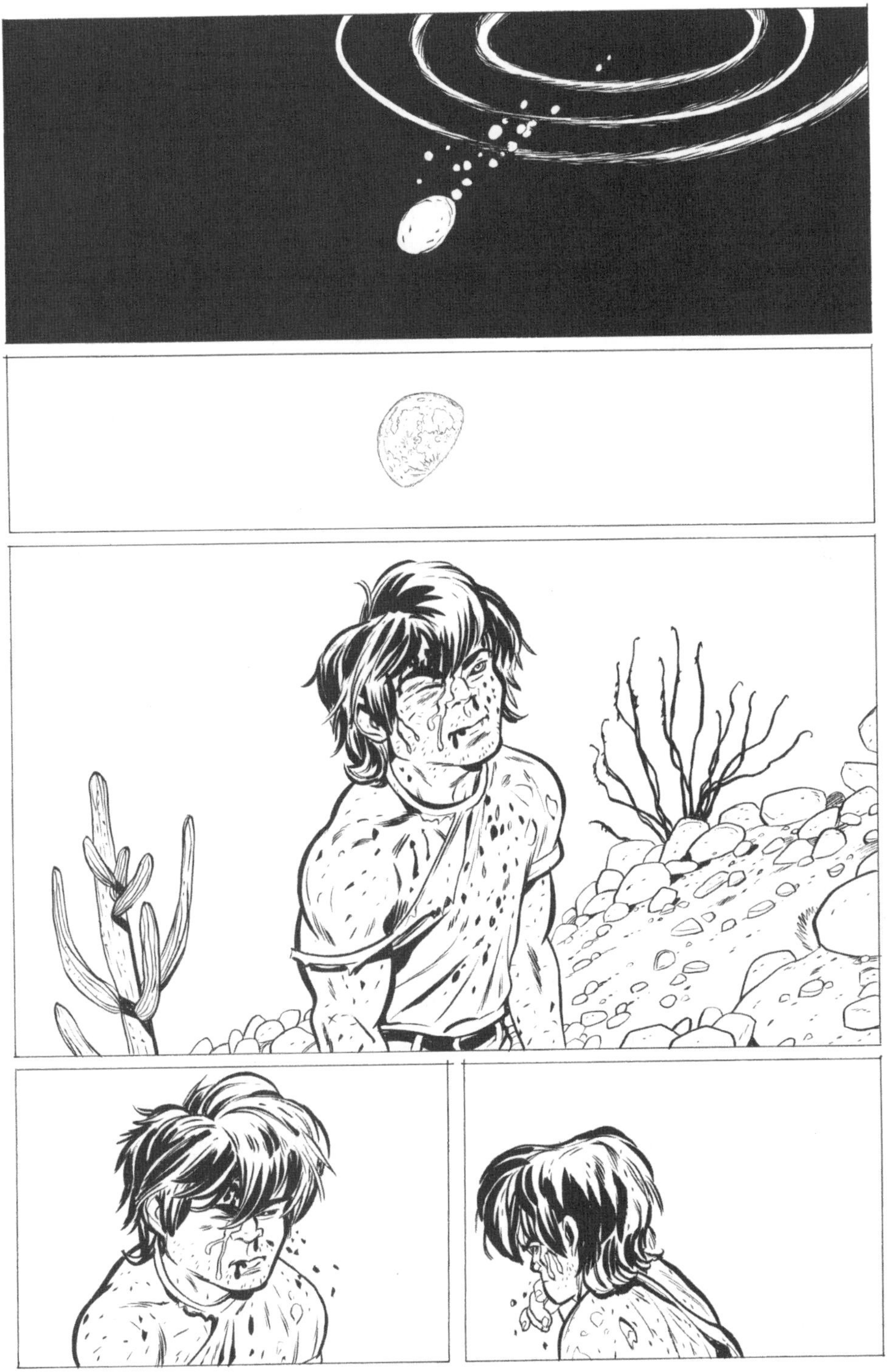

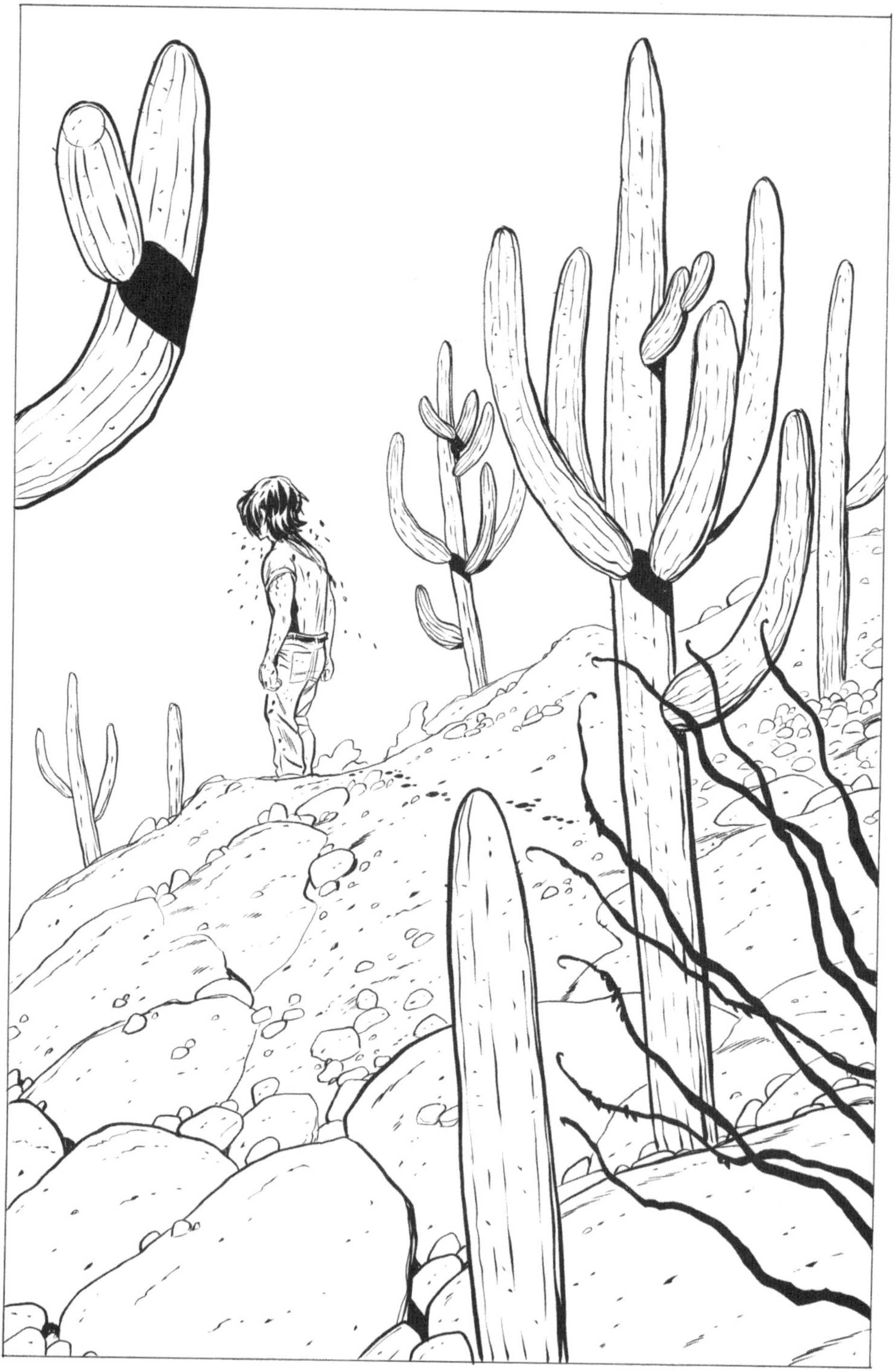

2.
ANNIE

$\nabla \cdot B = 0$
$\nabla \cdot E = \frac{\rho}{\epsilon_0}$
$\nabla \times E = -\frac{\partial B}{\partial t}$
$\nabla \times B = \mu_0 J + \mu_0 \epsilon_0 \frac{\partial E}{\partial t}$

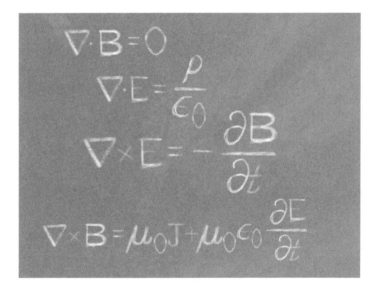

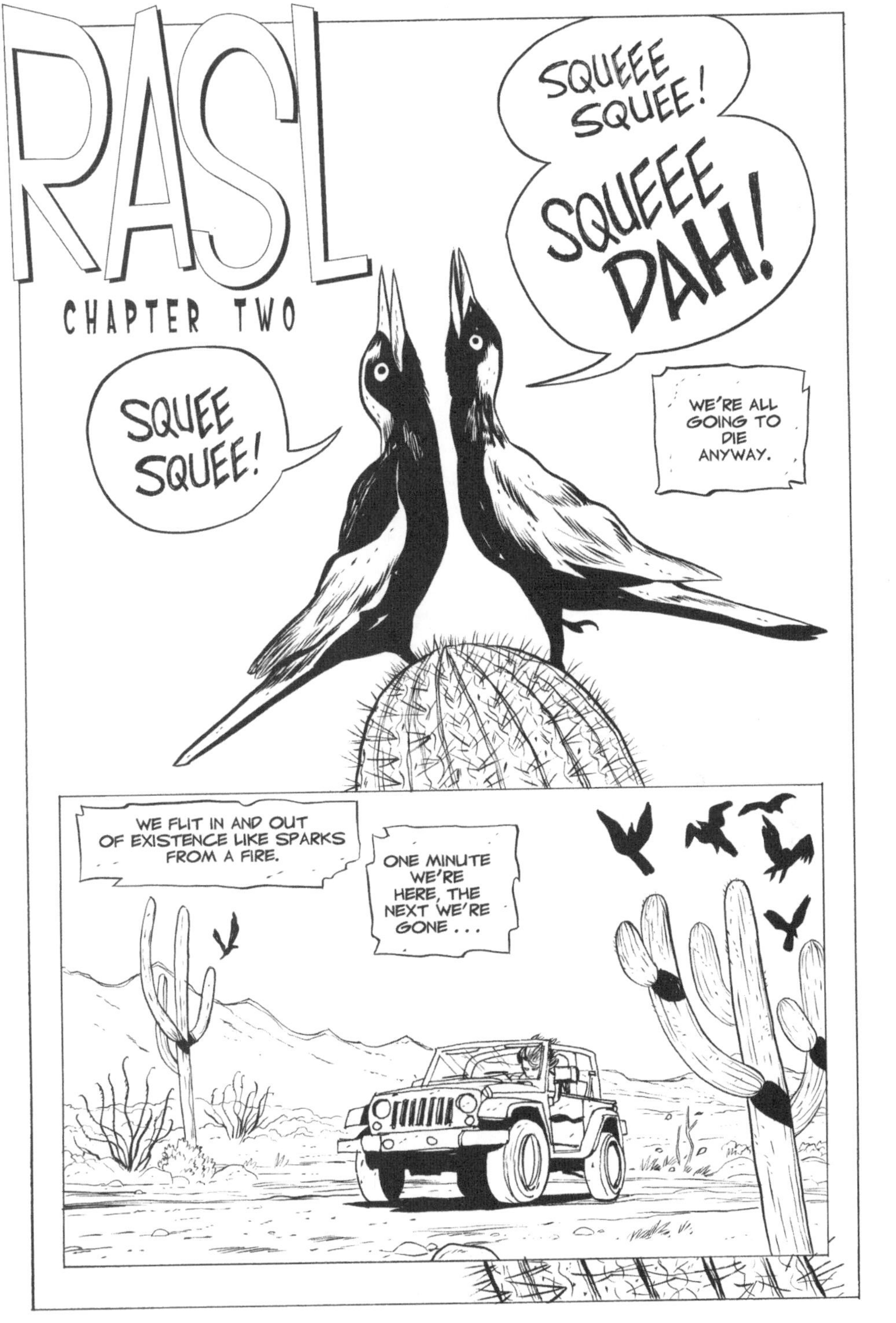
RASL
CHAPTER TWO
SQUEEE SQUEE! SQUEEE DAH!
SQUEE SQUEE!
WE'RE ALL GOING TO DIE ANYWAY.
WE FLIT IN AND OUT OF EXISTENCE LIKE SPARKS FROM A FIRE.
ONE MINUTE WE'RE HERE, THE NEXT WE'RE GONE . . .

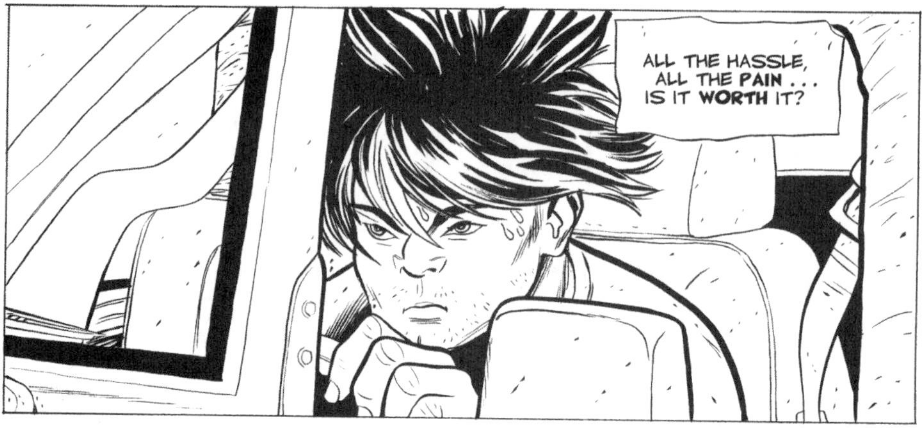
ALL THE HASSLE,
ALL THE **PAIN** . . .
IS IT **WORTH** IT?

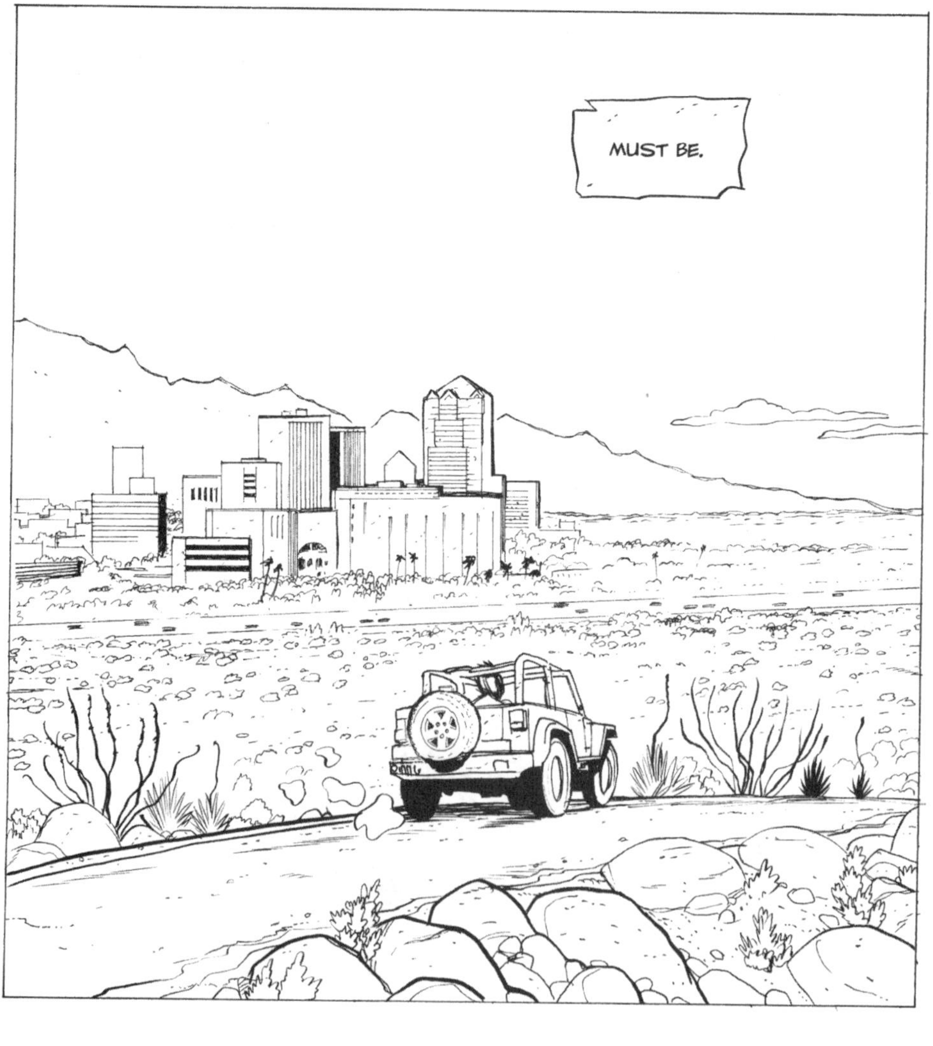
MUST BE.

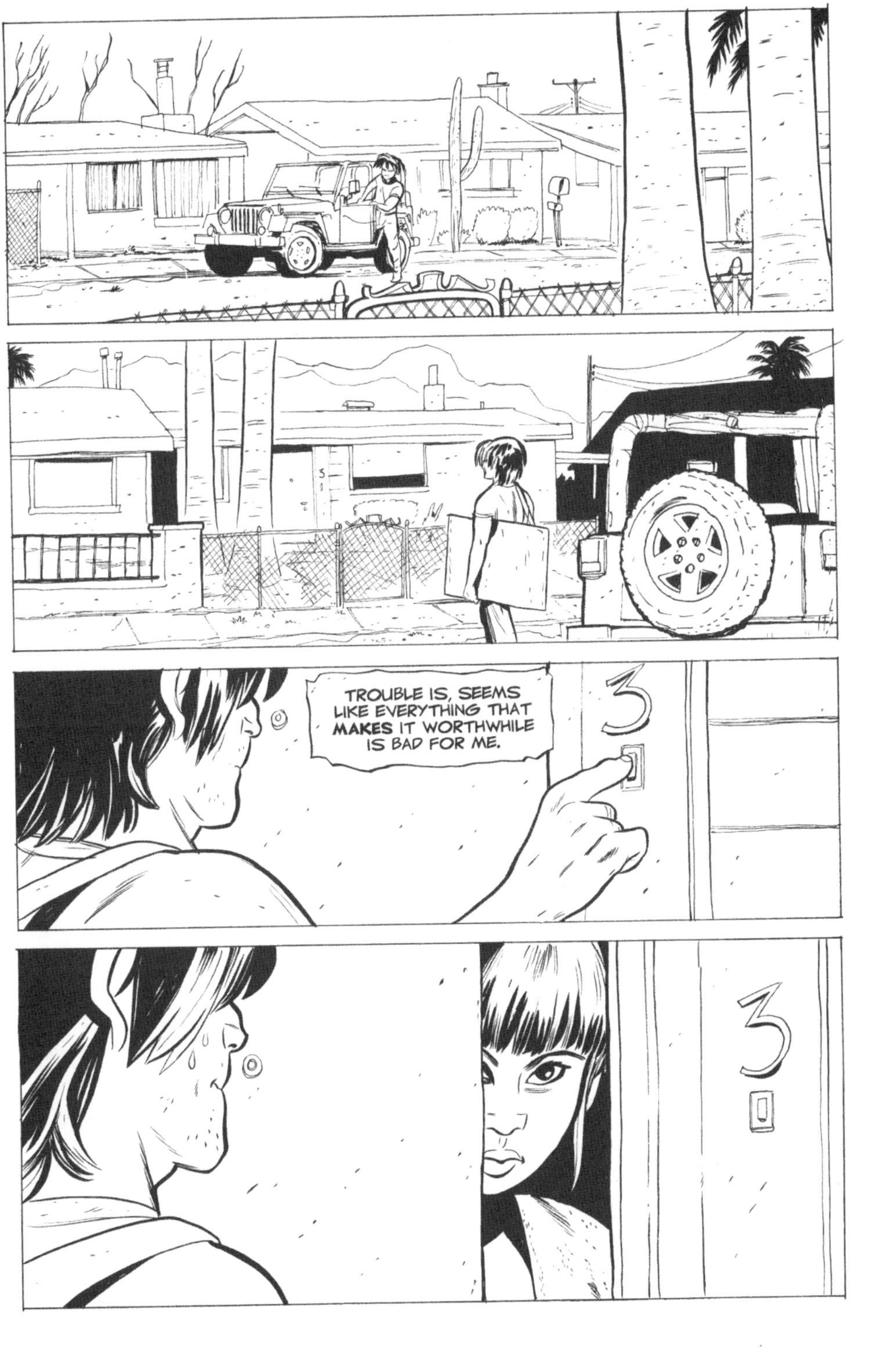
TROUBLE IS, SEEMS LIKE EVERYTHING THAT **MAKES** IT WORTHWHILE IS BAD FOR ME.

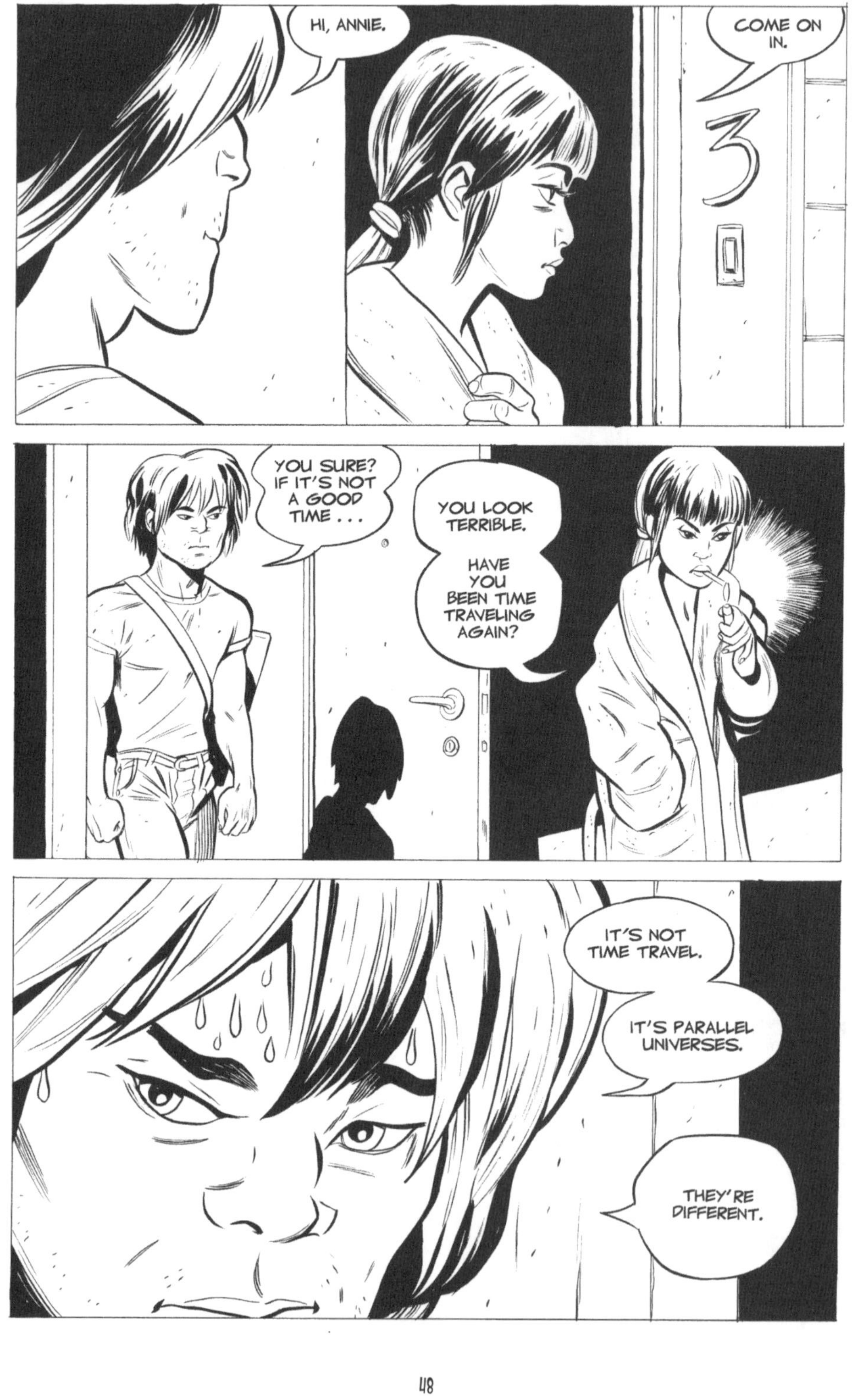
HI, ANNIE.
COME ON IN.
YOU SURE? IF IT'S NOT A GOOD TIME . . .
YOU LOOK TERRIBLE.
HAVE YOU BEEN TIME TRAVELING AGAIN?
IT'S NOT TIME TRAVEL.
IT'S PARALLEL UNIVERSES.
THEY'RE DIFFERENT.

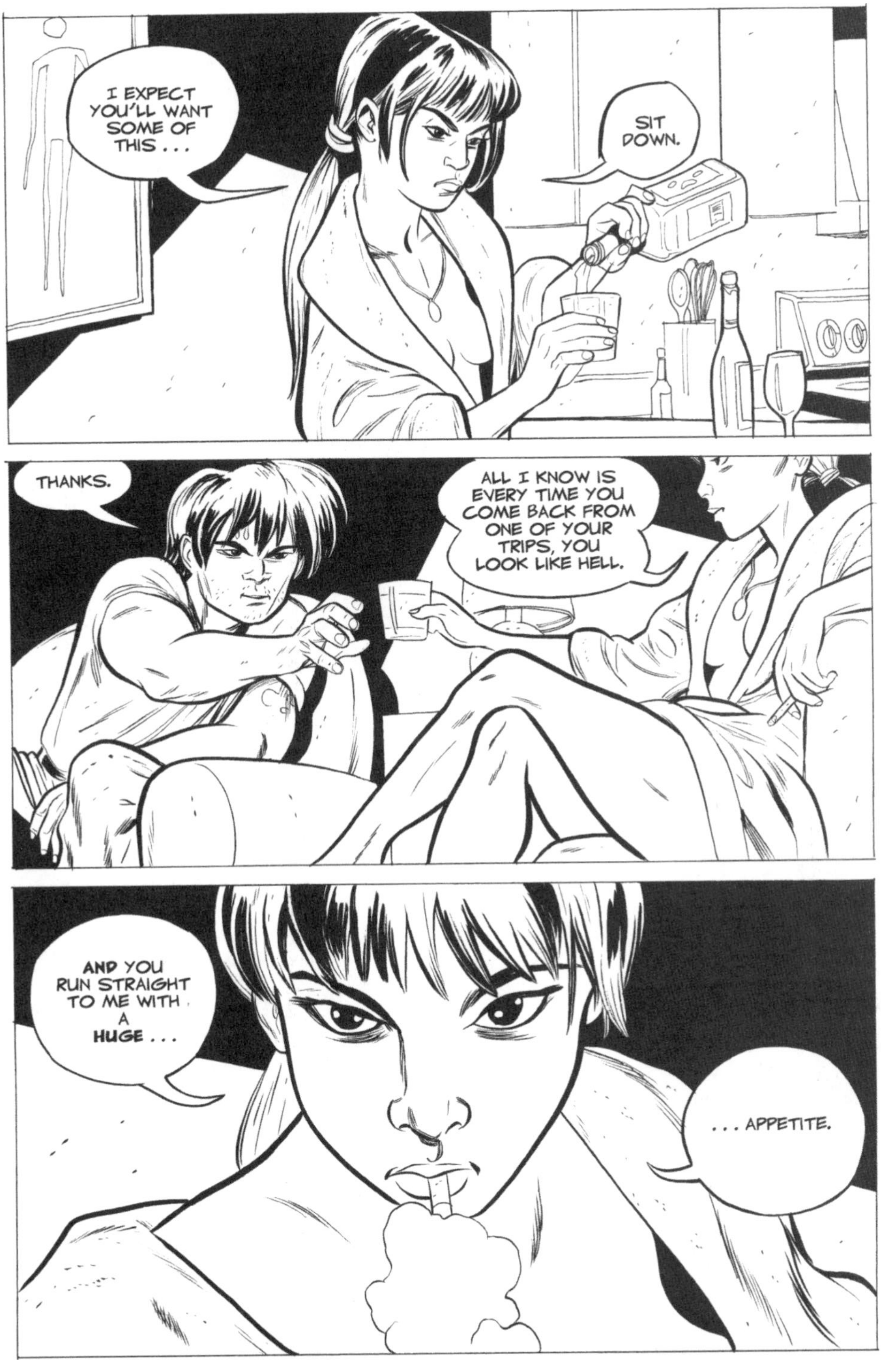
I EXPECT YOU'LL WANT SOME OF THIS . . .
SIT DOWN.
THANKS.
ALL I KNOW IS EVERY TIME YOU COME BACK FROM ONE OF YOUR TRIPS, YOU LOOK LIKE HELL.
AND YOU RUN STRAIGHT TO ME WITH A HUGE . . .
. . . APPETITE.

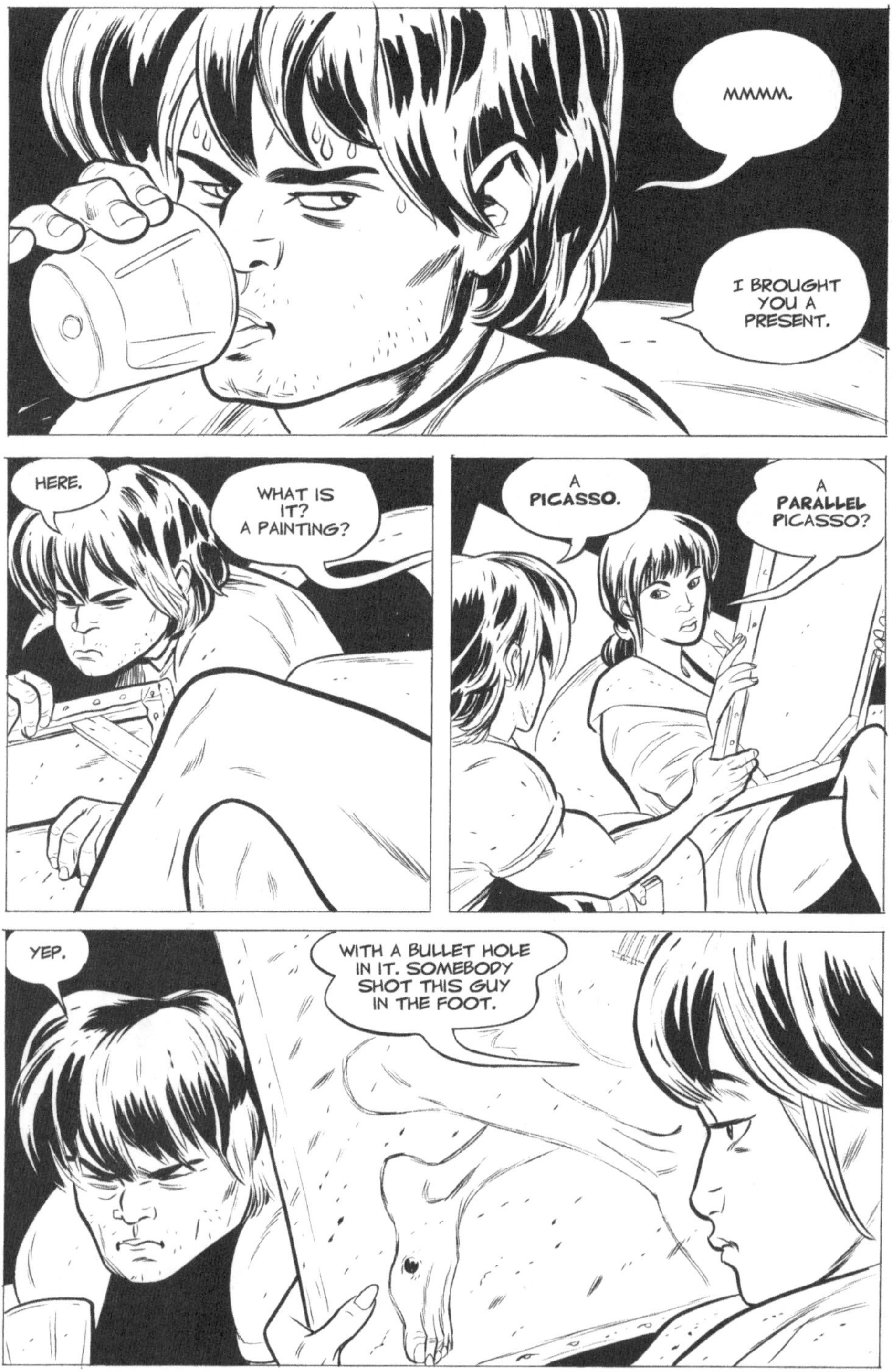
MMMM.
I BROUGHT YOU A PRESENT.
HERE.
WHAT IS IT? A PAINTING?
A PICASSO.
A PARALLEL PICASSO?
YEP.
WITH A BULLET HOLE IN IT. SOMEBODY SHOT THIS GUY IN THE FOOT.

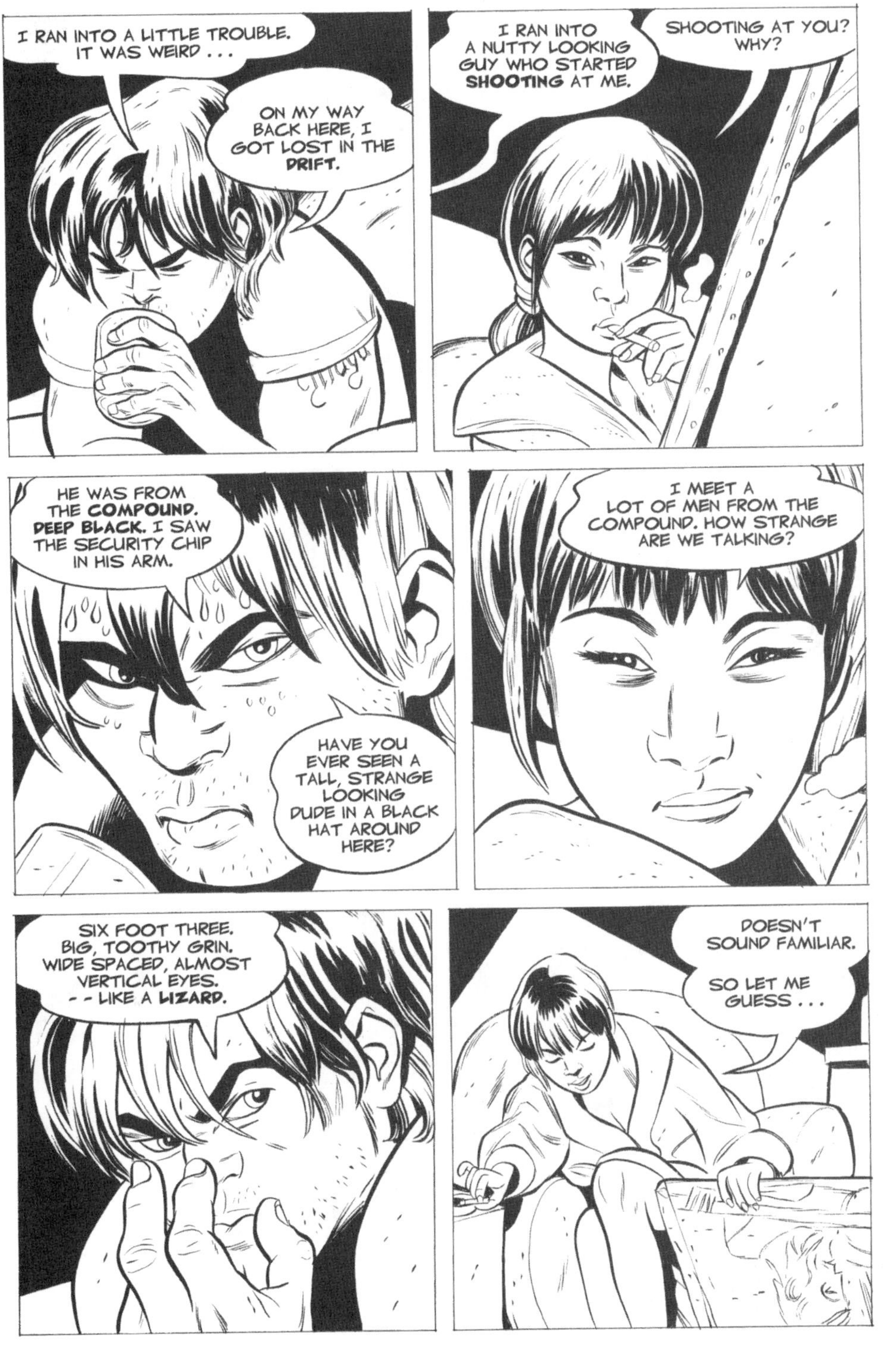
I RAN INTO A LITTLE TROUBLE. IT WAS WEIRD . . .
ON MY WAY BACK HERE, I GOT LOST IN THE DRIFT.
I RAN INTO A NUTTY LOOKING GUY WHO STARTED SHOOTING AT ME.
SHOOTING AT YOU? WHY?
HE WAS FROM THE COMPOUND. DEEP BLACK. I SAW THE SECURITY CHIP IN HIS ARM.
HAVE YOU EVER SEEN A TALL, STRANGE LOOKING DUDE IN A BLACK HAT AROUND HERE?
I MEET A LOT OF MEN FROM THE COMPOUND. HOW STRANGE ARE WE TALKING?
SIX FOOT THREE. BIG, TOOTHY GRIN. WIDE SPACED, ALMOST VERTICAL EYES. - - LIKE A LIZARD.
DOESN'T SOUND FAMILIAR.
SO LET ME GUESS . . .

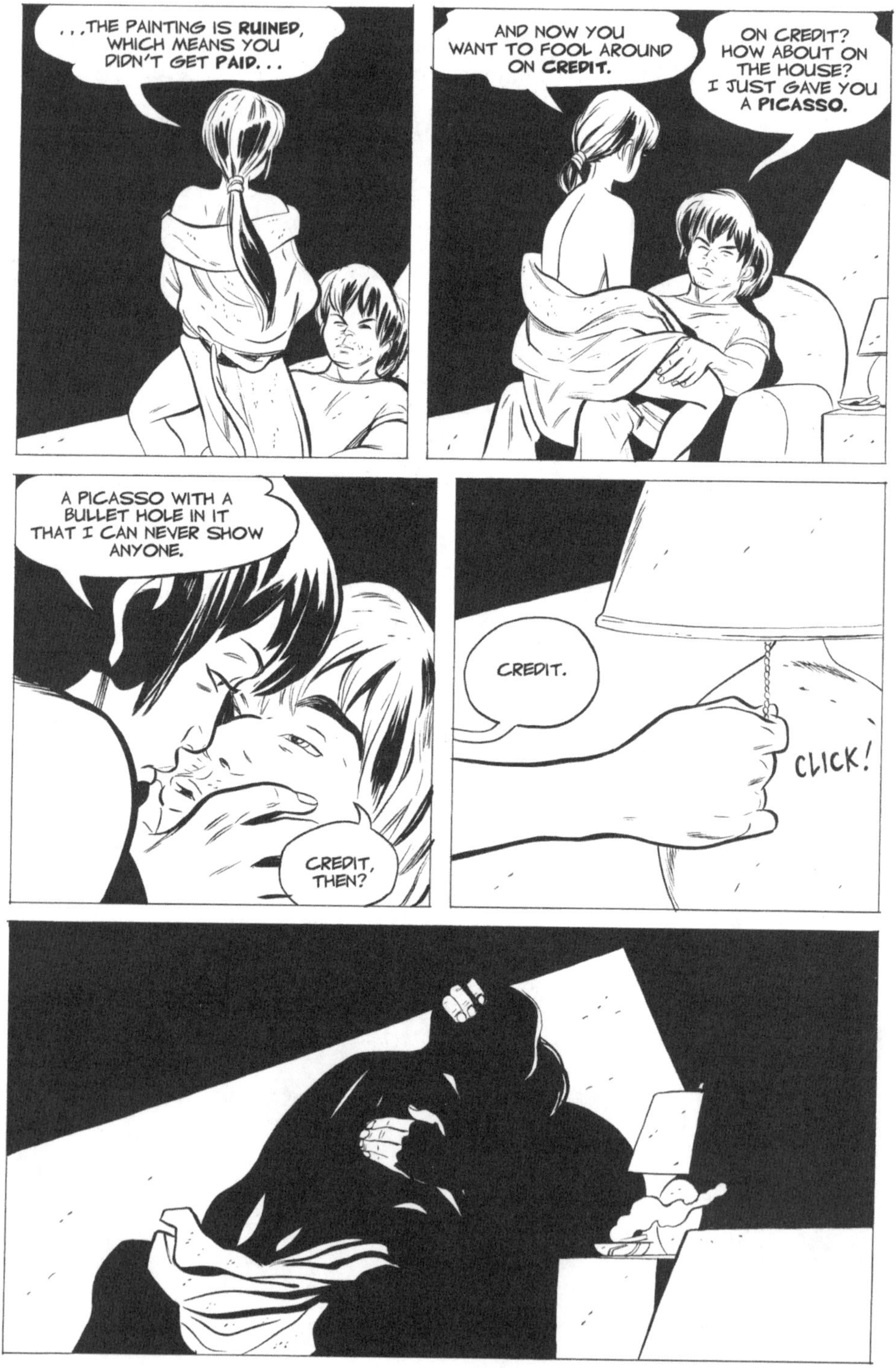

. . .THE PAINTING IS RUINED, WHICH MEANS YOU DIDN'T GET PAID. . .
AND NOW YOU WANT TO FOOL AROUND ON CREDIT.
ON CREDIT? HOW ABOUT ON THE HOUSE? I JUST GAVE YOU A PICASSO.
A PICASSO WITH A BULLET HOLE IN IT THAT I CAN NEVER SHOW ANYONE.
CREDIT, THEN?
CREDIT.
CLICK!

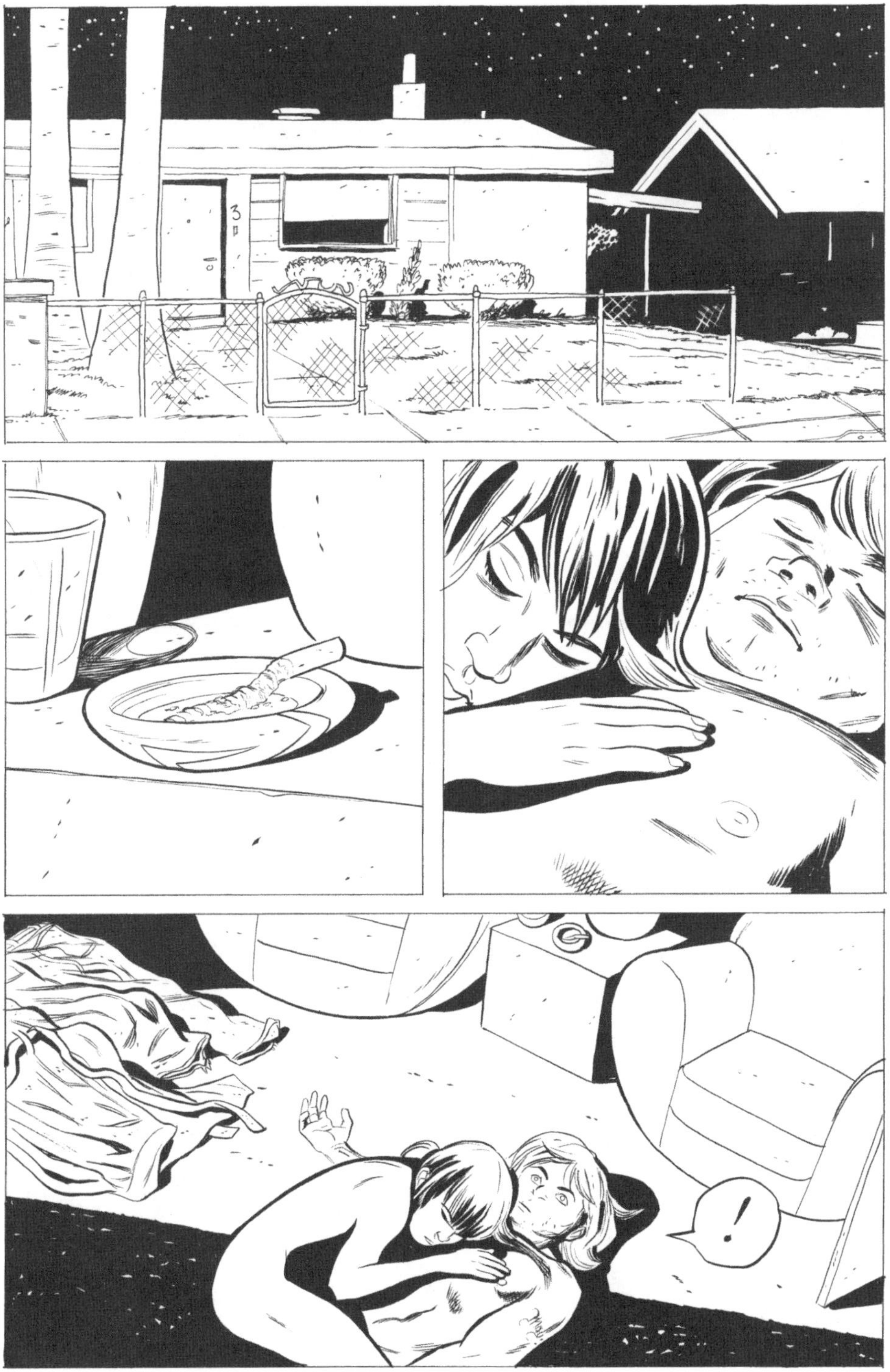
!

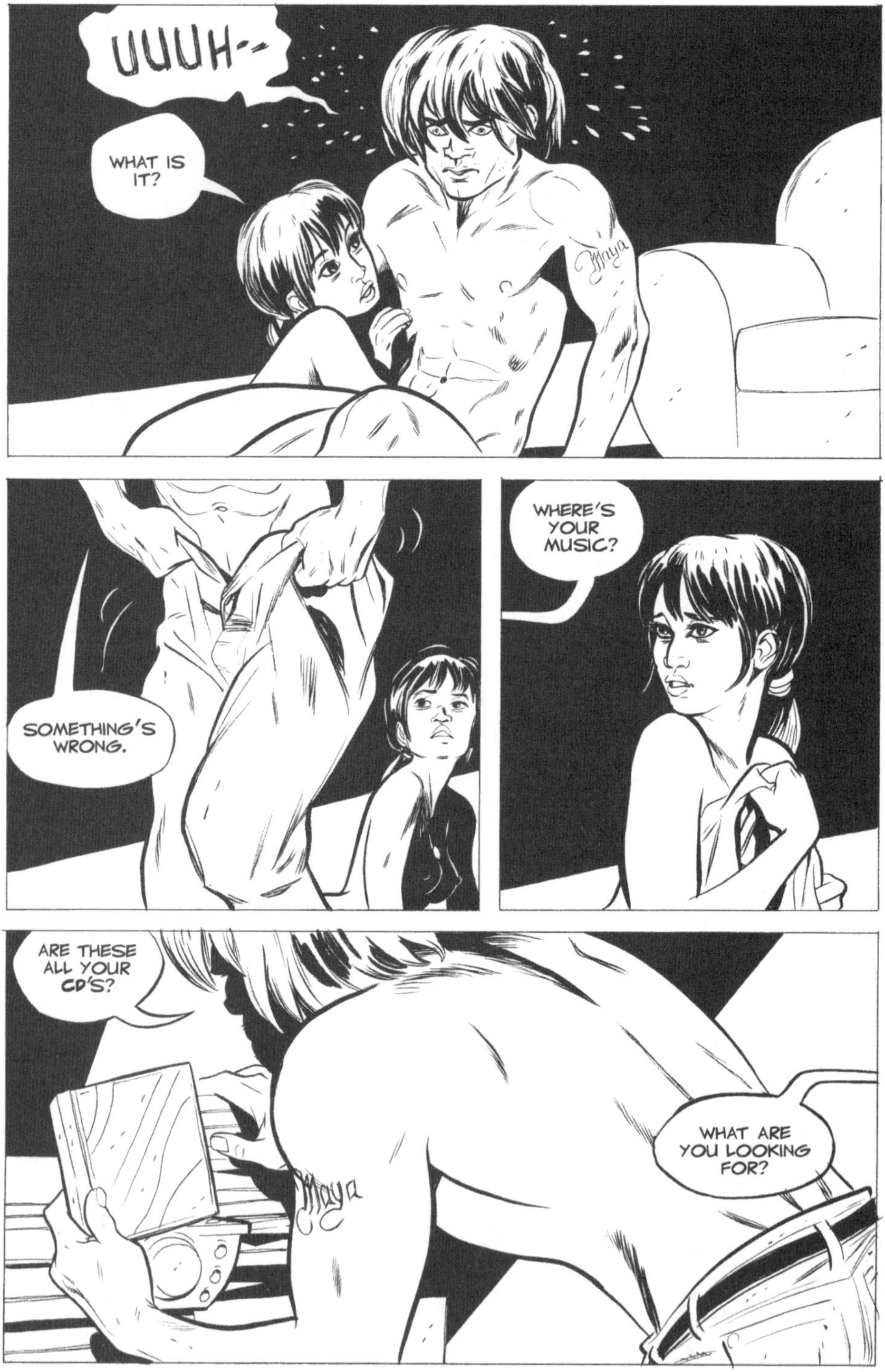
UUUH--
WHAT IS IT?
SOMETHING'S WRONG.
WHERE'S YOUR MUSIC?
ARE THESE ALL YOUR CD'S?
WHAT ARE YOU LOOKING FOR?

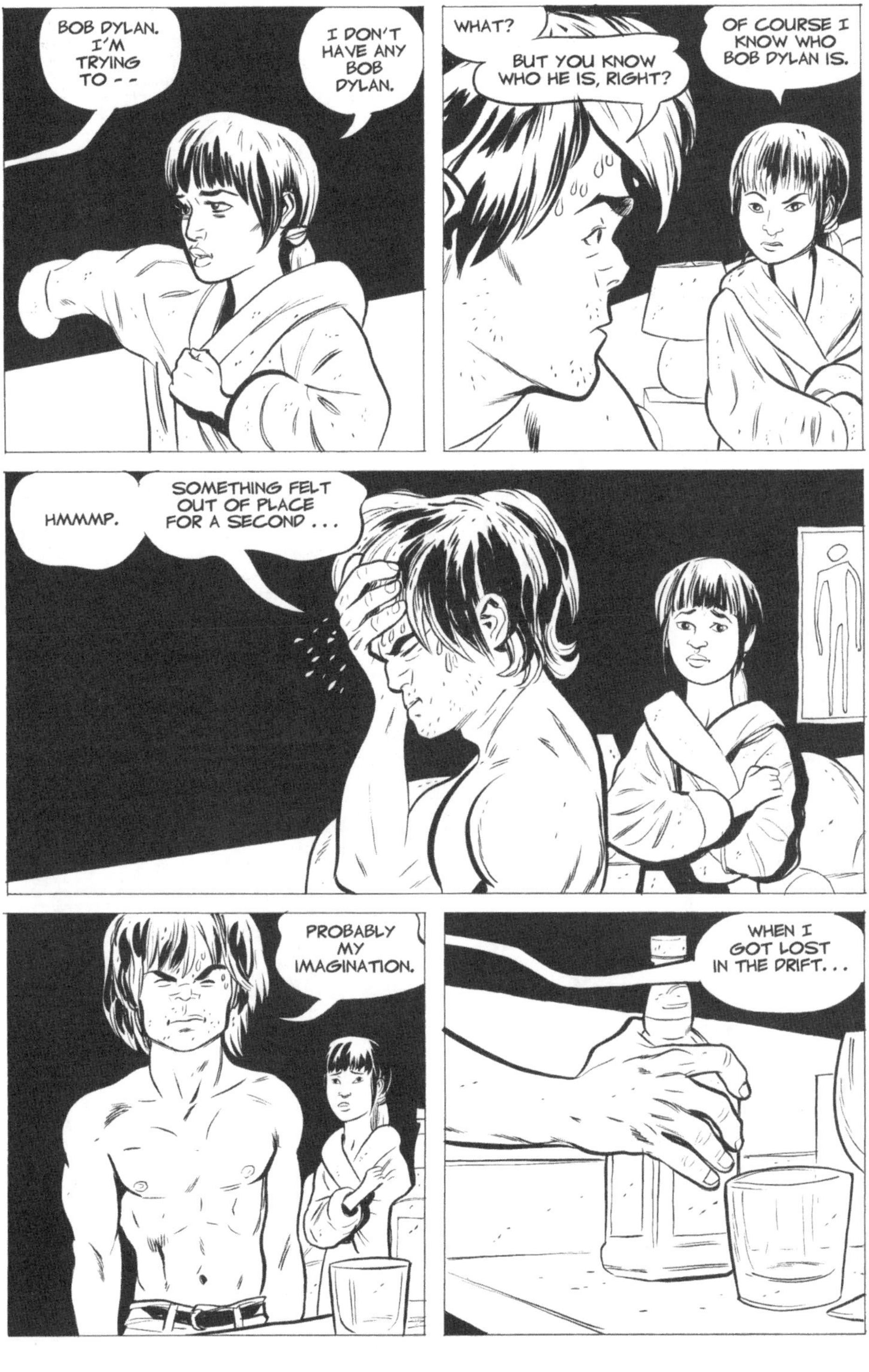
BOB DYLAN. I'M TRYING TO - -
I DON'T HAVE ANY BOB DYLAN.
WHAT?
BUT YOU KNOW WHO HE IS, RIGHT?
OF COURSE I KNOW WHO BOB DYLAN IS.
HMMMP.
SOMETHING FELT OUT OF PLACE FOR A SECOND . . .
PROBABLY MY IMAGINATION.
WHEN I GOT LOST IN THE DRIFT. . .

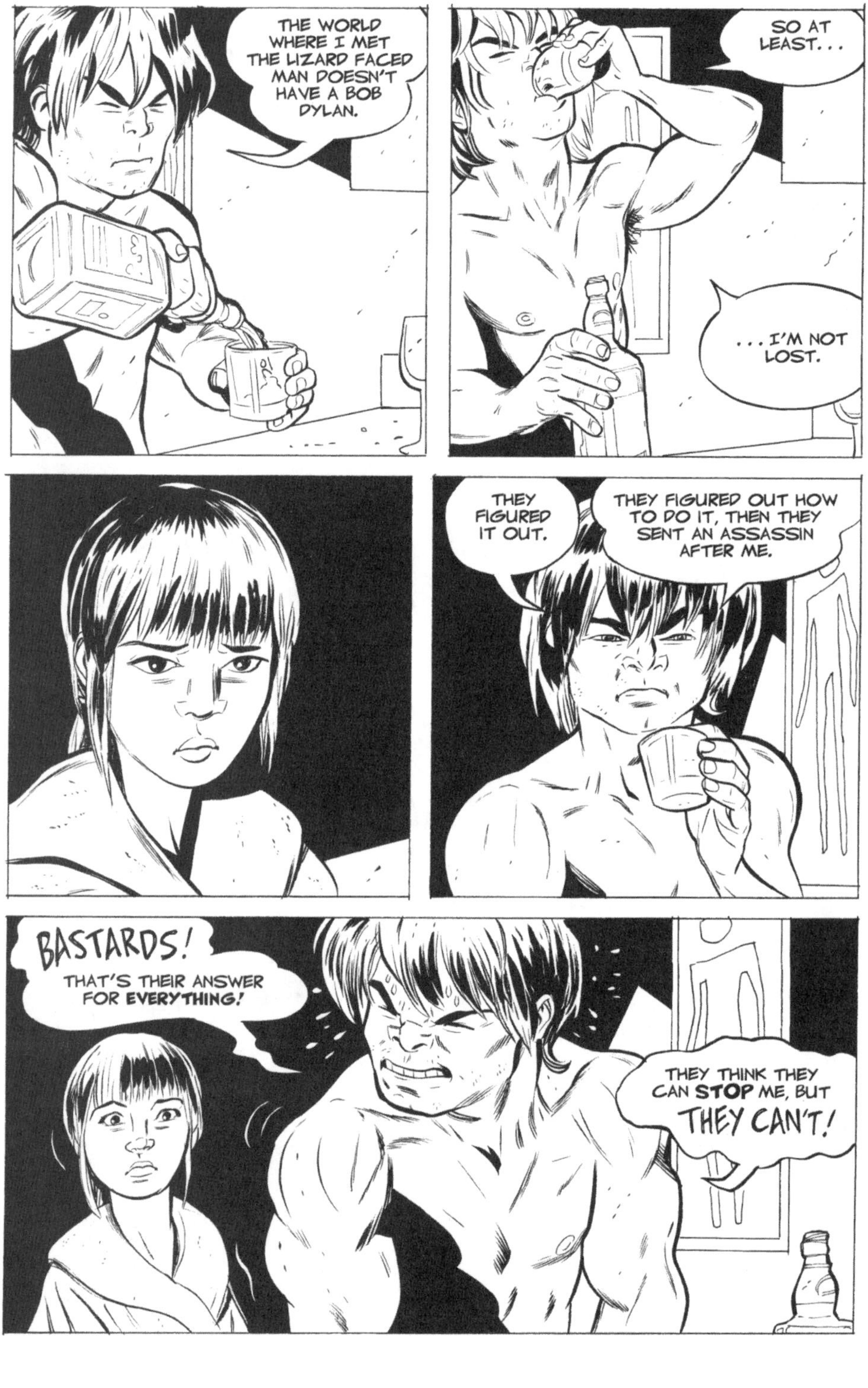
THE WORLD WHERE I MET THE LIZARD FACED MAN DOESN'T HAVE A BOB DYLAN.
SO AT LEAST...
...I'M NOT LOST.
THEY FIGURED IT OUT.
THEY FIGURED OUT HOW TO DO IT, THEN THEY SENT AN ASSASSIN AFTER ME.
BASTARDS! THAT'S THEIR ANSWER FOR EVERYTHING!
THEY THINK THEY CAN STOP ME, BUT THEY CAN'T!

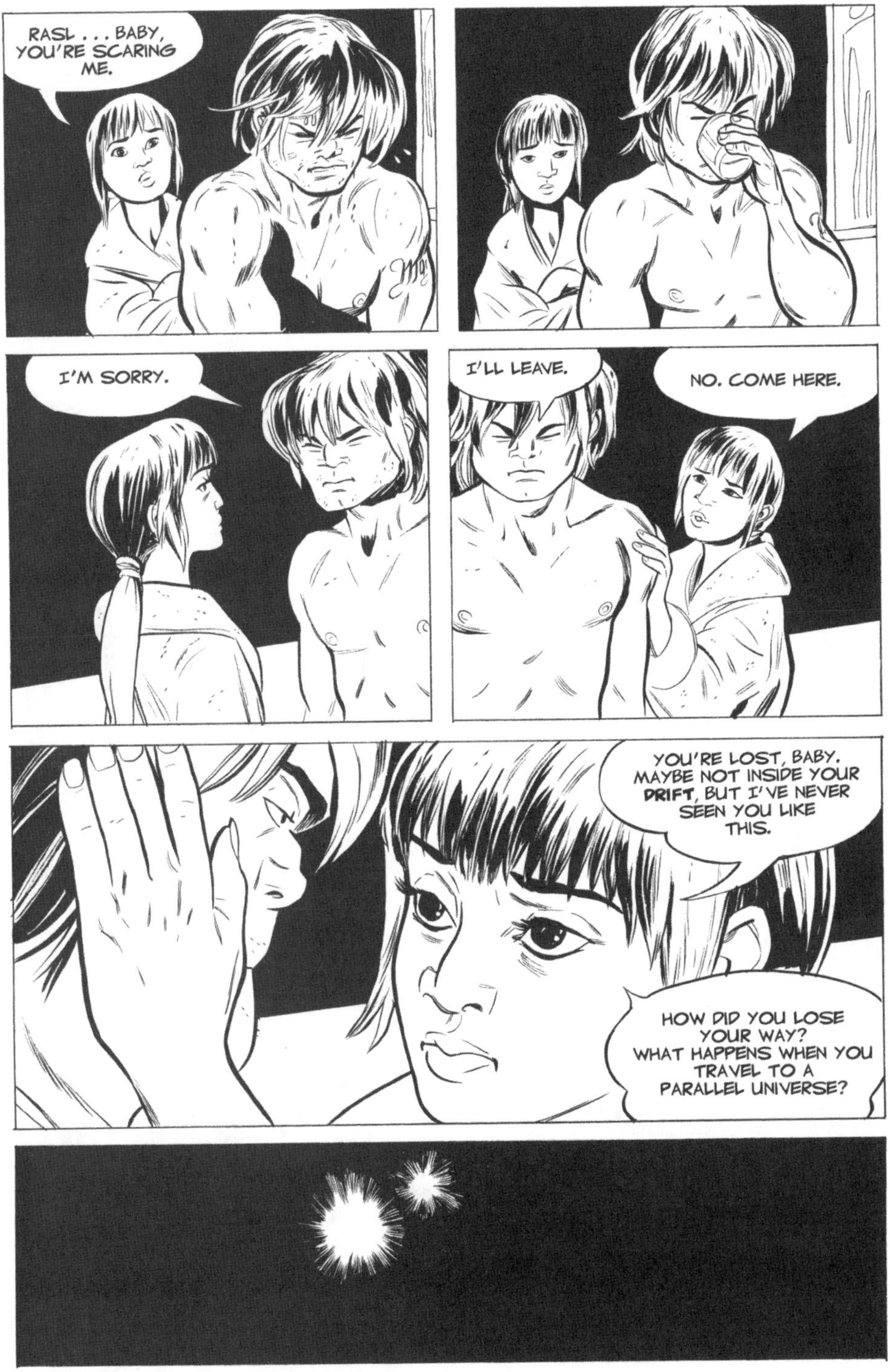
RASL . . . BABY, YOU'RE SCARING ME.
I'M SORRY.
I'LL LEAVE.
NO. COME HERE.
YOU'RE LOST, BABY. MAYBE NOT INSIDE YOUR **DRIFT**, BUT I'VE NEVER SEEN YOU LIKE THIS.
HOW DID YOU LOSE YOUR WAY? WHAT HAPPENS WHEN YOU TRAVEL TO A PARALLEL UNIVERSE?

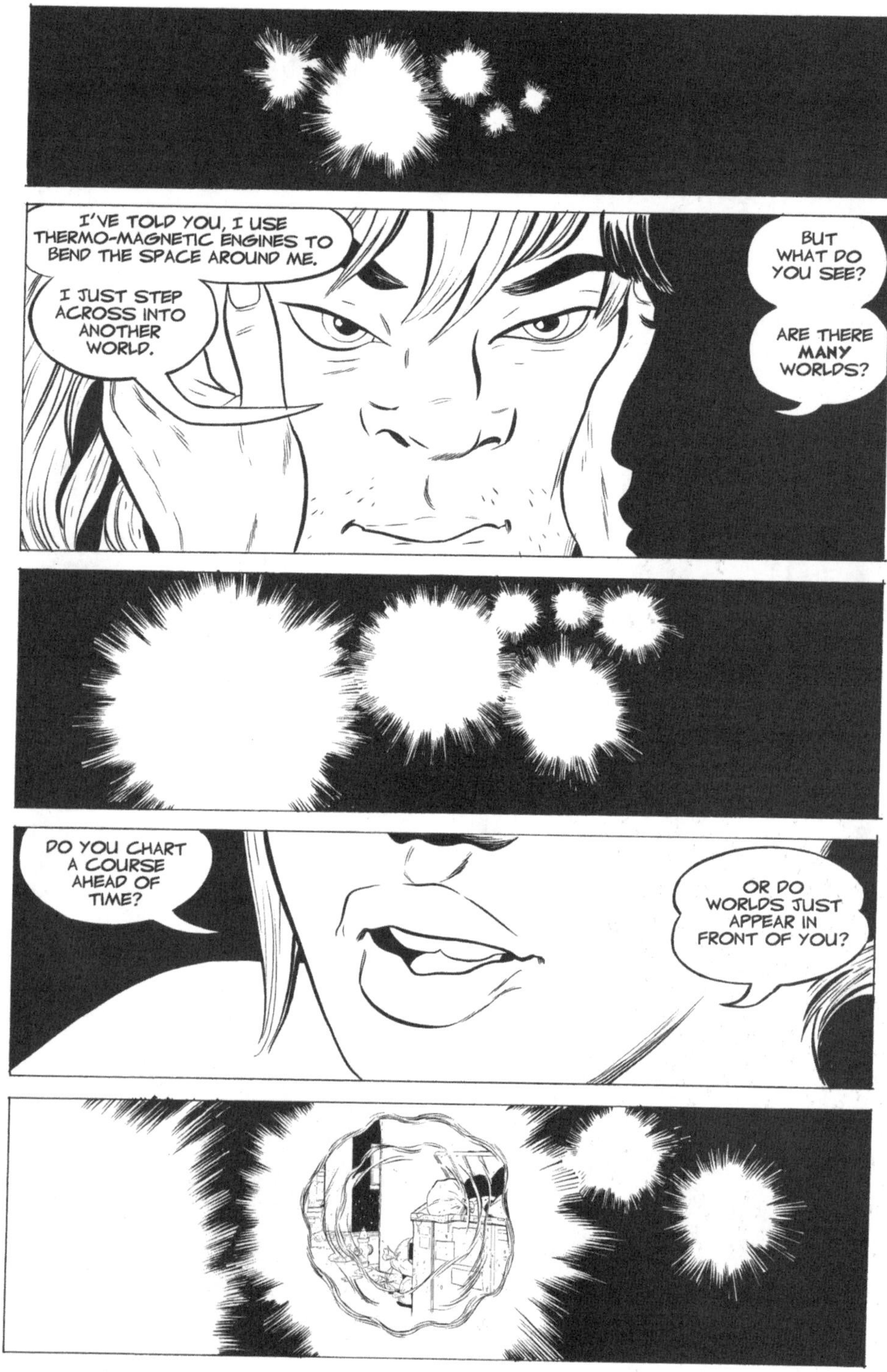
I'VE TOLD YOU, I USE THERMO-MAGNETIC ENGINES TO BEND THE SPACE AROUND ME.
I JUST STEP ACROSS INTO ANOTHER WORLD.
BUT WHAT DO YOU SEE?
ARE THERE **MANY** WORLDS?
DO YOU CHART A COURSE AHEAD OF TIME?
OR DO WORLDS JUST APPEAR IN FRONT OF YOU?

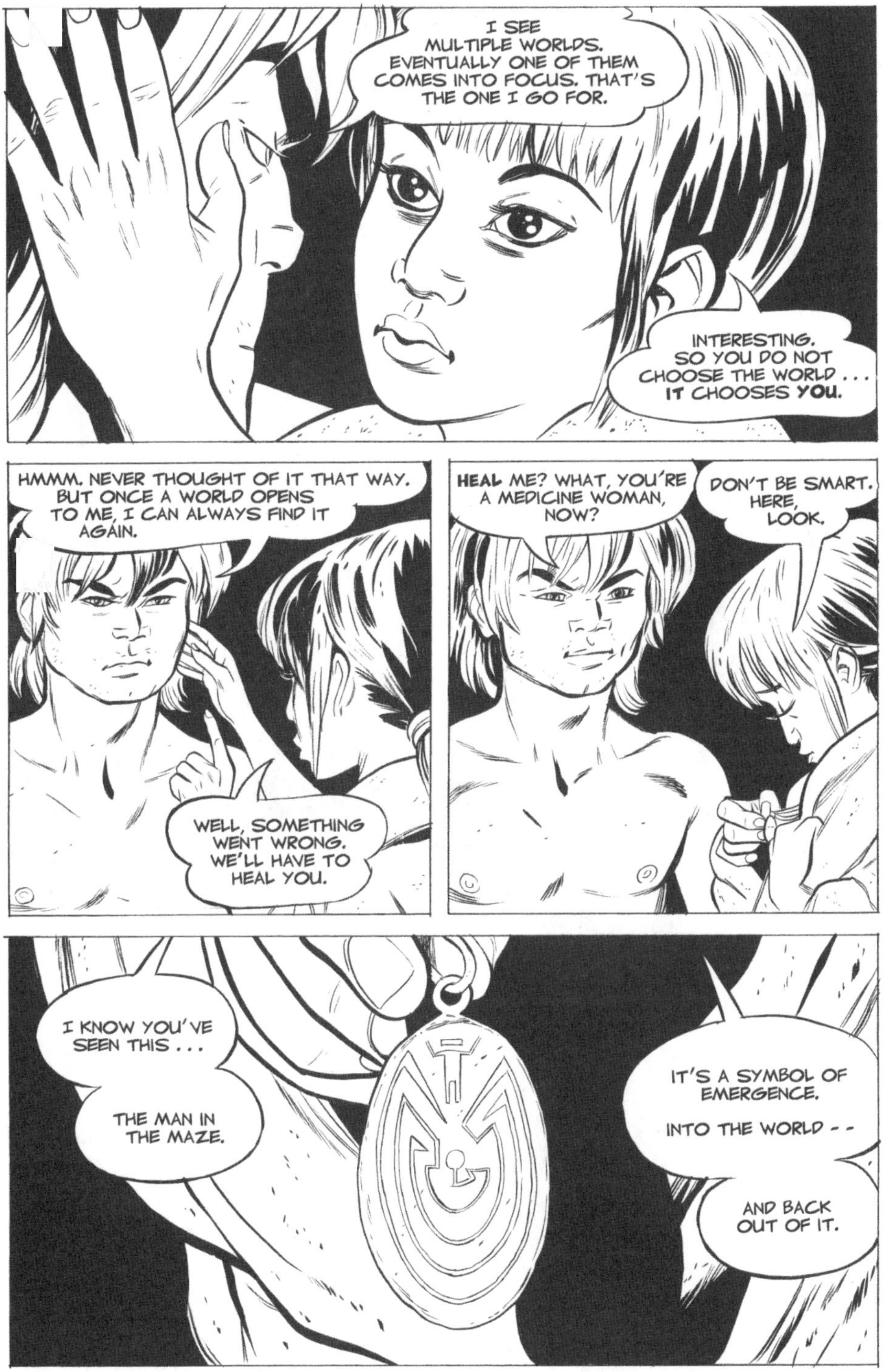
I SEE MULTIPLE WORLDS. EVENTUALLY ONE OF THEM COMES INTO FOCUS. THAT'S THE ONE I GO FOR.
INTERESTING. SO YOU DO NOT CHOOSE THE WORLD . . . IT CHOOSES YOU.
HMMM. NEVER THOUGHT OF IT THAT WAY. BUT ONCE A WORLD OPENS TO ME, I CAN ALWAYS FIND IT AGAIN.
WELL, SOMETHING WENT WRONG. WE'LL HAVE TO HEAL YOU.
HEAL ME? WHAT, YOU'RE A MEDICINE WOMAN, NOW?
DON'T BE SMART. HERE, LOOK.
I KNOW YOU'VE SEEN THIS . . .
THE MAN IN THE MAZE.
IT'S A SYMBOL OF EMERGENCE.
INTO THE WORLD - -
AND BACK OUT OF IT.

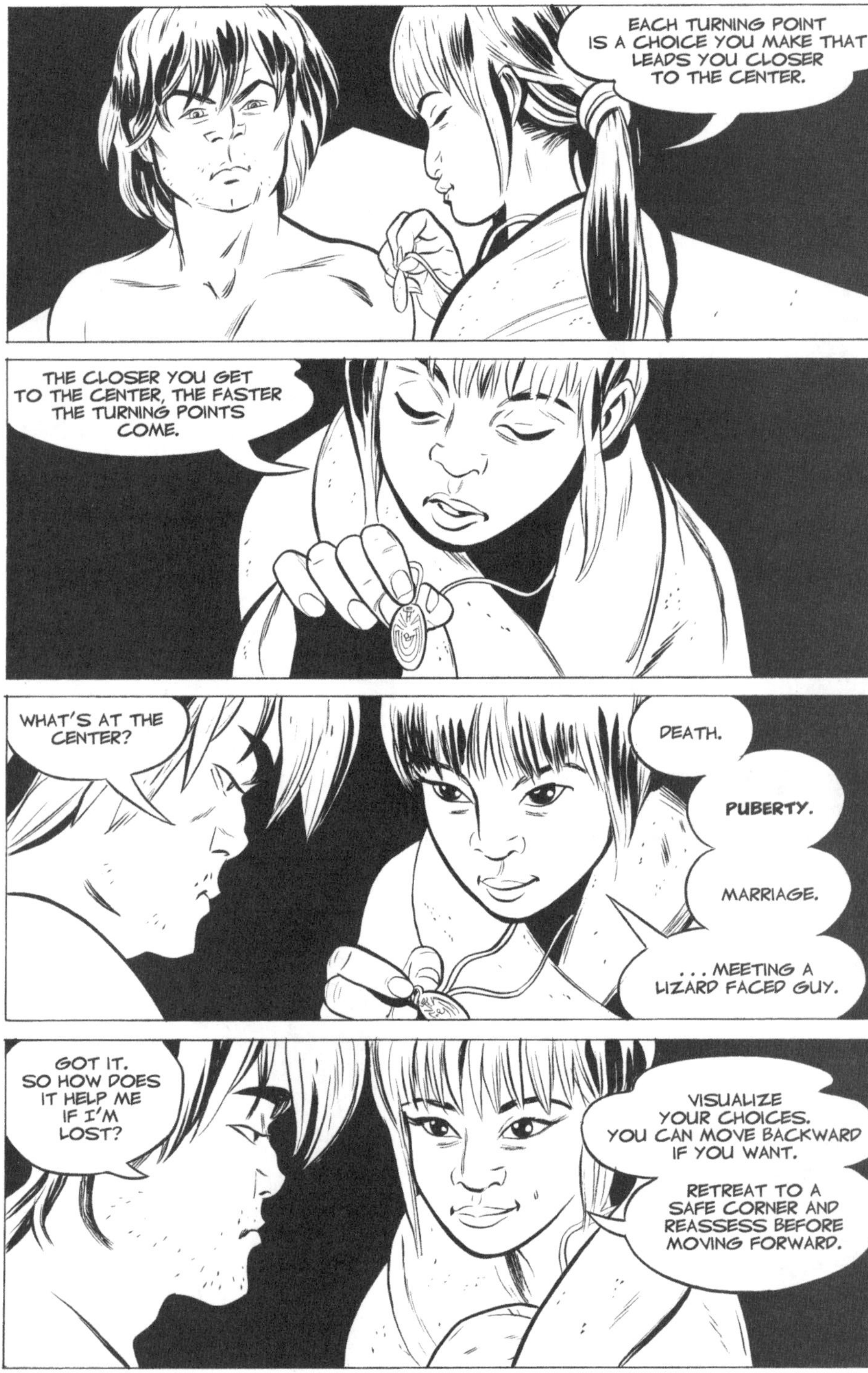
EACH TURNING POINT IS A CHOICE YOU MAKE THAT LEADS YOU CLOSER TO THE CENTER.
THE CLOSER YOU GET TO THE CENTER, THE FASTER THE TURNING POINTS COME.
WHAT'S AT THE CENTER?
DEATH.
PUBERTY.
MARRIAGE.
. . . MEETING A LIZARD FACED GUY.
GOT IT. SO HOW DOES IT HELP ME IF I'M LOST?
VISUALIZE YOUR CHOICES. YOU CAN MOVE BACKWARD IF YOU WANT.
RETREAT TO A SAFE CORNER AND REASSESS BEFORE MOVING FORWARD.

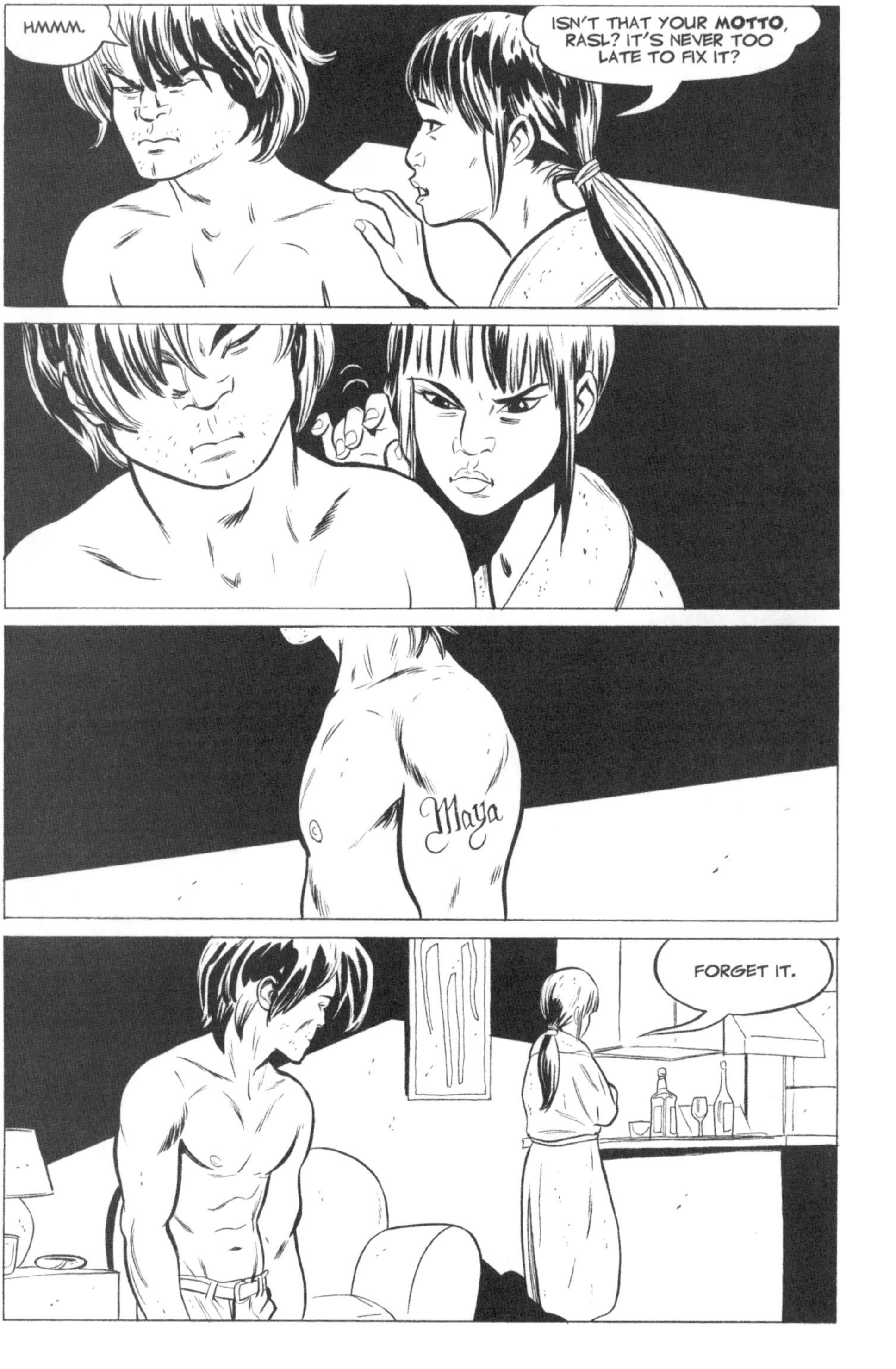
HMMM.
ISN'T THAT YOUR MOTTO, RASL? IT'S NEVER TOO LATE TO FIX IT?
Maya
FORGET IT.

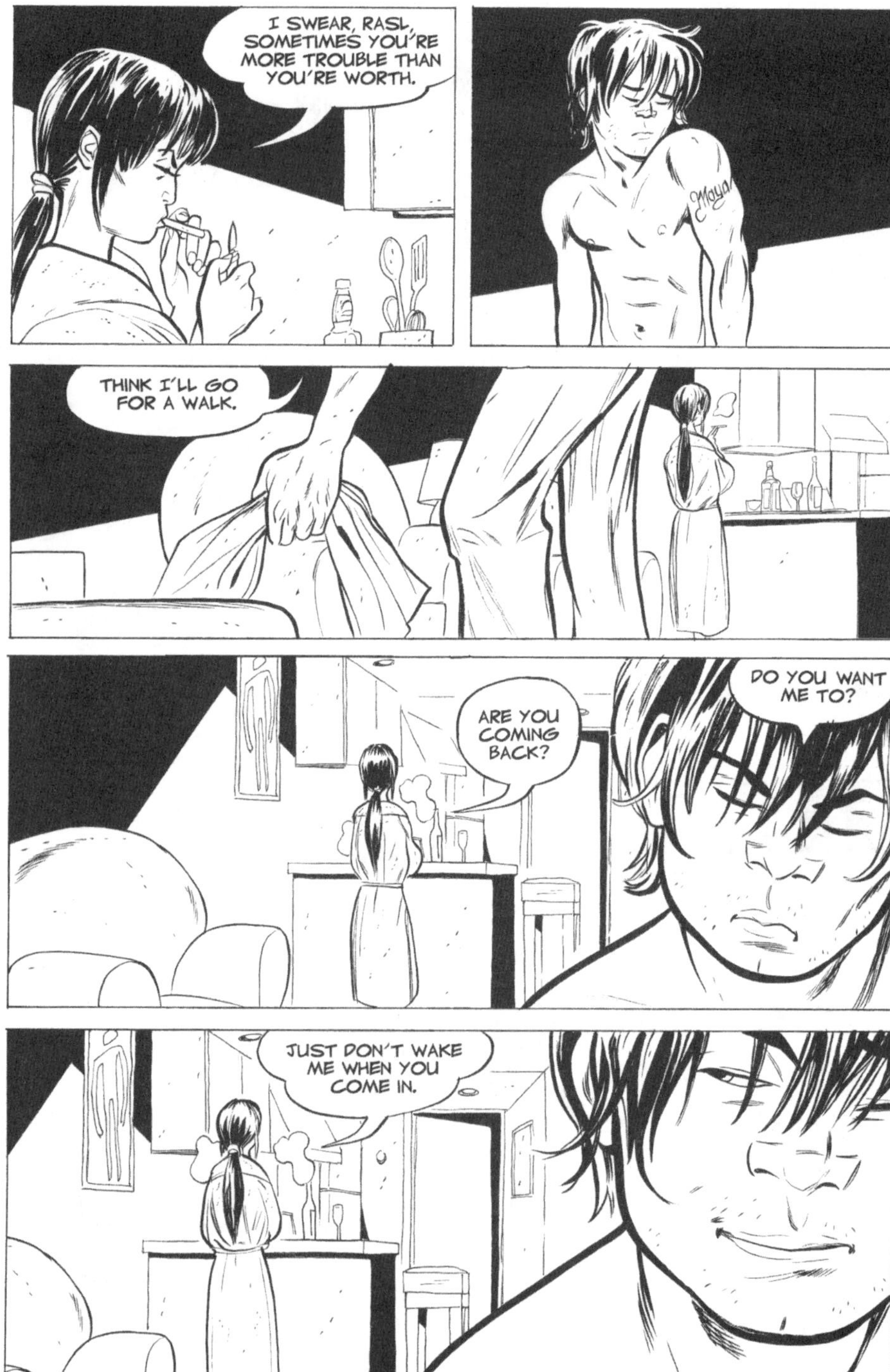
I SWEAR, RASL, SOMETIMES YOU'RE MORE TROUBLE THAN YOU'RE WORTH.
Maya
THINK I'LL GO FOR A WALK.
ARE YOU COMING BACK?
DO YOU WANT ME TO?
JUST DON'T WAKE ME WHEN YOU COME IN.

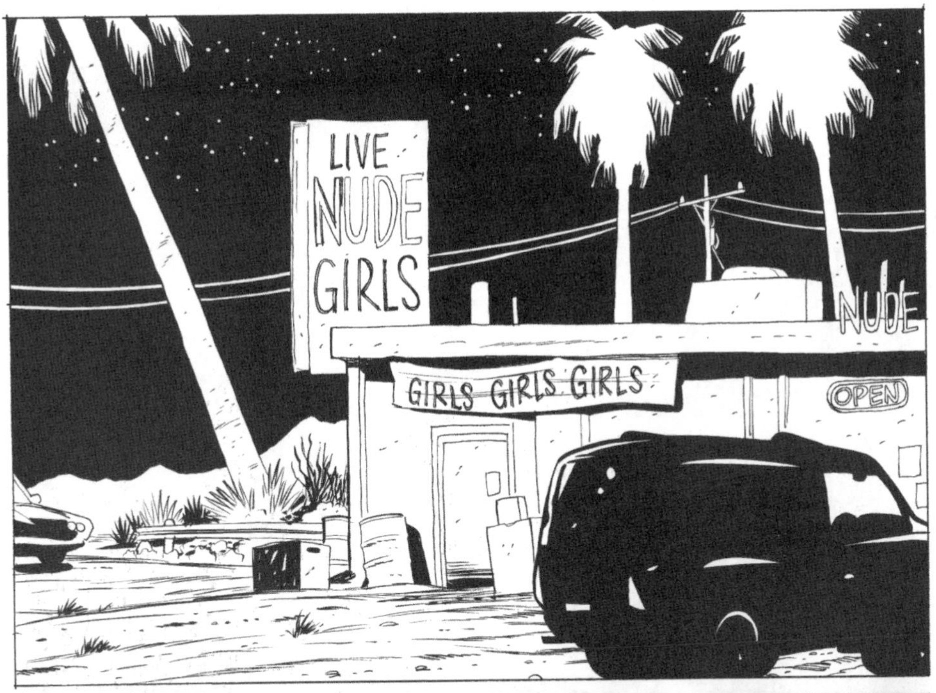
LIVE NUDE GIRLS
NUDE
GIRLS GIRLS GIRLS
OPEN

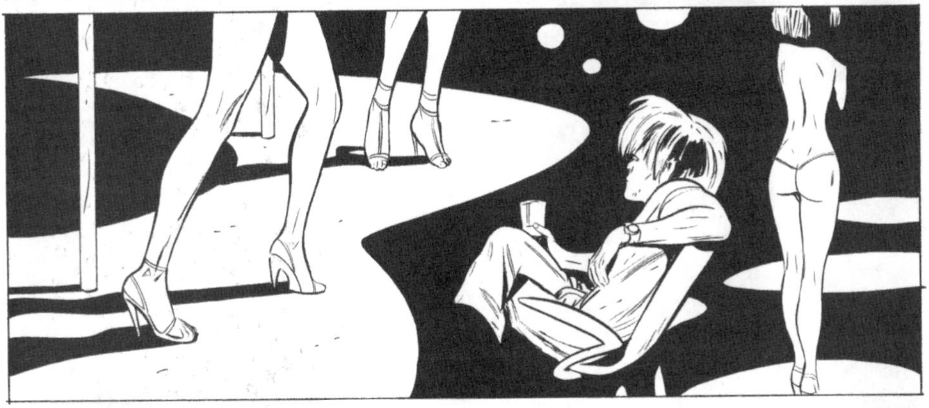

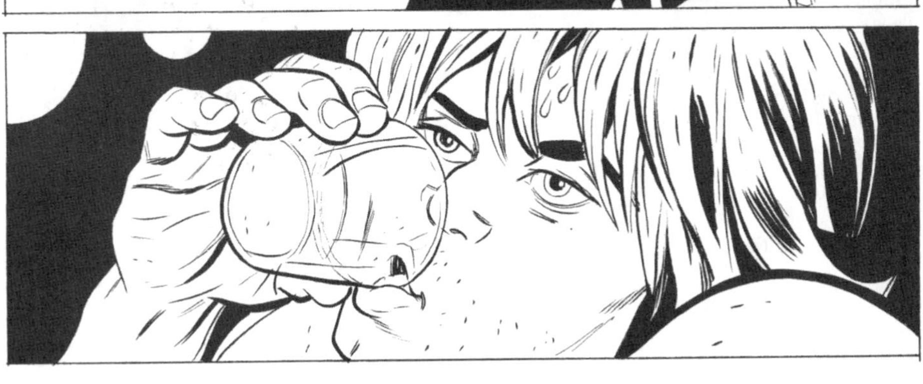

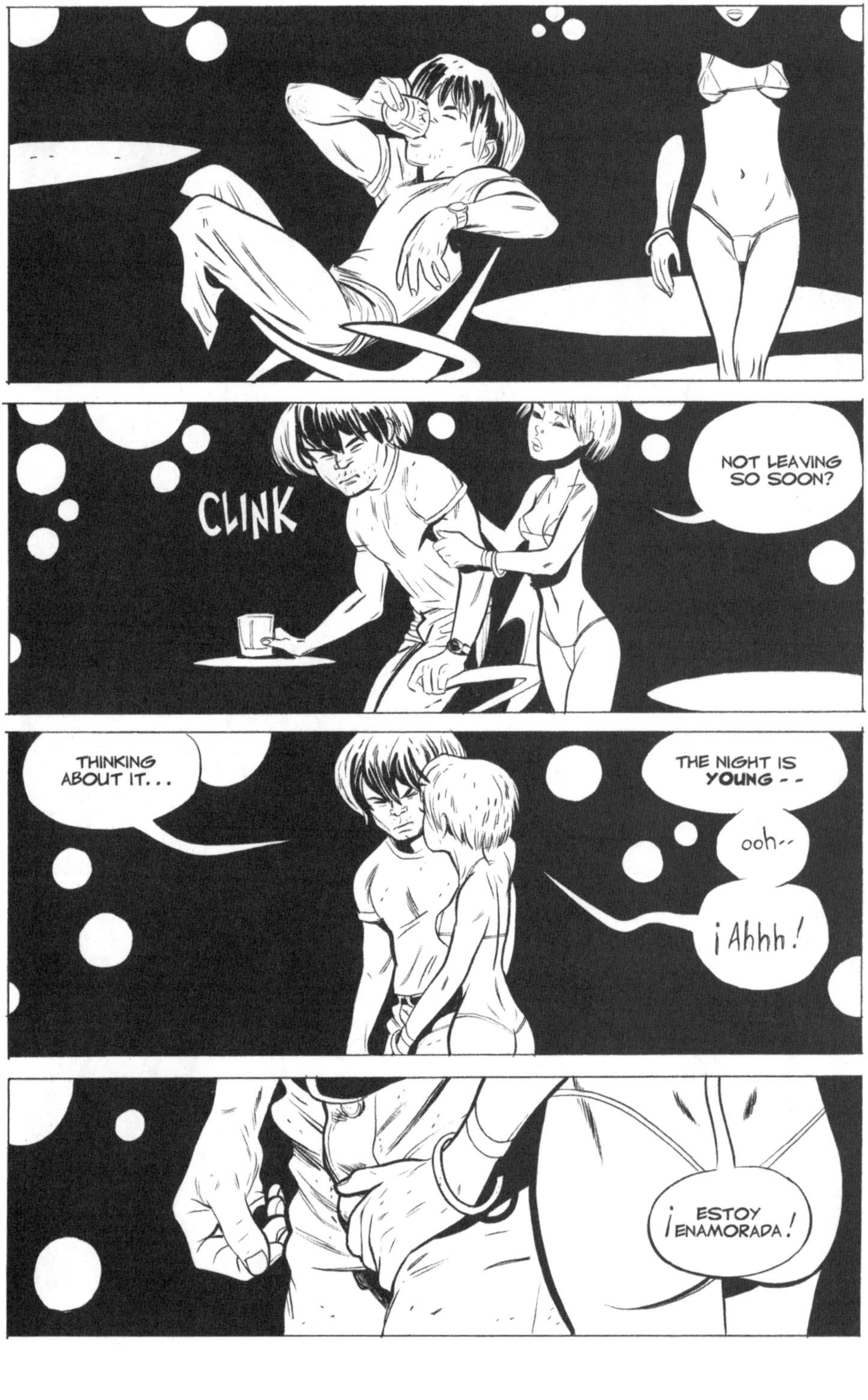
CLINK
NOT LEAVING SO SOON?
THINKING ABOUT IT...
THE NIGHT IS **YOUNG** --
ooh--
¡Ahhh!
¡ESTOY ENAMORADA!

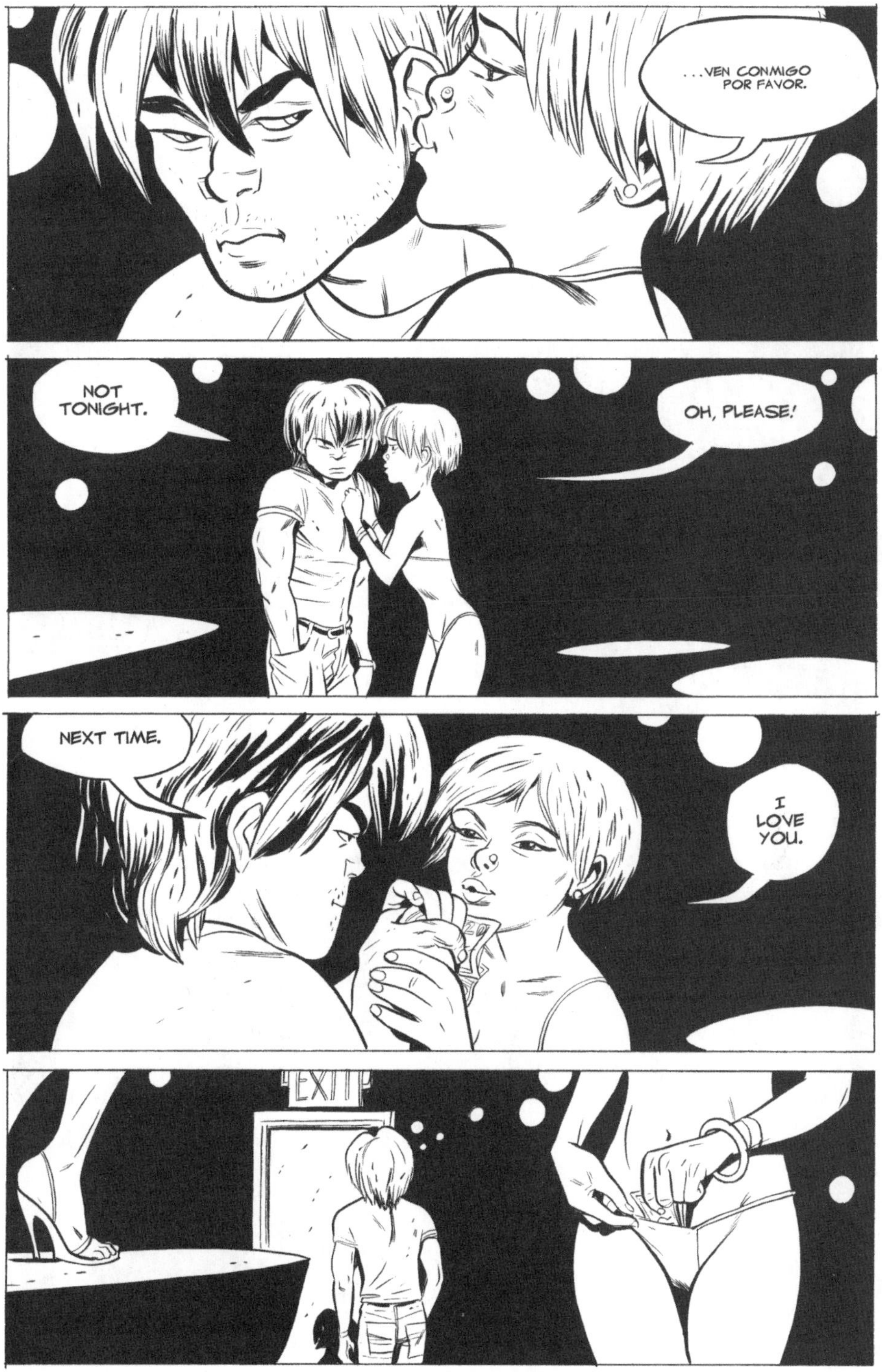
...VEN CONMIGO POR FAVOR.
NOT TONIGHT.
OH, PLEASE!
NEXT TIME.
I LOVE YOU.
EXIT

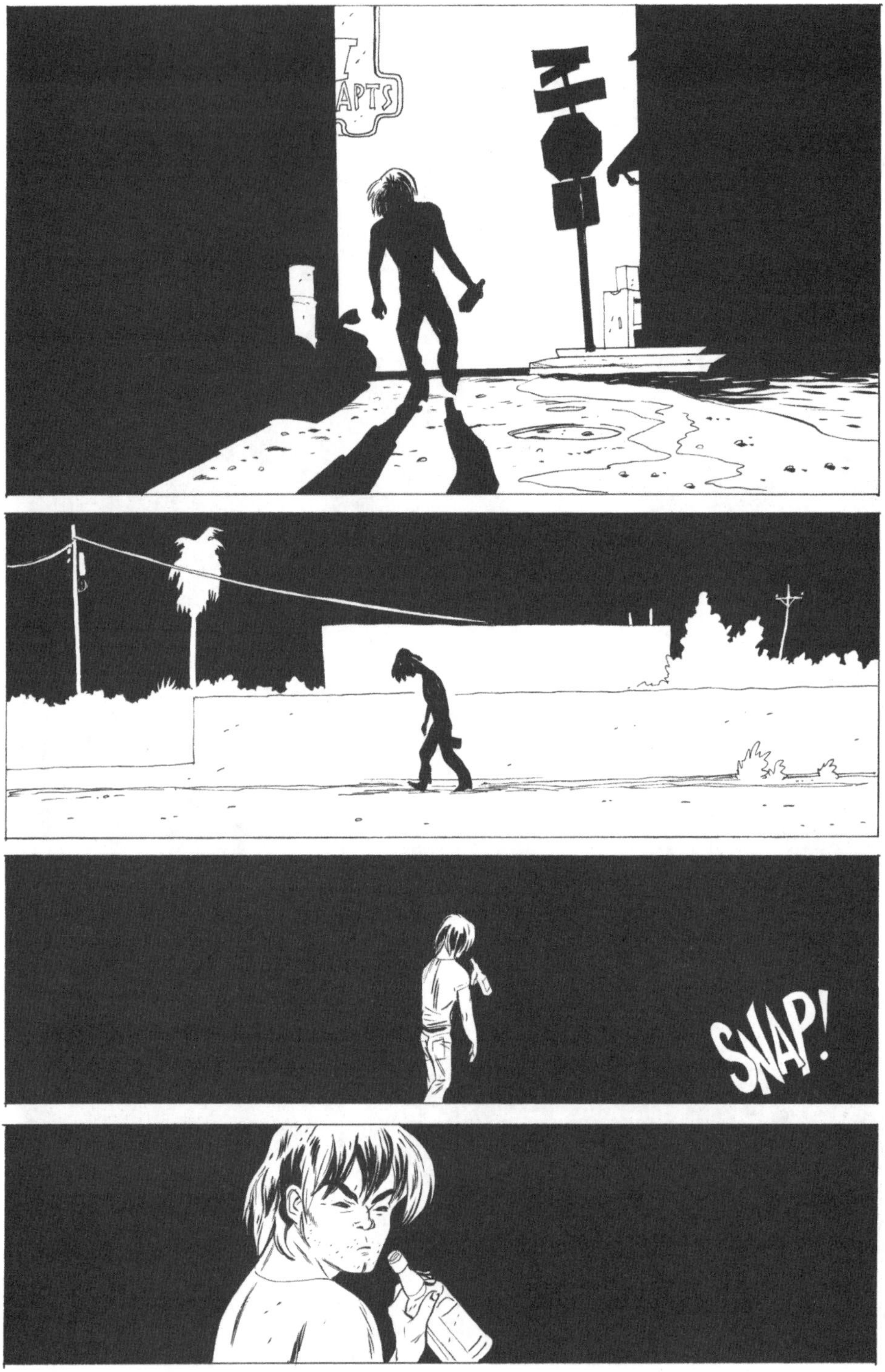
APTS
SNAP!

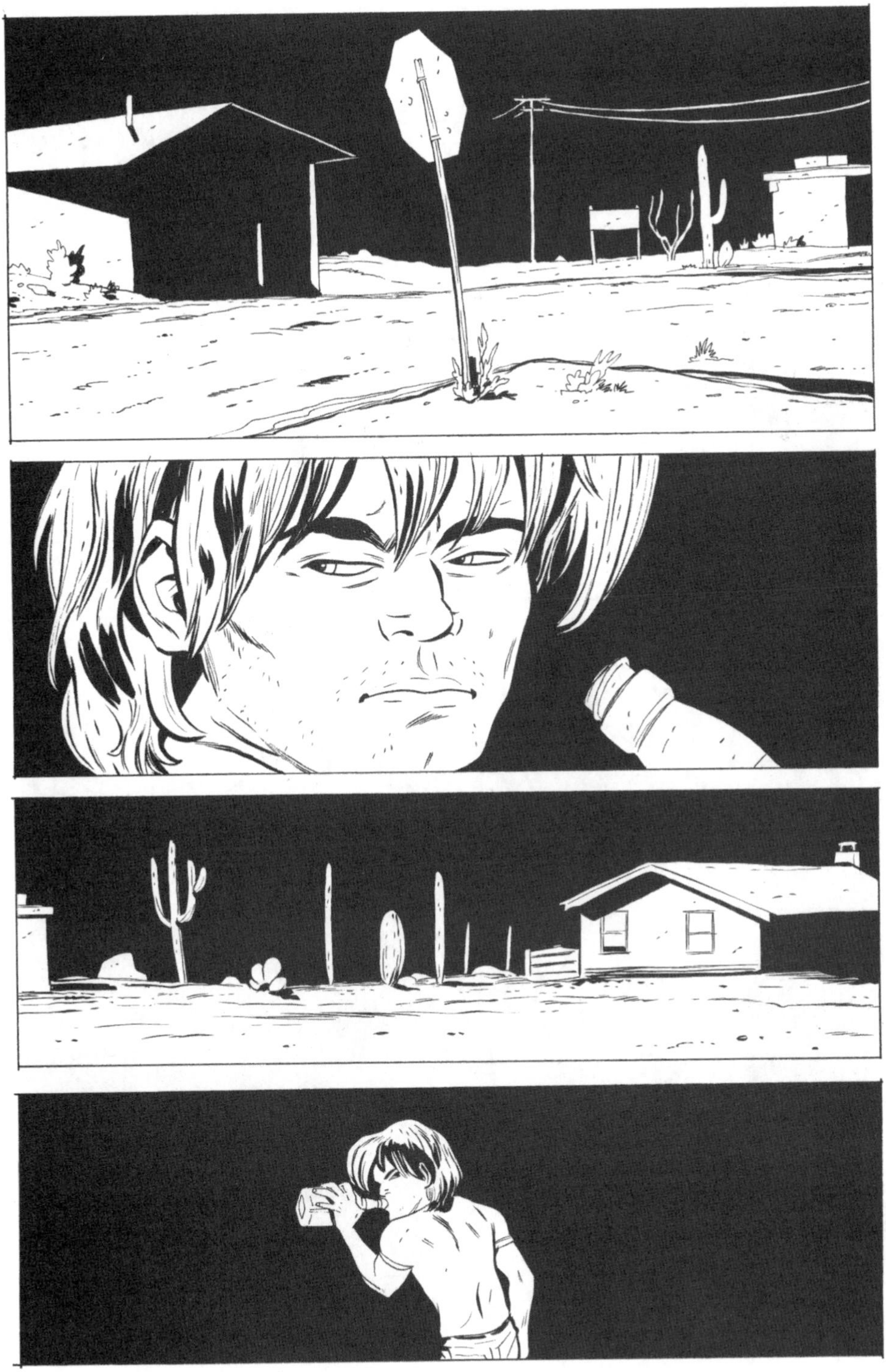

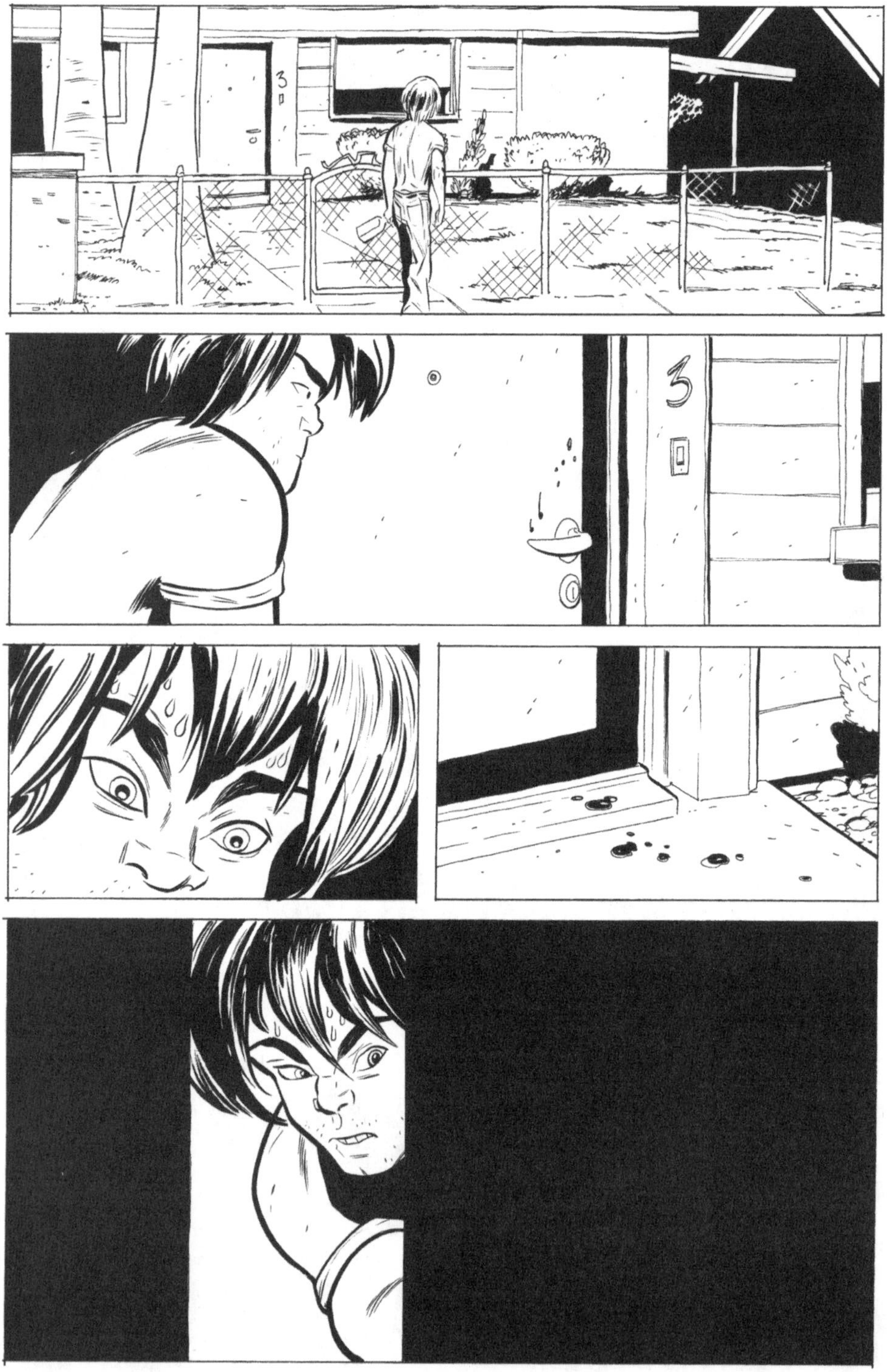
3

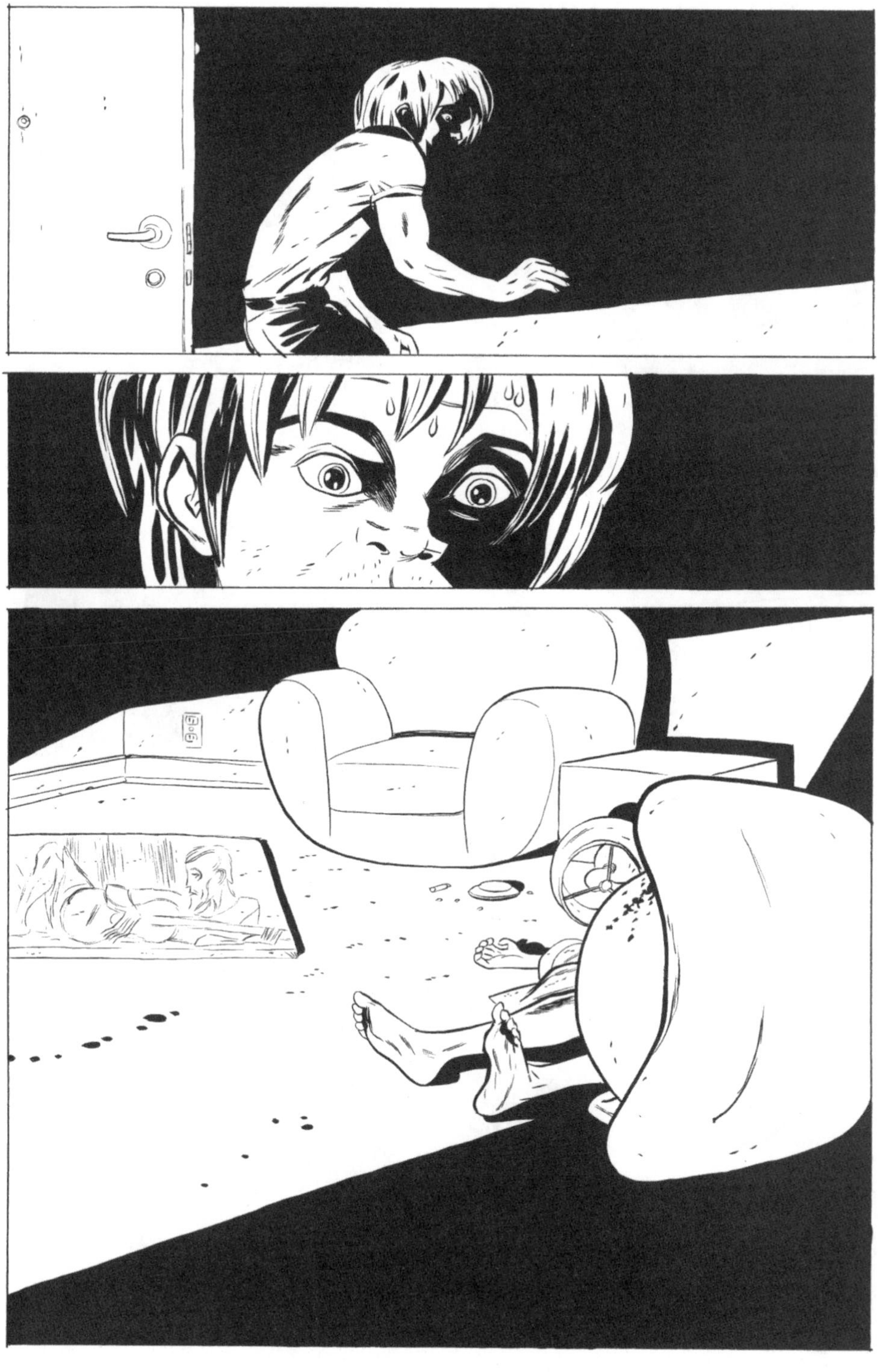

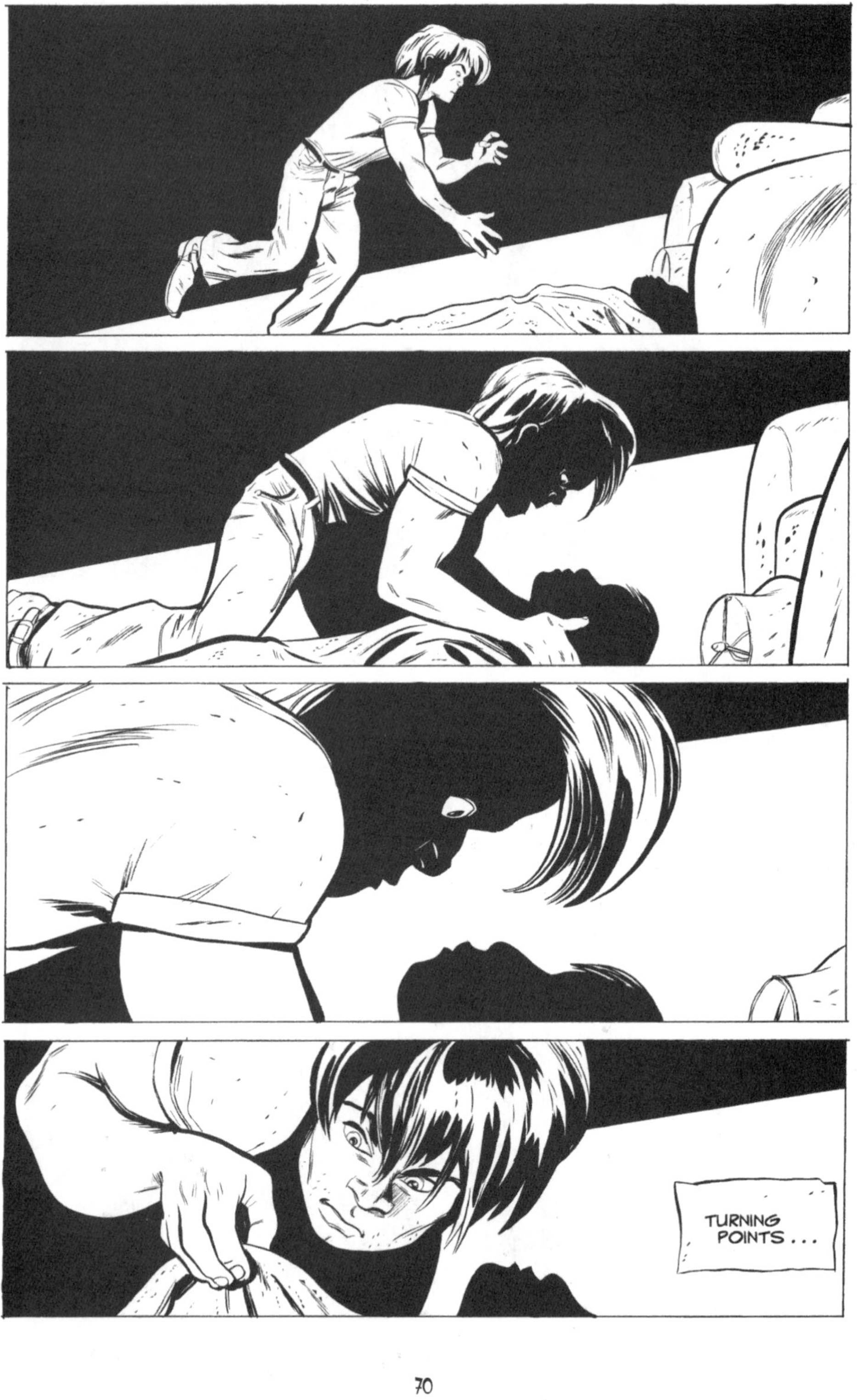
TURNING POINTS . . .

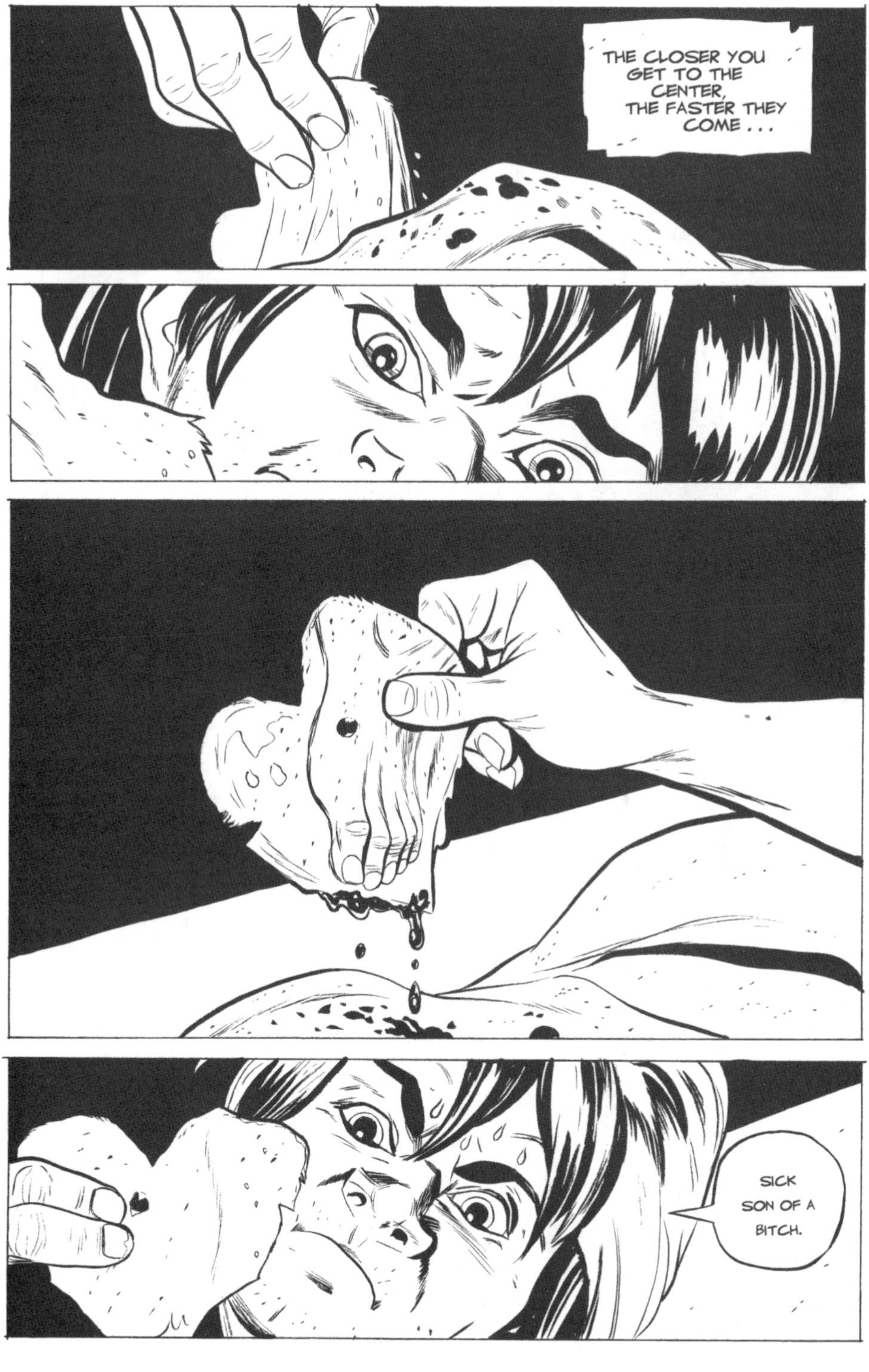
THE CLOSER YOU GET TO THE CENTER, THE FASTER THEY COME . . .
SICK SON OF A BITCH.

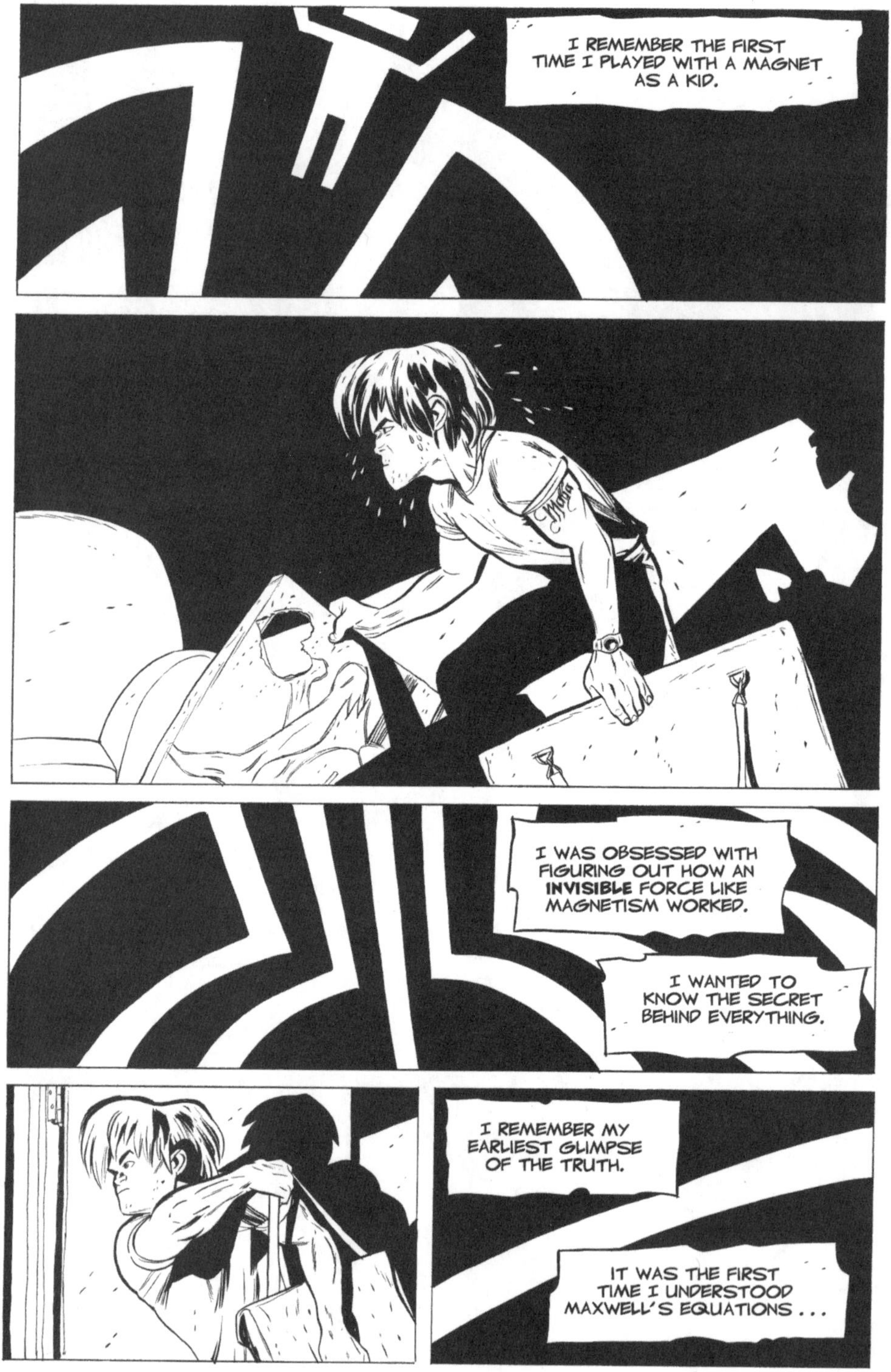
I REMEMBER THE FIRST TIME I PLAYED WITH A MAGNET AS A KID.
I WAS OBSESSED WITH FIGURING OUT HOW AN INVISIBLE FORCE LIKE MAGNETISM WORKED.
I WANTED TO KNOW THE SECRET BEHIND EVERYTHING.
I REMEMBER MY EARLIEST GLIMPSE OF THE TRUTH.
IT WAS THE FIRST TIME I UNDERSTOOD MAXWELL'S EQUATIONS . . .

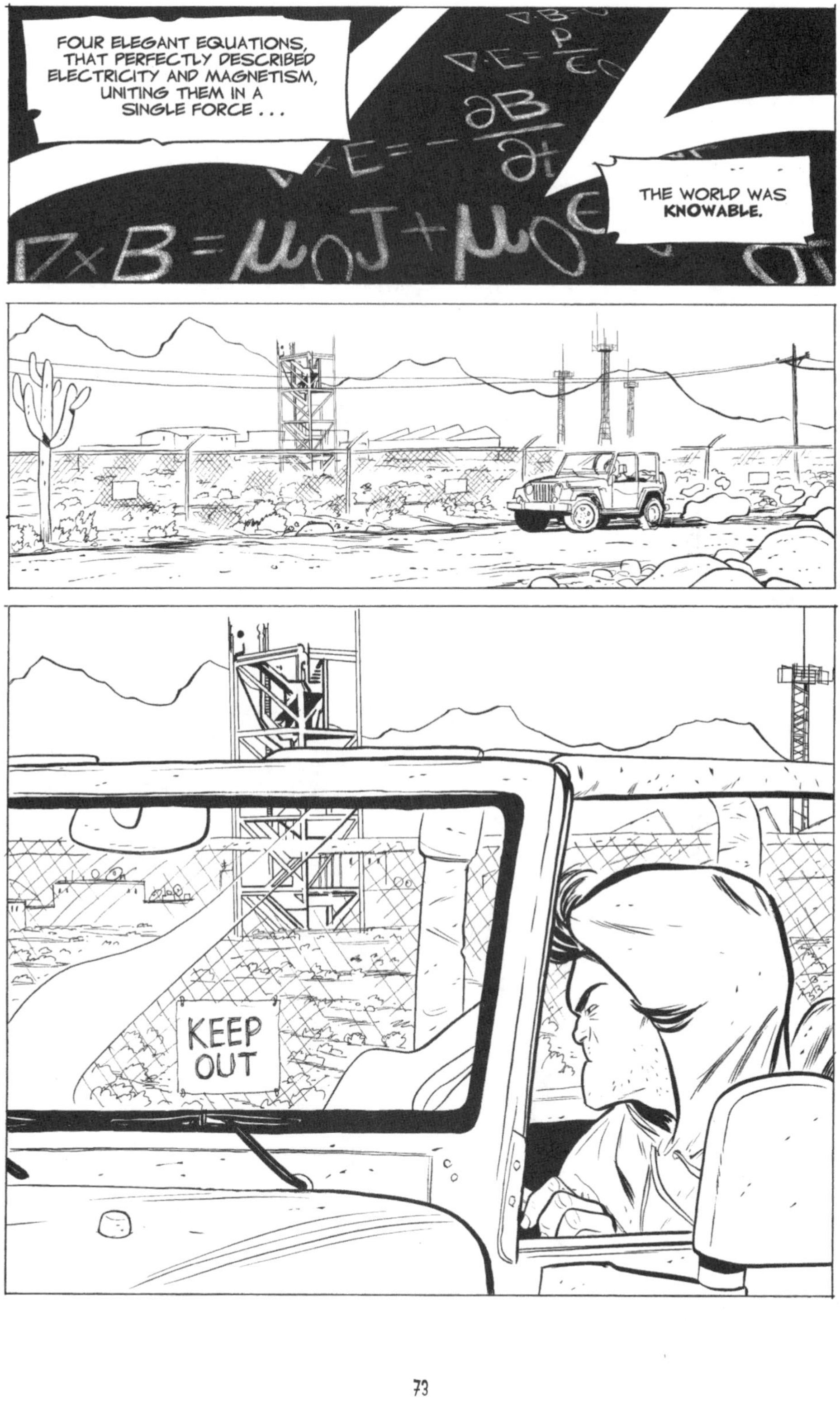
FOUR ELEGANT EQUATIONS, THAT PERFECTLY DESCRIBED ELECTRICITY AND MAGNETISM, UNITING THEM IN A SINGLE FORCE . . .
THE WORLD WAS **KNOWABLE.**
KEEP OUT

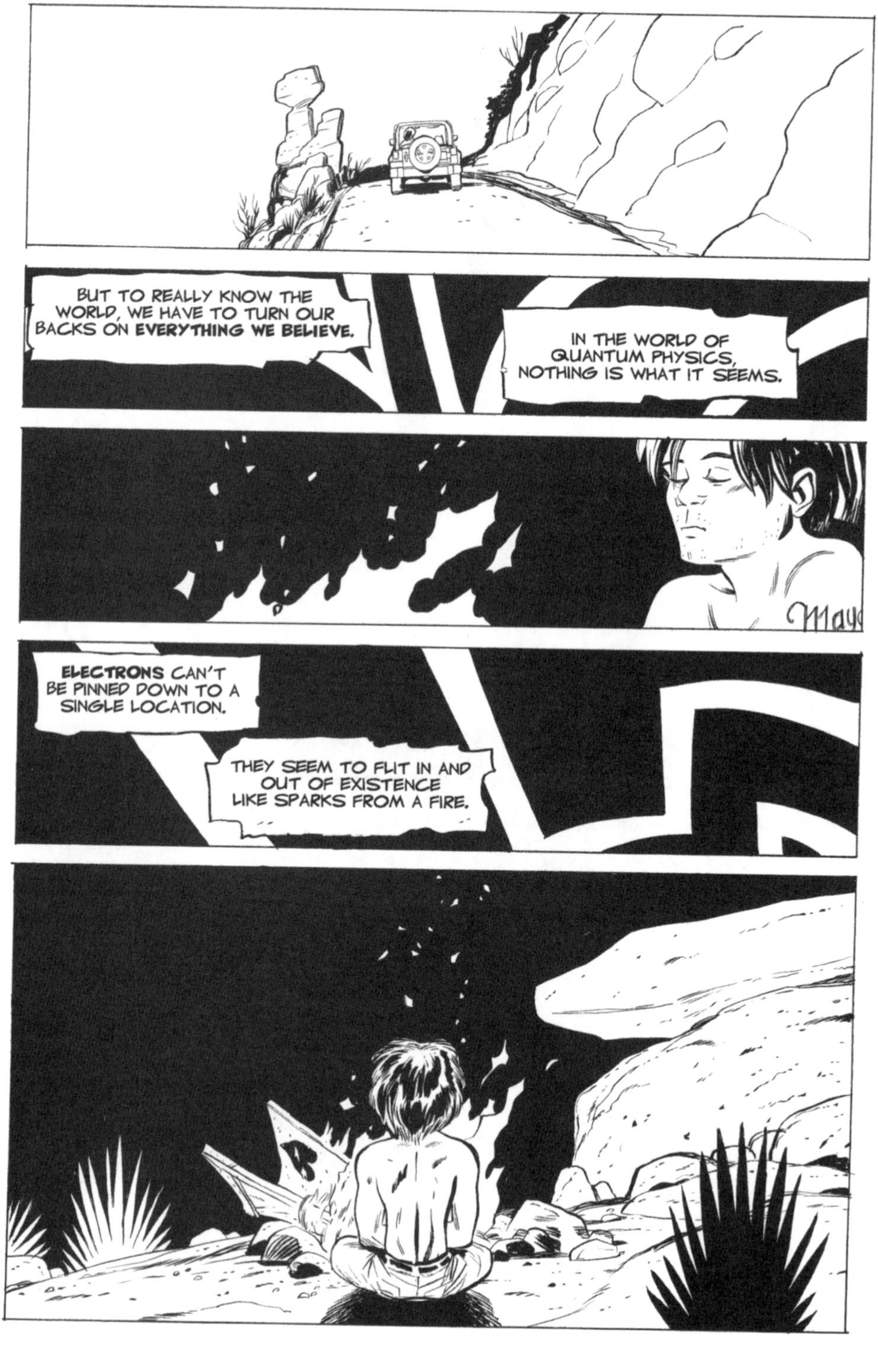
BUT TO REALLY KNOW THE WORLD, WE HAVE TO TURN OUR BACKS ON **EVERYTHING WE BELIEVE.**
IN THE WORLD OF QUANTUM PHYSICS, NOTHING IS WHAT IT SEEMS.
ELECTRONS CAN'T BE PINNED DOWN TO A SINGLE LOCATION.
THEY SEEM TO FLIT IN AND OUT OF EXISTENCE LIKE SPARKS FROM A FIRE.

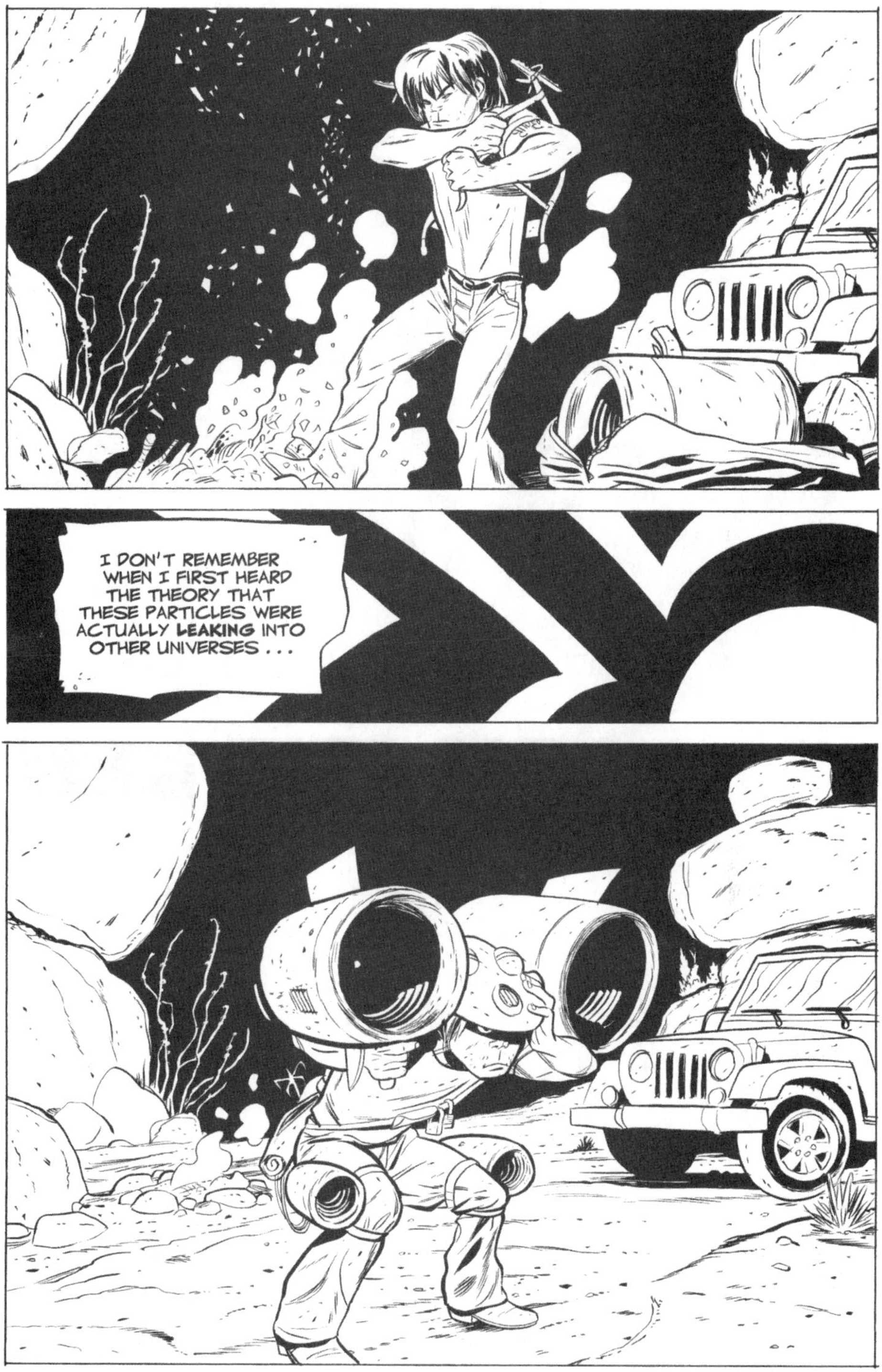
I DON'T REMEMBER WHEN I FIRST HEARD THE THEORY THAT THESE PARTICLES WERE ACTUALLY LEAKING INTO OTHER UNIVERSES . . .

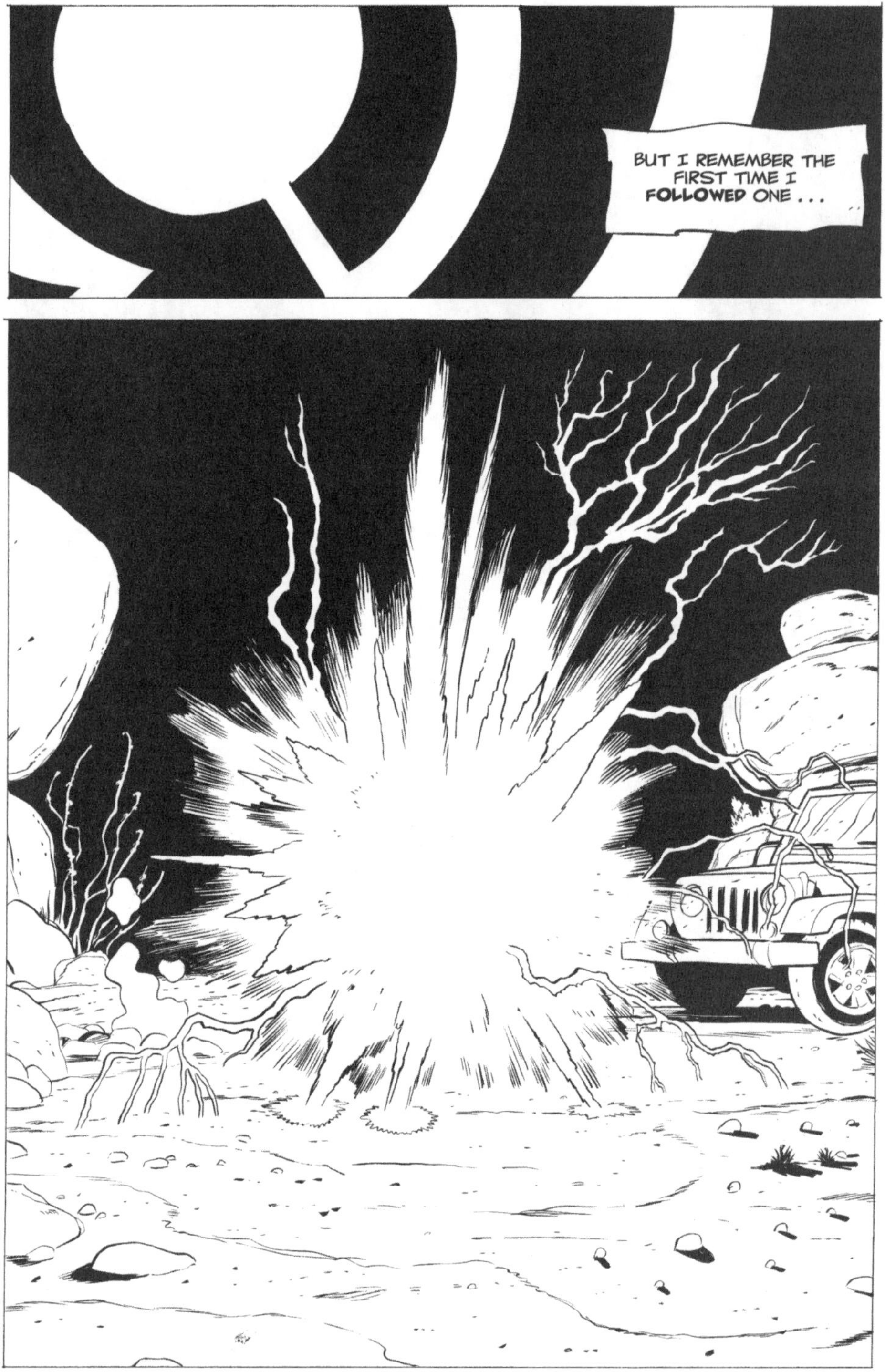
BUT I REMEMBER THE FIRST TIME I FOLLOWED ONE . . .

3.
MAYA

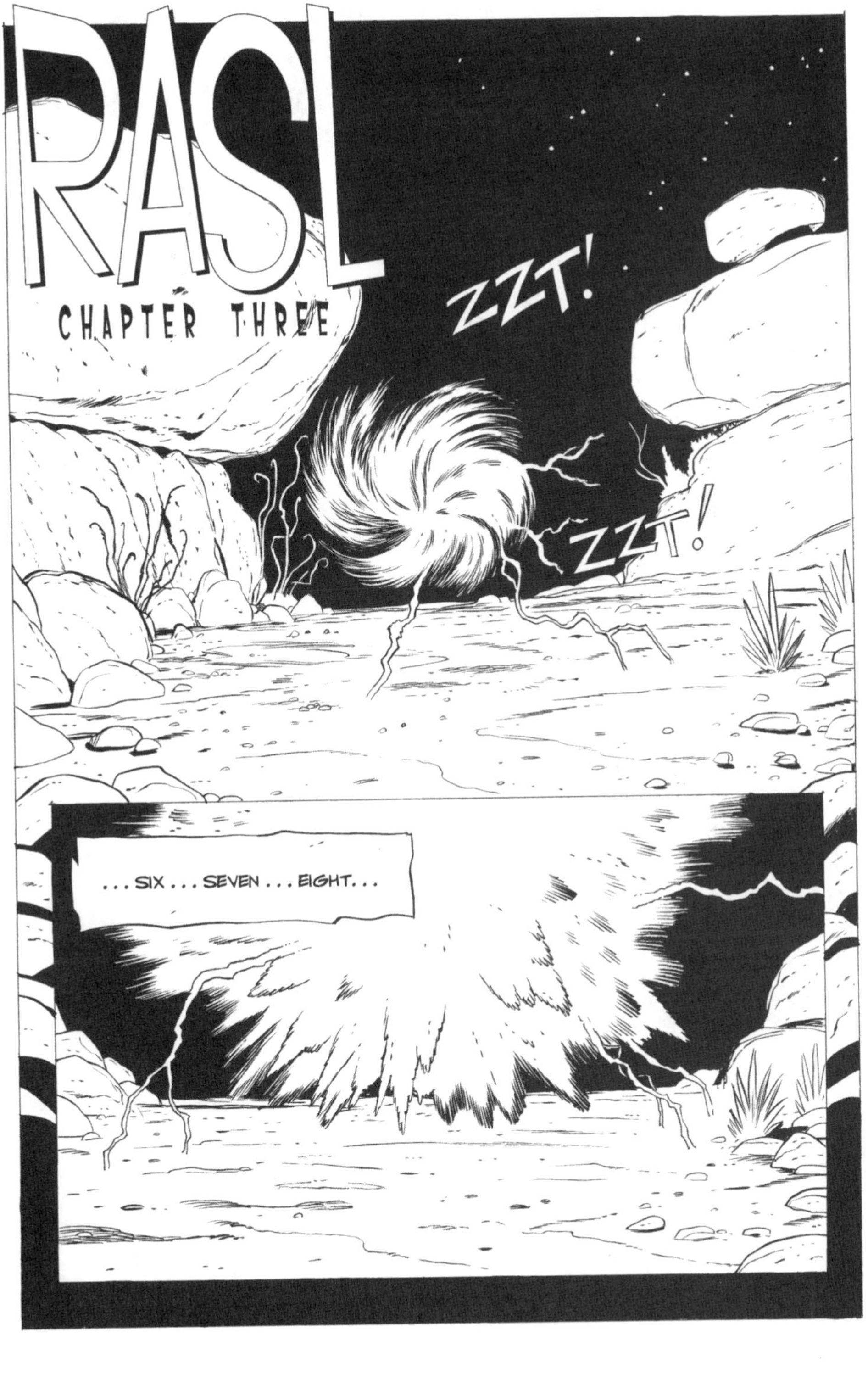

RASL
CHAPTER THREE
ZZT!
ZZT!
. . . SIX . . . SEVEN . . . EIGHT . . .

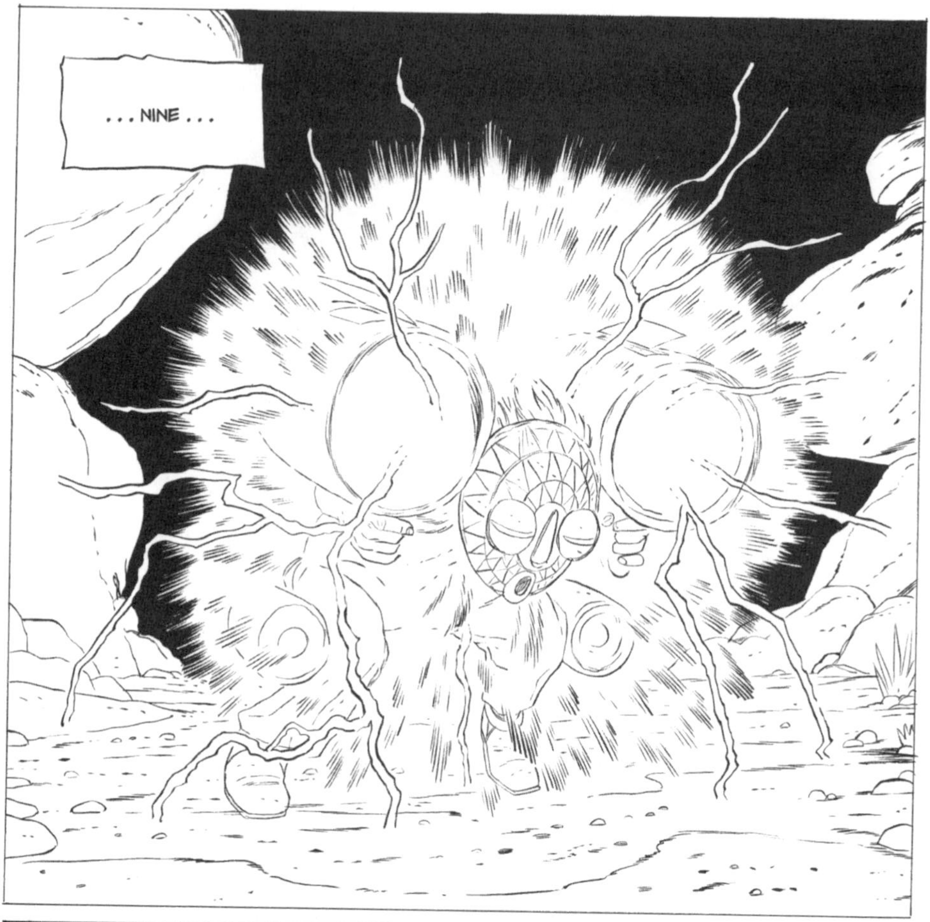
. . . NINE . . .
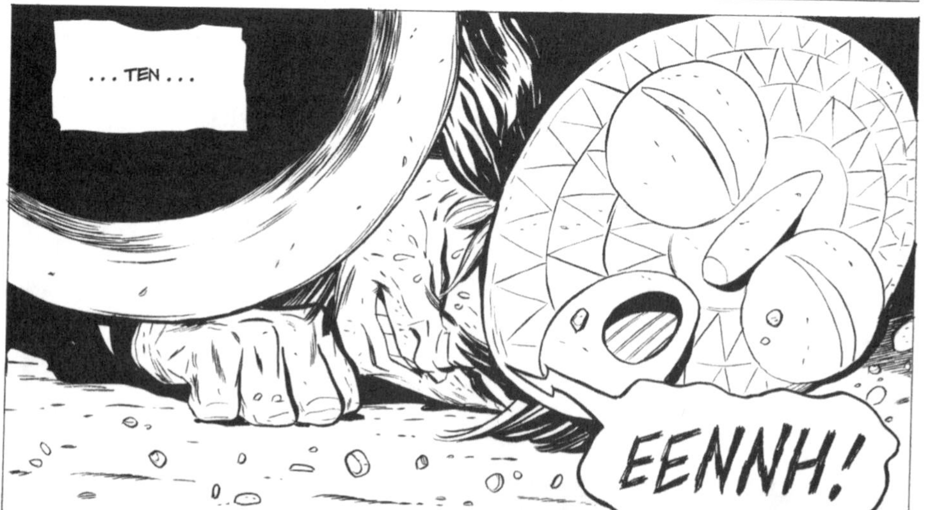
. . . TEN . . .
EENNH!

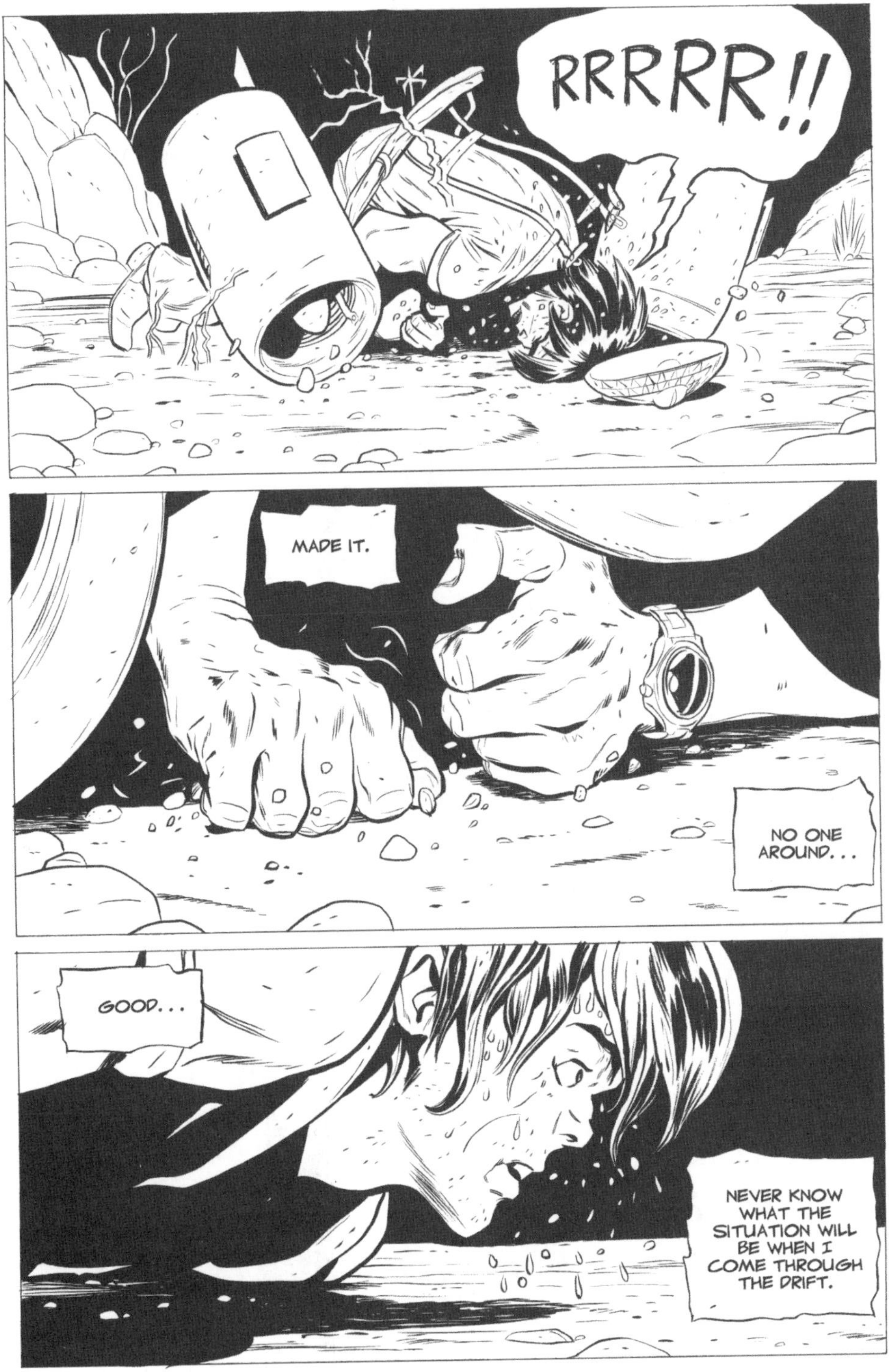
RRRRR!!
MADE IT.
NO ONE AROUND...
GOOD...
NEVER KNOW WHAT THE SITUATION WILL BE WHEN I COME THROUGH THE DRIFT.

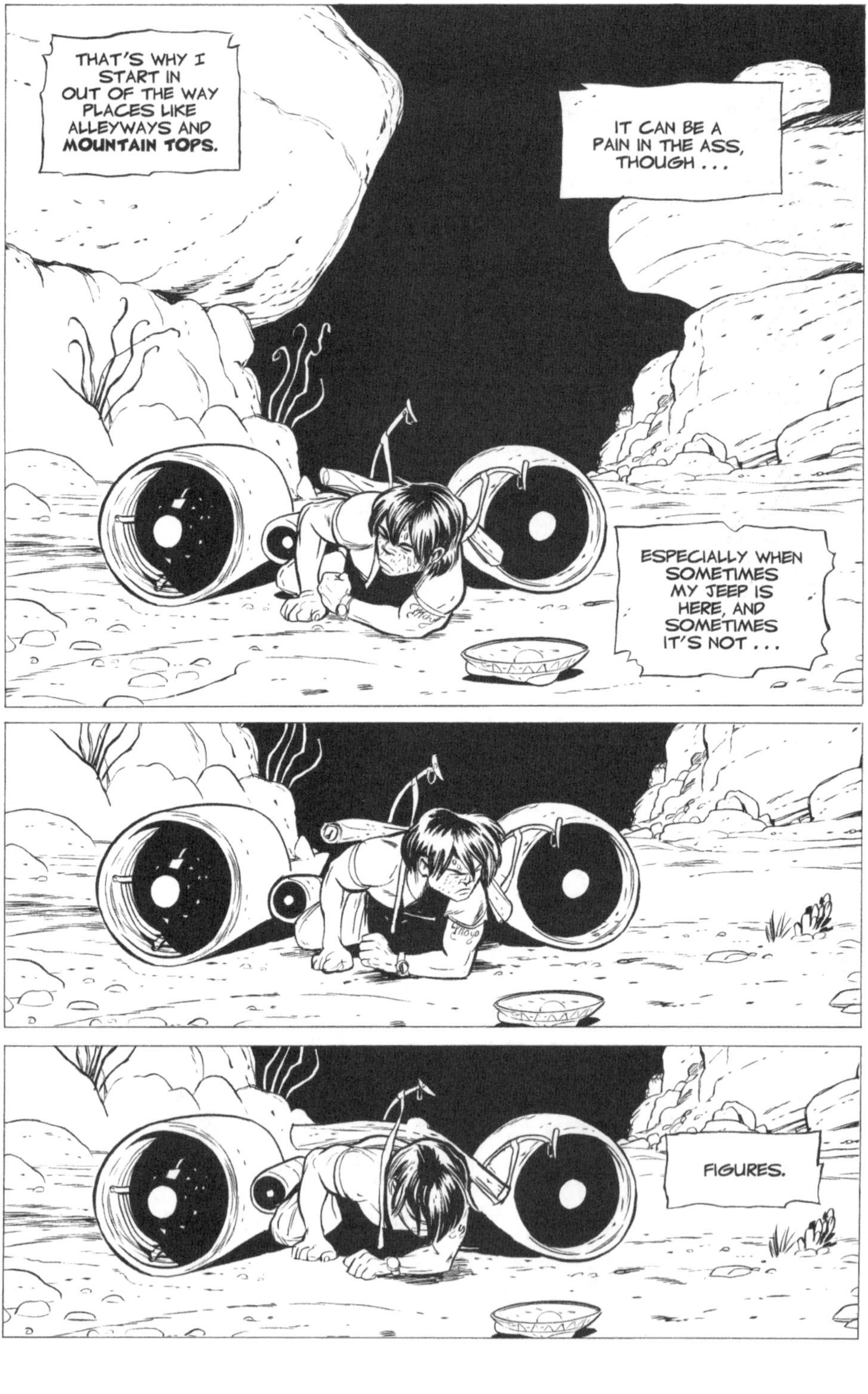
THAT'S WHY I START IN OUT OF THE WAY PLACES LIKE ALLEYWAYS AND **MOUNTAIN TOPS.**
IT CAN BE A PAIN IN THE ASS, THOUGH . . .
ESPECIALLY WHEN SOMETIMES MY JEEP IS HERE, AND SOMETIMES IT'S NOT . . .
FIGURES.

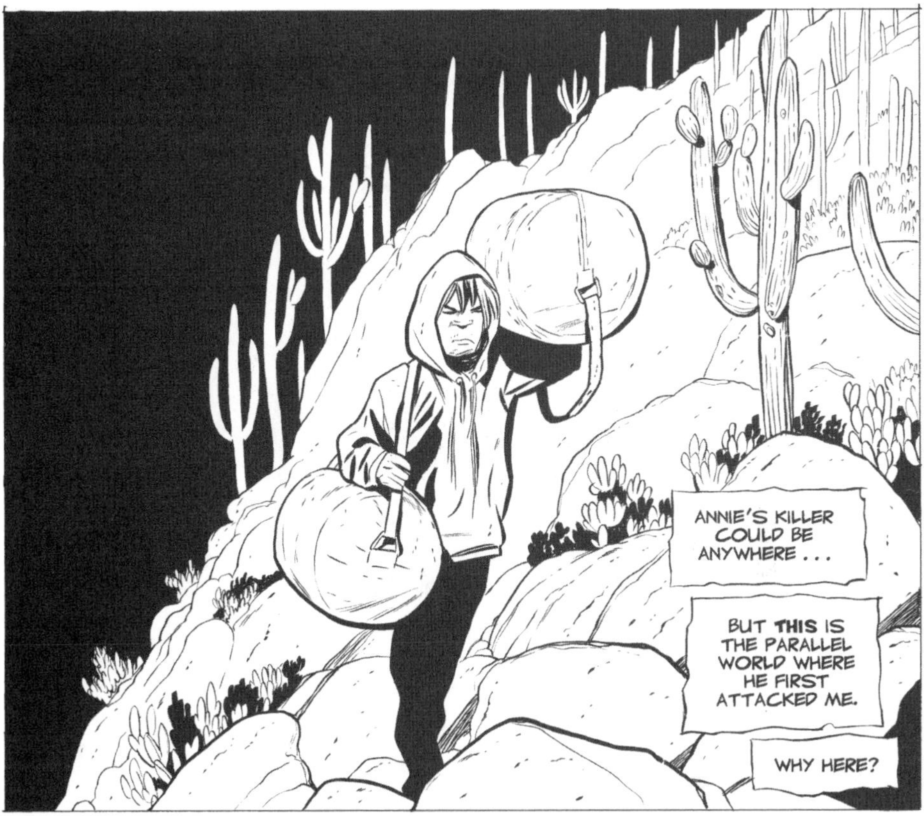
ANNIE'S KILLER COULD BE ANYWHERE . . .
BUT **THIS** IS THE PARALLEL WORLD WHERE HE FIRST ATTACKED ME.
WHY HERE?

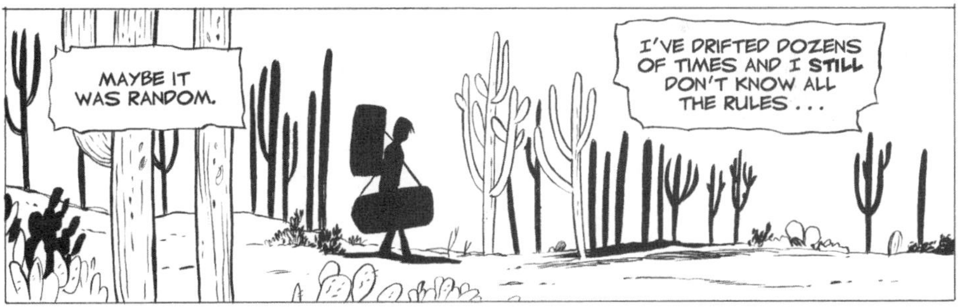
MAYBE IT WAS RANDOM.
I'VE DRIFTED DOZENS OF TIMES AND I **STILL** DON'T KNOW ALL THE RULES . . .

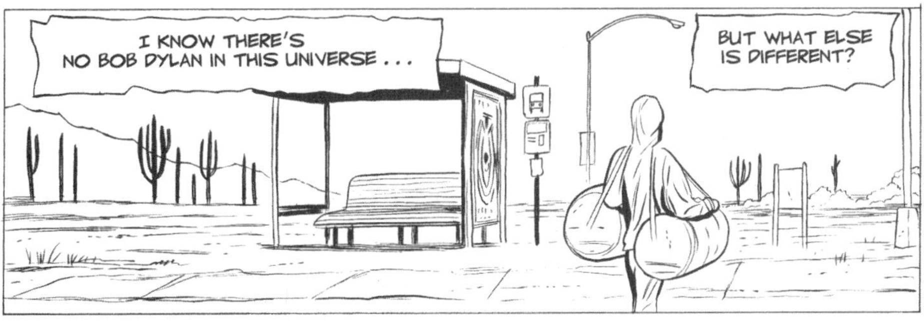
I KNOW THERE'S NO BOB DYLAN IN THIS UNIVERSE . . .
BUT WHAT ELSE IS DIFFERENT?

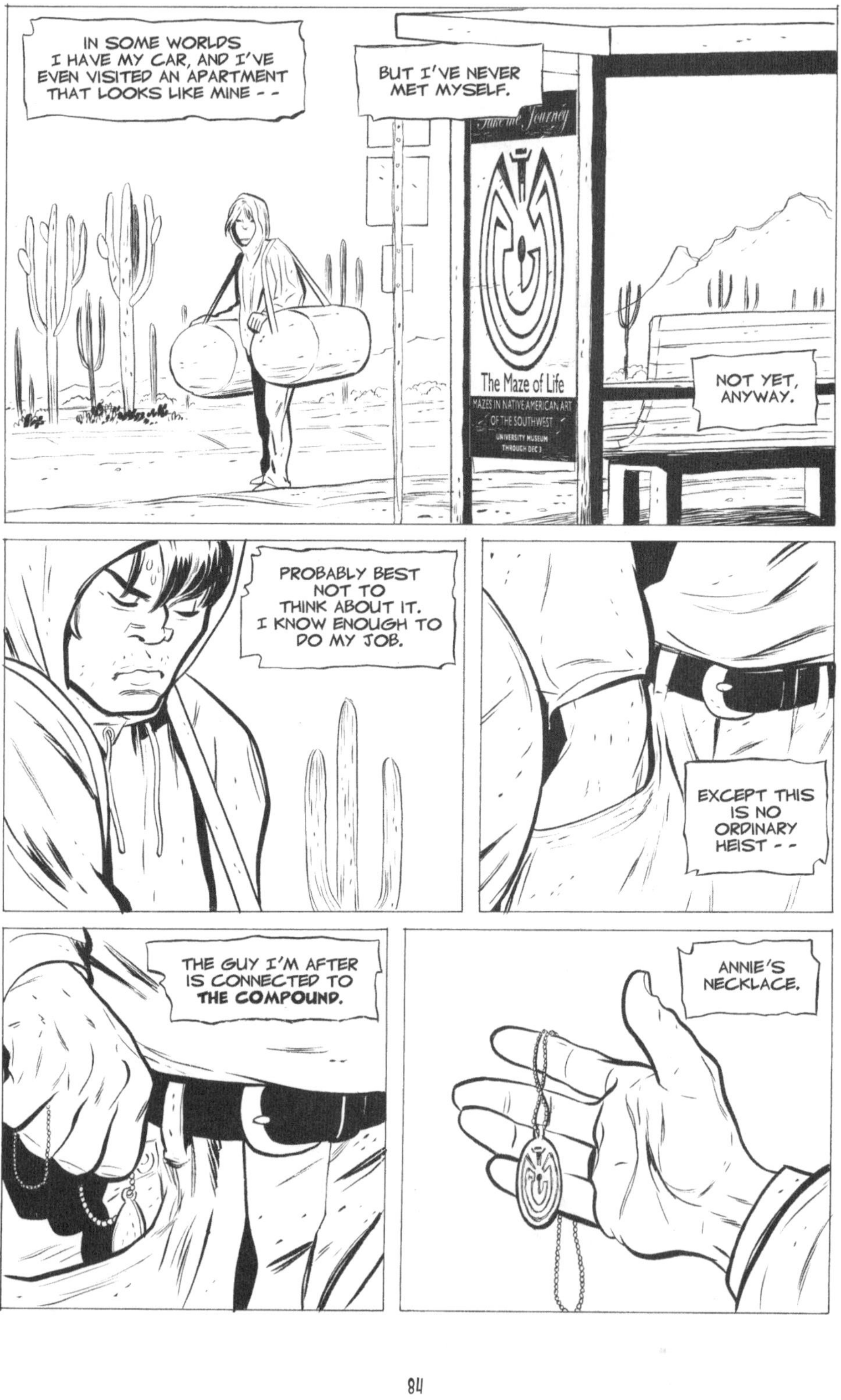
IN SOME WORLDS I HAVE MY CAR, AND I'VE EVEN VISITED AN APARTMENT THAT LOOKS LIKE MINE - -
BUT I'VE NEVER MET MYSELF.
The Maze of Life
MAZES IN NATIVE AMERICAN ART OF THE SOUTHWEST
UNIVERSITY MUSEUM
THROUGH DEC 3
NOT YET, ANYWAY.
PROBABLY BEST NOT TO THINK ABOUT IT. I KNOW ENOUGH TO DO MY JOB.
EXCEPT THIS IS NO ORDINARY HEIST - -
THE GUY I'M AFTER IS CONNECTED TO **THE COMPOUND.**
ANNIE'S NECKLACE.

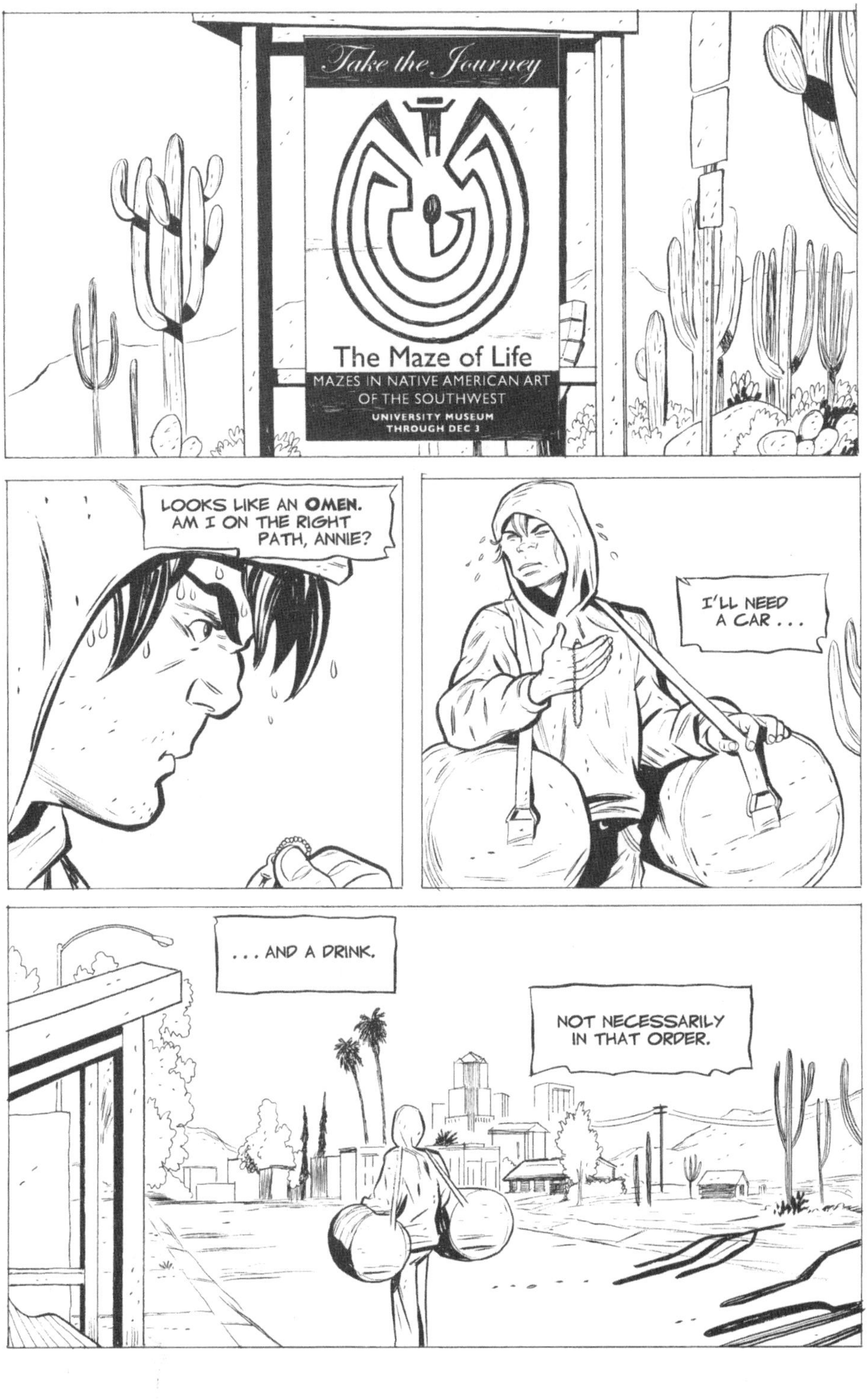
Take the Journey
The Maze of Life
MAZES IN NATIVE AMERICAN ART OF THE SOUTHWEST
UNIVERSITY MUSEUM
THROUGH DEC 3
LOOKS LIKE AN OMEN. AM I ON THE RIGHT PATH, ANNIE?
I'LL NEED A CAR . . .
. . . AND A DRINK.
NOT NECESSARILY IN THAT ORDER.

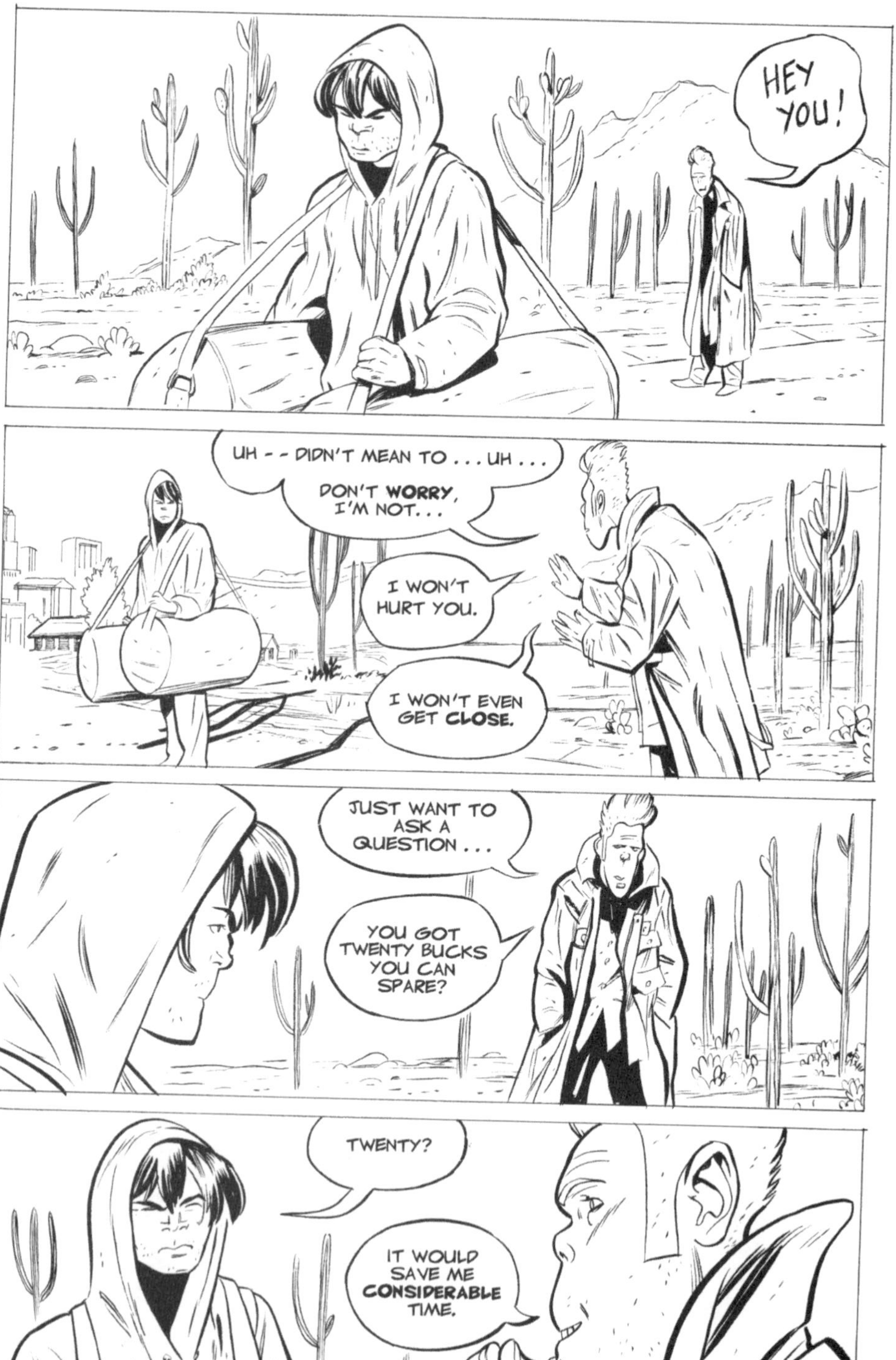
HEY YOU!
UH -- DIDN'T MEAN TO . . . UH . . .
DON'T WORRY, I'M NOT . . .
I WON'T HURT YOU.
I WON'T EVEN GET CLOSE.
JUST WANT TO ASK A QUESTION . . .
YOU GOT TWENTY BUCKS YOU CAN SPARE?
TWENTY?
IT WOULD SAVE ME CONSIDERABLE TIME.

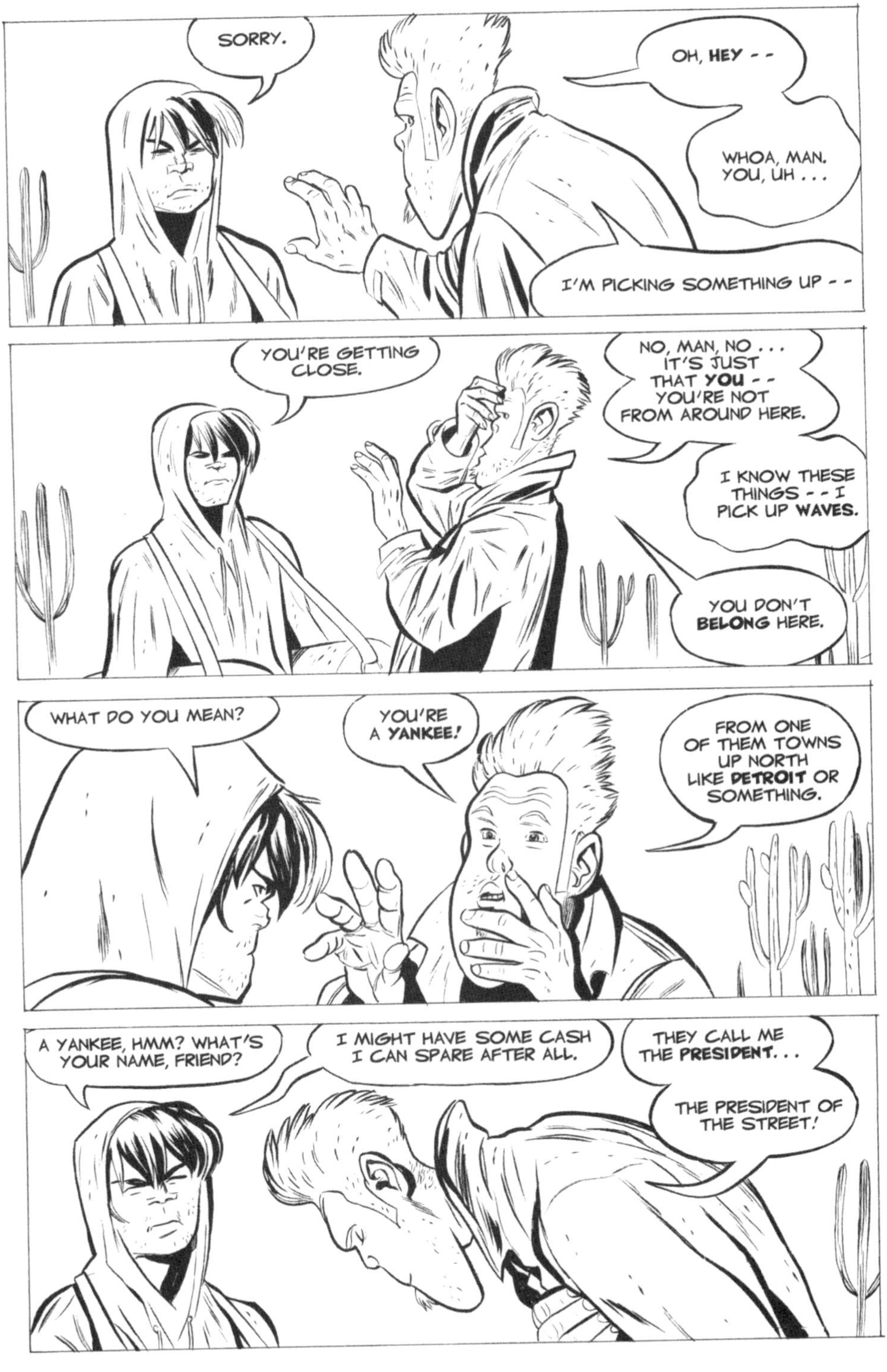
SORRY.
OH, HEY - -
WHOA, MAN. YOU, UH . . .
I'M PICKING SOMETHING UP - -
YOU'RE GETTING CLOSE.
NO, MAN, NO . . . IT'S JUST THAT YOU - - YOU'RE NOT FROM AROUND HERE.
I KNOW THESE THINGS - - I PICK UP WAVES.
YOU DON'T BELONG HERE.
WHAT DO YOU MEAN?
YOU'RE A YANKEE!
FROM ONE OF THEM TOWNS UP NORTH LIKE DETROIT OR SOMETHING.
A YANKEE, HMM? WHAT'S YOUR NAME, FRIEND?
I MIGHT HAVE SOME CASH I CAN SPARE AFTER ALL.
THEY CALL ME THE PRESIDENT. . .
THE PRESIDENT OF THE STREET!

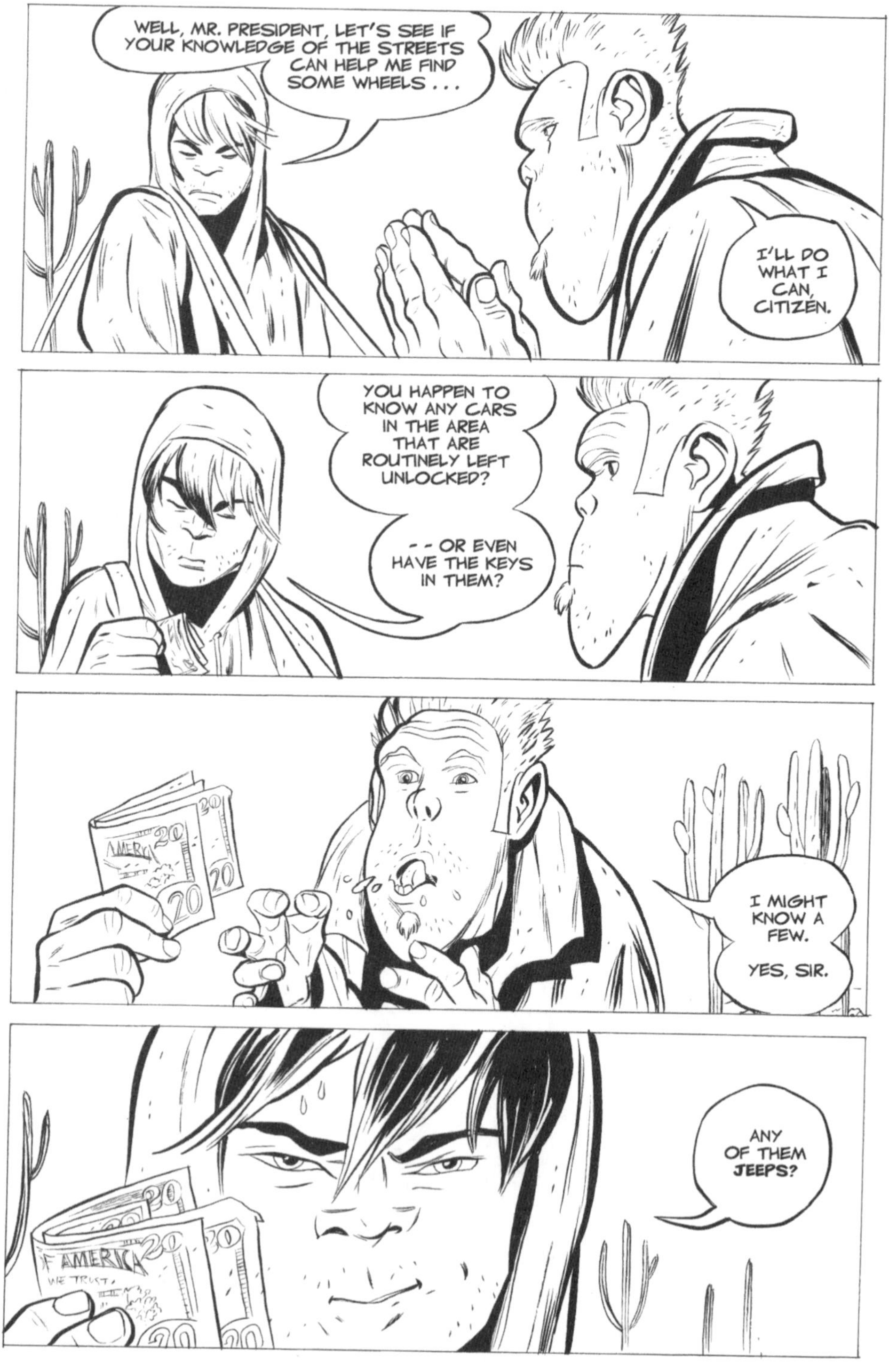
WELL, MR. PRESIDENT, LET'S SEE IF YOUR KNOWLEDGE OF THE STREETS CAN HELP ME FIND SOME WHEELS . . .
I'LL DO WHAT I CAN, CITIZEN.
YOU HAPPEN TO KNOW ANY CARS IN THE AREA THAT ARE ROUTINELY LEFT UNLOCKED?
- - OR EVEN HAVE THE KEYS IN THEM?
I MIGHT KNOW A FEW.
YES, SIR.
ANY OF THEM JEEPS?

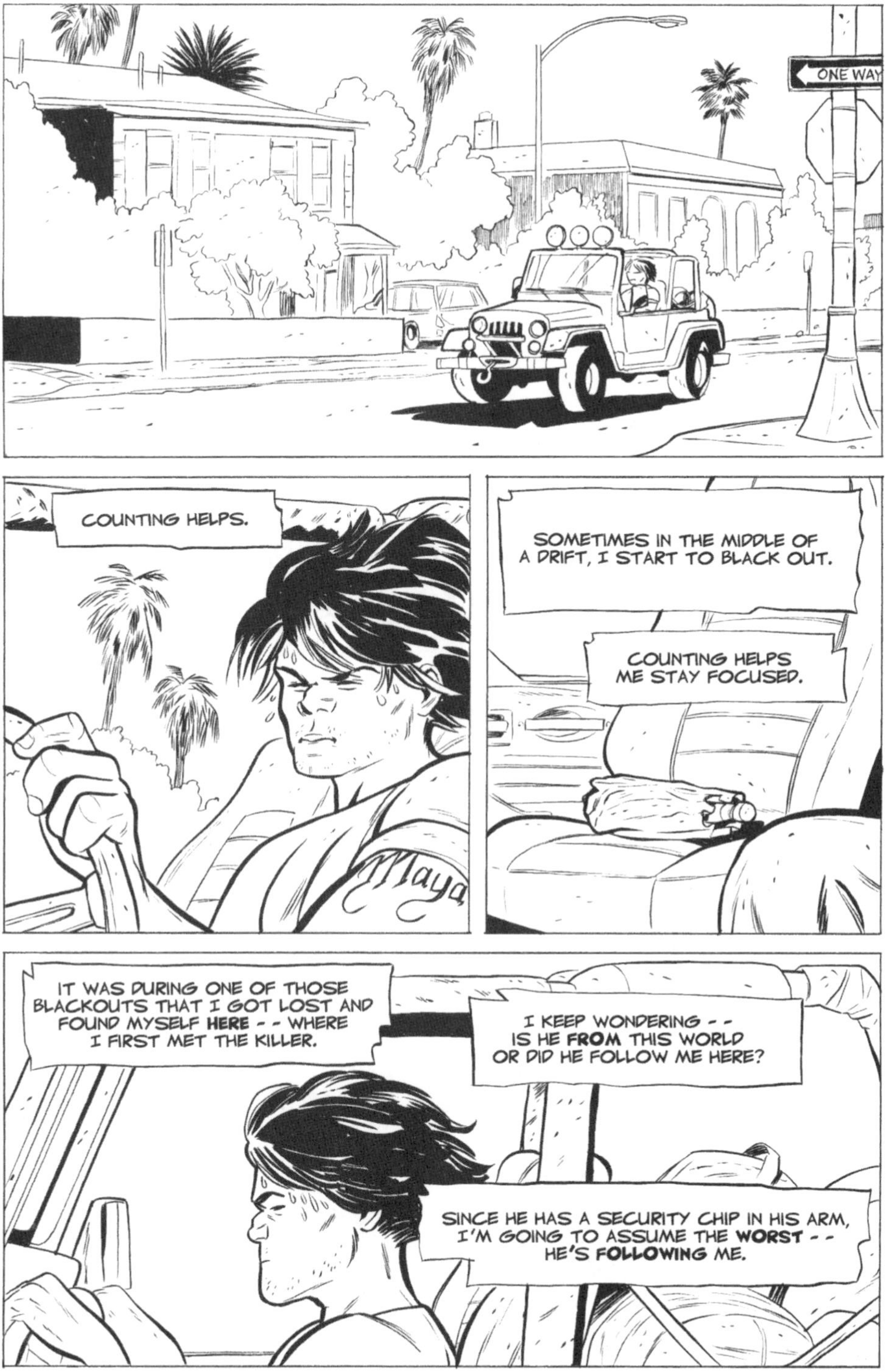
ONE WAY
COUNTING HELPS.
Maya
SOMETIMES IN THE MIDDLE OF A DRIFT, I START TO BLACK OUT.
COUNTING HELPS ME STAY FOCUSED.
IT WAS DURING ONE OF THOSE BLACKOUTS THAT I GOT LOST AND FOUND MYSELF **HERE** - - WHERE I FIRST MET THE KILLER.
I KEEP WONDERING - - IS HE **FROM** THIS WORLD OR DID HE FOLLOW ME HERE?
SINCE HE HAS A SECURITY CHIP IN HIS ARM, I'M GOING TO ASSUME THE **WORST** - - HE'S **FOLLOWING** ME.

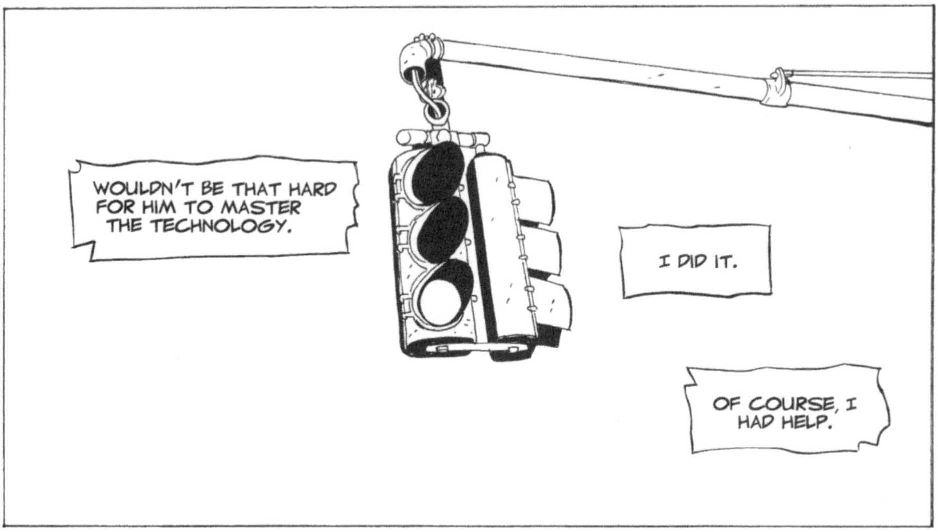
WOULDN'T BE THAT HARD FOR HIM TO MASTER THE TECHNOLOGY.
I DID IT.
OF COURSE, I HAD HELP.

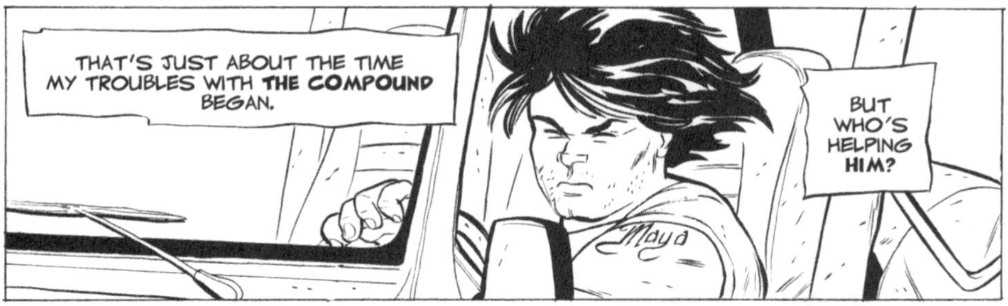
THAT'S JUST ABOUT THE TIME MY TROUBLES WITH **THE COMPOUND** BEGAN.
BUT WHO'S HELPING **HIM?**
Maya

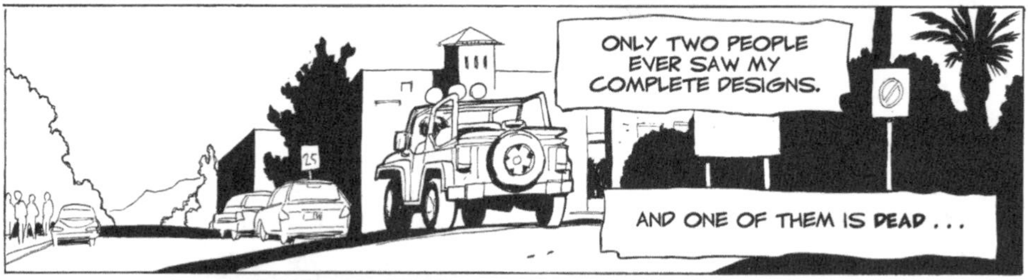
25
ONLY TWO PEOPLE EVER SAW MY COMPLETE DESIGNS.
AND ONE OF THEM IS **DEAD** . . .

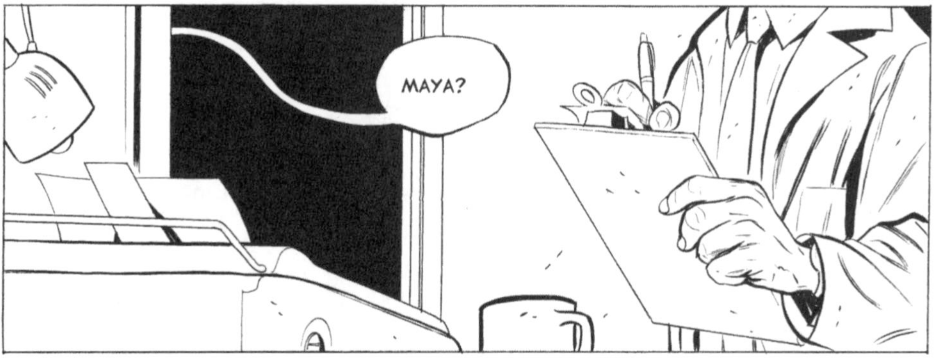
MAYA?

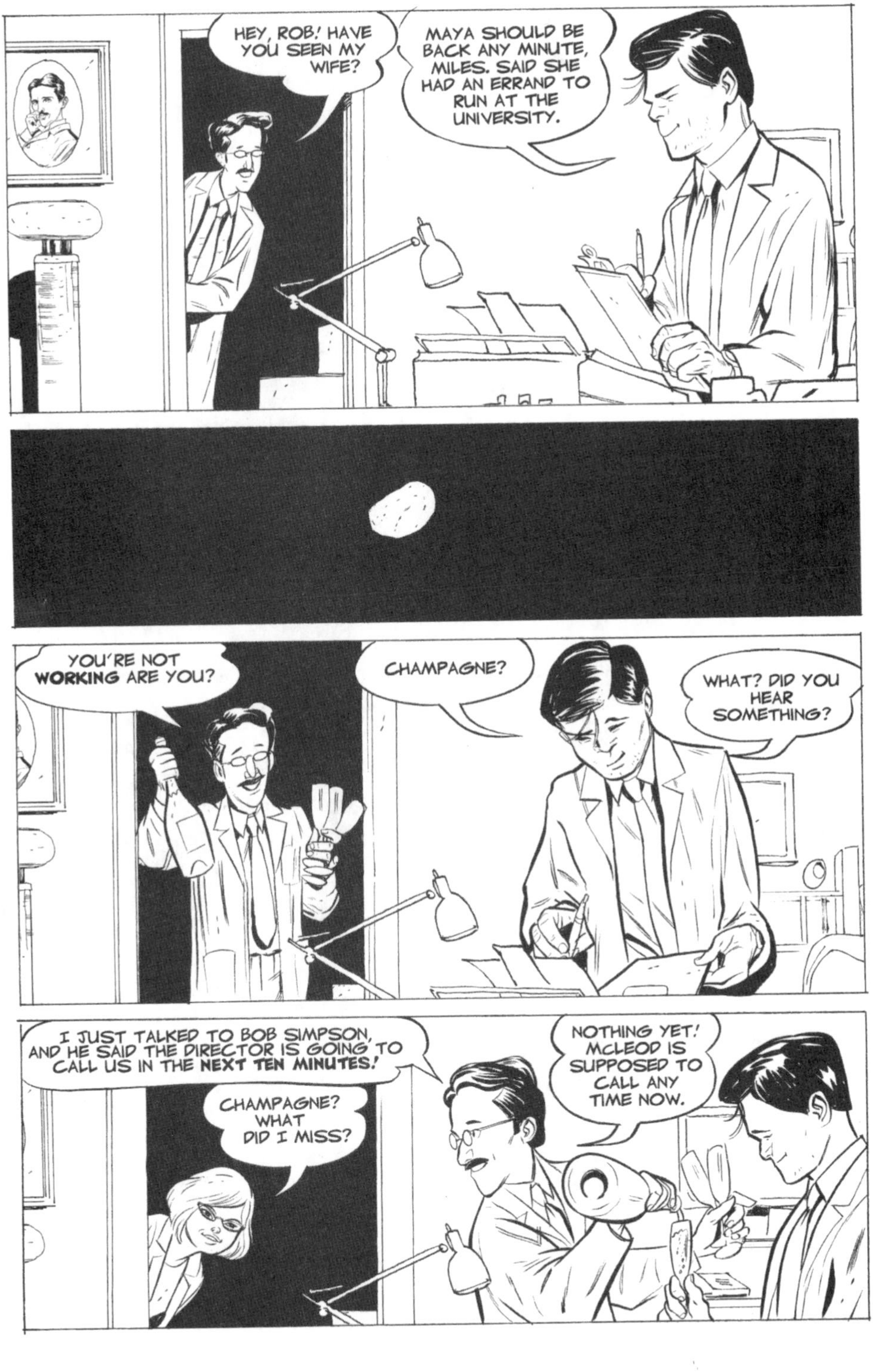
HEY, ROB! HAVE YOU SEEN MY WIFE?
MAYA SHOULD BE BACK ANY MINUTE, MILES. SAID SHE HAD AN ERRAND TO RUN AT THE UNIVERSITY.
YOU'RE NOT WORKING ARE YOU?
CHAMPAGNE?
WHAT? DID YOU HEAR SOMETHING?
I JUST TALKED TO BOB SIMPSON, AND HE SAID THE DIRECTOR IS GOING TO CALL US IN THE NEXT TEN MINUTES!
NOTHING YET! McLEOD IS SUPPOSED TO CALL ANY TIME NOW.
CHAMPAGNE? WHAT DID I MISS?

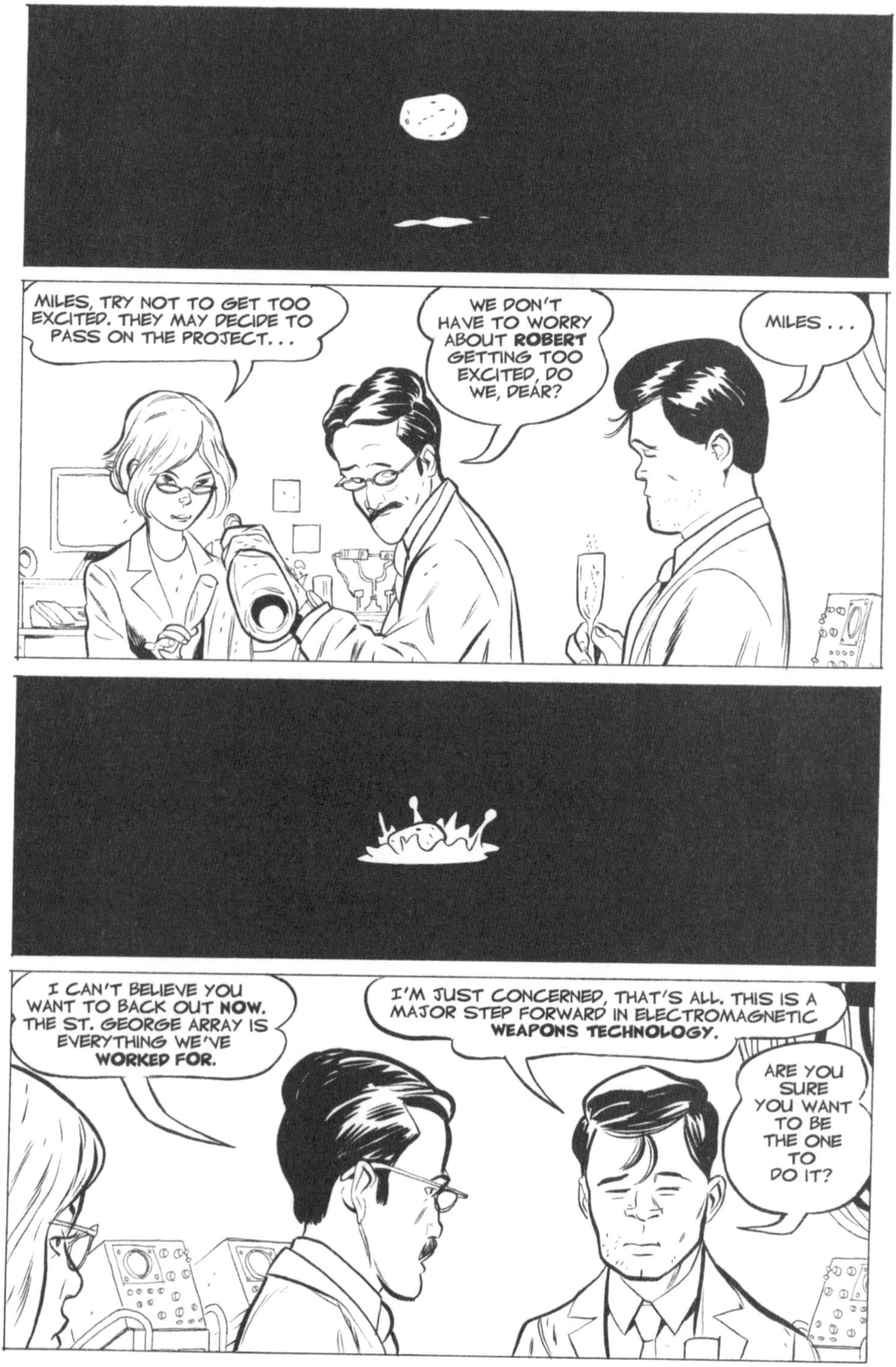
MILES, TRY NOT TO GET TOO EXCITED. THEY MAY DECIDE TO PASS ON THE PROJECT...
WE DON'T HAVE TO WORRY ABOUT ROBERT GETTING TOO EXCITED, DO WE, DEAR?
MILES...
I CAN'T BELIEVE YOU WANT TO BACK OUT NOW. THE ST. GEORGE ARRAY IS EVERYTHING WE'VE WORKED FOR.
I'M JUST CONCERNED, THAT'S ALL. THIS IS A MAJOR STEP FORWARD IN ELECTROMAGNETIC WEAPONS TECHNOLOGY.
ARE YOU SURE YOU WANT TO BE THE ONE TO DO IT?

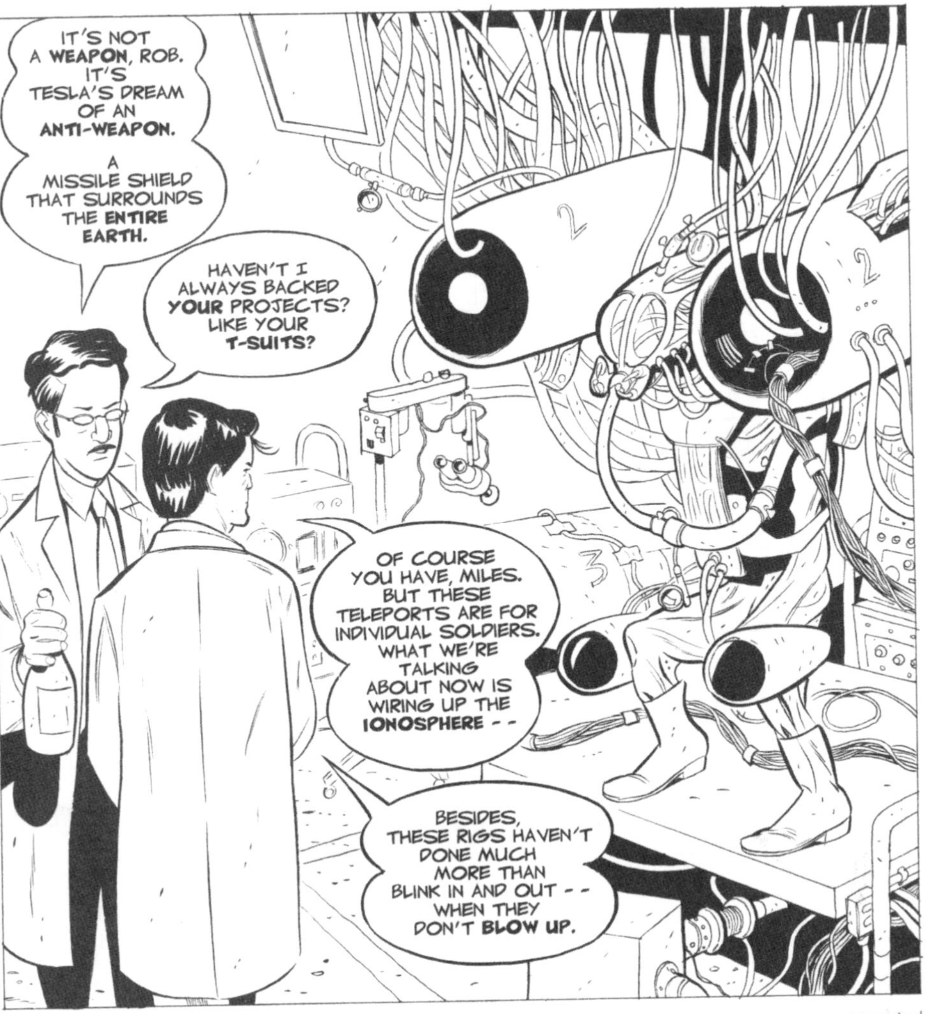
IT'S NOT A **WEAPON**, ROB. IT'S TESLA'S DREAM OF AN **ANTI-WEAPON.**
A MISSILE SHIELD THAT SURROUNDS THE **ENTIRE EARTH.**
HAVEN'T I ALWAYS BACKED **YOUR** PROJECTS? LIKE YOUR **T-SUITS?**
OF COURSE YOU HAVE, MILES. BUT THESE TELEPORTS ARE FOR INDIVIDUAL SOLDIERS. WHAT WE'RE TALKING ABOUT NOW IS WIRING UP THE **IONOSPHERE --**
BESIDES, THESE RIGS HAVEN'T DONE MUCH MORE THAN BLINK IN AND OUT -- WHEN THEY DON'T **BLOW UP.**

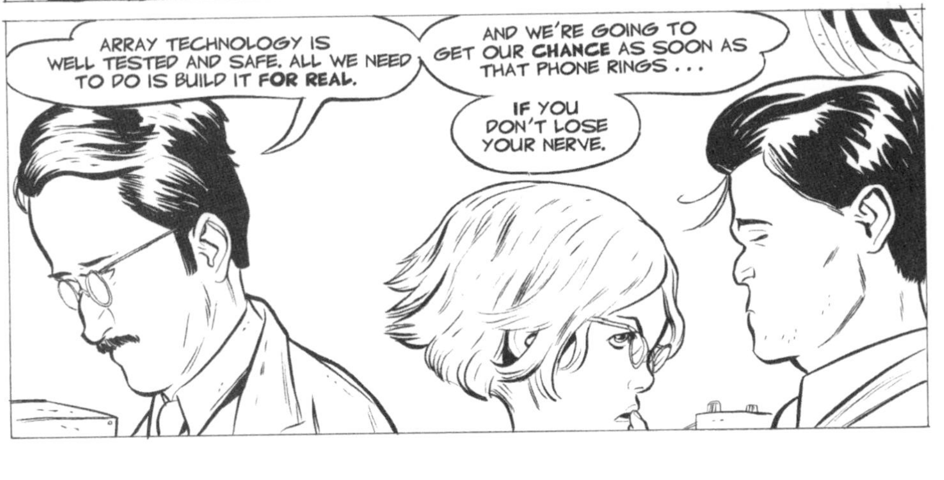
ARRAY TECHNOLOGY IS WELL TESTED AND SAFE. ALL WE NEED TO DO IS BUILD IT **FOR REAL.**
AND WE'RE GOING TO GET OUR **CHANCE** AS SOON AS THAT PHONE RINGS . . .
IF YOU DON'T LOSE YOUR NERVE.

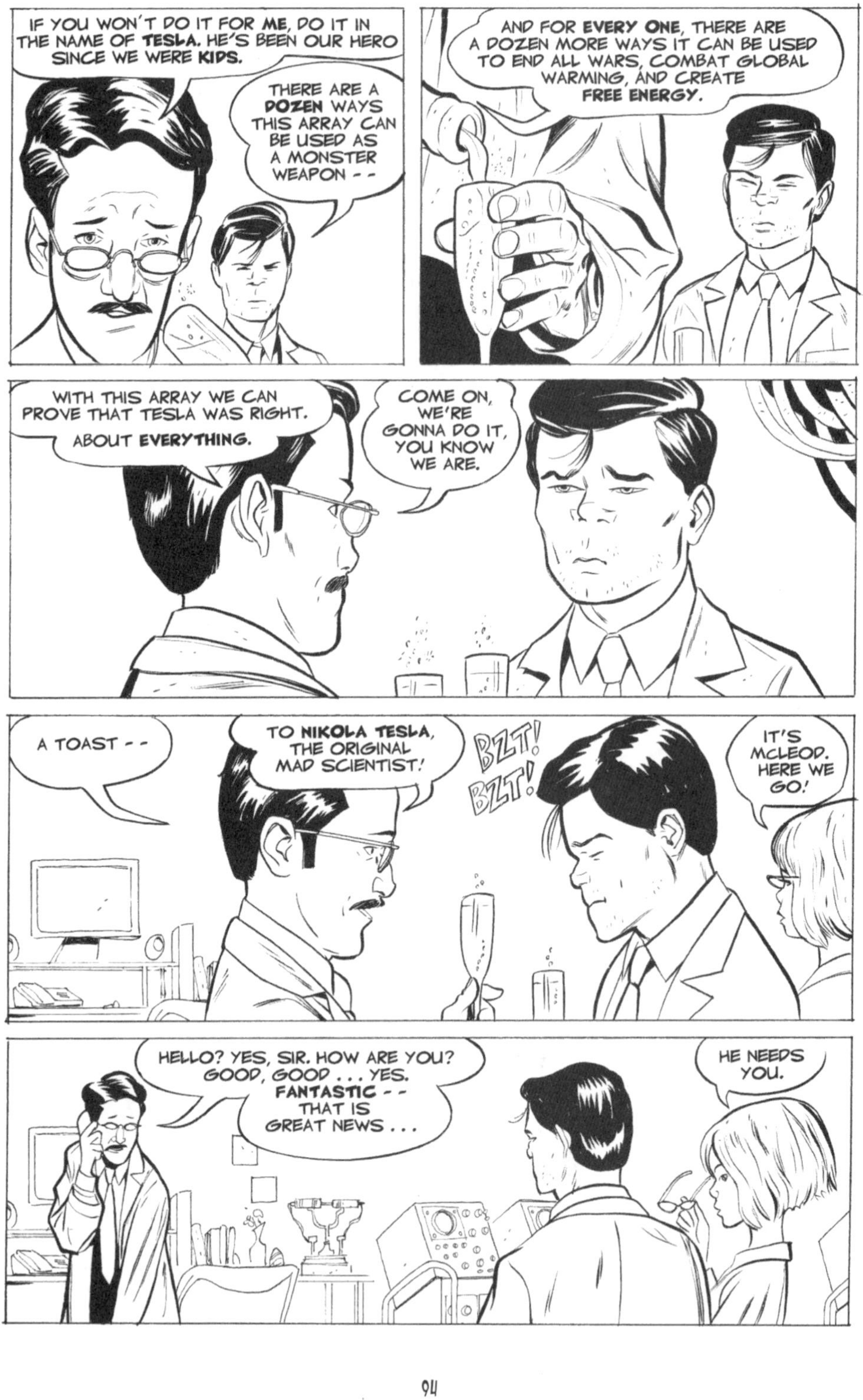
IF YOU WON'T DO IT FOR ME, DO IT IN THE NAME OF TESLA. HE'S BEEN OUR HERO SINCE WE WERE KIDS.
THERE ARE A DOZEN WAYS THIS ARRAY CAN BE USED AS A MONSTER WEAPON - -
AND FOR EVERY ONE, THERE ARE A DOZEN MORE WAYS IT CAN BE USED TO END ALL WARS, COMBAT GLOBAL WARMING, AND CREATE FREE ENERGY.
WITH THIS ARRAY WE CAN PROVE THAT TESLA WAS RIGHT.
ABOUT EVERYTHING.
COME ON, WE'RE GONNA DO IT, YOU KNOW WE ARE.
A TOAST - -
TO NIKOLA TESLA, THE ORIGINAL MAD SCIENTIST!
BZT! BZT!
IT'S MCLEOD. HERE WE GO!
HELLO? YES, SIR. HOW ARE YOU? GOOD, GOOD . . . YES. FANTASTIC - - THAT IS GREAT NEWS . . .
HE NEEDS YOU.

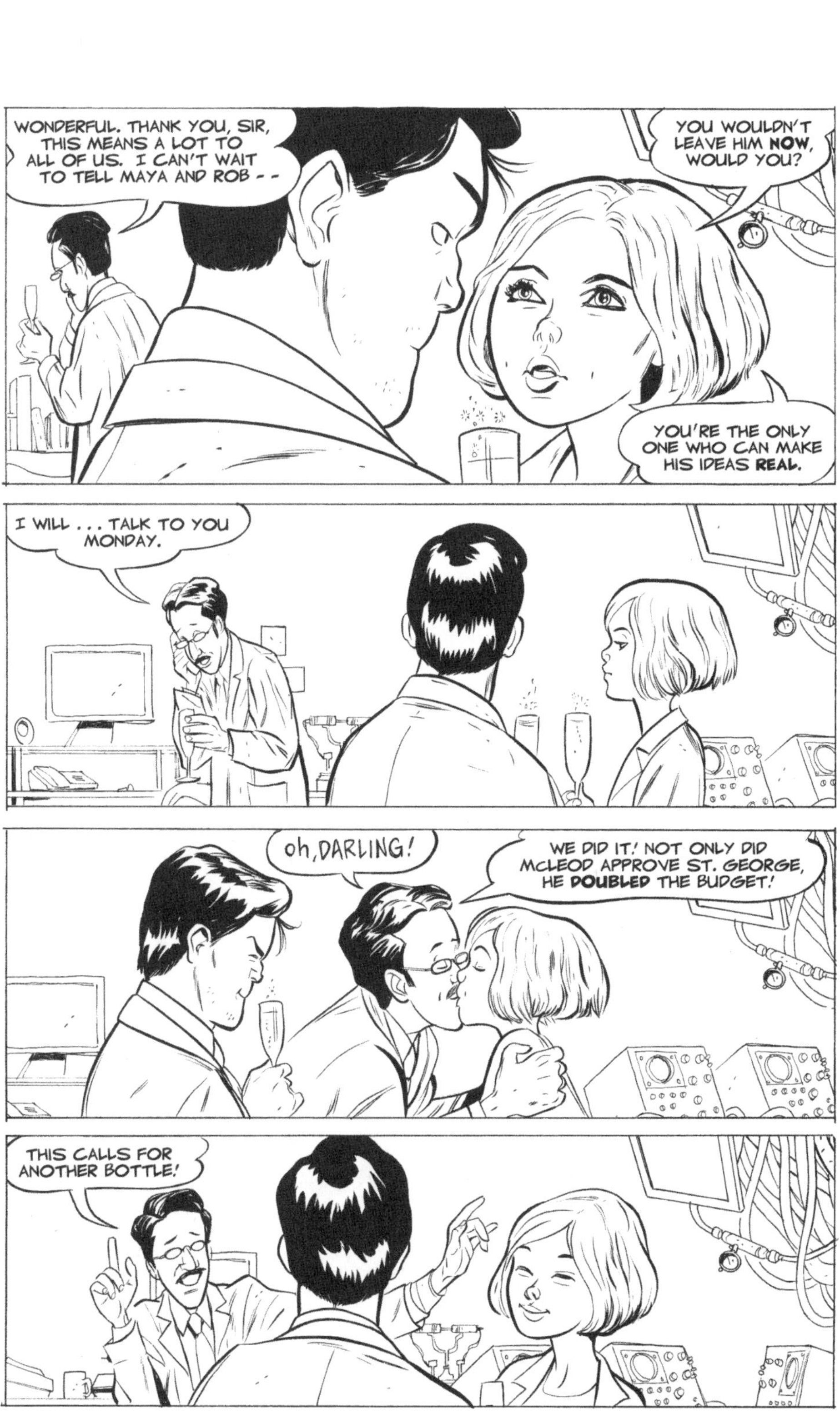
WONDERFUL. THANK YOU, SIR, THIS MEANS A LOT TO ALL OF US. I CAN'T WAIT TO TELL MAYA AND ROB - -
YOU WOULDN'T LEAVE HIM NOW, WOULD YOU?
YOU'RE THE ONLY ONE WHO CAN MAKE HIS IDEAS REAL.
I WILL . . . TALK TO YOU MONDAY.
oh, DARLING!
WE DID IT! NOT ONLY DID McLEOD APPROVE ST. GEORGE, HE DOUBLED THE BUDGET!
THIS CALLS FOR ANOTHER BOTTLE!

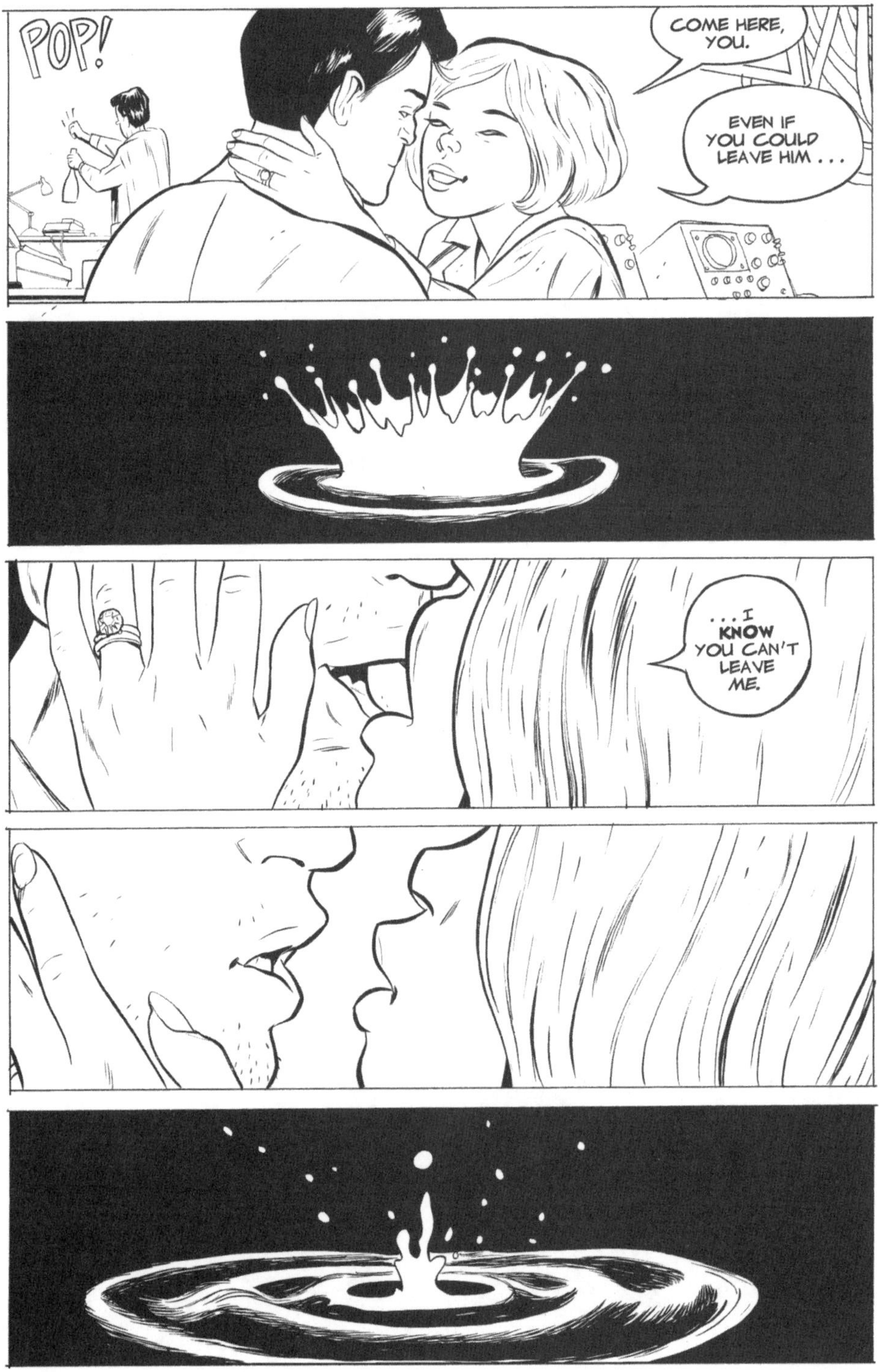
POP!
COME HERE, YOU.
EVEN IF YOU COULD LEAVE HIM . . .
. . . I KNOW YOU CAN'T LEAVE ME.

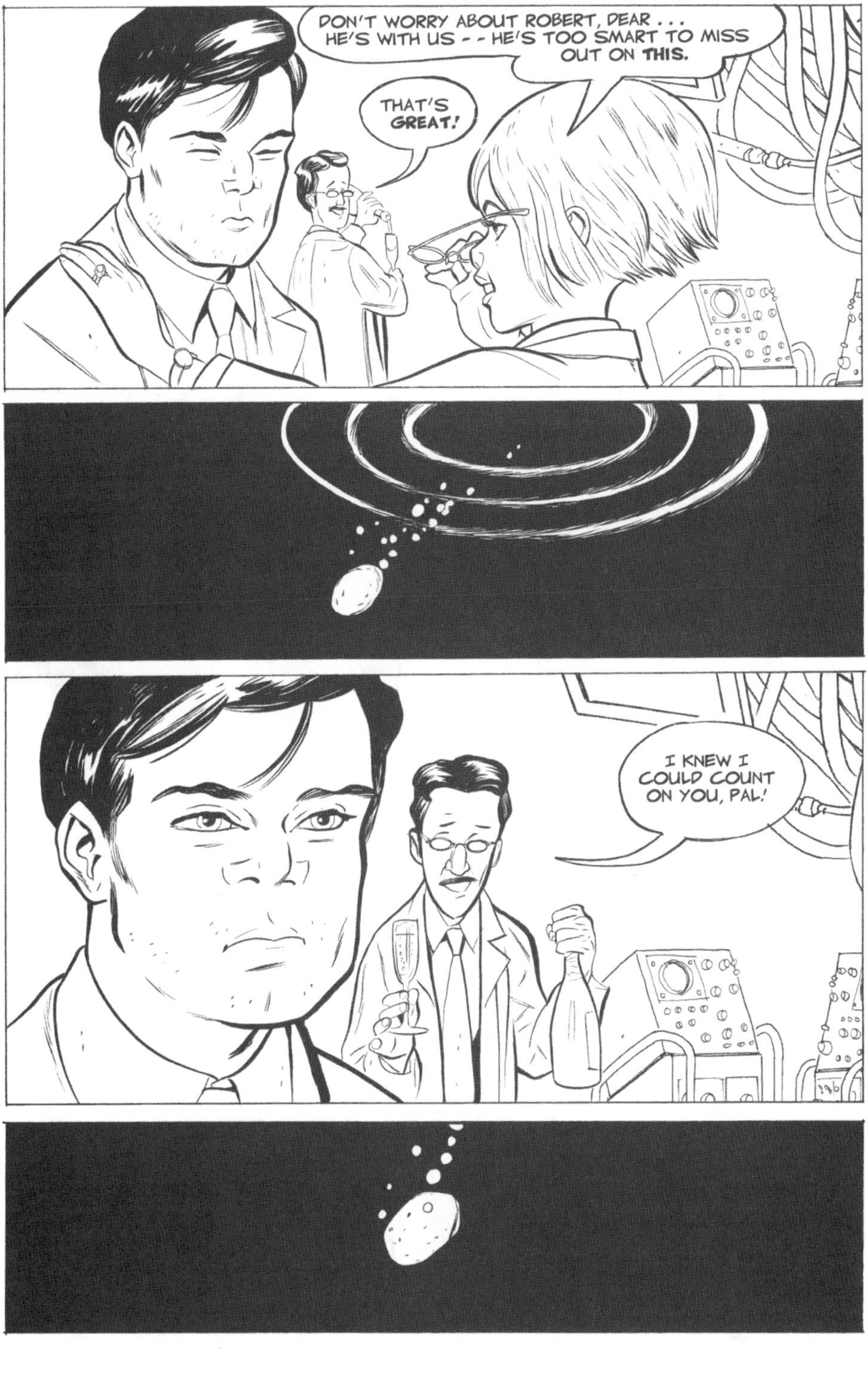
DON'T WORRY ABOUT ROBERT, DEAR . . . HE'S WITH US - - HE'S TOO SMART TO MISS OUT ON **THIS.**
THAT'S **GREAT!**
I KNEW I COULD COUNT ON YOU, PAL!

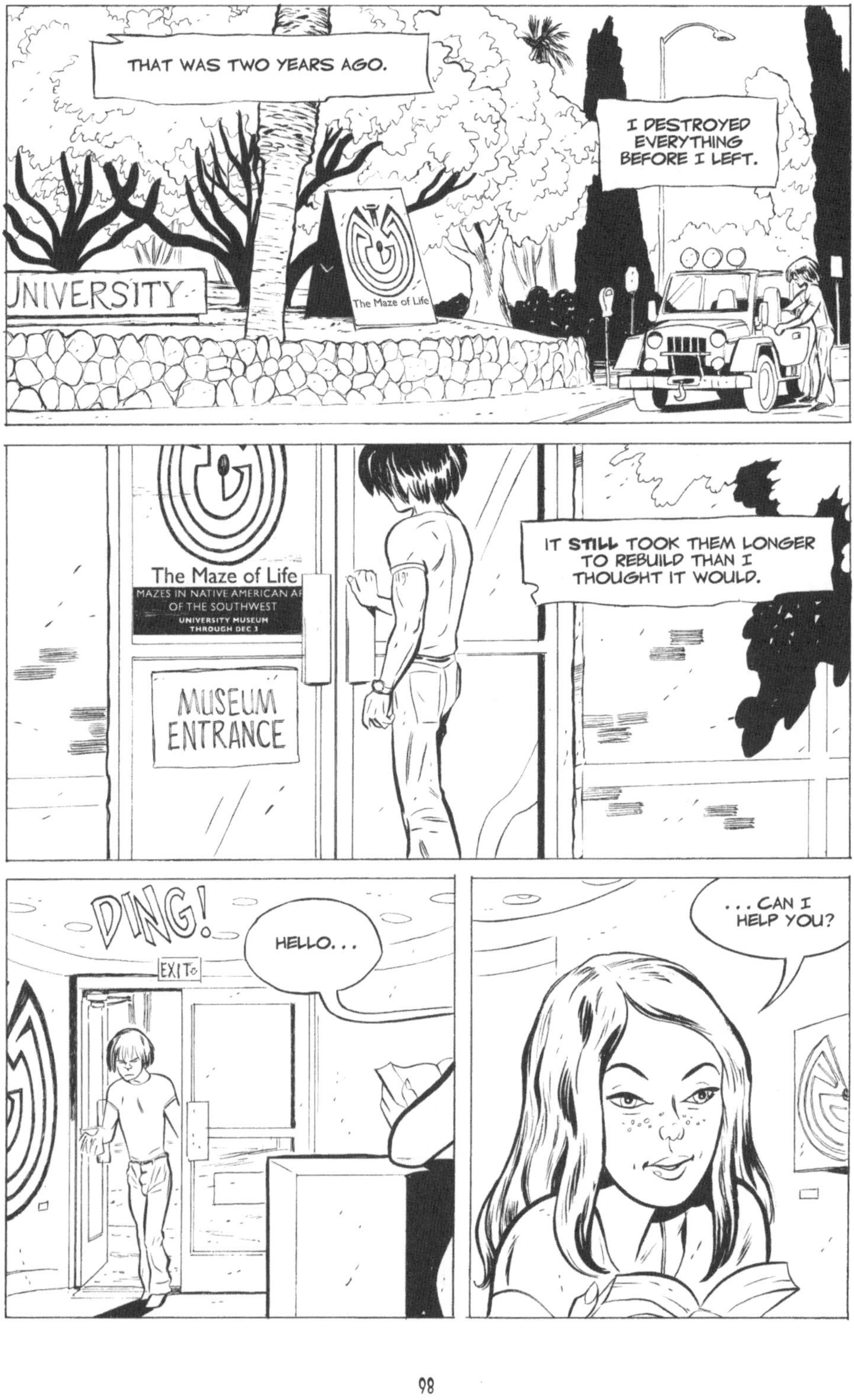
THAT WAS TWO YEARS AGO.
I DESTROYED EVERYTHING BEFORE I LEFT.
UNIVERSITY
The Maze of Life
The Maze of Life
MAZES IN NATIVE AMERICAN A
OF THE SOUTHWEST
UNIVERSITY MUSEUM
THROUGH DEC 3
MUSEUM ENTRANCE
IT **STILL** TOOK THEM LONGER TO REBUILD THAN I THOUGHT IT WOULD.
DING!
EXIT
HELLO...
...CAN I HELP YOU?

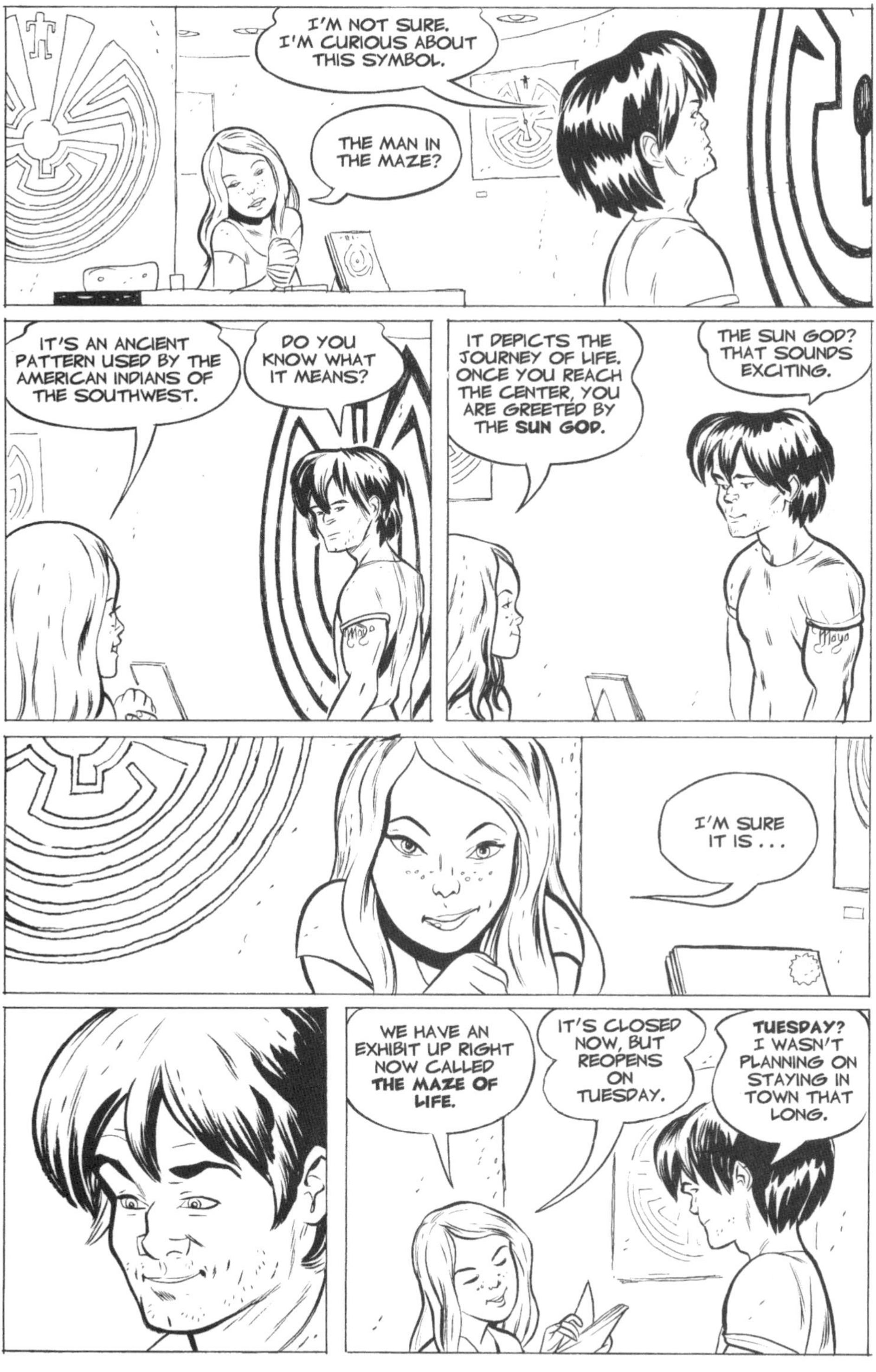
I'M NOT SURE. I'M CURIOUS ABOUT THIS SYMBOL.
THE MAN IN THE MAZE?
IT'S AN ANCIENT PATTERN USED BY THE AMERICAN INDIANS OF THE SOUTHWEST.
DO YOU KNOW WHAT IT MEANS?
IT DEPICTS THE JOURNEY OF LIFE. ONCE YOU REACH THE CENTER, YOU ARE GREETED BY THE SUN GOD.
THE SUN GOD? THAT SOUNDS EXCITING.
I'M SURE IT IS . . .
WE HAVE AN EXHIBIT UP RIGHT NOW CALLED THE MAZE OF LIFE.
IT'S CLOSED NOW, BUT REOPENS ON TUESDAY.
TUESDAY? I WASN'T PLANNING ON STAYING IN TOWN THAT LONG.

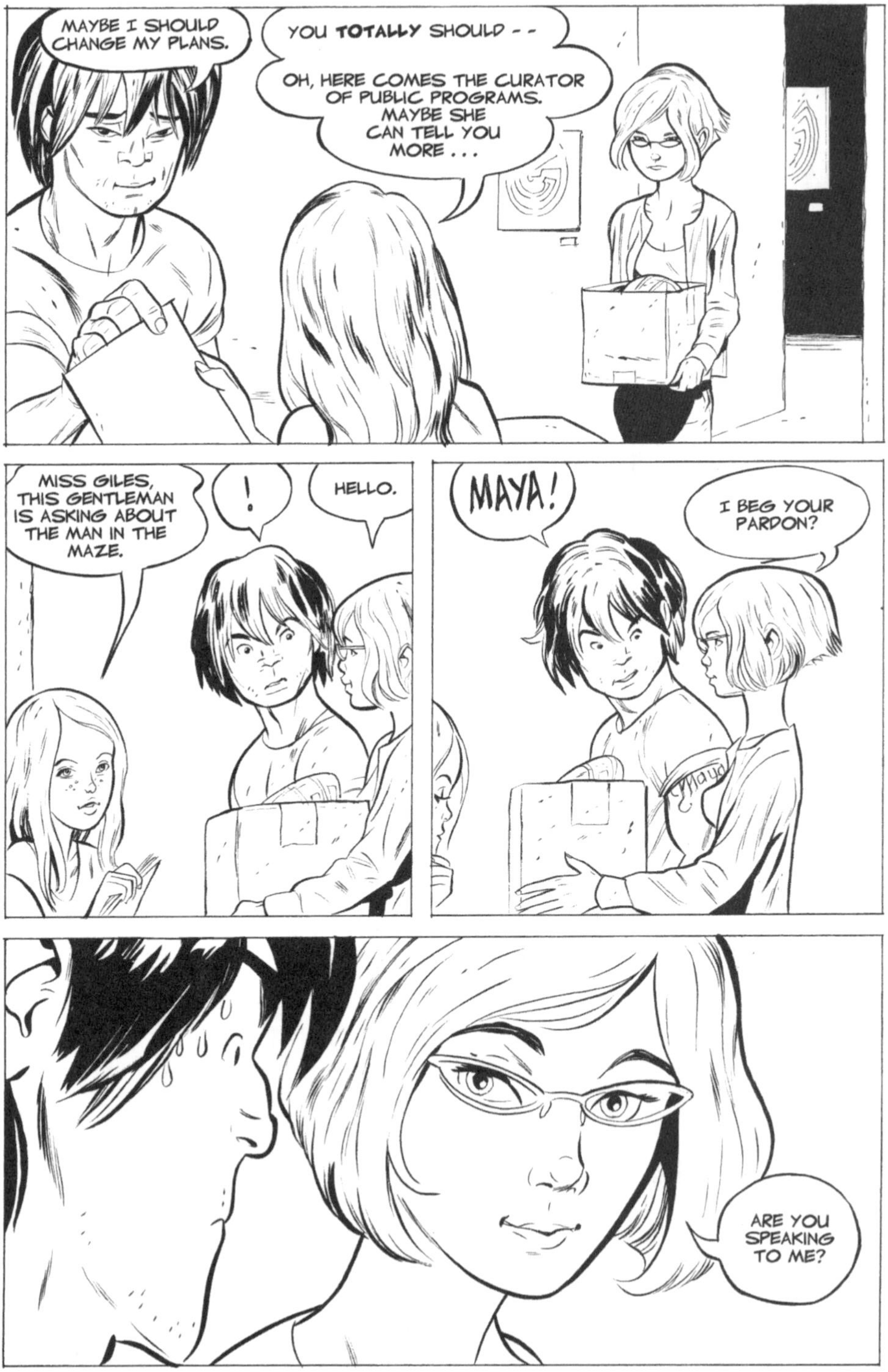
MAYBE I SHOULD CHANGE MY PLANS.
YOU **TOTALLY** SHOULD - -
OH, HERE COMES THE CURATOR OF PUBLIC PROGRAMS. MAYBE SHE CAN TELL YOU MORE . . .
MISS GILES, THIS GENTLEMAN IS ASKING ABOUT THE MAN IN THE MAZE.
!
HELLO.
MAYA!
I BEG YOUR PARDON?
ARE YOU SPEAKING TO ME?

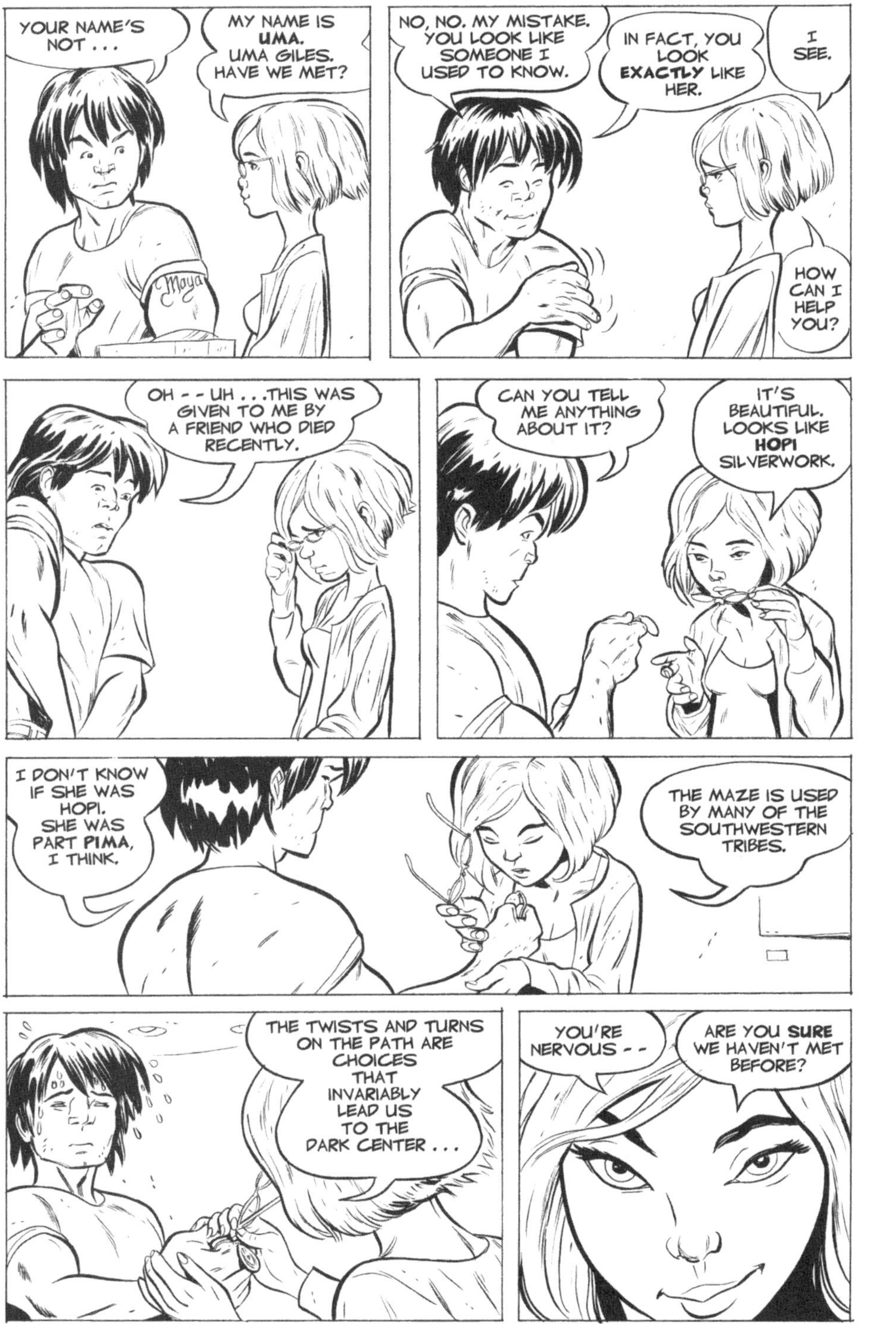
YOUR NAME'S NOT . . .
MY NAME IS UMA. UMA GILES. HAVE WE MET?
Maya
NO, NO. MY MISTAKE. YOU LOOK LIKE SOMEONE I USED TO KNOW.
IN FACT, YOU LOOK EXACTLY LIKE HER.
I SEE.
HOW CAN I HELP YOU?
OH - - UH . . .THIS WAS GIVEN TO ME BY A FRIEND WHO DIED RECENTLY.
CAN YOU TELL ME ANYTHING ABOUT IT?
IT'S BEAUTIFUL. LOOKS LIKE HOPI SILVERWORK.
I DON'T KNOW IF SHE WAS HOPI. SHE WAS PART PIMA, I THINK.
THE MAZE IS USED BY MANY OF THE SOUTHWESTERN TRIBES.
THE TWISTS AND TURNS ON THE PATH ARE CHOICES THAT INVARIABLY LEAD US TO THE DARK CENTER . . .
YOU'RE NERVOUS - -
ARE YOU SURE WE HAVEN'T MET BEFORE?

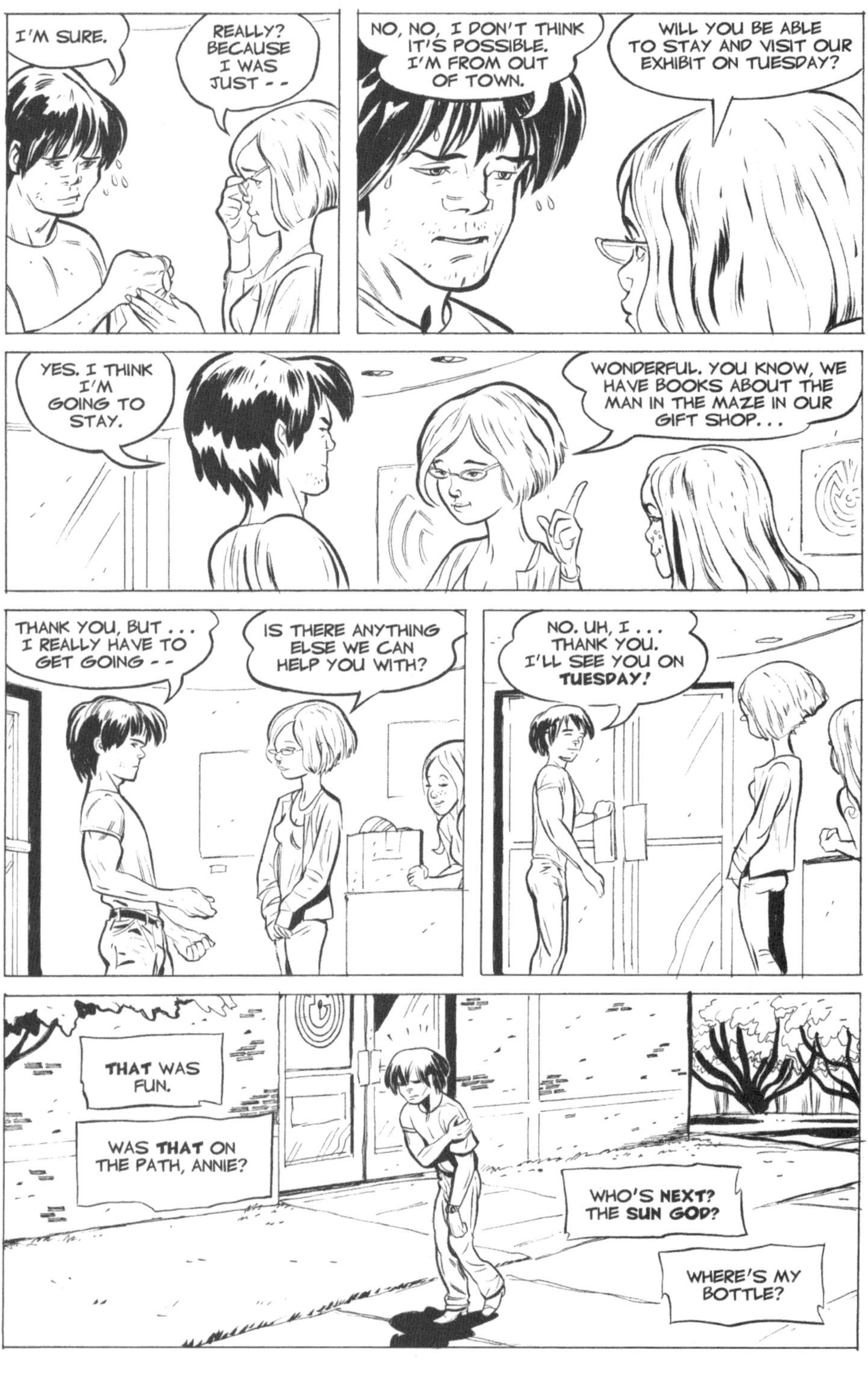
I'M SURE.
REALLY? BECAUSE I WAS JUST - -
NO, NO, I DON'T THINK IT'S POSSIBLE. I'M FROM OUT OF TOWN.
WILL YOU BE ABLE TO STAY AND VISIT OUR EXHIBIT ON TUESDAY?
YES. I THINK I'M GOING TO STAY.
WONDERFUL. YOU KNOW, WE HAVE BOOKS ABOUT THE MAN IN THE MAZE IN OUR GIFT SHOP...
THANK YOU, BUT... I REALLY HAVE TO GET GOING - -
IS THERE ANYTHING ELSE WE CAN HELP YOU WITH?
NO. UH, I... THANK YOU. I'LL SEE YOU ON **TUESDAY**!
THAT WAS FUN.
WAS **THAT** ON THE PATH, ANNIE?
WHO'S **NEXT**? THE **SUN GOD**?
WHERE'S MY BOTTLE?

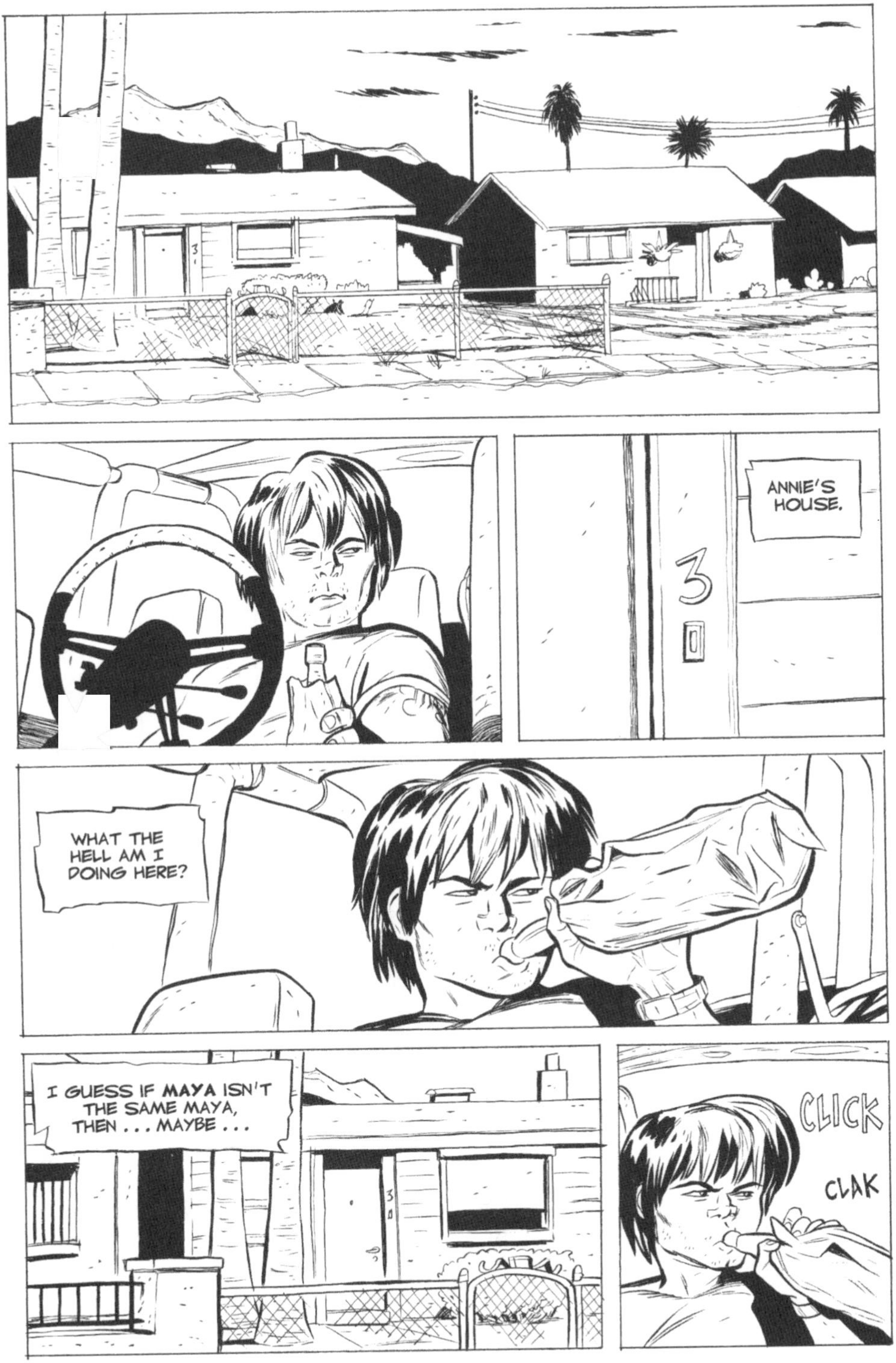
ANNIE'S HOUSE.
WHAT THE HELL AM I DOING HERE?
I GUESS IF MAYA ISN'T THE SAME MAYA, THEN . . . MAYBE . . .
CLICK
CLAK

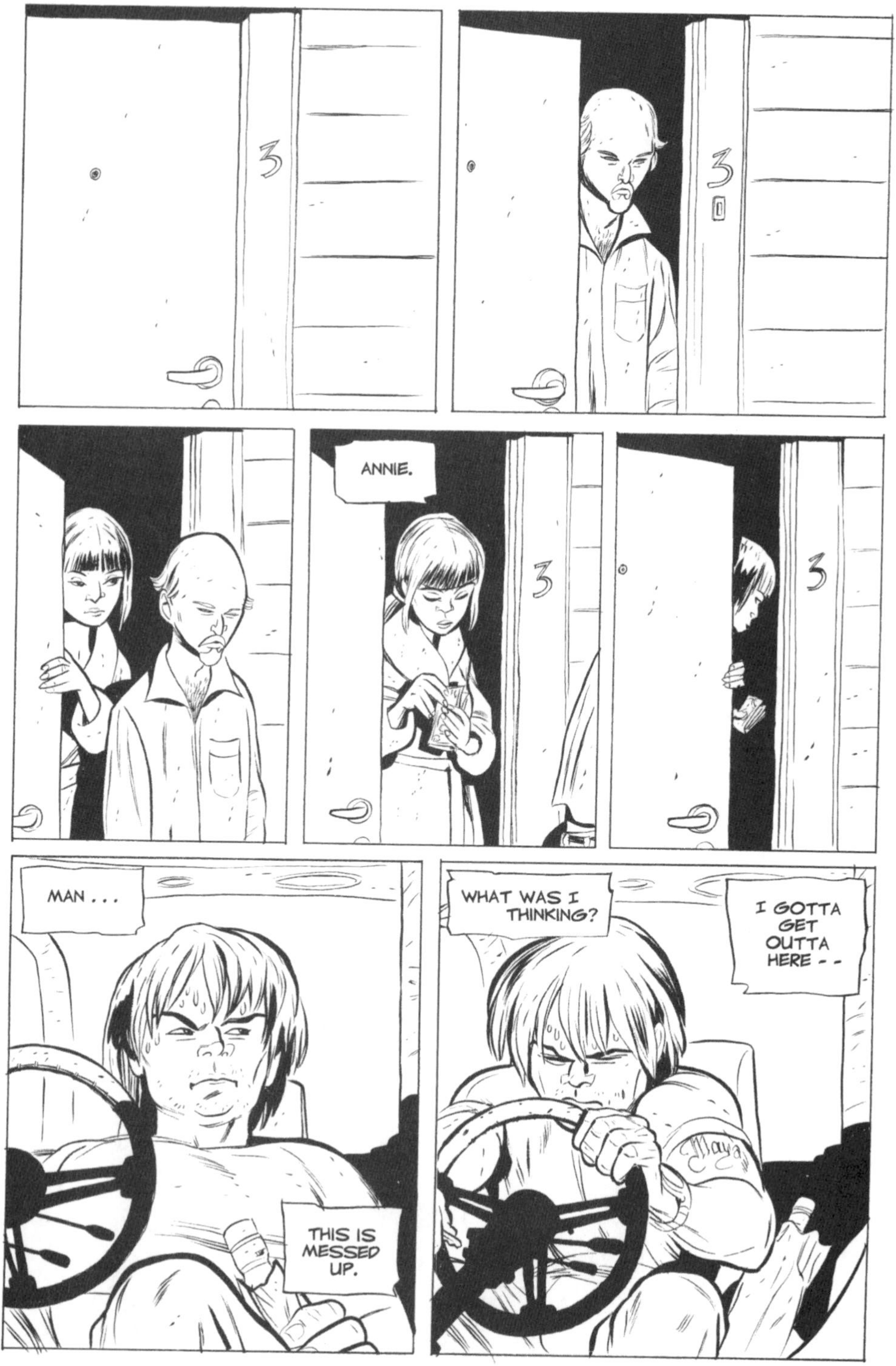
ANNIE.
MAN . . .
THIS IS MESSED UP.
WHAT WAS I THINKING?
I GOTTA GET OUTTA HERE - -
Maya

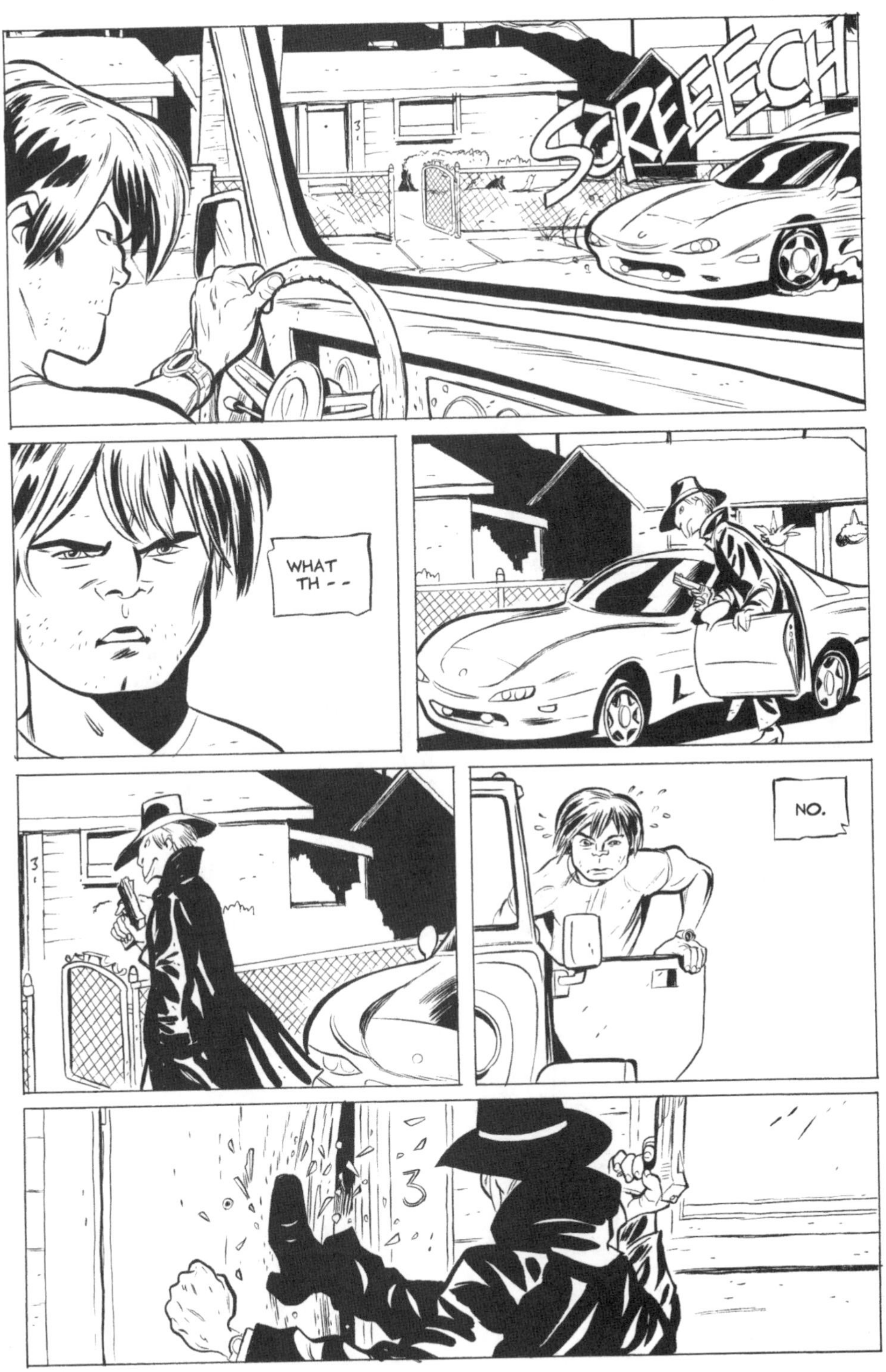
SCREEECH
WHAT TH --
NO.

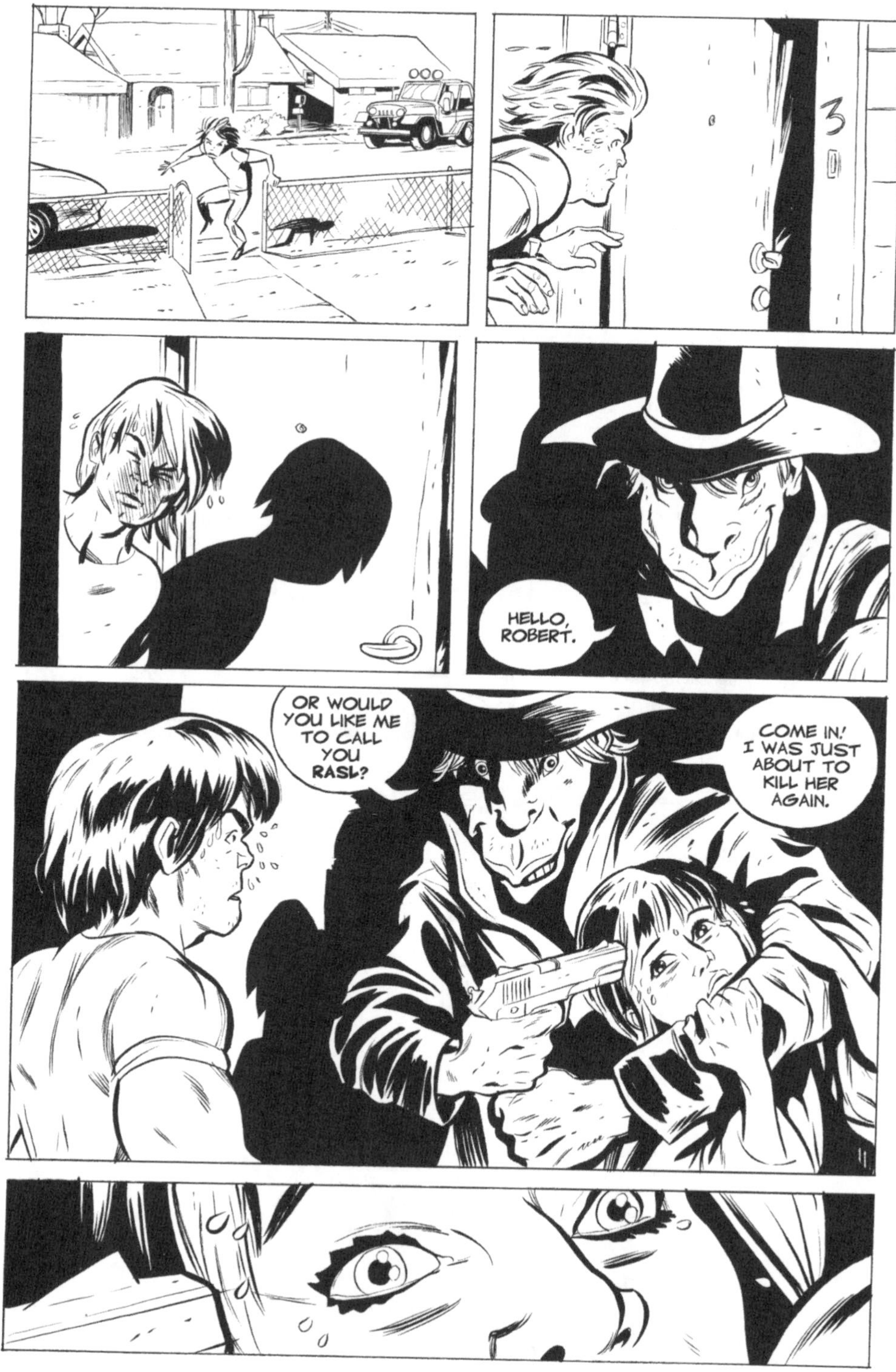
HELLO, ROBERT.
OR WOULD YOU LIKE ME TO CALL YOU RASL?
COME IN! I WAS JUST ABOUT TO KILL HER AGAIN.

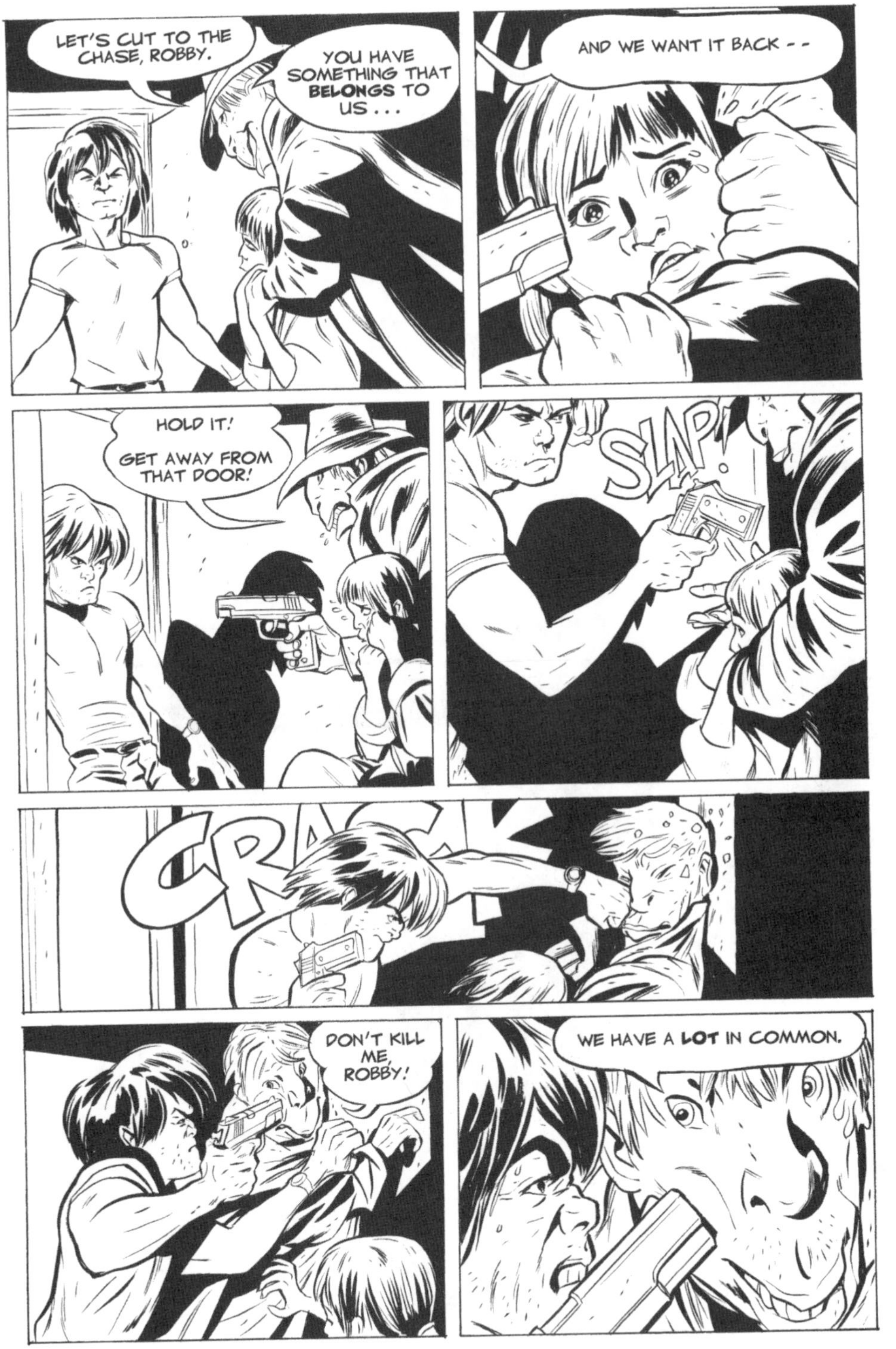
LET'S CUT TO THE CHASE, ROBBY.
YOU HAVE SOMETHING THAT **BELONGS** TO US . . .
AND WE WANT IT BACK - -
HOLD IT! GET AWAY FROM THAT DOOR!
SLAP!
CRACK
DON'T KILL ME ROBBY!
WE HAVE A **LOT** IN COMMON.

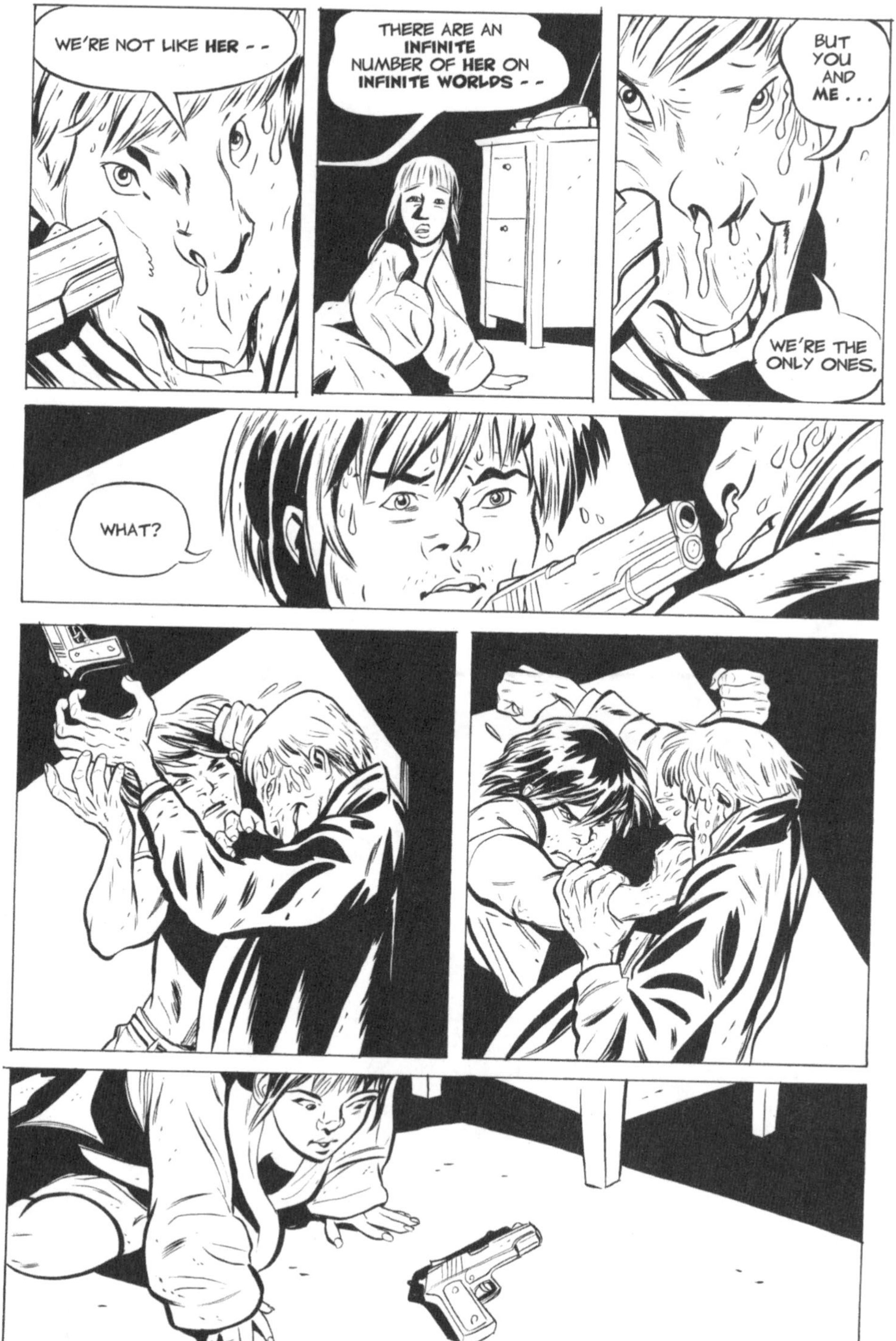
WE'RE NOT LIKE HER - -
THERE ARE AN INFINITE NUMBER OF HER ON INFINITE WORLDS - -
BUT YOU AND ME . . .
WE'RE THE ONLY ONES.
WHAT?

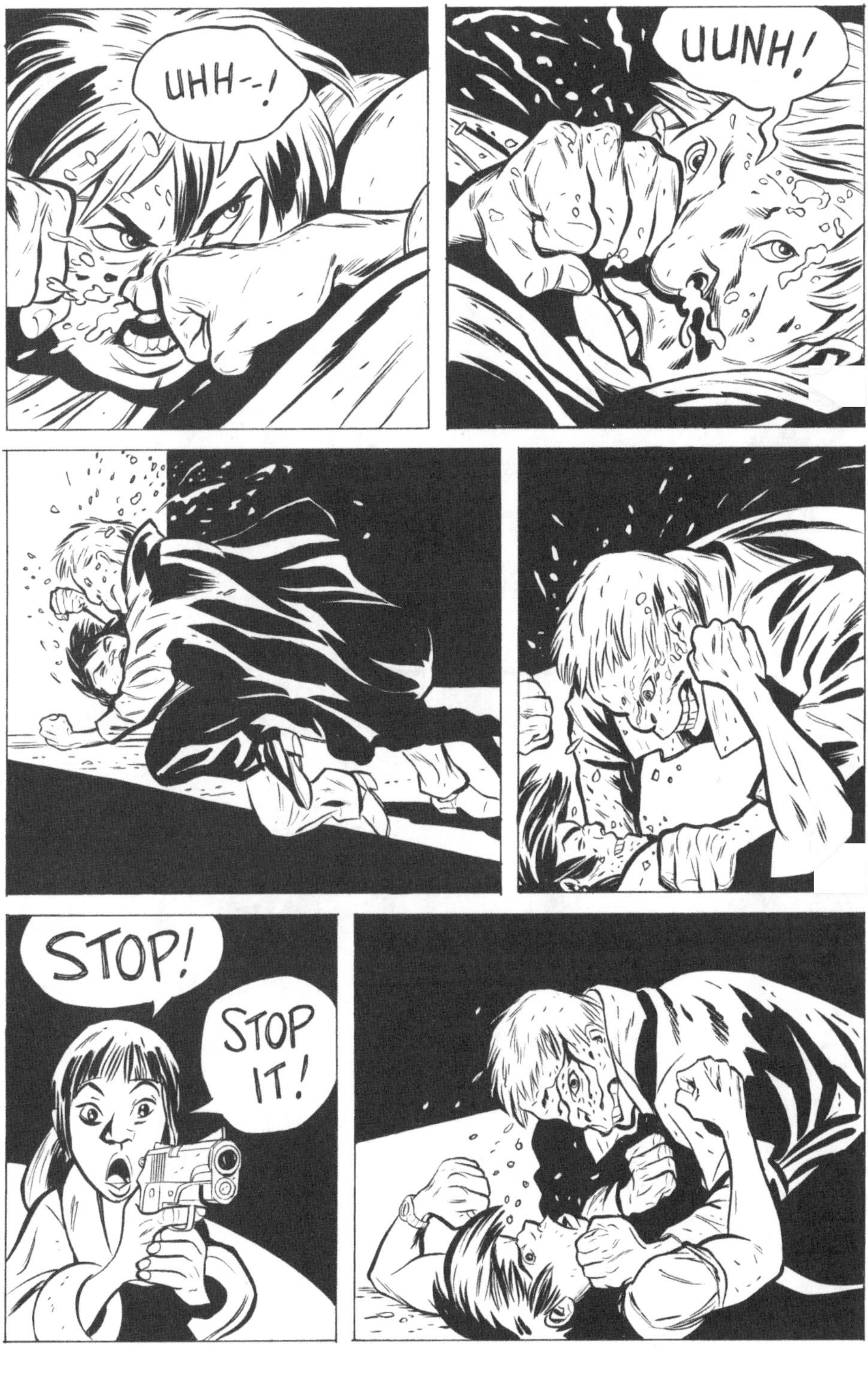
UHH--!
UUNH!
STOP!
STOP IT!

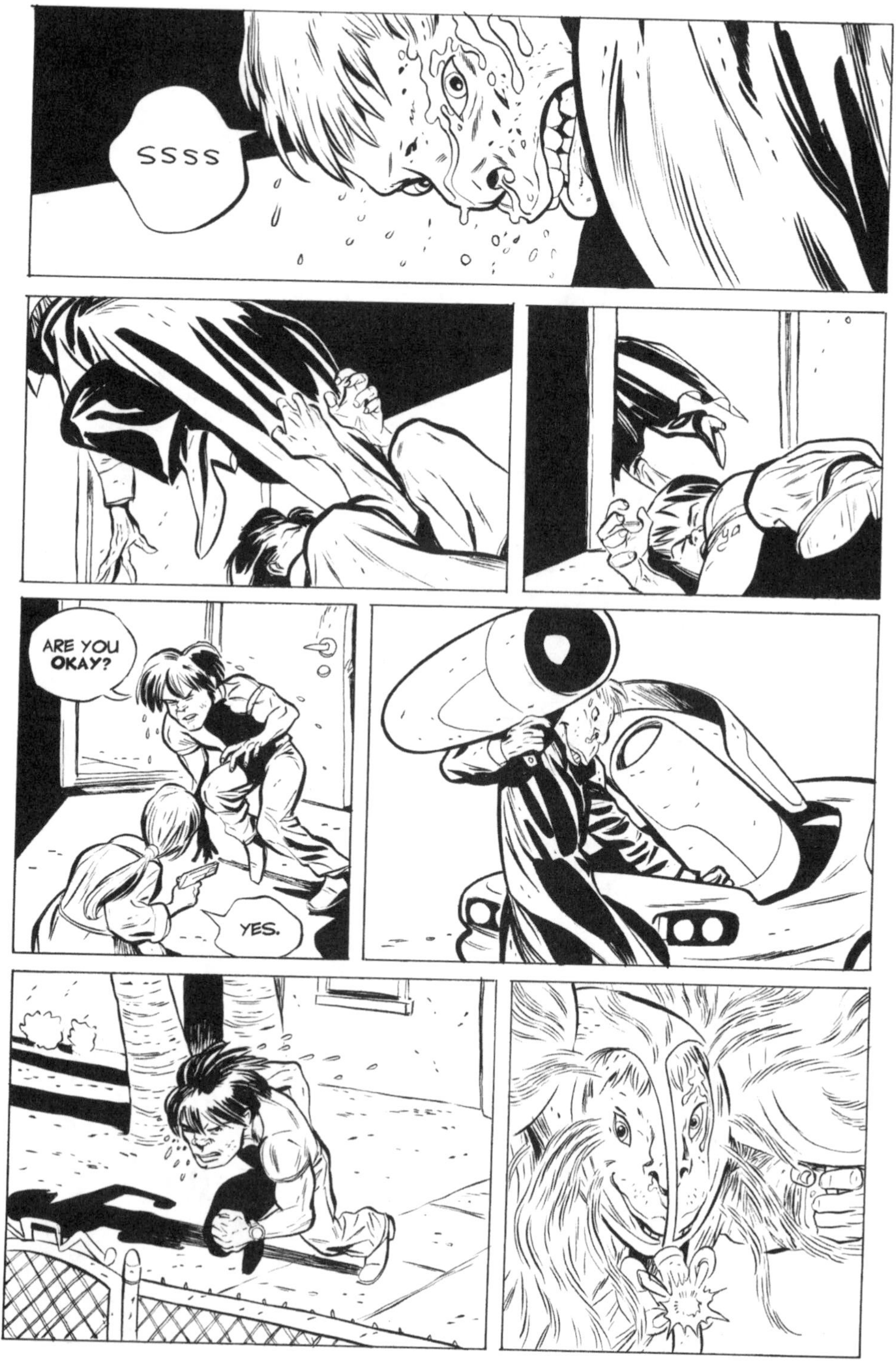
SSSS
ARE YOU OKAY?
YES.

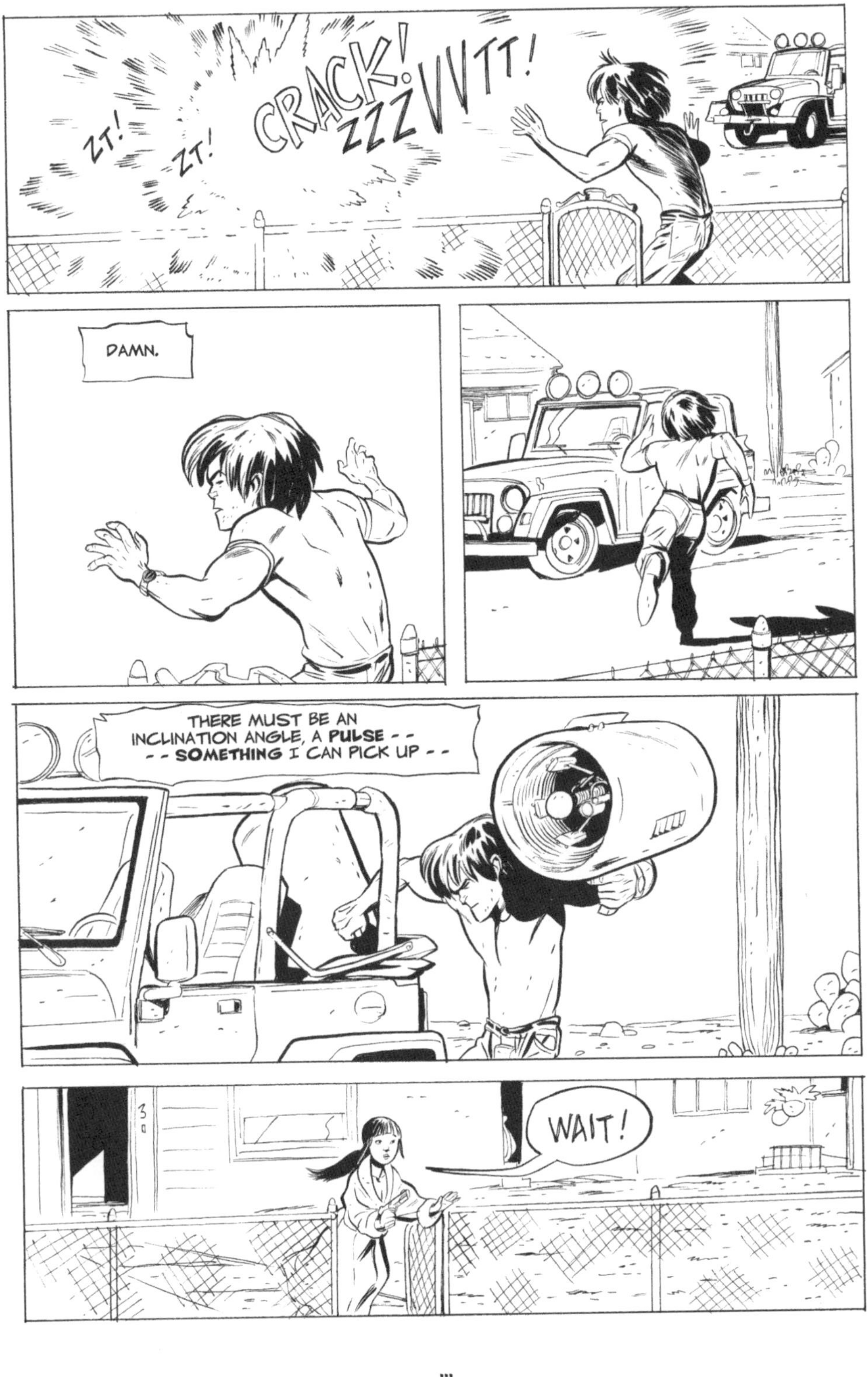
ZT!
ZT!
CRACK!
ZZZVVTT!
DAMN.
THERE MUST BE AN INCLINATION ANGLE, A PULSE - - - - SOMETHING I CAN PICK UP - -
WAIT!

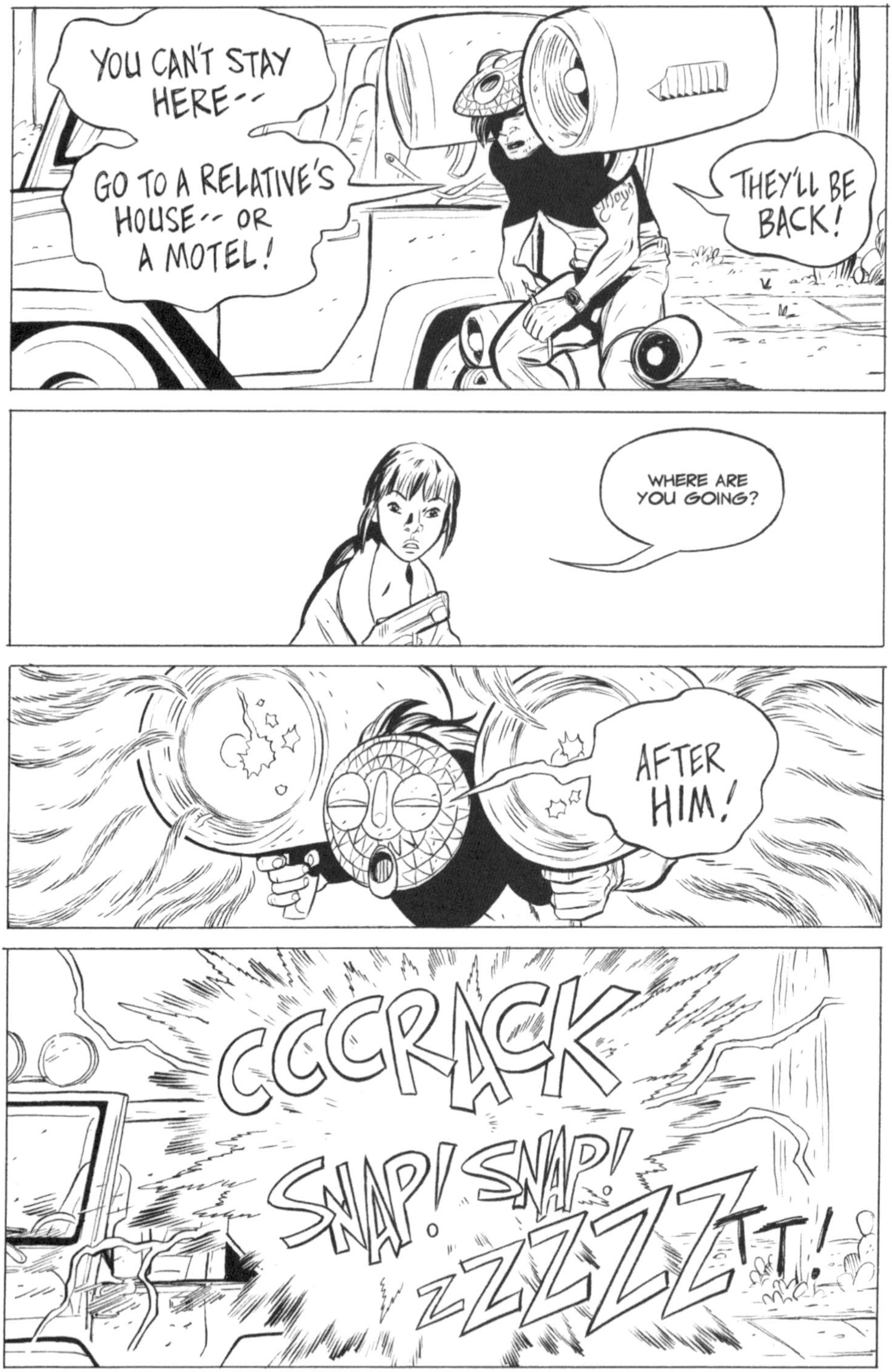
YOU CAN'T STAY HERE--
GO TO A RELATIVE'S HOUSE-- OR A MOTEL!
THEY'LL BE BACK!
WHERE ARE YOU GOING?
AFTER HIM!
CCCRACK
SNAP! SNAP!
zZZZZTTT!

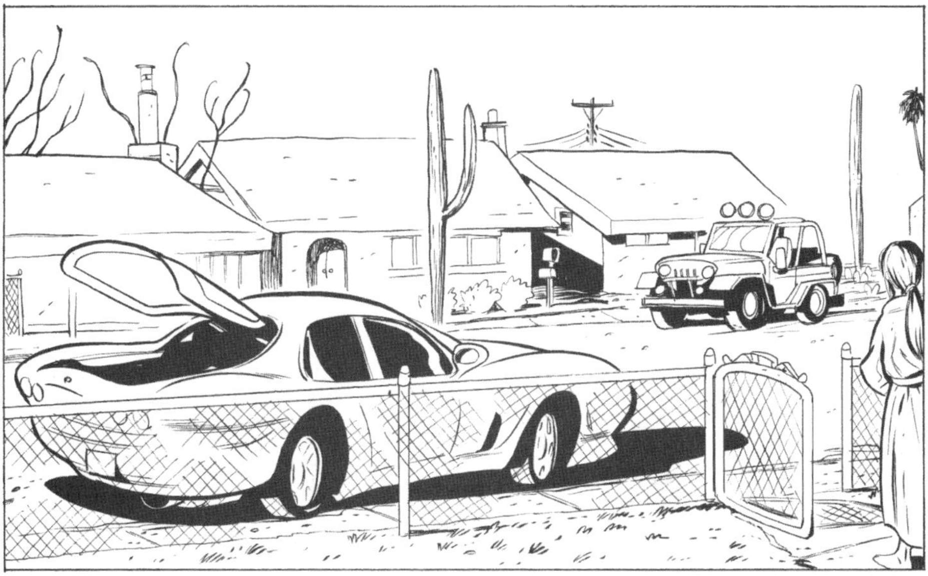

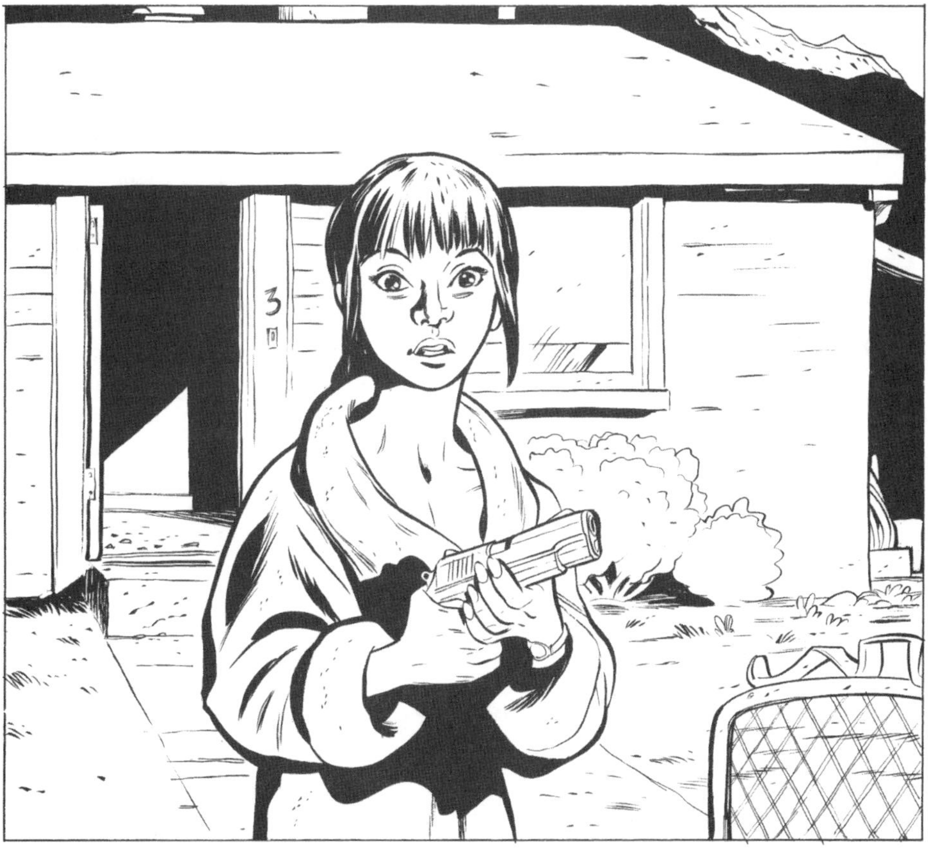

PART 2

RASL AND THE FIRE OF ST. GEORGE

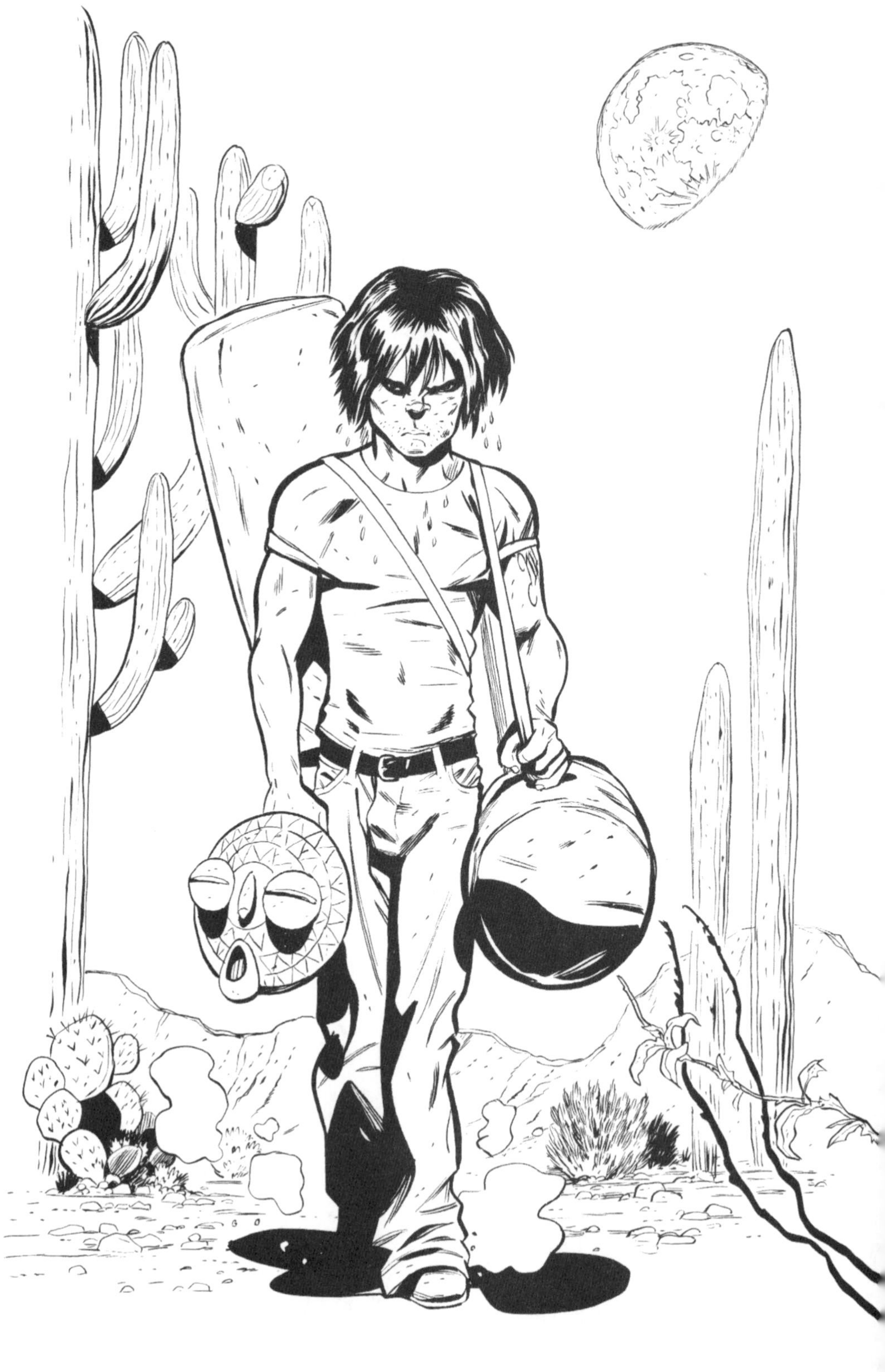

"THE SPREAD OF CIVILIZATION MAY BE LIKENED TO A FIRE

FIRST A FEEBLE SPARK, NEXT A FLICKERING FLAME, THEN A MIGHTY BLAZE, EVER INCREASING IN SPEED AND POWER."

-NIKOLA TESLA

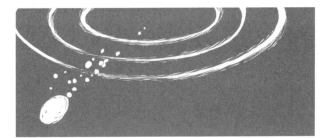

4.
OPENING DOORS

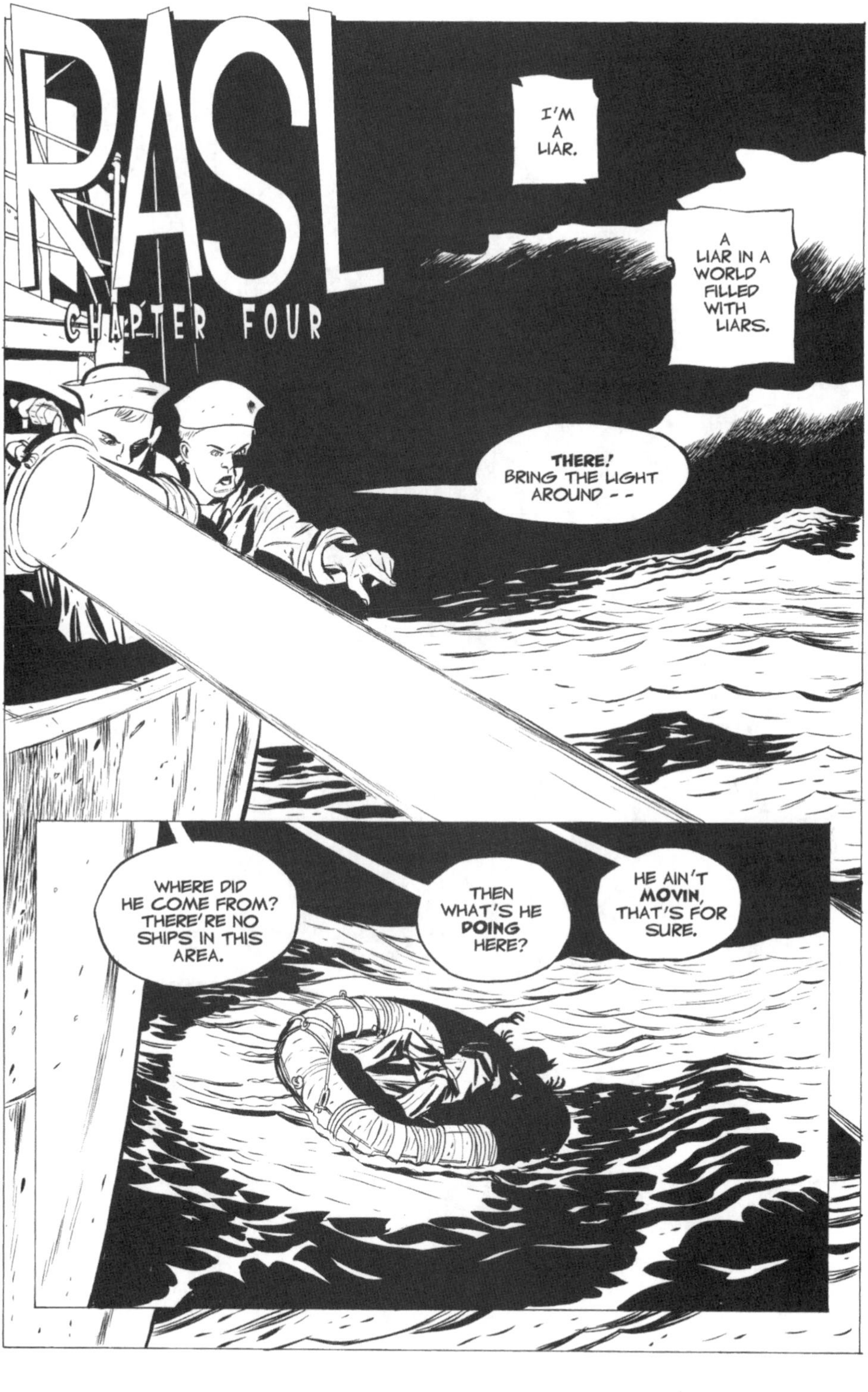
RASL
CHAPTER FOUR
I'M A LIAR.
A LIAR IN A WORLD FILLED WITH LIARS.
THERE! BRING THE LIGHT AROUND --
WHERE DID HE COME FROM? THERE'RE NO SHIPS IN THIS AREA.
THEN WHAT'S HE DOING HERE?
HE AIN'T MOVIN, THAT'S FOR SURE.

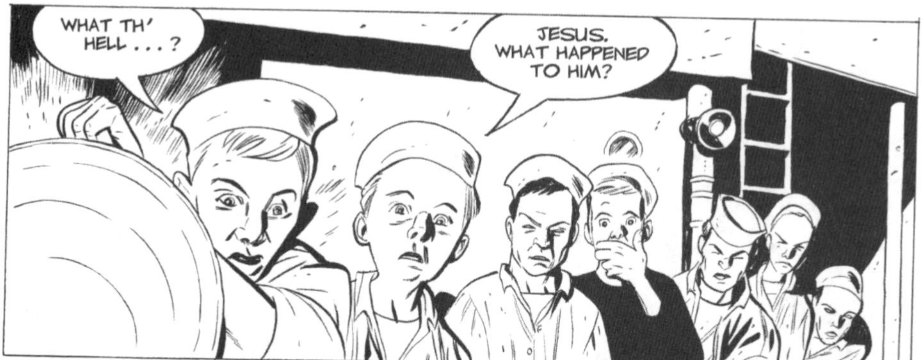
WHAT TH' HELL . . . ?
JESUS. WHAT HAPPENED TO HIM?

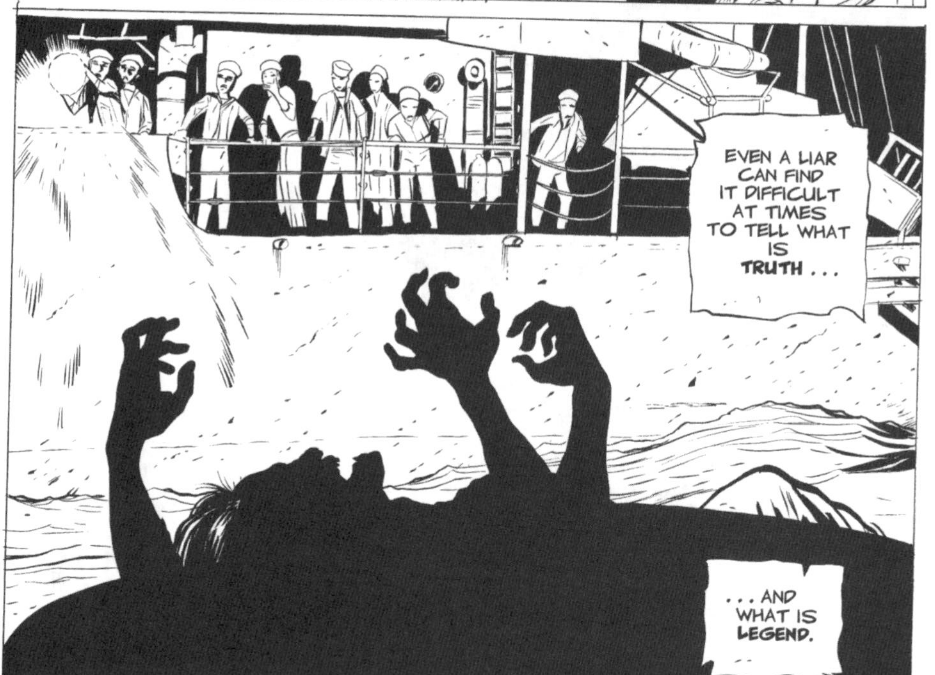
EVEN A LIAR CAN FIND IT DIFFICULT AT TIMES TO TELL WHAT IS **TRUTH** . . .
. . . AND WHAT IS **LEGEND**.

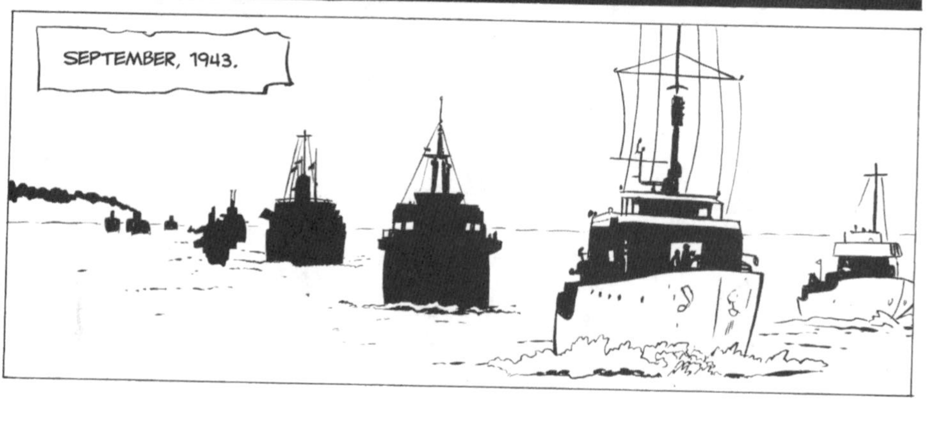
SEPTEMBER, 1943.

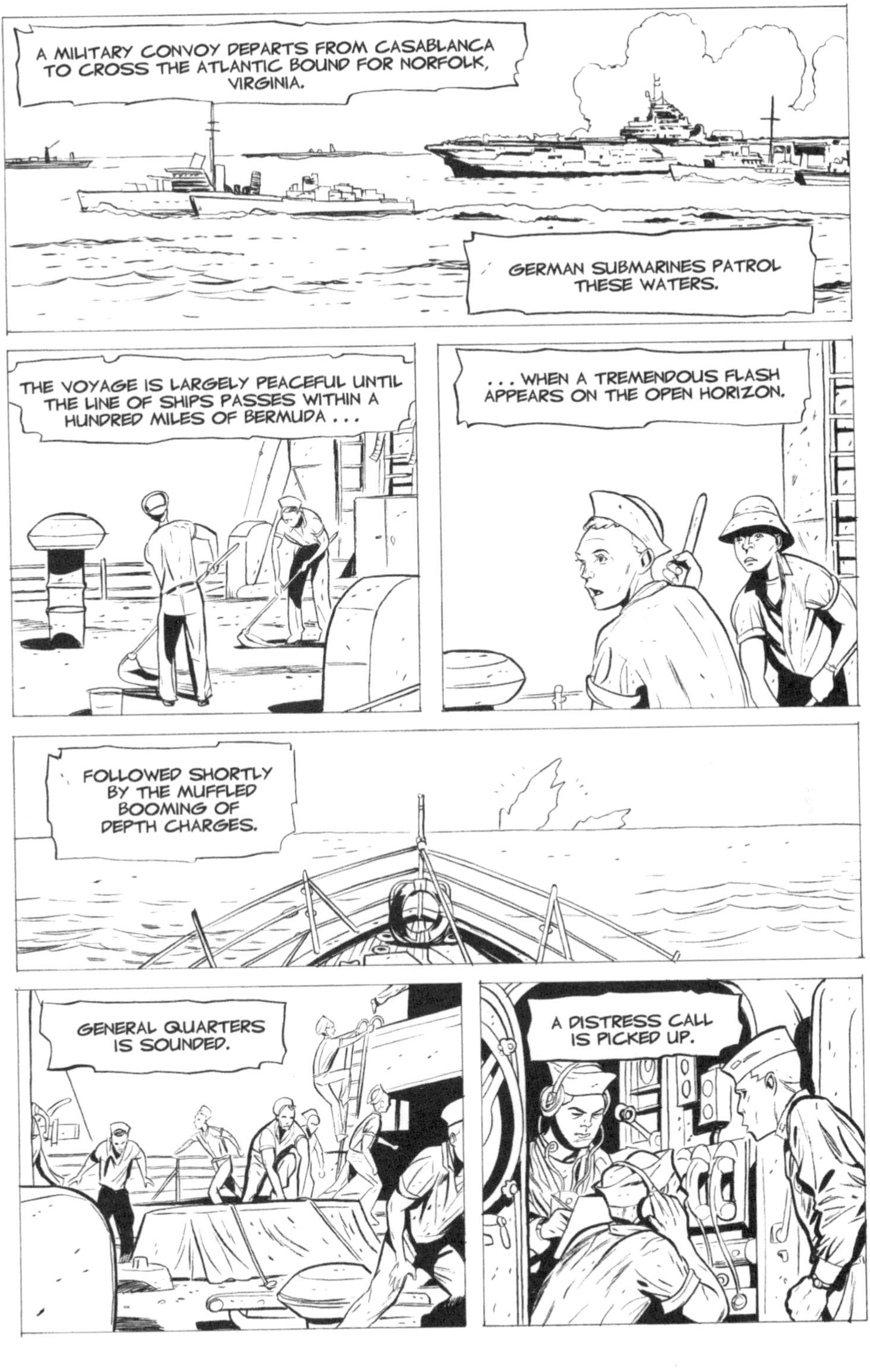
A MILITARY CONVOY DEPARTS FROM CASABLANCA TO CROSS THE ATLANTIC BOUND FOR NORFOLK, VIRGINIA.
GERMAN SUBMARINES PATROL THESE WATERS.
THE VOYAGE IS LARGELY PEACEFUL UNTIL THE LINE OF SHIPS PASSES WITHIN A HUNDRED MILES OF BERMUDA . . .
. . . WHEN A TREMENDOUS FLASH APPEARS ON THE OPEN HORIZON.
FOLLOWED SHORTLY BY THE MUFFLED BOOMING OF DEPTH CHARGES.
GENERAL QUARTERS IS SOUNDED.
A DISTRESS CALL IS PICKED UP.

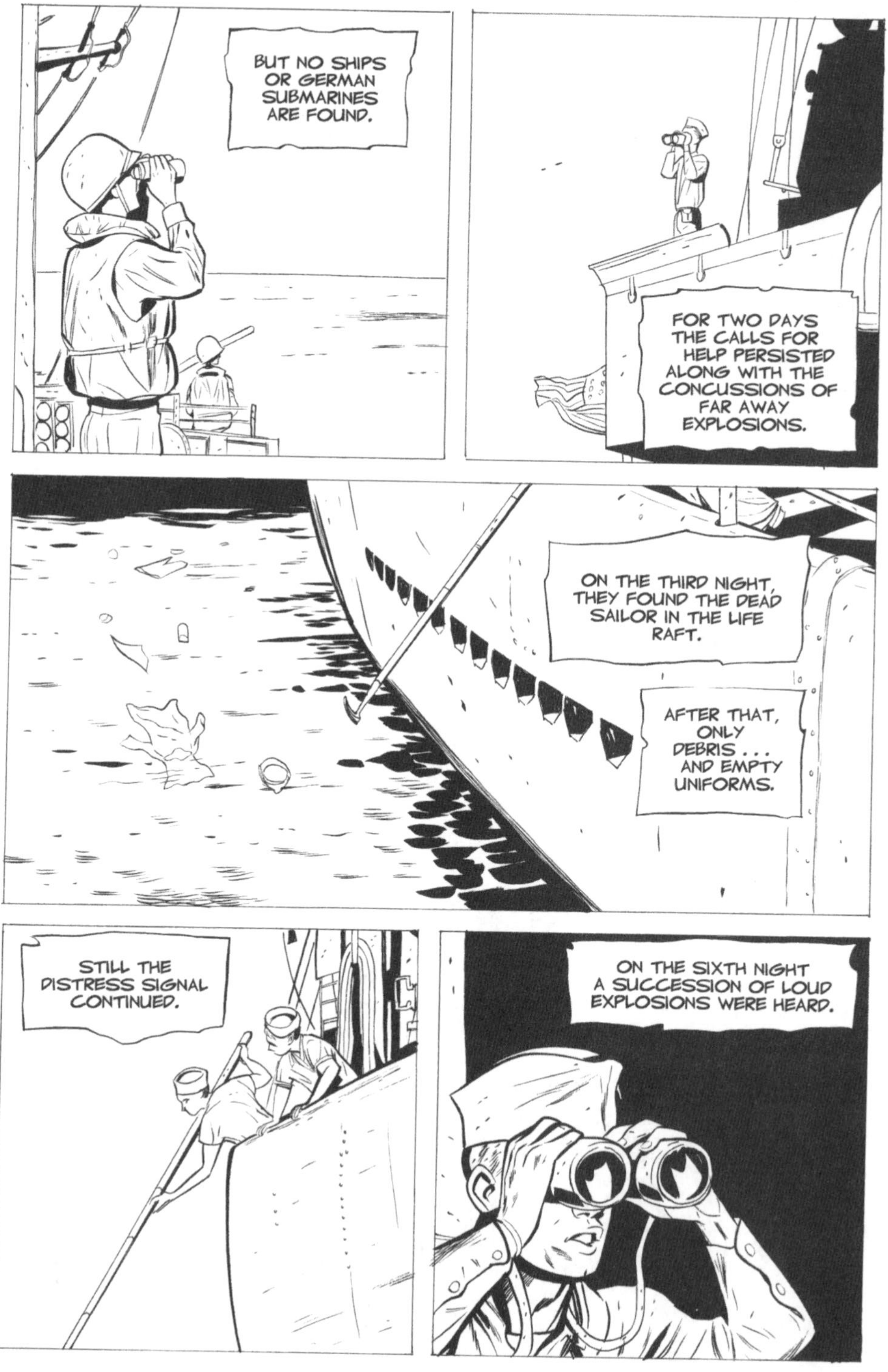
BUT NO SHIPS OR GERMAN SUBMARINES ARE FOUND.
FOR TWO DAYS THE CALLS FOR HELP PERSISTED ALONG WITH THE CONCUSSIONS OF FAR AWAY EXPLOSIONS.
ON THE THIRD NIGHT, THEY FOUND THE DEAD SAILOR IN THE LIFE RAFT.
AFTER THAT, ONLY DEBRIS . . . AND EMPTY UNIFORMS.
STILL THE DISTRESS SIGNAL CONTINUED.
ON THE SIXTH NIGHT A SUCCESSION OF LOUD EXPLOSIONS WERE HEARD.

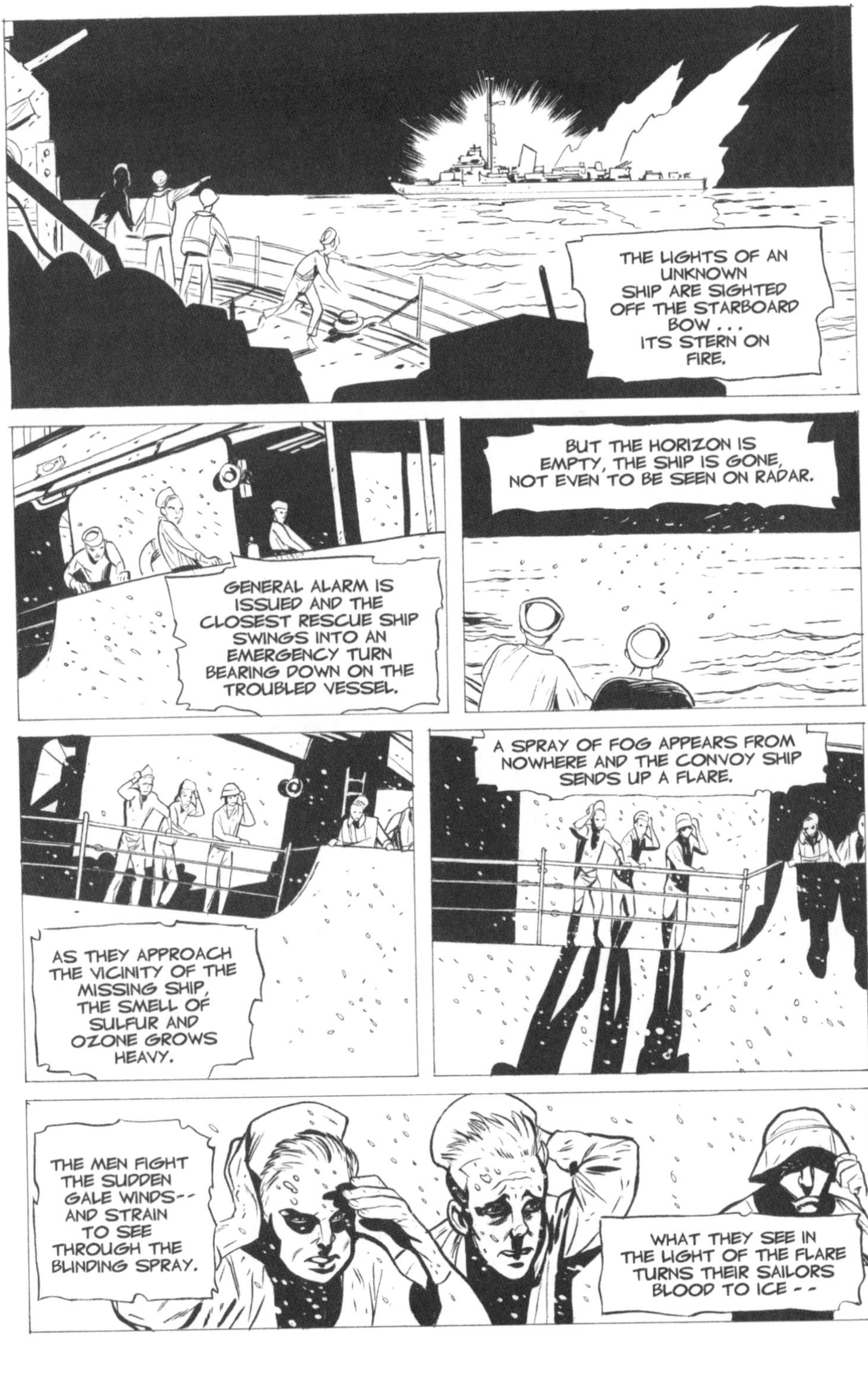
THE LIGHTS OF AN UNKNOWN SHIP ARE SIGHTED OFF THE STARBOARD BOW . . . ITS STERN ON FIRE.
GENERAL ALARM IS ISSUED AND THE CLOSEST RESCUE SHIP SWINGS INTO AN EMERGENCY TURN BEARING DOWN ON THE TROUBLED VESSEL.
BUT THE HORIZON IS EMPTY, THE SHIP IS GONE, NOT EVEN TO BE SEEN ON RADAR.
AS THEY APPROACH THE VICINITY OF THE MISSING SHIP, THE SMELL OF SULFUR AND OZONE GROWS HEAVY.
A SPRAY OF FOG APPEARS FROM NOWHERE AND THE CONVOY SHIP SENDS UP A FLARE.
THE MEN FIGHT THE SUDDEN GALE WINDS-- AND STRAIN TO SEE THROUGH THE BLINDING SPRAY.
WHAT THEY SEE IN THE LIGHT OF THE FLARE TURNS THEIR SAILORS BLOOD TO ICE --

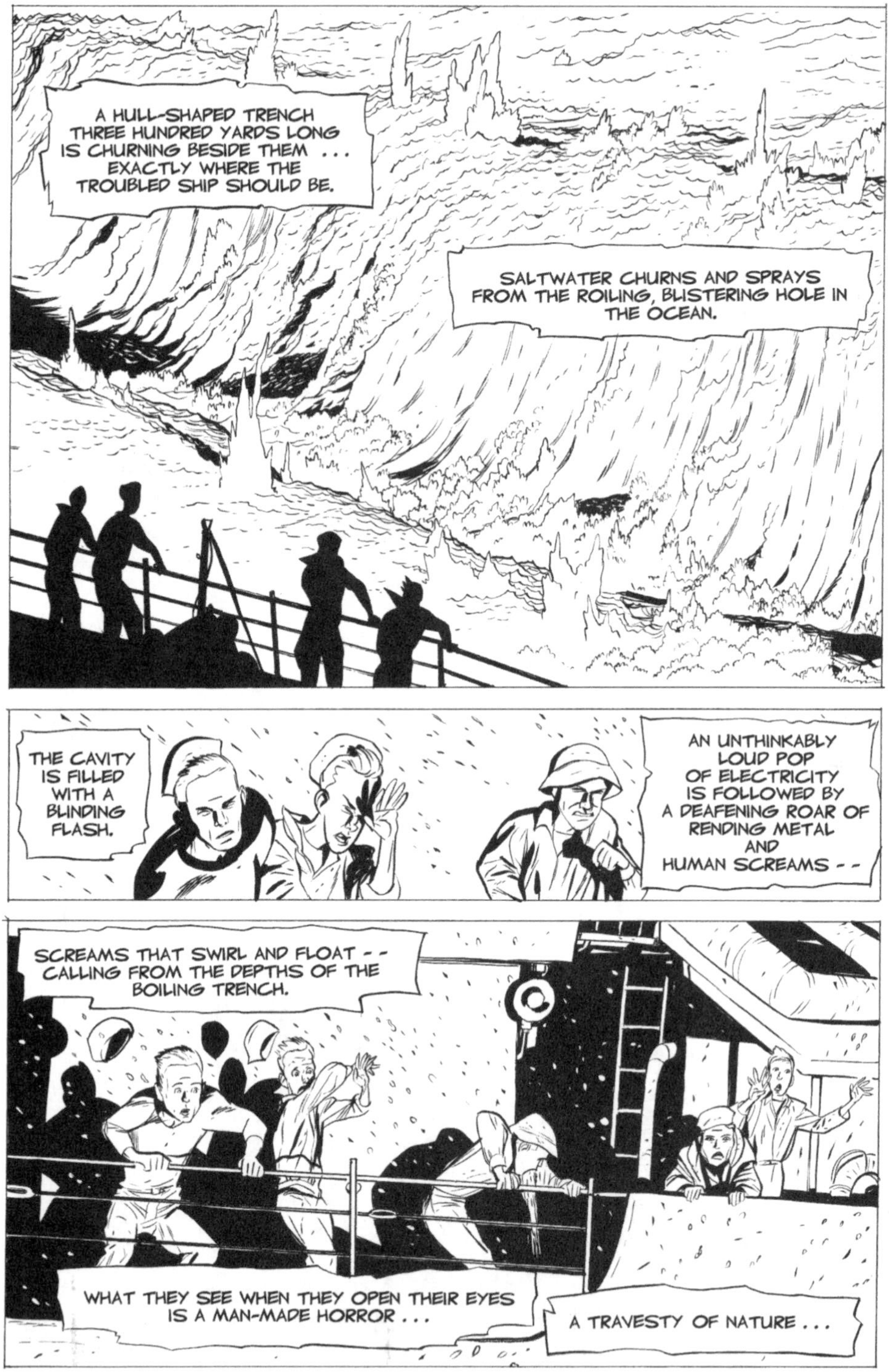
A HULL-SHAPED TRENCH THREE HUNDRED YARDS LONG IS CHURNING BESIDE THEM . . . EXACTLY WHERE THE TROUBLED SHIP SHOULD BE.
SALTWATER CHURNS AND SPRAYS FROM THE ROILING, BLISTERING HOLE IN THE OCEAN.
THE CAVITY IS FILLED WITH A BLINDING FLASH.
AN UNTHINKABLY LOUD POP OF ELECTRICITY IS FOLLOWED BY A DEAFENING ROAR OF RENDING METAL AND HUMAN SCREAMS - -
SCREAMS THAT SWIRL AND FLOAT - - CALLING FROM THE DEPTHS OF THE BOILING TRENCH.
WHAT THEY SEE WHEN THEY OPEN THEIR EYES IS A MAN-MADE HORROR . . .
A TRAVESTY OF NATURE . . .

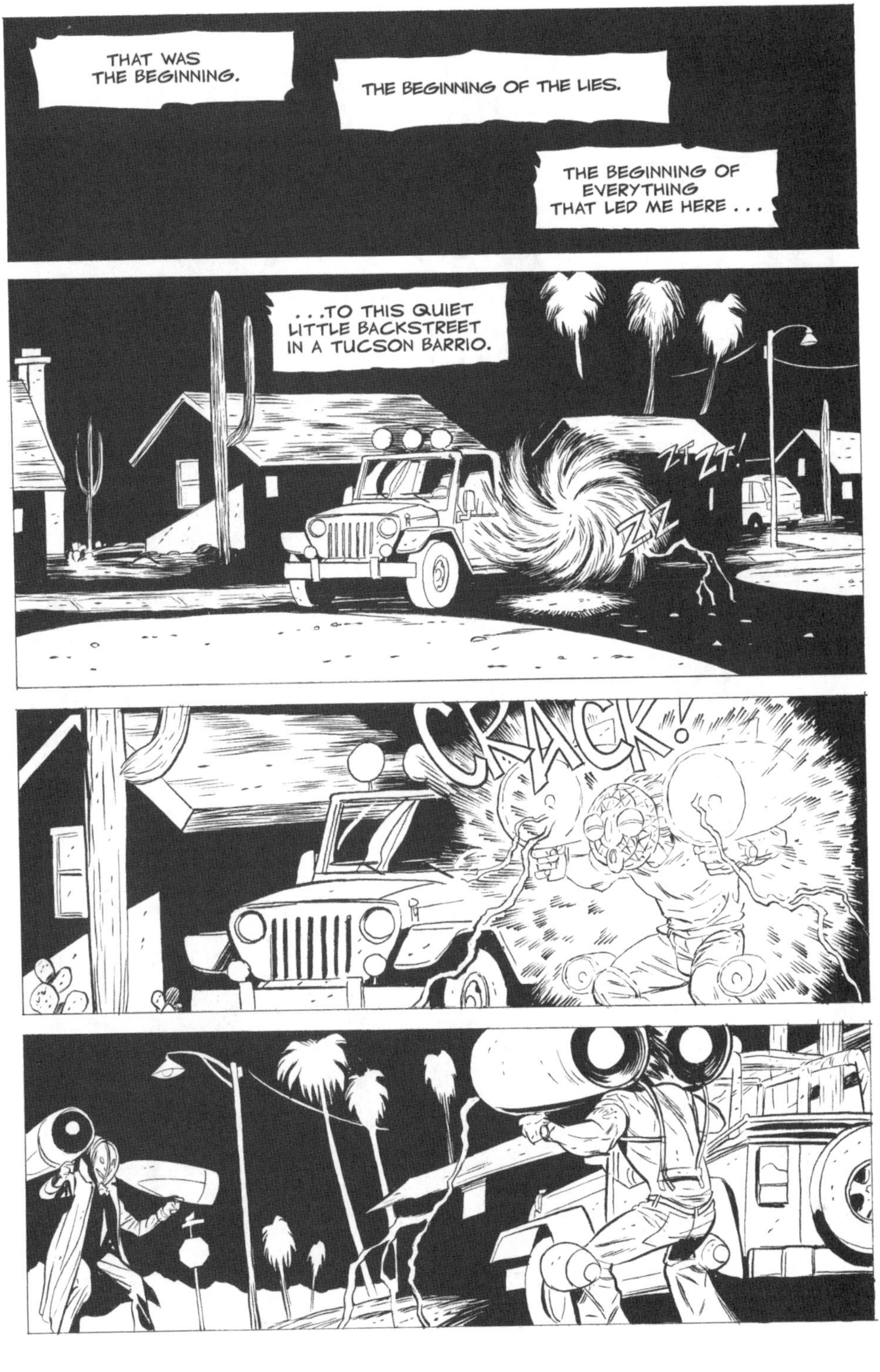
THAT WAS THE BEGINNING.
THE BEGINNING OF THE LIES.
THE BEGINNING OF EVERYTHING THAT LED ME HERE . . .
. . .TO THIS QUIET LITTLE BACKSTREET IN A TUCSON BARRIO.
ZT ZT!
ZZ
CRACK!

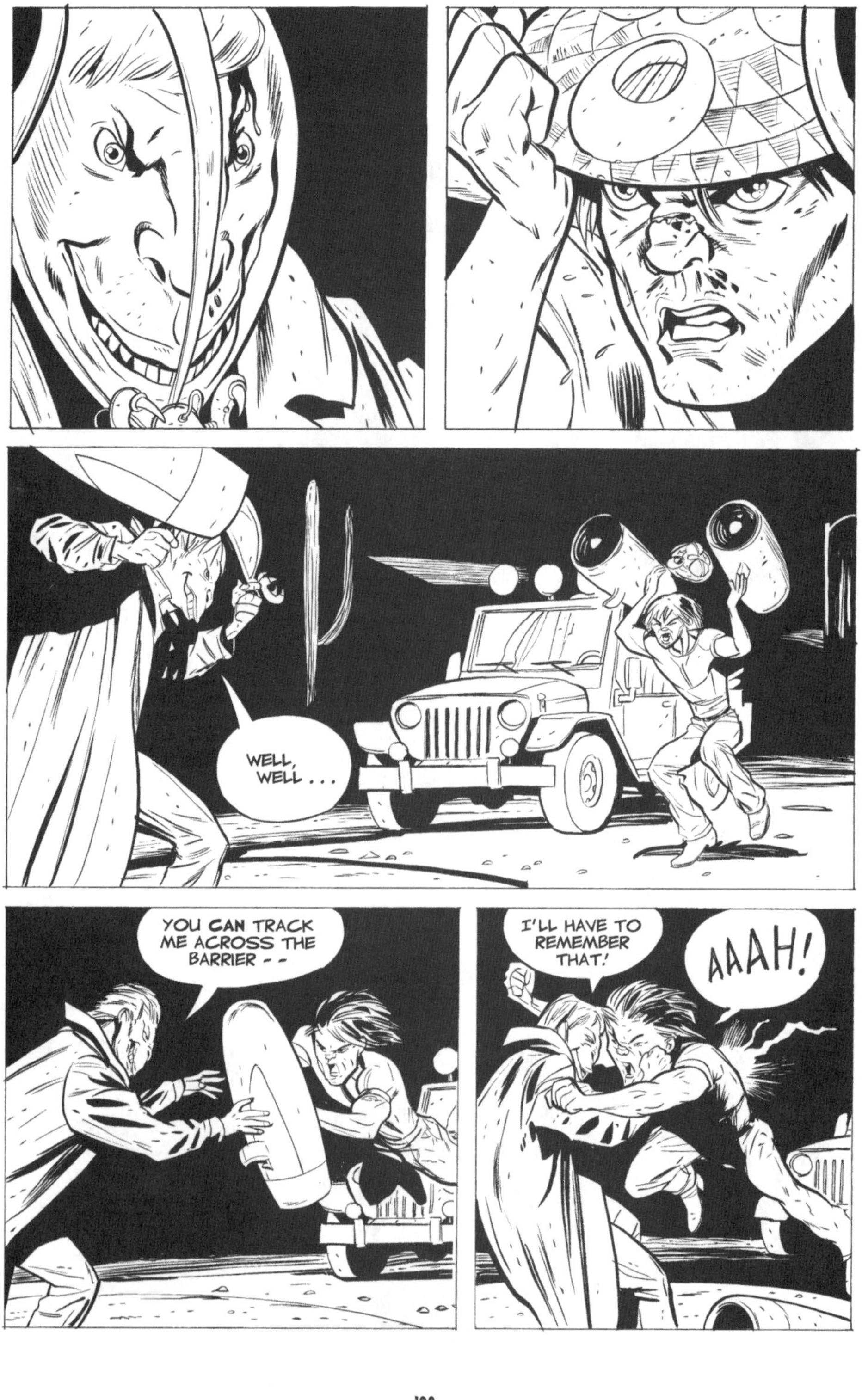
WELL, WELL . . .
YOU CAN TRACK ME ACROSS THE BARRIER - -
I'LL HAVE TO REMEMBER THAT!
AAAH!

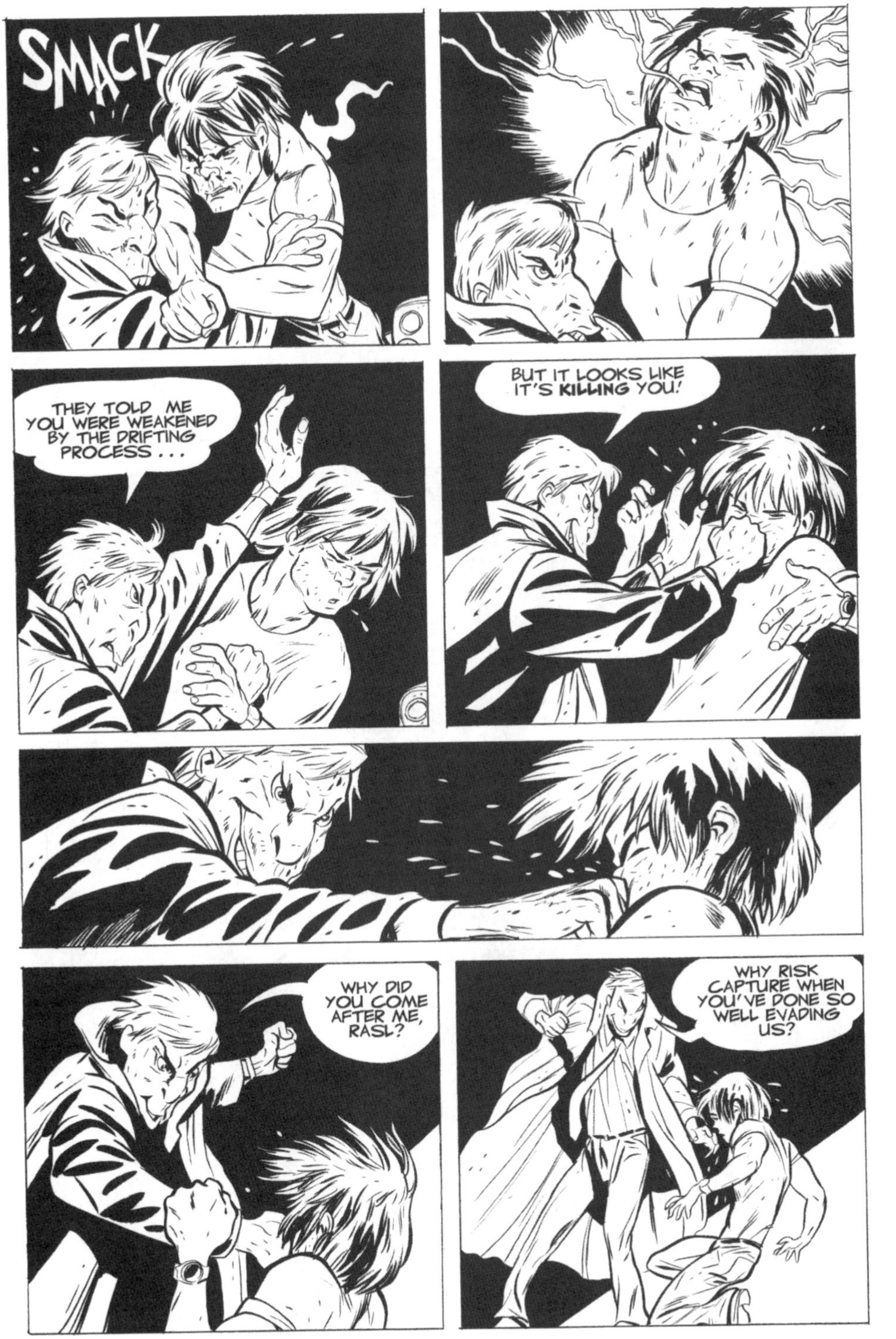
SMACK
THEY TOLD ME YOU WERE WEAKENED BY THE DRIFTING PROCESS . . .
BUT IT LOOKS LIKE IT'S **KILLING** YOU!
WHY DID YOU COME AFTER ME, RASL?
WHY RISK CAPTURE WHEN YOU'VE DONE SO WELL EVADING US?

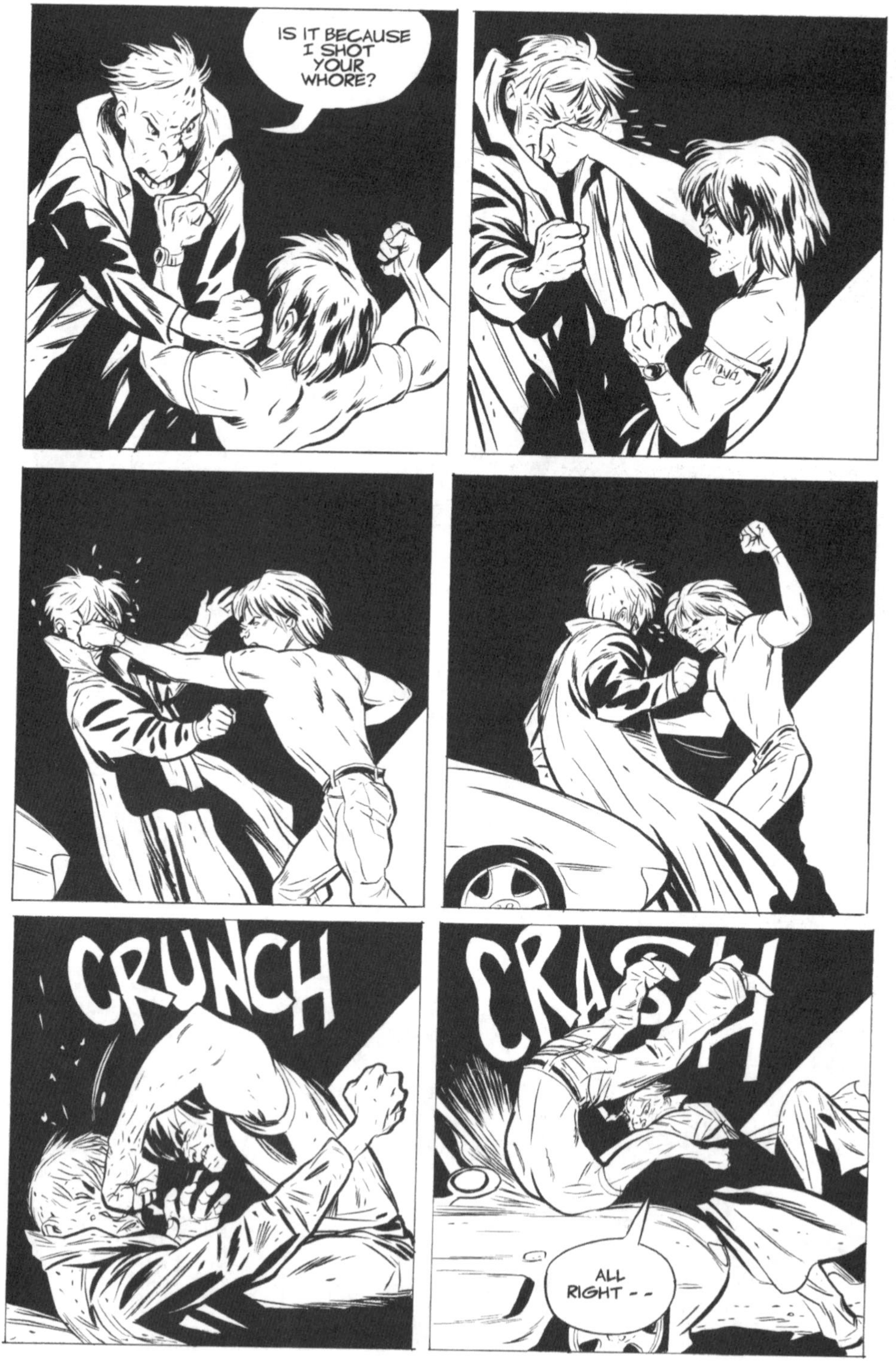
IS IT BECAUSE I SHOT YOUR WHORE?
CRUNCH
CRASH
ALL RIGHT - -

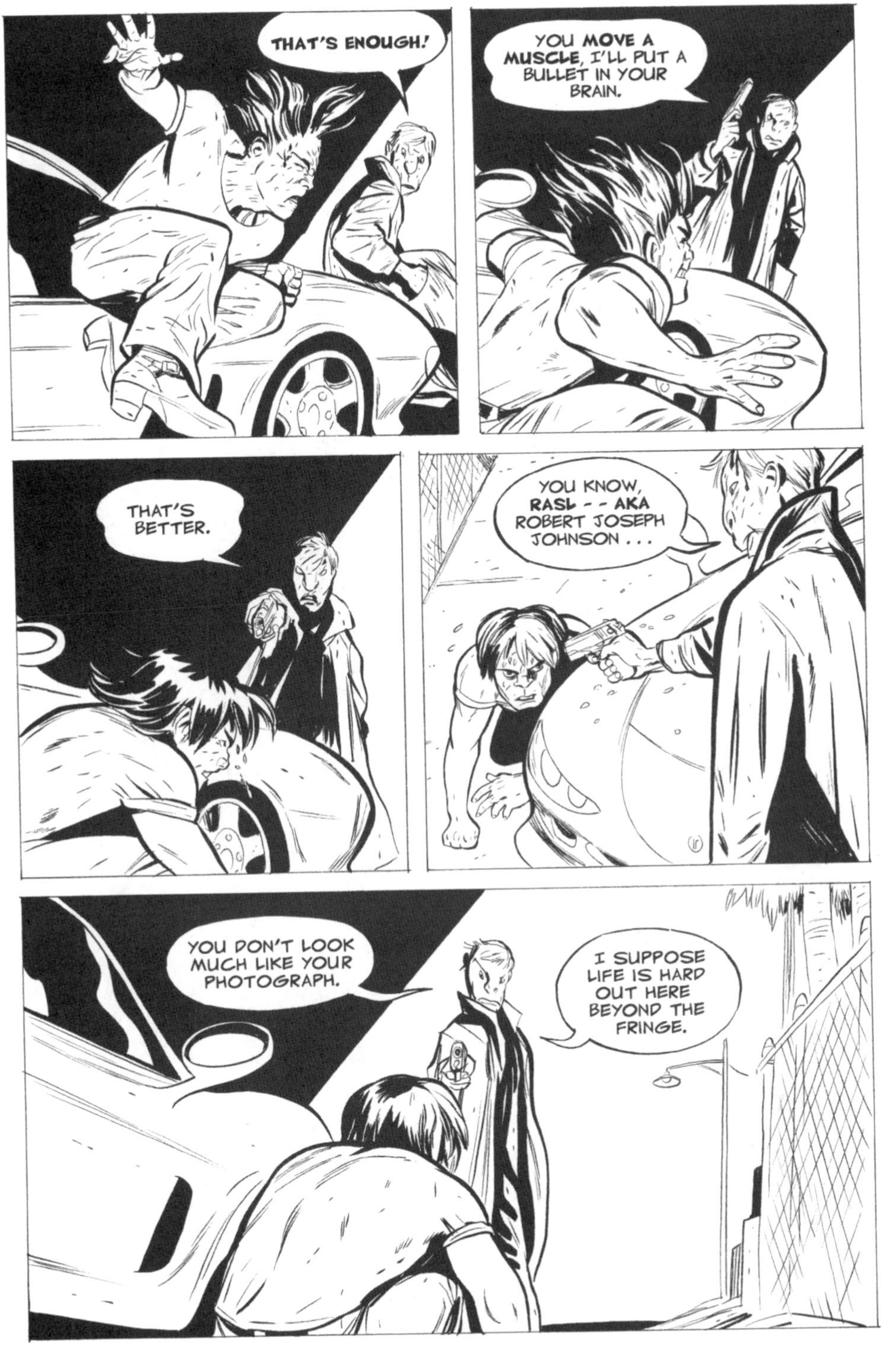
THAT'S ENOUGH!
YOU MOVE A MUSCLE, I'LL PUT A BULLET IN YOUR BRAIN.
THAT'S BETTER.
YOU KNOW, RASL -- AKA ROBERT JOSEPH JOHNSON . . .
YOU DON'T LOOK MUCH LIKE YOUR PHOTOGRAPH.
I SUPPOSE LIFE IS HARD OUT HERE BEYOND THE FRINGE.

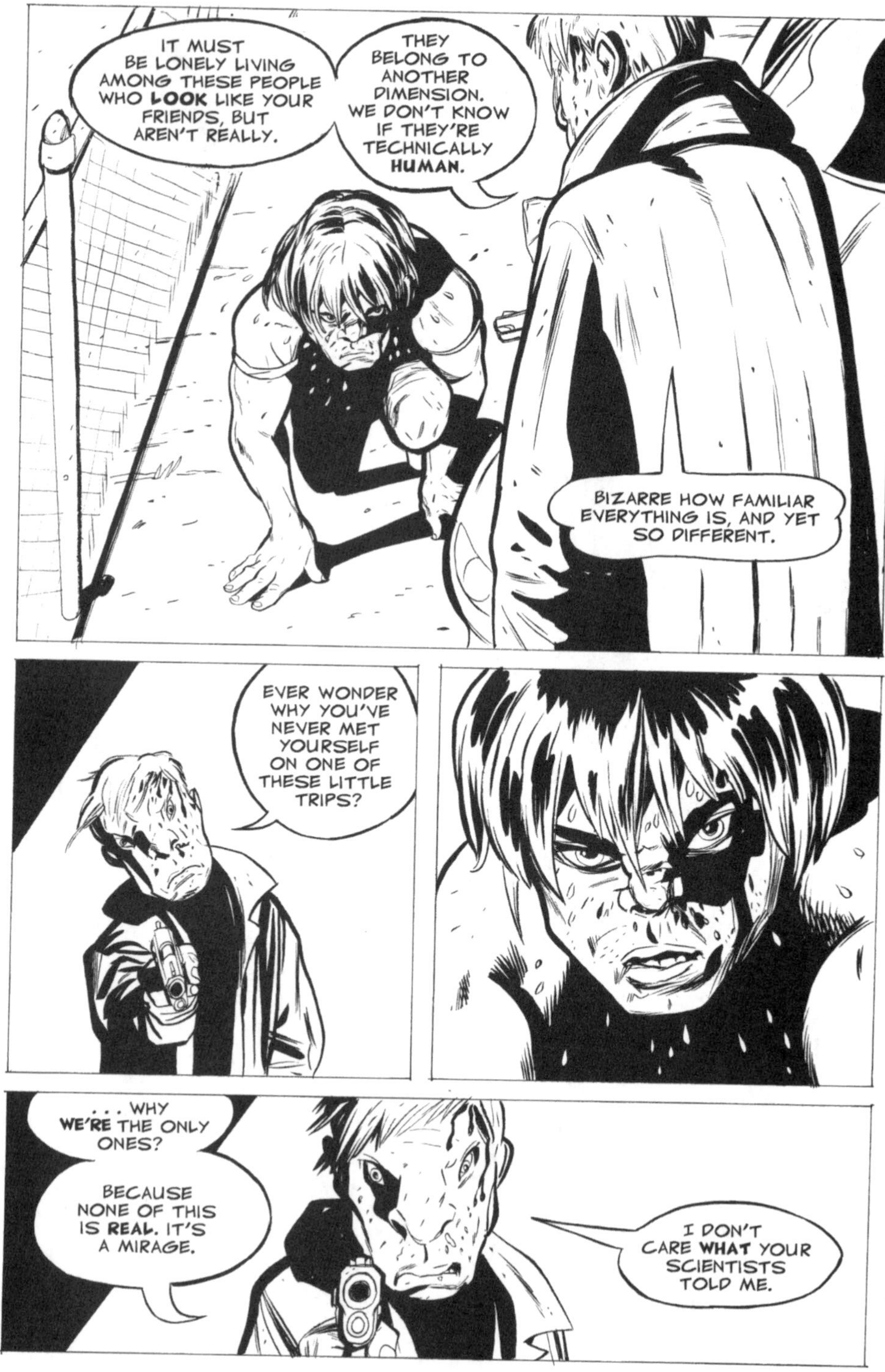
IT MUST BE LONELY LIVING AMONG THESE PEOPLE WHO **LOOK** LIKE YOUR FRIENDS, BUT AREN'T REALLY.
THEY BELONG TO ANOTHER DIMENSION. WE DON'T KNOW IF THEY'RE TECHNICALLY **HUMAN**.
BIZARRE HOW FAMILIAR EVERYTHING IS, AND YET SO DIFFERENT.
EVER WONDER WHY YOU'VE NEVER MET YOURSELF ON ONE OF THESE LITTLE TRIPS?
. . . WHY **WE'RE** THE ONLY ONES?
BECAUSE NONE OF THIS IS **REAL**. IT'S A MIRAGE.
I DON'T CARE **WHAT** YOUR SCIENTISTS TOLD ME.

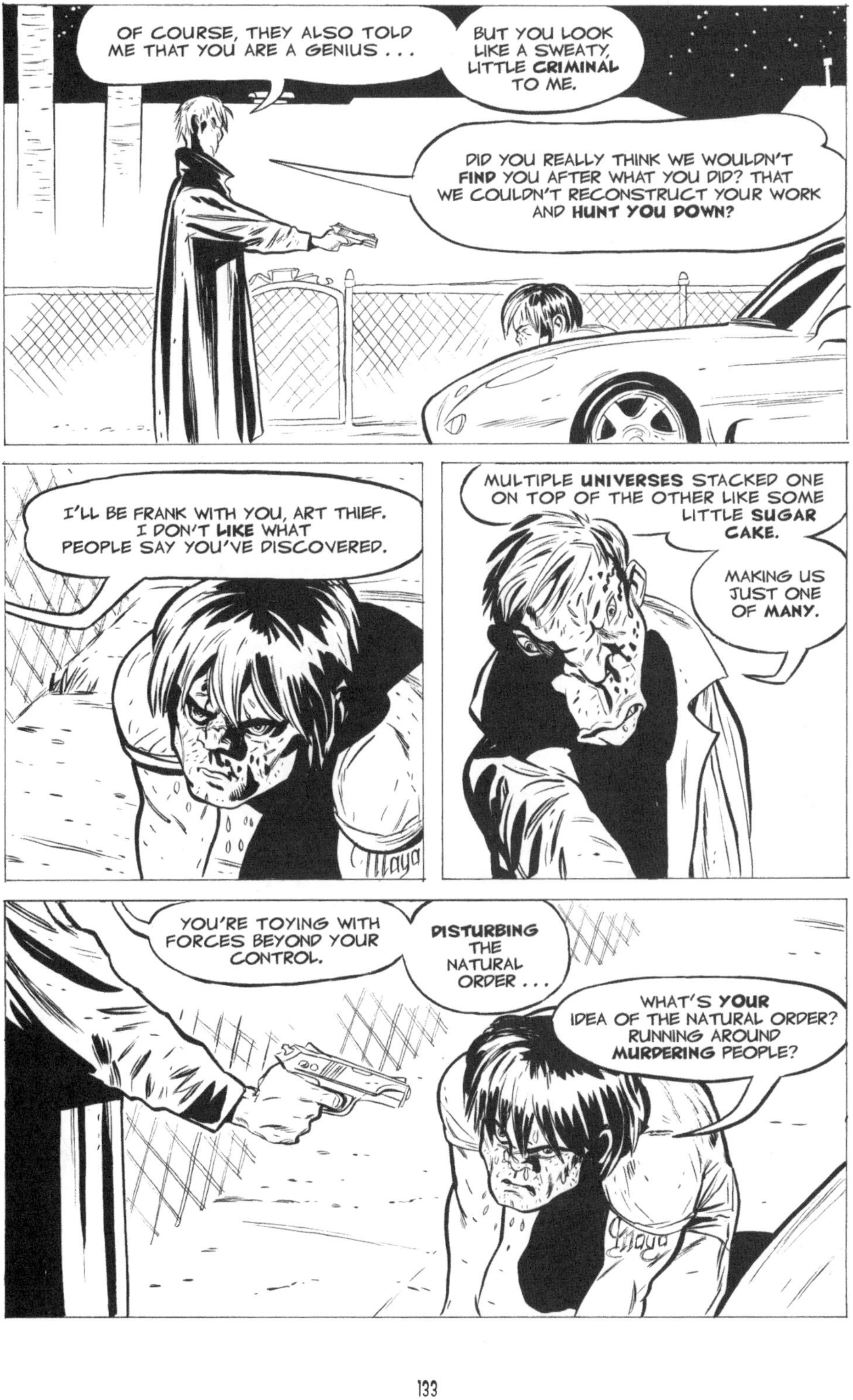
OF COURSE, THEY ALSO TOLD ME THAT YOU ARE A GENIUS . . .
BUT YOU LOOK LIKE A SWEATY, LITTLE **CRIMINAL** TO ME.
DID YOU REALLY THINK WE WOULDN'T **FIND** YOU AFTER WHAT YOU DID? THAT WE COULDN'T RECONSTRUCT YOUR WORK AND **HUNT YOU DOWN**?
I'LL BE FRANK WITH YOU, ART THIEF. I DON'T **LIKE** WHAT PEOPLE SAY YOU'VE DISCOVERED.
MULTIPLE **UNIVERSES** STACKED ONE ON TOP OF THE OTHER LIKE SOME LITTLE **SUGAR CAKE**.
MAKING US JUST ONE OF **MANY**.
YOU'RE TOYING WITH FORCES BEYOND YOUR CONTROL.
DISTURBING THE NATURAL ORDER . . .
WHAT'S **YOUR** IDEA OF THE NATURAL ORDER? RUNNING AROUND **MURDERING** PEOPLE?

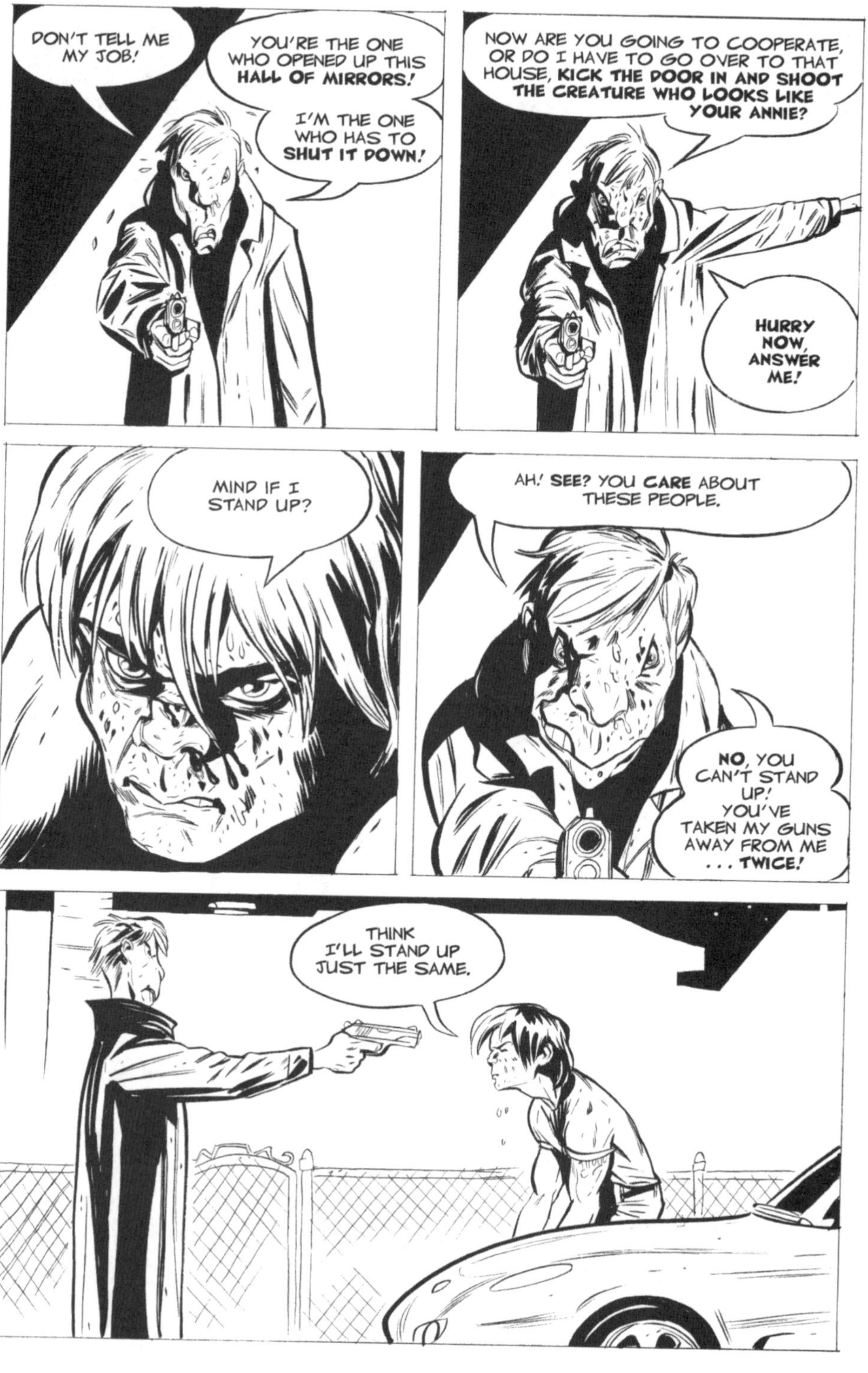
DON'T TELL ME MY JOB!
YOU'RE THE ONE WHO OPENED UP THIS HALL OF MIRRORS!
I'M THE ONE WHO HAS TO SHUT IT DOWN!
NOW ARE YOU GOING TO COOPERATE, OR DO I HAVE TO GO OVER TO THAT HOUSE, KICK THE DOOR IN AND SHOOT THE CREATURE WHO LOOKS LIKE YOUR ANNIE?
HURRY NOW, ANSWER ME!
MIND IF I STAND UP?
AH! SEE? YOU CARE ABOUT THESE PEOPLE.
NO, YOU CAN'T STAND UP! YOU'VE TAKEN MY GUNS AWAY FROM ME . . . TWICE!
THINK I'LL STAND UP JUST THE SAME.

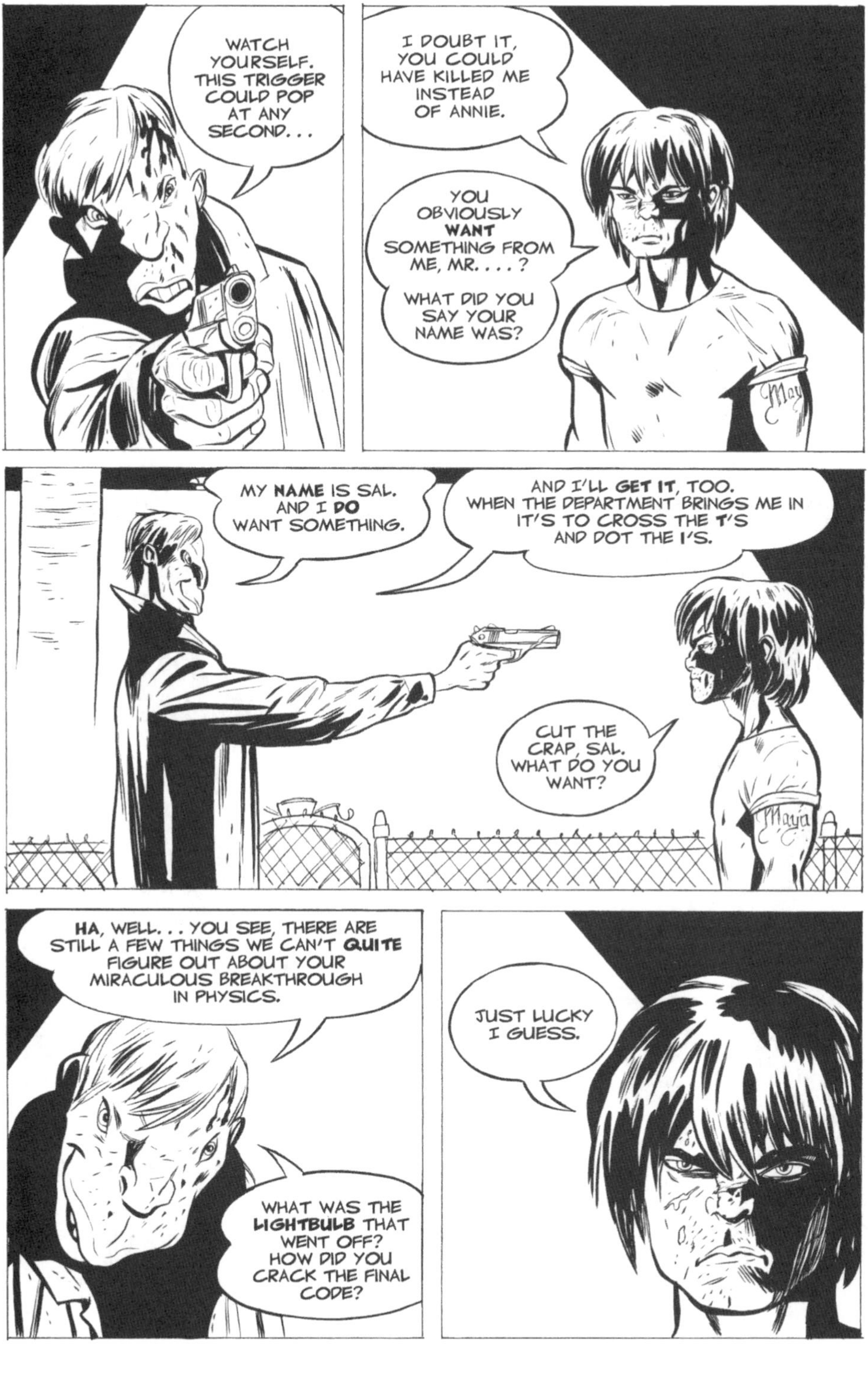
WATCH YOURSELF. THIS TRIGGER COULD POP AT ANY SECOND. . .
I DOUBT IT, YOU COULD HAVE KILLED ME INSTEAD OF ANNIE.
YOU OBVIOUSLY **WANT** SOMETHING FROM ME, MR. . . . ?
WHAT DID YOU SAY YOUR NAME WAS?
MY **NAME** IS SAL. AND I **DO** WANT SOMETHING.
AND I'LL **GET IT**, TOO. WHEN THE DEPARTMENT BRINGS ME IN IT'S TO CROSS THE **T**'S AND DOT THE **I**'S.
CUT THE CRAP, SAL. WHAT DO YOU WANT?
HA, WELL. . . YOU SEE, THERE ARE STILL A FEW THINGS WE CAN'T **QUITE** FIGURE OUT ABOUT YOUR MIRACULOUS BREAKTHROUGH IN PHYSICS.
WHAT WAS THE **LIGHTBULB** THAT WENT OFF? HOW DID YOU CRACK THE FINAL CODE?
JUST LUCKY I GUESS.

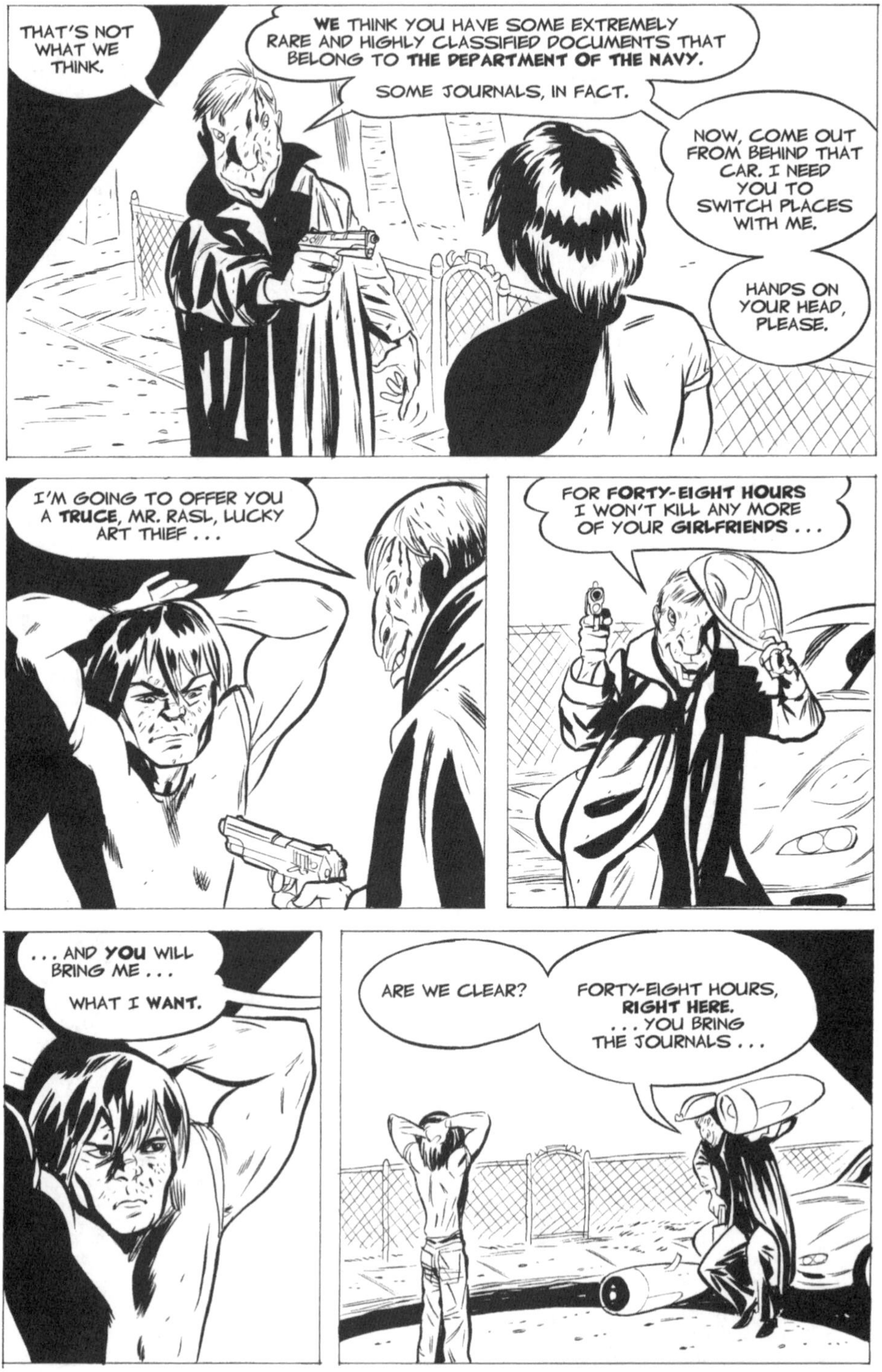
THAT'S NOT WHAT WE THINK.
WE THINK YOU HAVE SOME EXTREMELY RARE AND HIGHLY CLASSIFIED DOCUMENTS THAT BELONG TO THE DEPARTMENT OF THE NAVY.
SOME JOURNALS, IN FACT.
NOW, COME OUT FROM BEHIND THAT CAR. I NEED YOU TO SWITCH PLACES WITH ME.
HANDS ON YOUR HEAD, PLEASE.
I'M GOING TO OFFER YOU A TRUCE, MR. RASL, LUCKY ART THIEF . . .
FOR FORTY-EIGHT HOURS I WON'T KILL ANY MORE OF YOUR GIRLFRIENDS . . .
. . . AND YOU WILL BRING ME . . .
WHAT I WANT.
ARE WE CLEAR?
FORTY-EIGHT HOURS, RIGHT HERE. . . . YOU BRING THE JOURNALS . . .

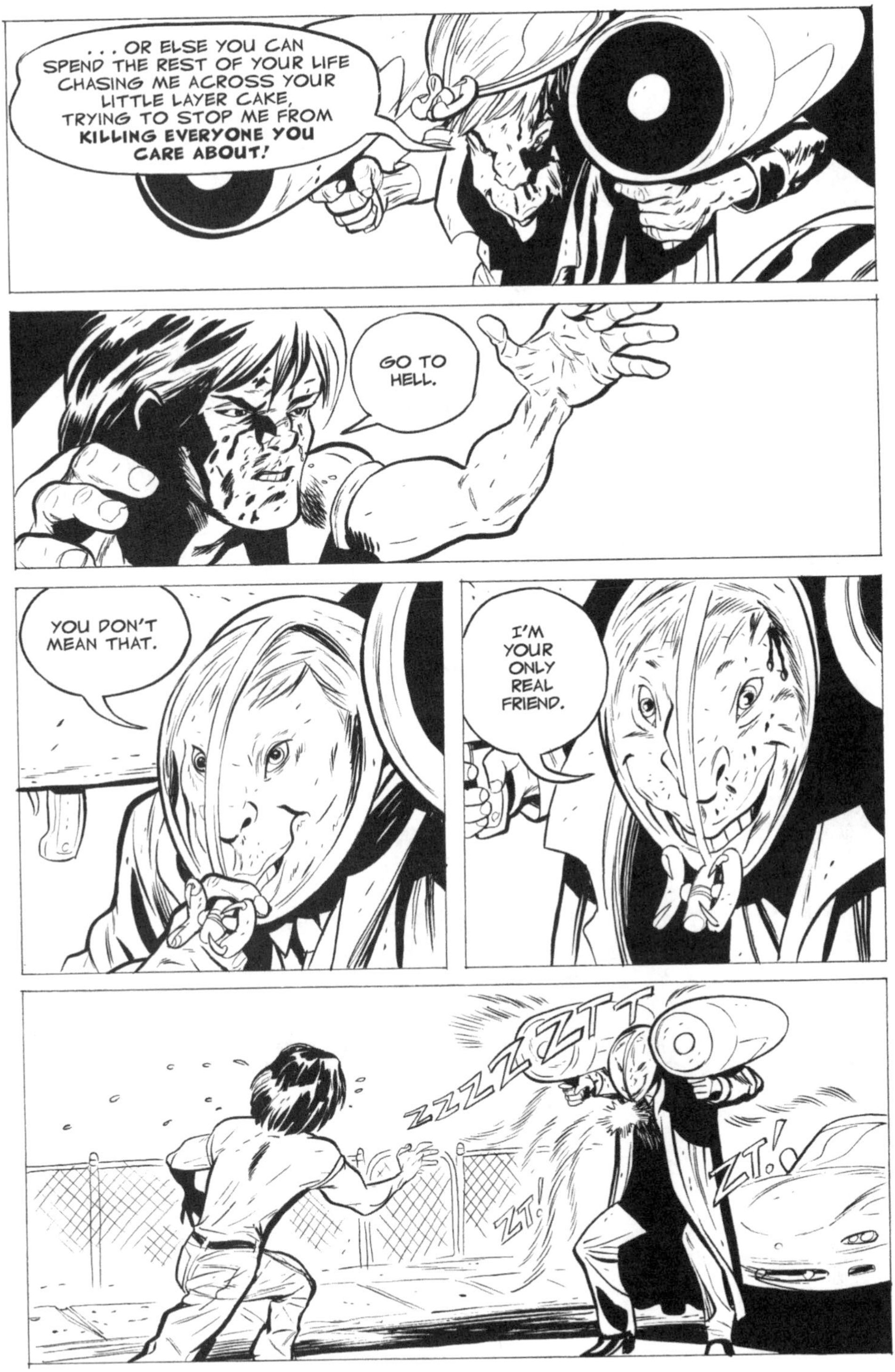
. . . OR ELSE YOU CAN SPEND THE REST OF YOUR LIFE CHASING ME ACROSS YOUR LITTLE LAYER CAKE, TRYING TO STOP ME FROM KILLING EVERYONE YOU CARE ABOUT!
GO TO HELL.
YOU DON'T MEAN THAT.
I'M YOUR ONLY REAL FRIEND.
ZZZZZZTTT
ZT!
ZT!

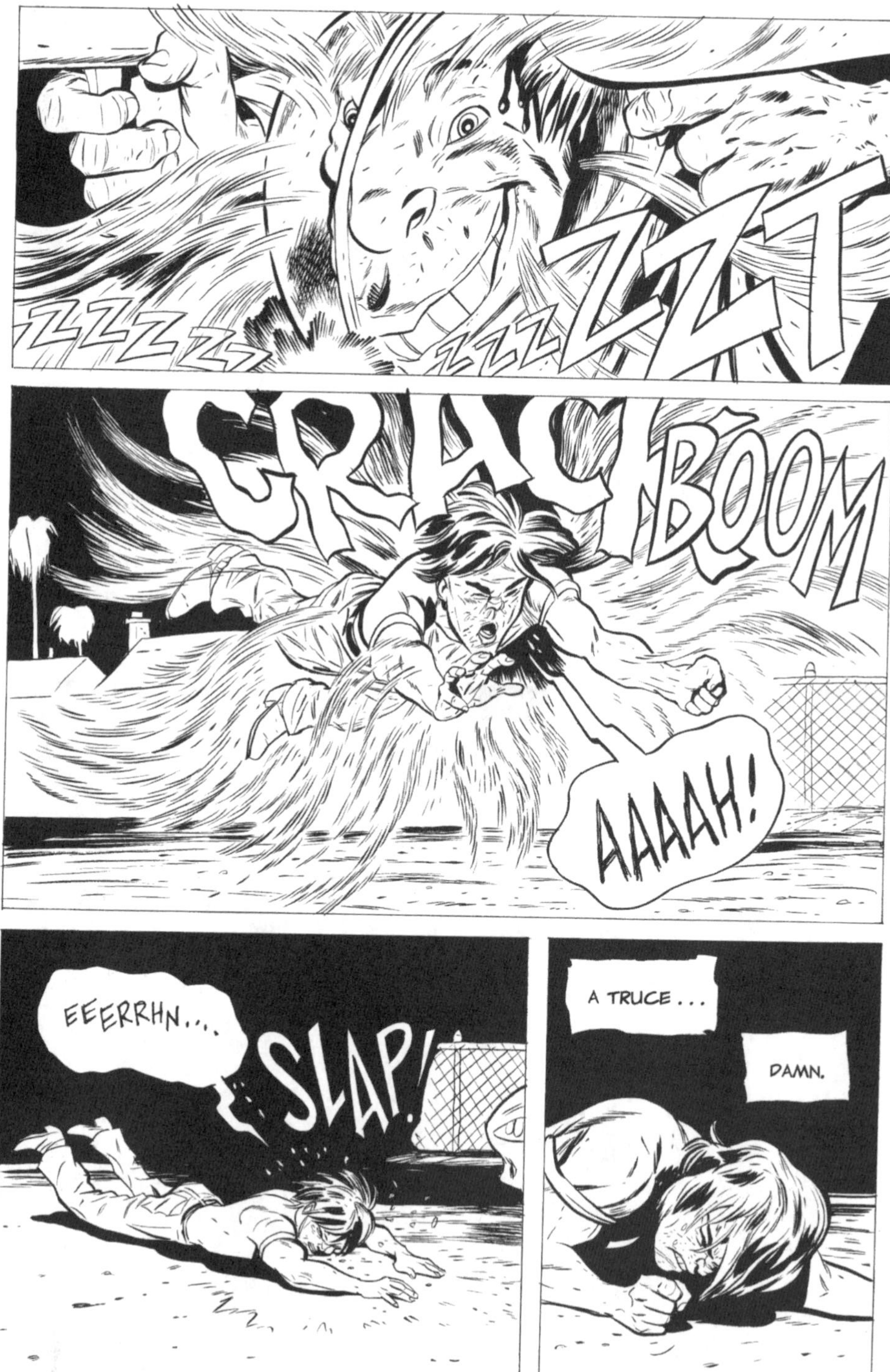
ZZZZZZZZZZZZT
CRAC
BOOM
AAAAH!
EEERRHN....
SLAP!
A TRUCE...
DAMN.

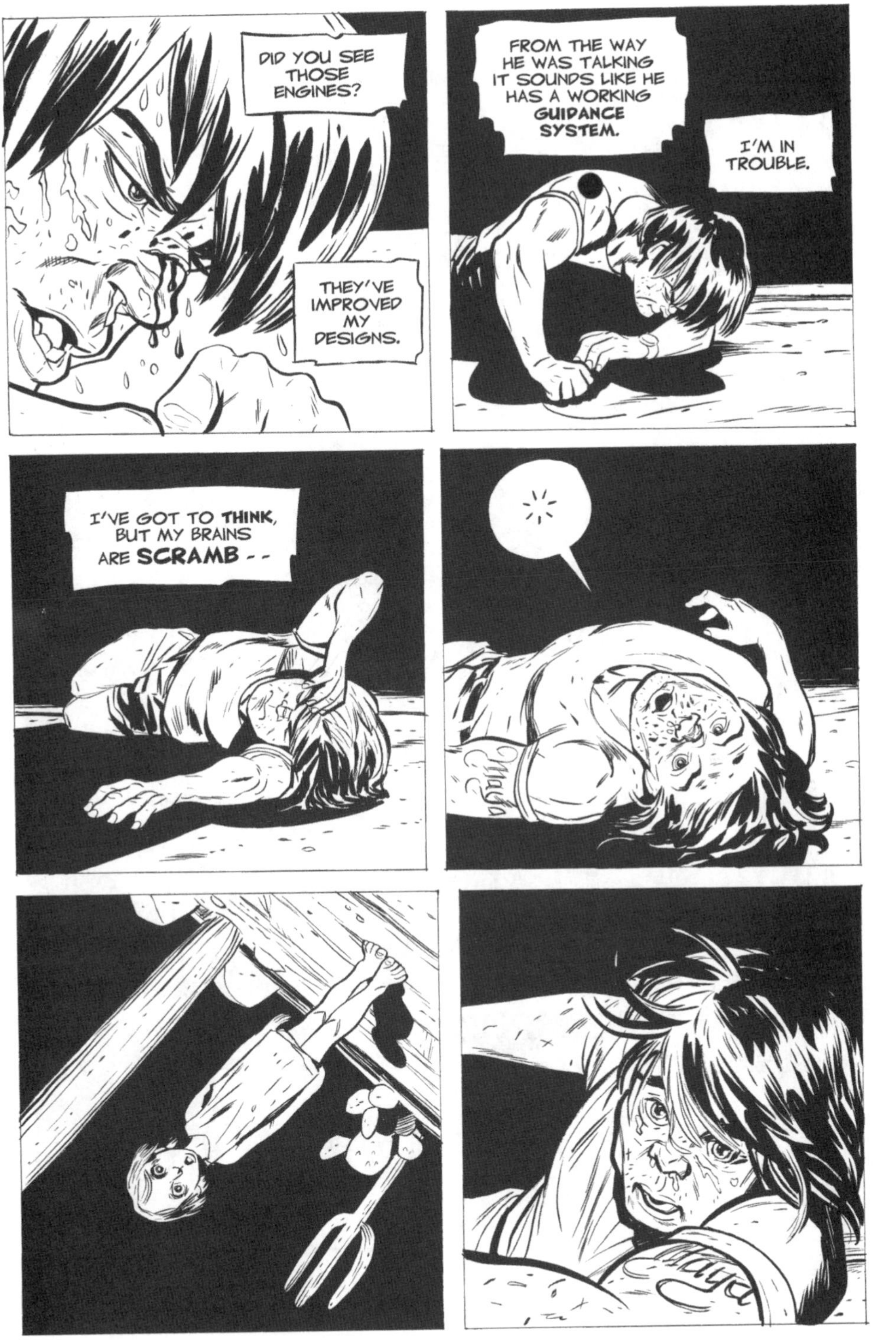
DID YOU SEE THOSE ENGINES?
THEY'VE IMPROVED MY DESIGNS.
FROM THE WAY HE WAS TALKING IT SOUNDS LIKE HE HAS A WORKING GUIDANCE SYSTEM.
I'M IN TROUBLE.
I'VE GOT TO THINK, BUT MY BRAINS ARE SCRAMB --
Maya
Maya

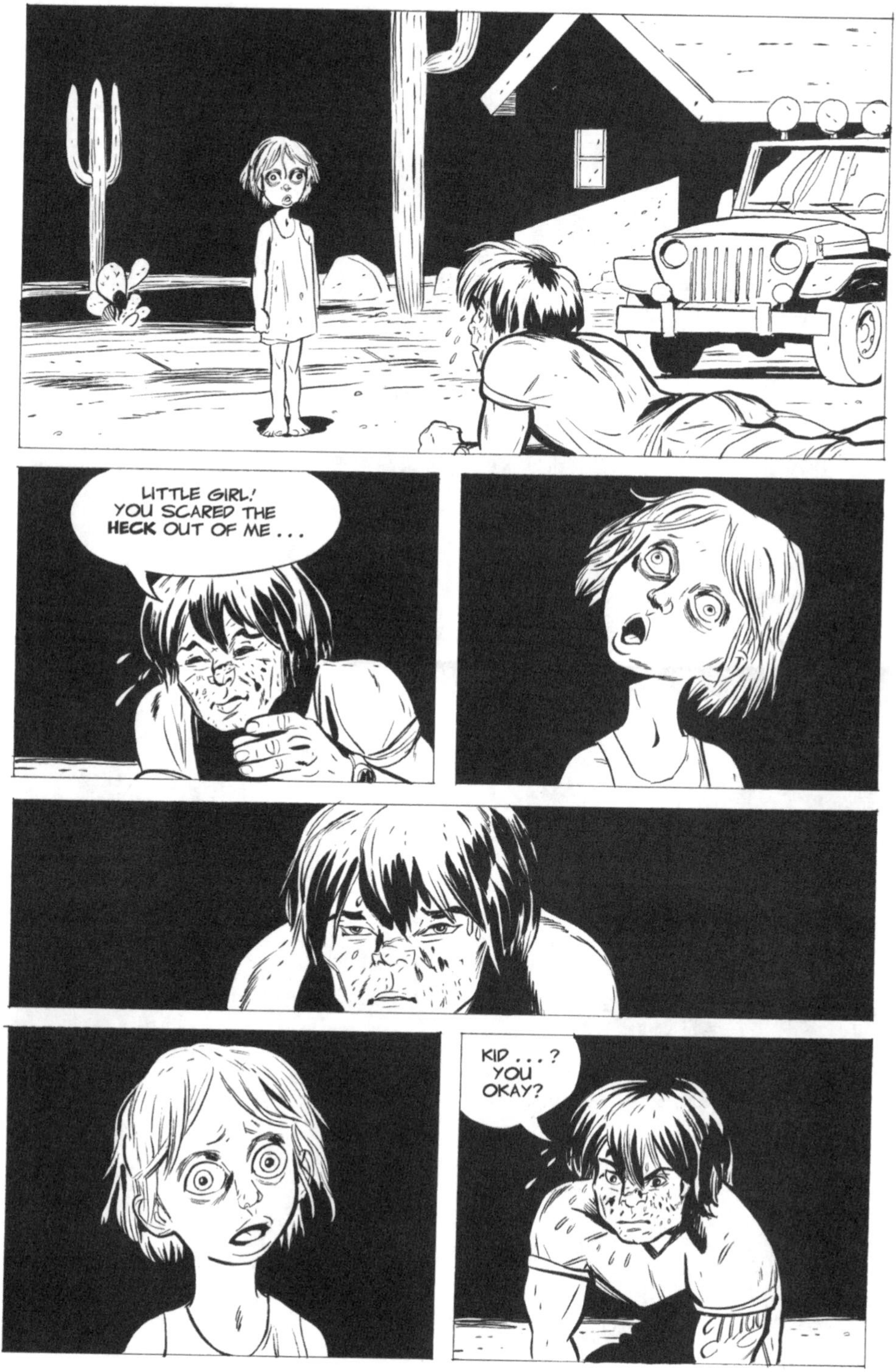
LITTLE GIRL! YOU SCARED THE **HECK** OUT OF ME . . .
KID . . . ? YOU OKAY?

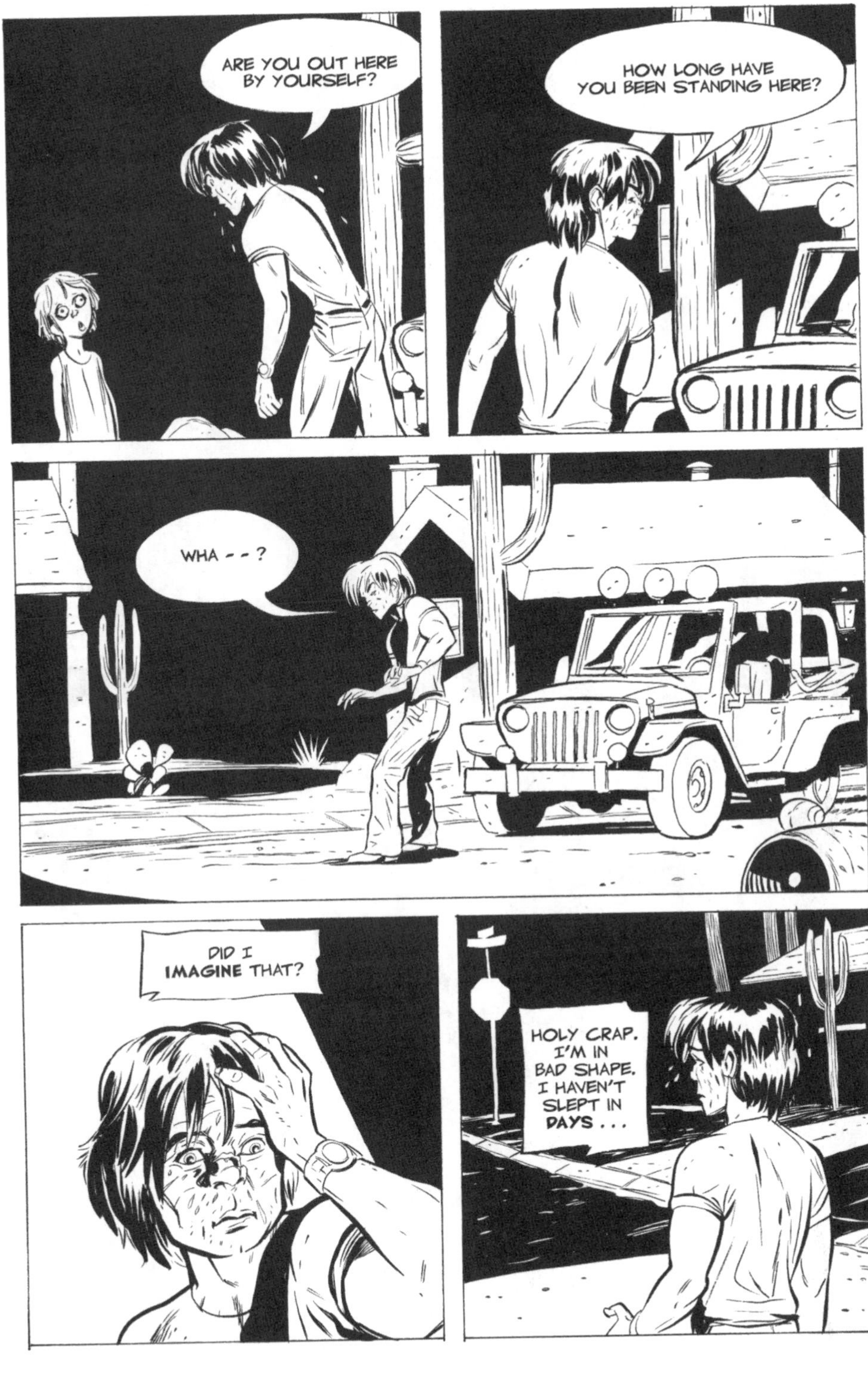
ARE YOU OUT HERE BY YOURSELF?
HOW LONG HAVE YOU BEEN STANDING HERE?
WHA - - ?
DID I IMAGINE THAT?
HOLY CRAP. I'M IN BAD SHAPE. I HAVEN'T SLEPT IN DAYS . . .

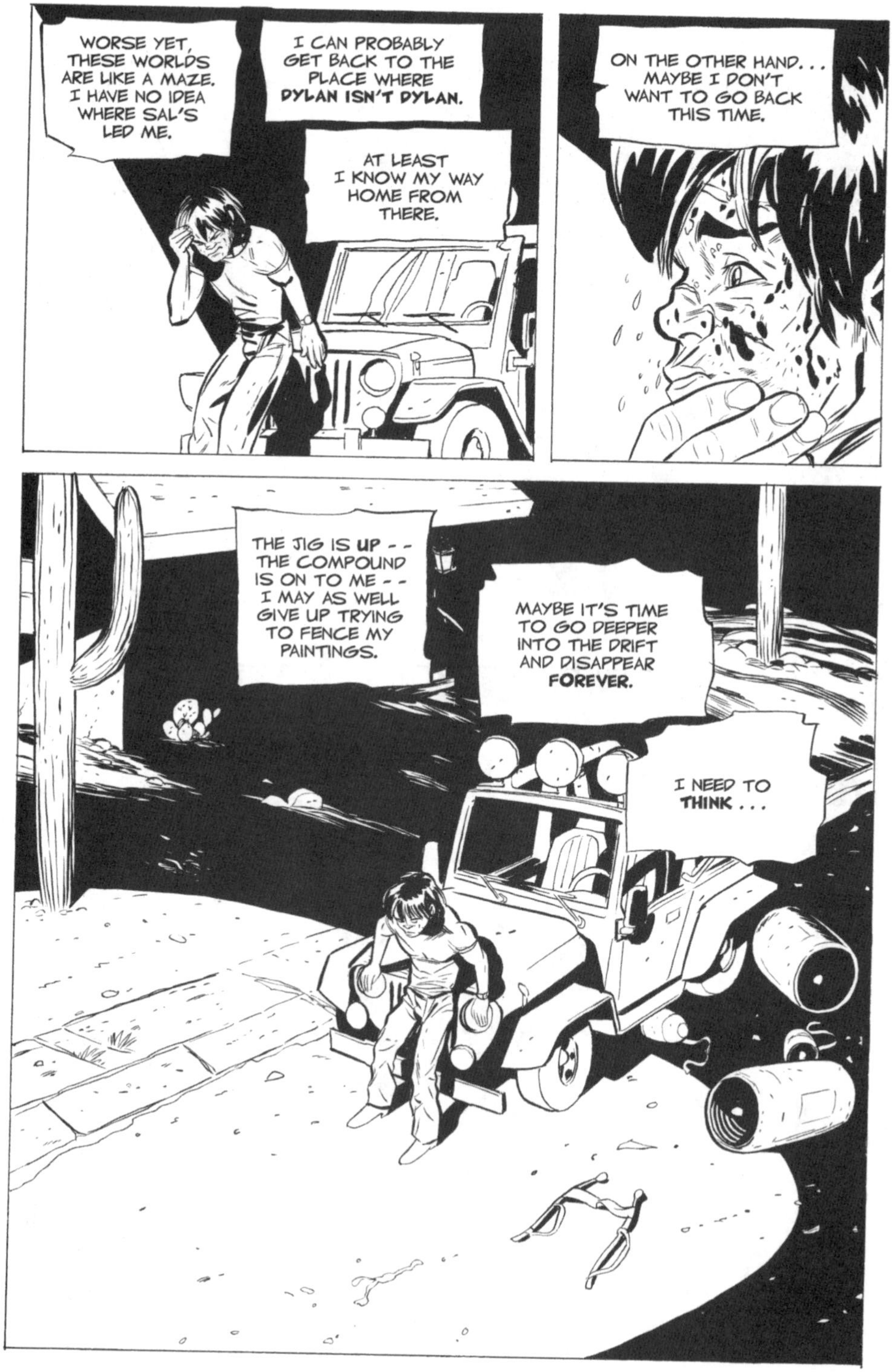
WORSE YET, THESE WORLDS ARE LIKE A MAZE. I HAVE NO IDEA WHERE SAL'S LED ME.
I CAN PROBABLY GET BACK TO THE PLACE WHERE **DYLAN ISN'T DYLAN.**
AT LEAST I KNOW MY WAY HOME FROM THERE.
ON THE OTHER HAND... MAYBE I DON'T WANT TO GO BACK THIS TIME.
THE JIG IS **UP** -- THE COMPOUND IS ON TO ME -- I MAY AS WELL GIVE UP TRYING TO FENCE MY PAINTINGS.
MAYBE IT'S TIME TO GO DEEPER INTO THE DRIFT AND DISAPPEAR **FOREVER.**
I NEED TO **THINK** ...

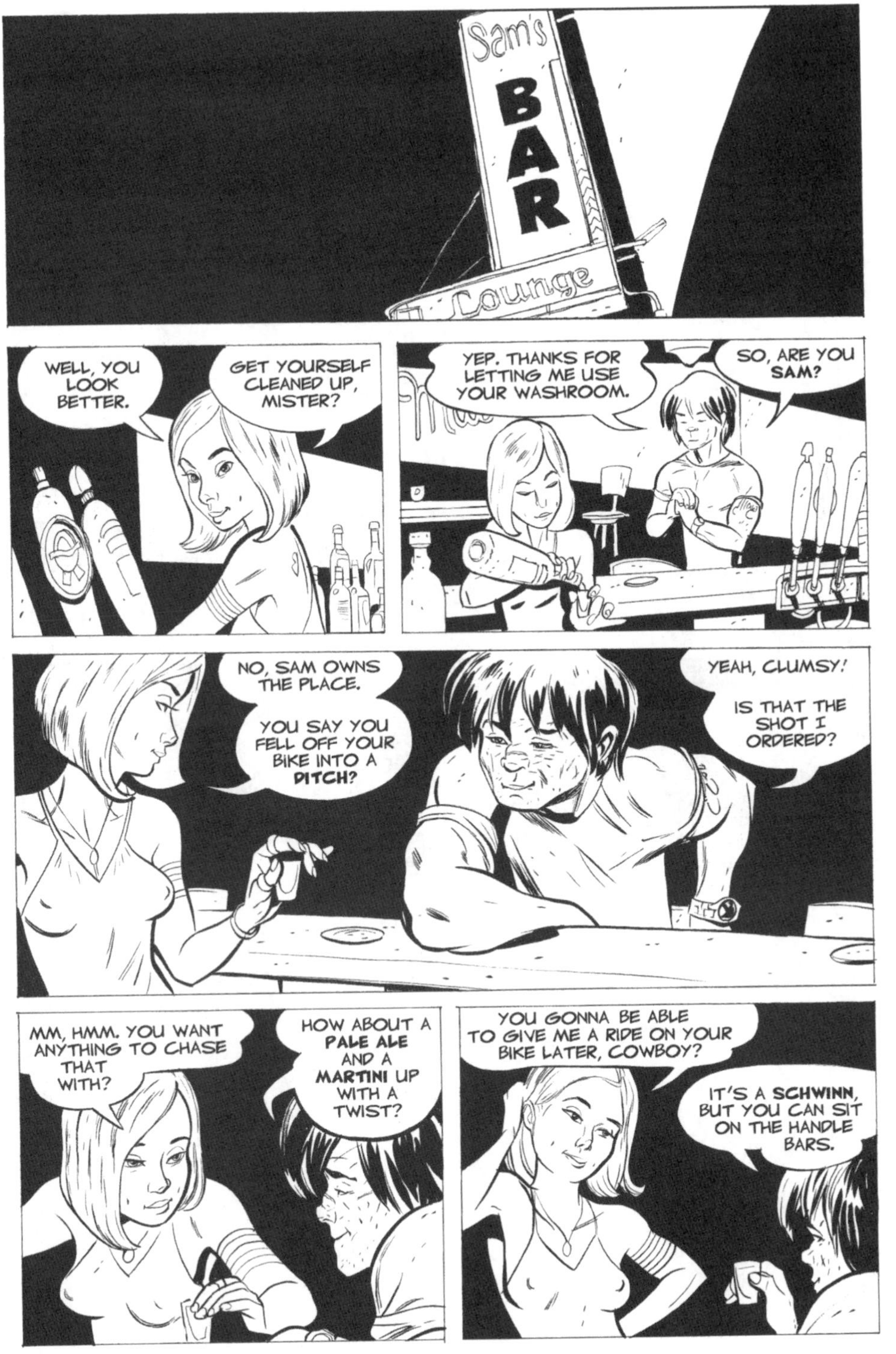
Sam's
BAR
Lounge
WELL, YOU LOOK BETTER.
GET YOURSELF CLEANED UP, MISTER?
YEP. THANKS FOR LETTING ME USE YOUR WASHROOM.
SO, ARE YOU **SAM**?
NO, SAM OWNS THE PLACE.
YOU SAY YOU FELL OFF YOUR BIKE INTO A **DITCH**?
YEAH, CLUMSY!
IS THAT THE SHOT I ORDERED?
MM, HMM. YOU WANT ANYTHING TO CHASE THAT WITH?
HOW ABOUT A **PALE ALE** AND A **MARTINI** UP WITH A TWIST?
YOU GONNA BE ABLE TO GIVE ME A RIDE ON YOUR BIKE LATER, COWBOY?
IT'S A **SCHWINN**, BUT YOU CAN SIT ON THE HANDLE BARS.

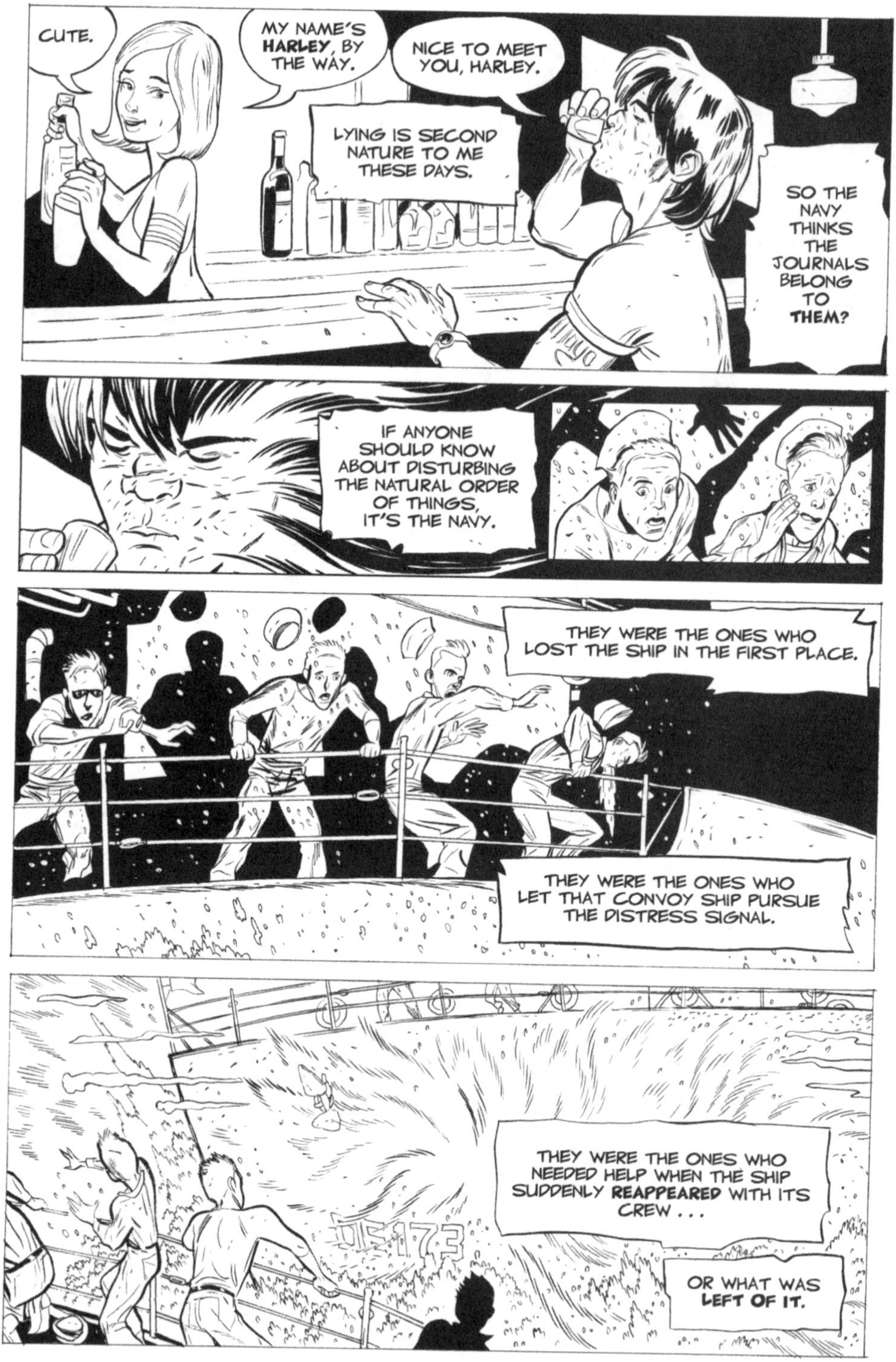
CUTE.
MY NAME'S **HARLEY**, BY THE WAY.
NICE TO MEET YOU, HARLEY.
LYING IS SECOND NATURE TO ME THESE DAYS.
SO THE NAVY THINKS THE JOURNALS BELONG TO **THEM?**
IF ANYONE SHOULD KNOW ABOUT DISTURBING THE NATURAL ORDER OF THINGS, IT'S THE NAVY.
THEY WERE THE ONES WHO LOST THE SHIP IN THE FIRST PLACE.
THEY WERE THE ONES WHO LET THAT CONVOY SHIP PURSUE THE DISTRESS SIGNAL.
THEY WERE THE ONES WHO NEEDED HELP WHEN THE SHIP SUDDENLY **REAPPEARED** WITH ITS CREW . . .
OR WHAT WAS **LEFT OF IT.**

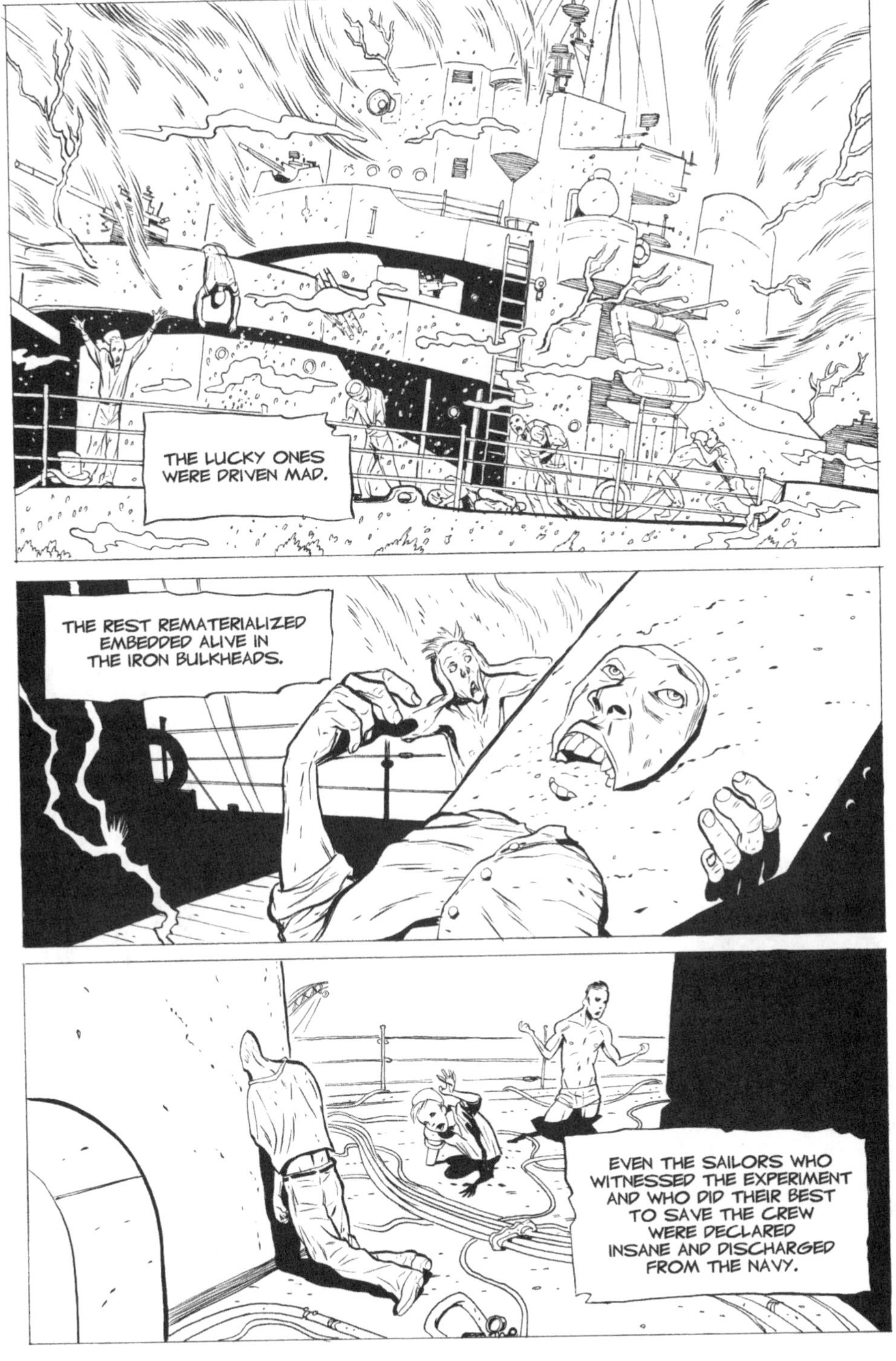
THE LUCKY ONES WERE DRIVEN MAD.
THE REST REMATERIALIZED EMBEDDED ALIVE IN THE IRON BULKHEADS.
EVEN THE SAILORS WHO WITNESSED THE EXPERIMENT AND WHO DID THEIR BEST TO SAVE THE CREW WERE DECLARED INSANE AND DISCHARGED FROM THE NAVY.

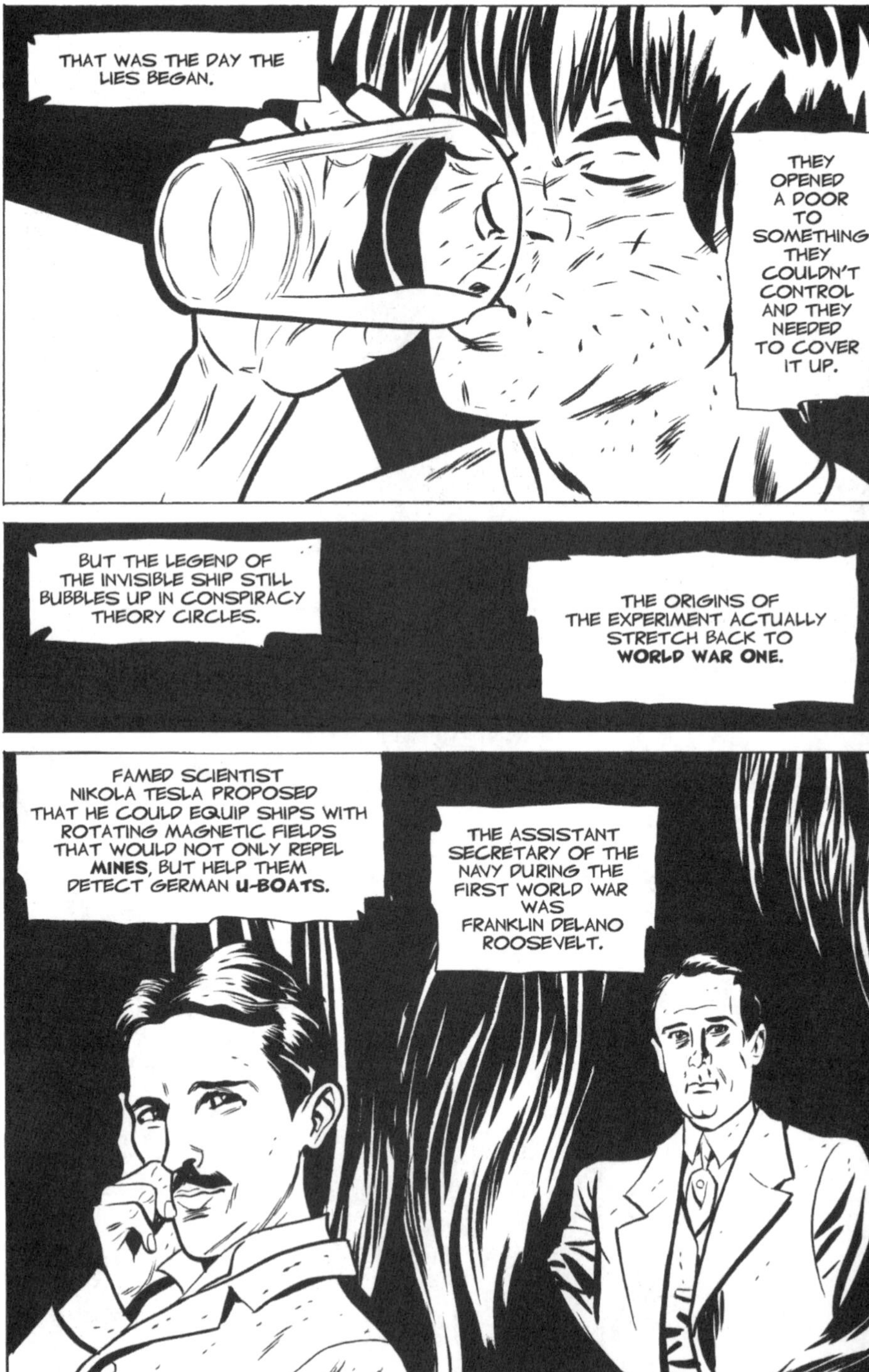
THAT WAS THE DAY THE LIES BEGAN.
THEY OPENED A DOOR TO SOMETHING THEY COULDN'T CONTROL AND THEY NEEDED TO COVER IT UP.
BUT THE LEGEND OF THE INVISIBLE SHIP STILL BUBBLES UP IN CONSPIRACY THEORY CIRCLES.
THE ORIGINS OF THE EXPERIMENT ACTUALLY STRETCH BACK TO **WORLD WAR ONE.**
FAMED SCIENTIST NIKOLA TESLA PROPOSED THAT HE COULD EQUIP SHIPS WITH ROTATING MAGNETIC FIELDS THAT WOULD NOT ONLY REPEL **MINES**, BUT HELP THEM DETECT GERMAN **U-BOATS.**
THE ASSISTANT SECRETARY OF THE NAVY DURING THE FIRST WORLD WAR WAS FRANKLIN DELANO ROOSEVELT.

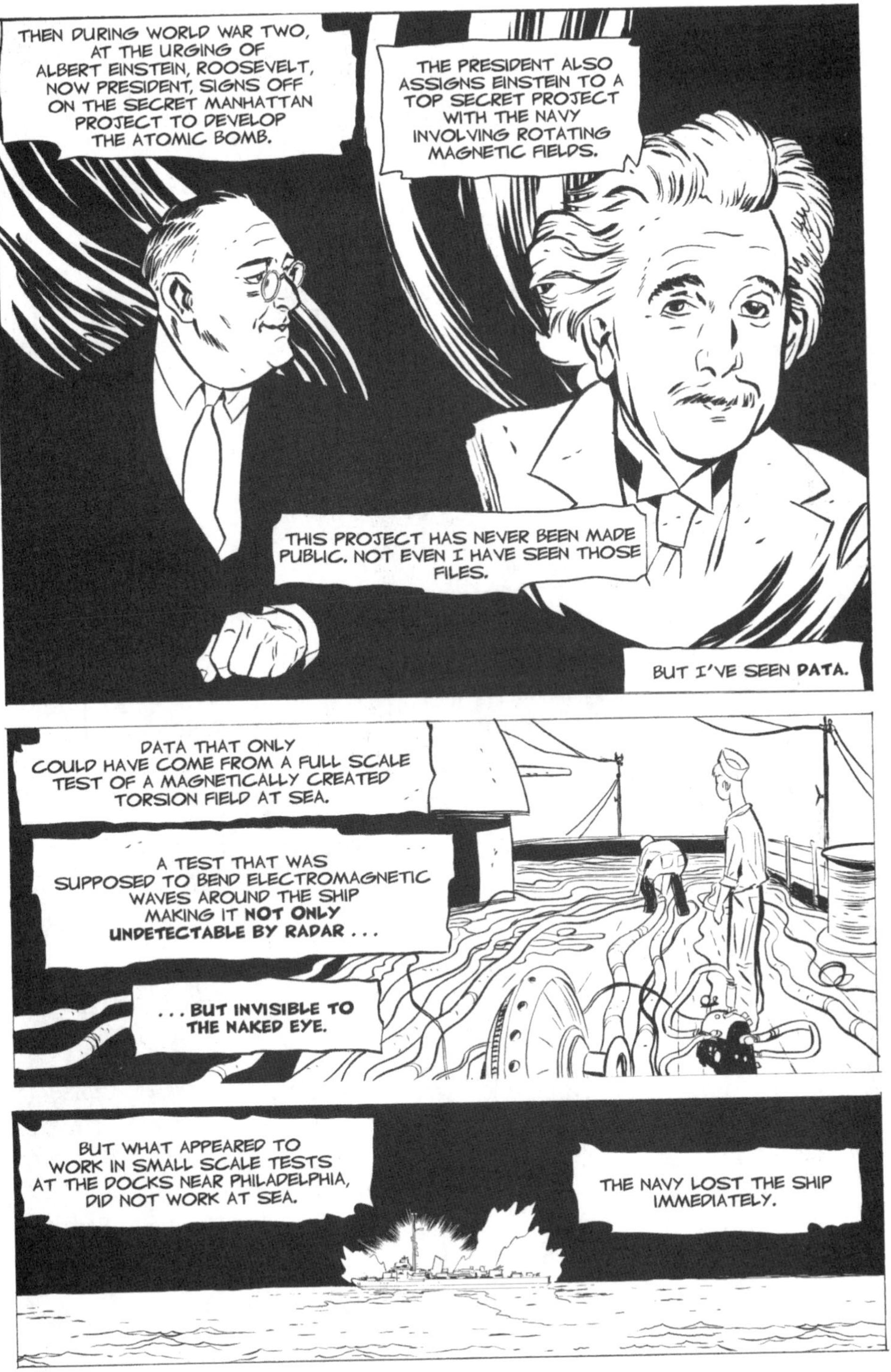
THEN DURING WORLD WAR TWO, AT THE URGING OF ALBERT EINSTEIN, ROOSEVELT, NOW PRESIDENT, SIGNS OFF ON THE SECRET MANHATTAN PROJECT TO DEVELOP THE ATOMIC BOMB.
THE PRESIDENT ALSO ASSIGNS EINSTEIN TO A TOP SECRET PROJECT WITH THE NAVY INVOLVING ROTATING MAGNETIC FIELDS.
THIS PROJECT HAS NEVER BEEN MADE PUBLIC. NOT EVEN I HAVE SEEN THOSE FILES.
BUT I'VE SEEN **DATA.**
DATA THAT ONLY COULD HAVE COME FROM A FULL SCALE TEST OF A MAGNETICALLY CREATED TORSION FIELD AT SEA.
A TEST THAT WAS SUPPOSED TO BEND ELECTROMAGNETIC WAVES AROUND THE SHIP MAKING IT **NOT ONLY UNDETECTABLE BY RADAR . . .**
. . . BUT INVISIBLE TO THE NAKED EYE.
BUT WHAT APPEARED TO WORK IN SMALL SCALE TESTS AT THE DOCKS NEAR PHILADELPHIA, DID NOT WORK AT SEA.
THE NAVY LOST THE SHIP IMMEDIATELY.

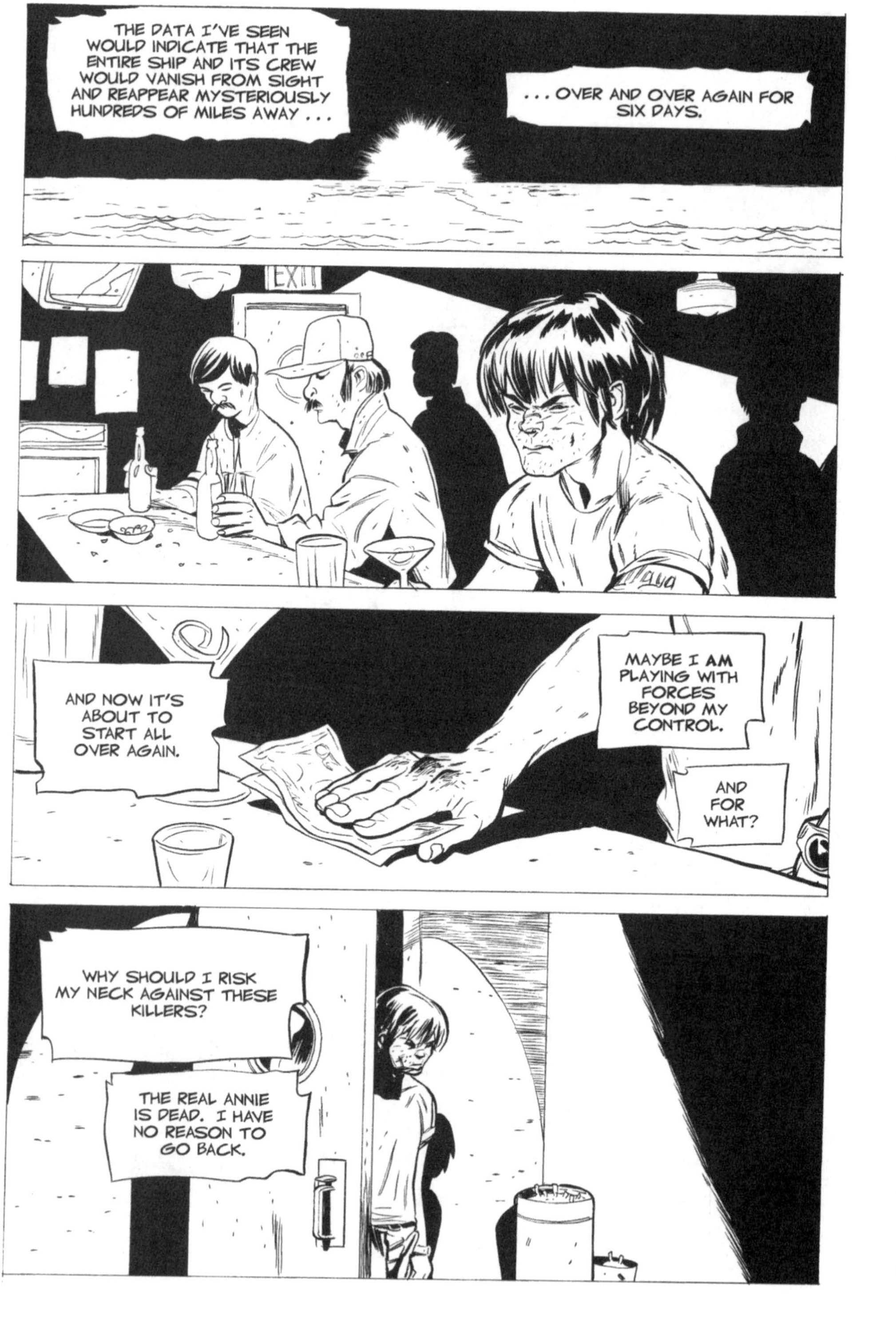
THE DATA I'VE SEEN WOULD INDICATE THAT THE ENTIRE SHIP AND ITS CREW WOULD VANISH FROM SIGHT AND REAPPEAR MYSTERIOUSLY HUNDREDS OF MILES AWAY . . .
. . . OVER AND OVER AGAIN FOR SIX DAYS.
EXIT
AND NOW IT'S ABOUT TO START ALL OVER AGAIN.
MAYBE I **AM** PLAYING WITH FORCES BEYOND MY CONTROL.
AND FOR WHAT?
WHY SHOULD I RISK MY NECK AGAINST THESE KILLERS?
THE REAL ANNIE IS DEAD. I HAVE NO REASON TO GO BACK.

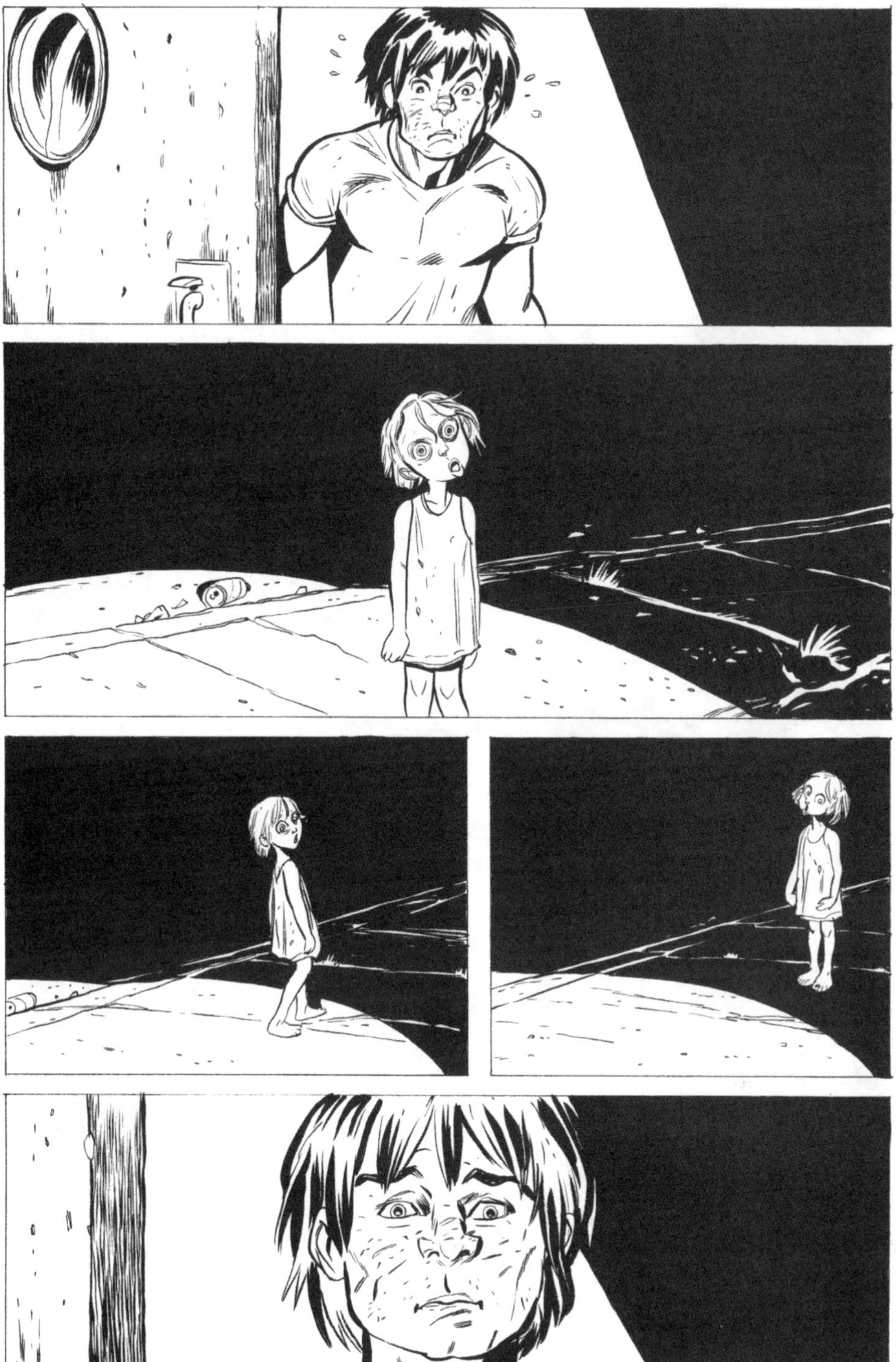

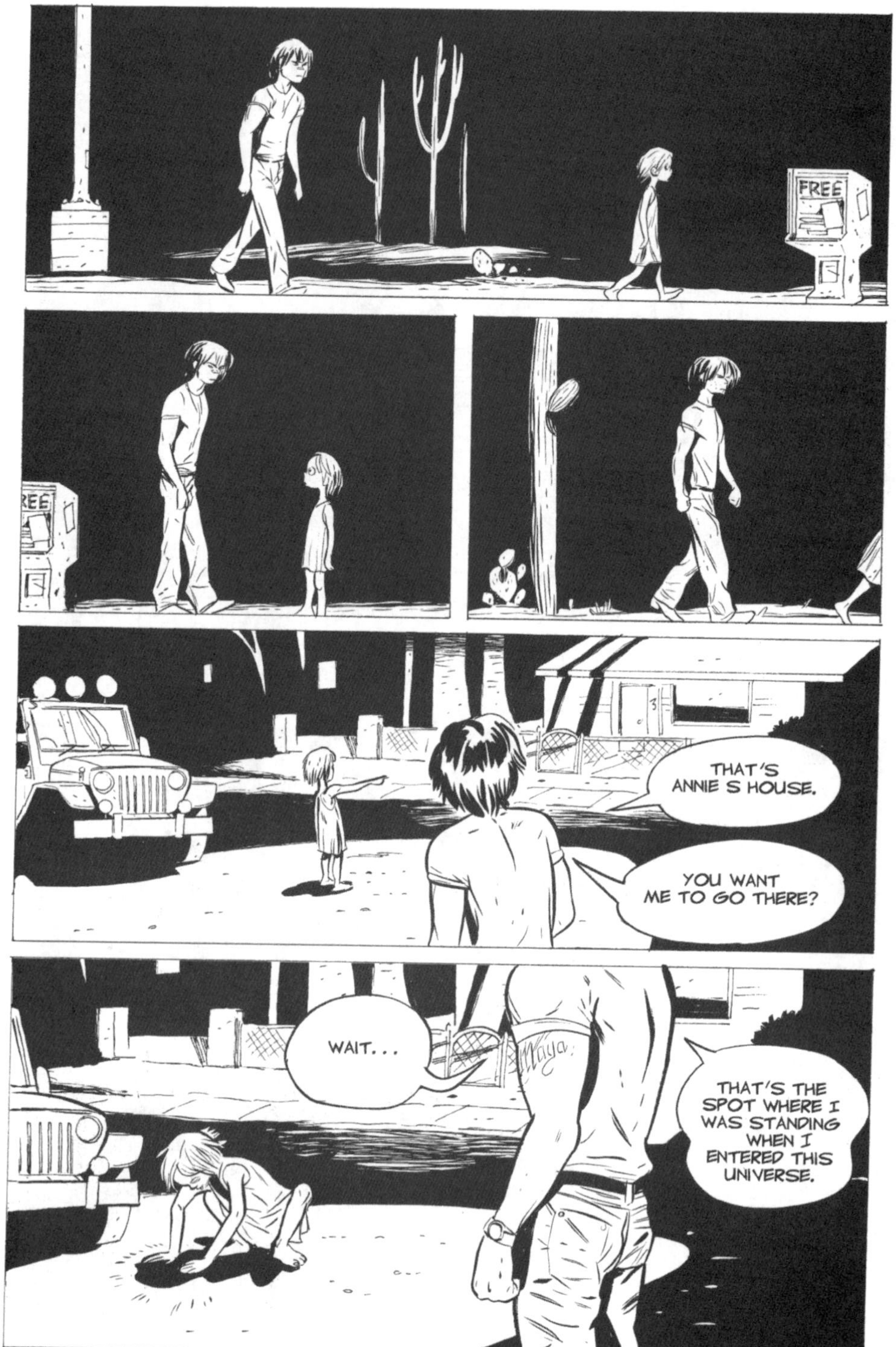
FREE
THAT'S ANNIE S HOUSE.
YOU WANT ME TO GO THERE?
WAIT...
THAT'S THE SPOT WHERE I WAS STANDING WHEN I ENTERED THIS UNIVERSE.

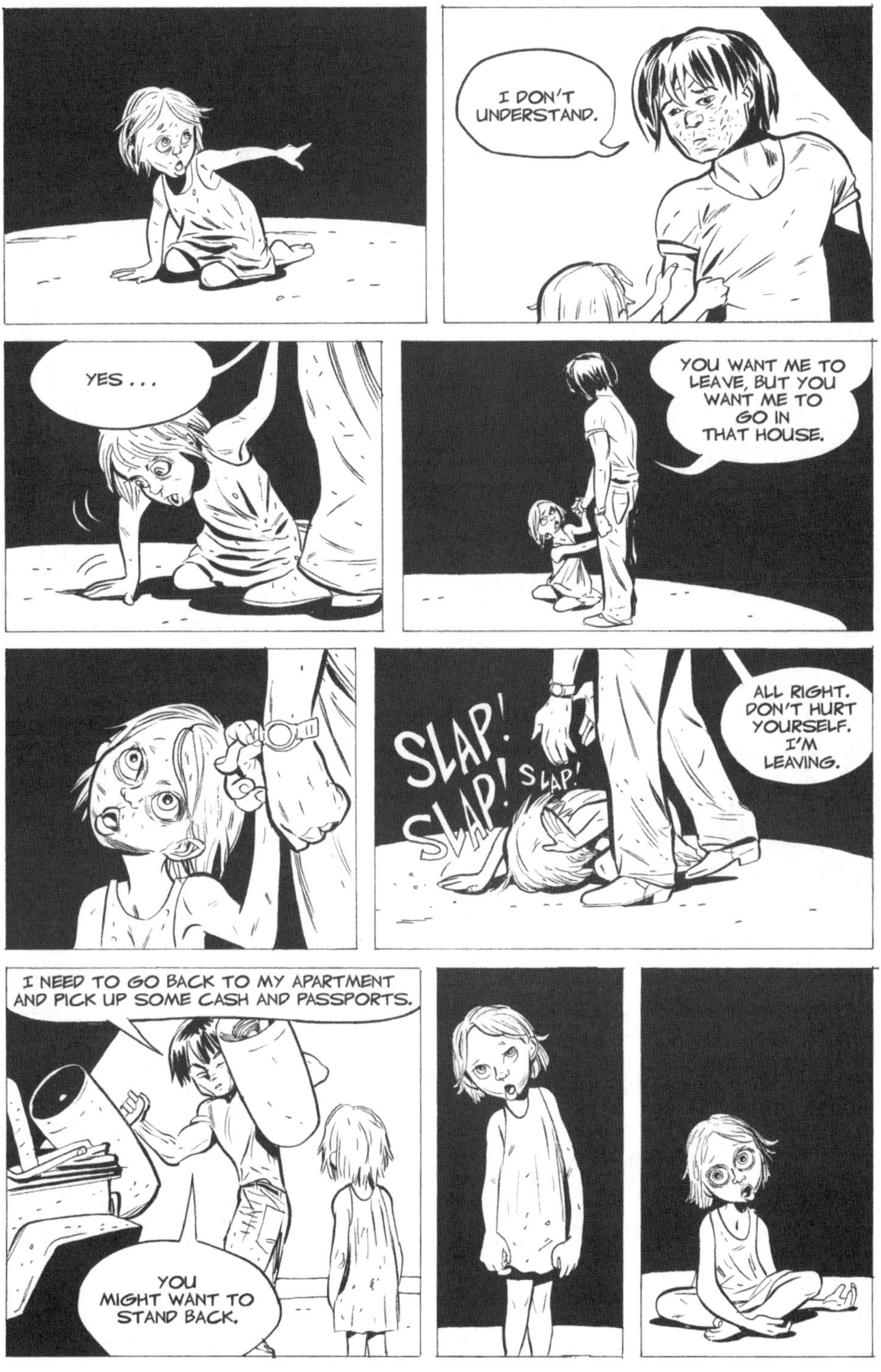
I DON'T UNDERSTAND.
YES . . .
YOU WANT ME TO LEAVE, BUT YOU WANT ME TO GO IN THAT HOUSE.
SLAP! SLAP! SLAP!
ALL RIGHT. DON'T HURT YOURSELF. I'M LEAVING.
I NEED TO GO BACK TO MY APARTMENT AND PICK UP SOME CASH AND PASSPORTS.
YOU MIGHT WANT TO STAND BACK.

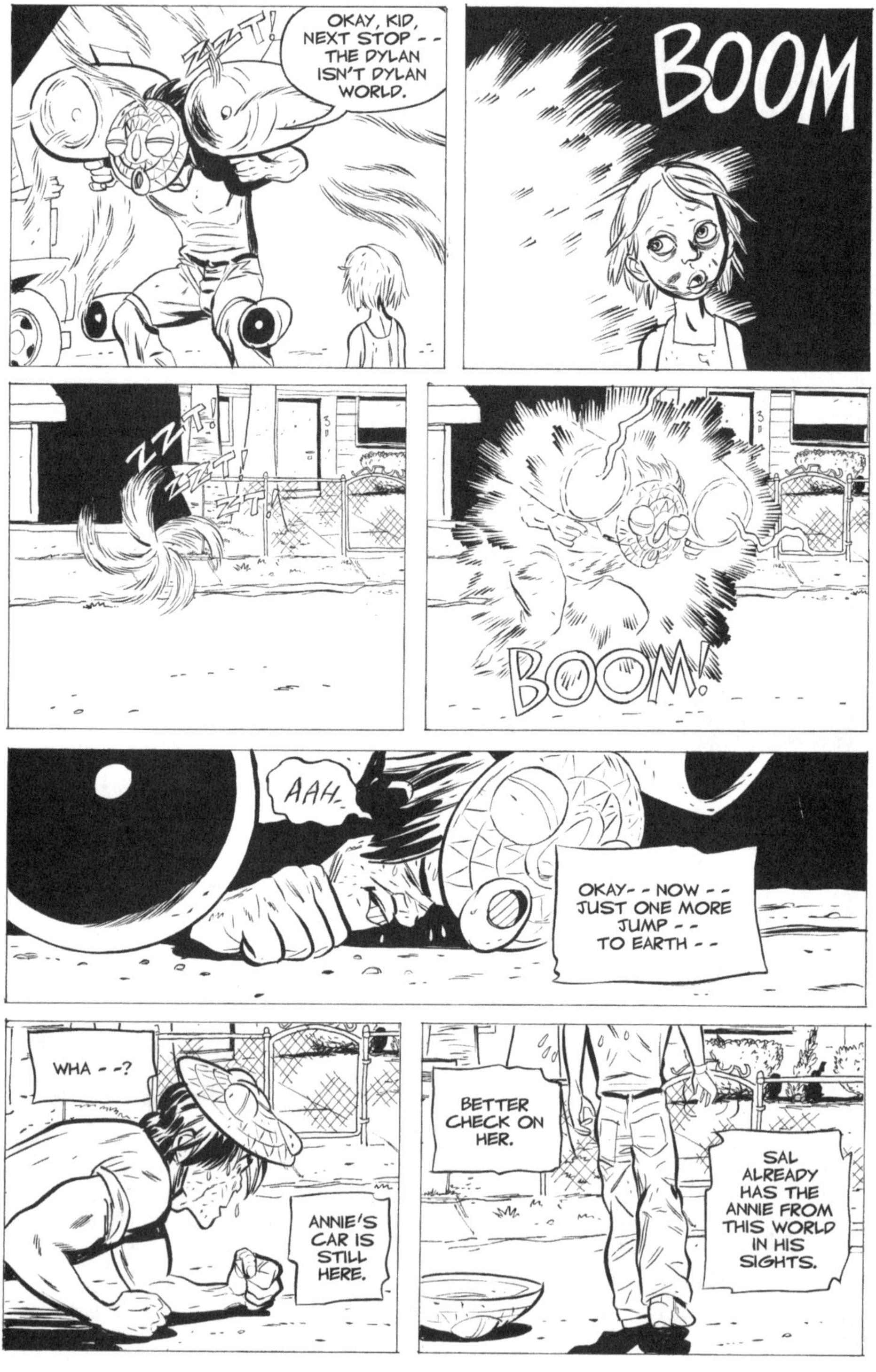
ZZZT!
OKAY, KID, NEXT STOP - - THE DYLAN ISN'T DYLAN WORLD.
BOOM
ZZZT!
ZZZT!
ZZT!
BOOM!
AAH.
OKAY- - NOW - - JUST ONE MORE JUMP - - TO EARTH - -
WHA - -?
ANNIE'S CAR IS STILL HERE.
BETTER CHECK ON HER.
SAL ALREADY HAS THE ANNIE FROM THIS WORLD IN HIS SIGHTS.

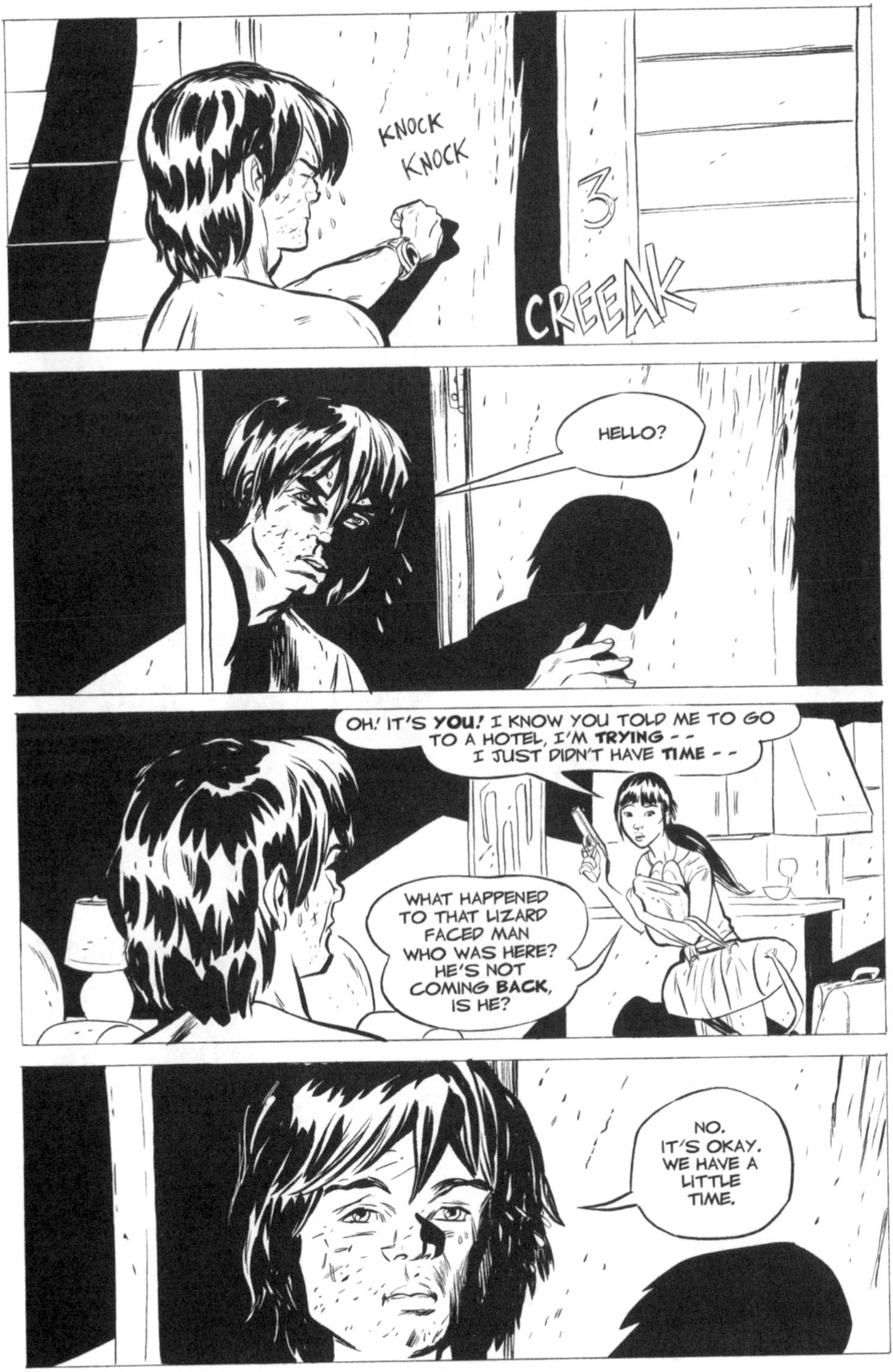
KNOCK
KNOCK
3
CREEAK
HELLO?
OH! IT'S YOU! I KNOW YOU TOLD ME TO GO TO A HOTEL, I'M TRYING -- I JUST DIDN'T HAVE TIME --
WHAT HAPPENED TO THAT LIZARD FACED MAN WHO WAS HERE? HE'S NOT COMING BACK, IS HE?
NO. IT'S OKAY. WE HAVE A LITTLE TIME.

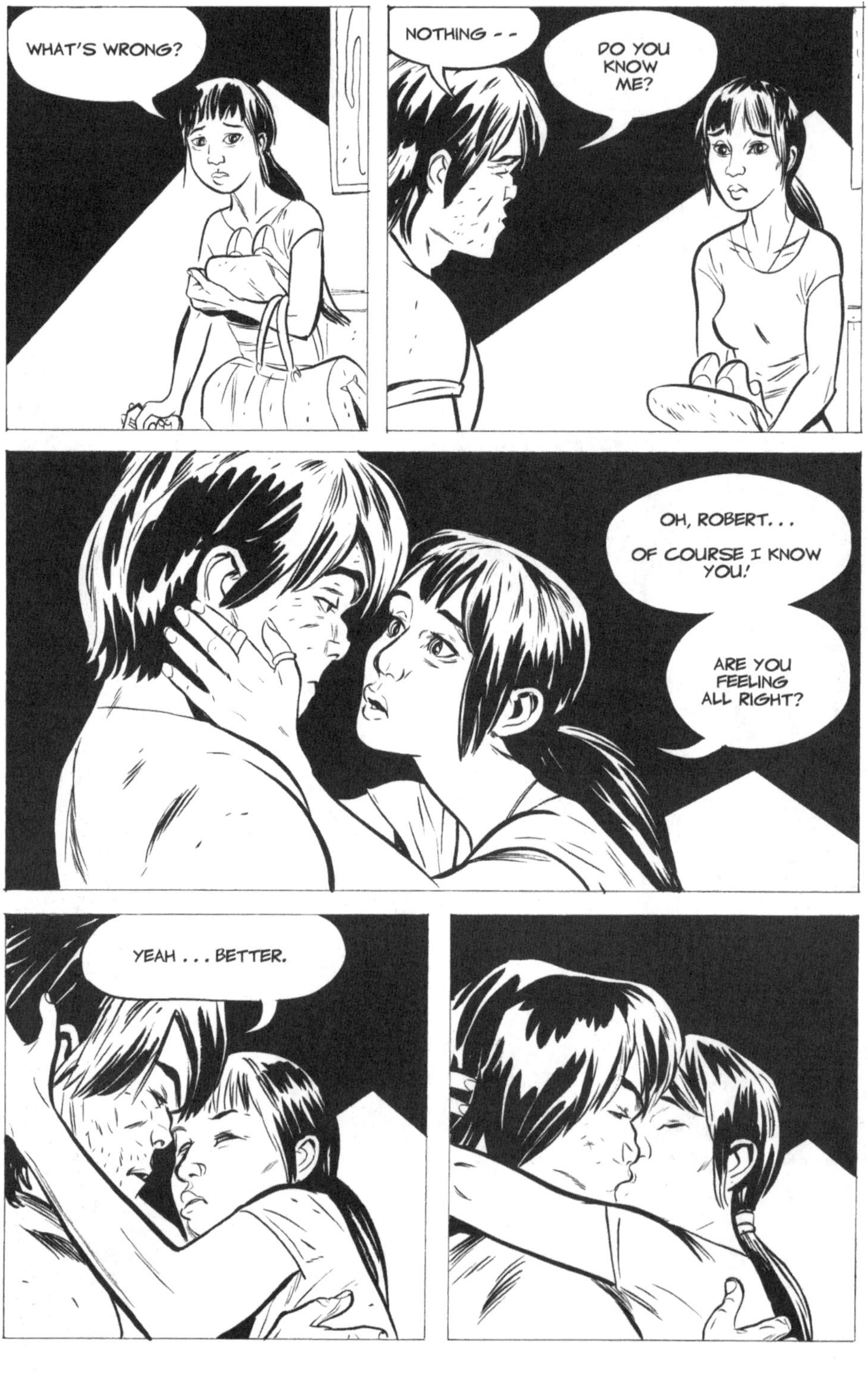
WHAT'S WRONG?
NOTHING - -
DO YOU KNOW ME?
OH, ROBERT...
OF COURSE I KNOW YOU!
ARE YOU FEELING ALL RIGHT?
YEAH... BETTER.

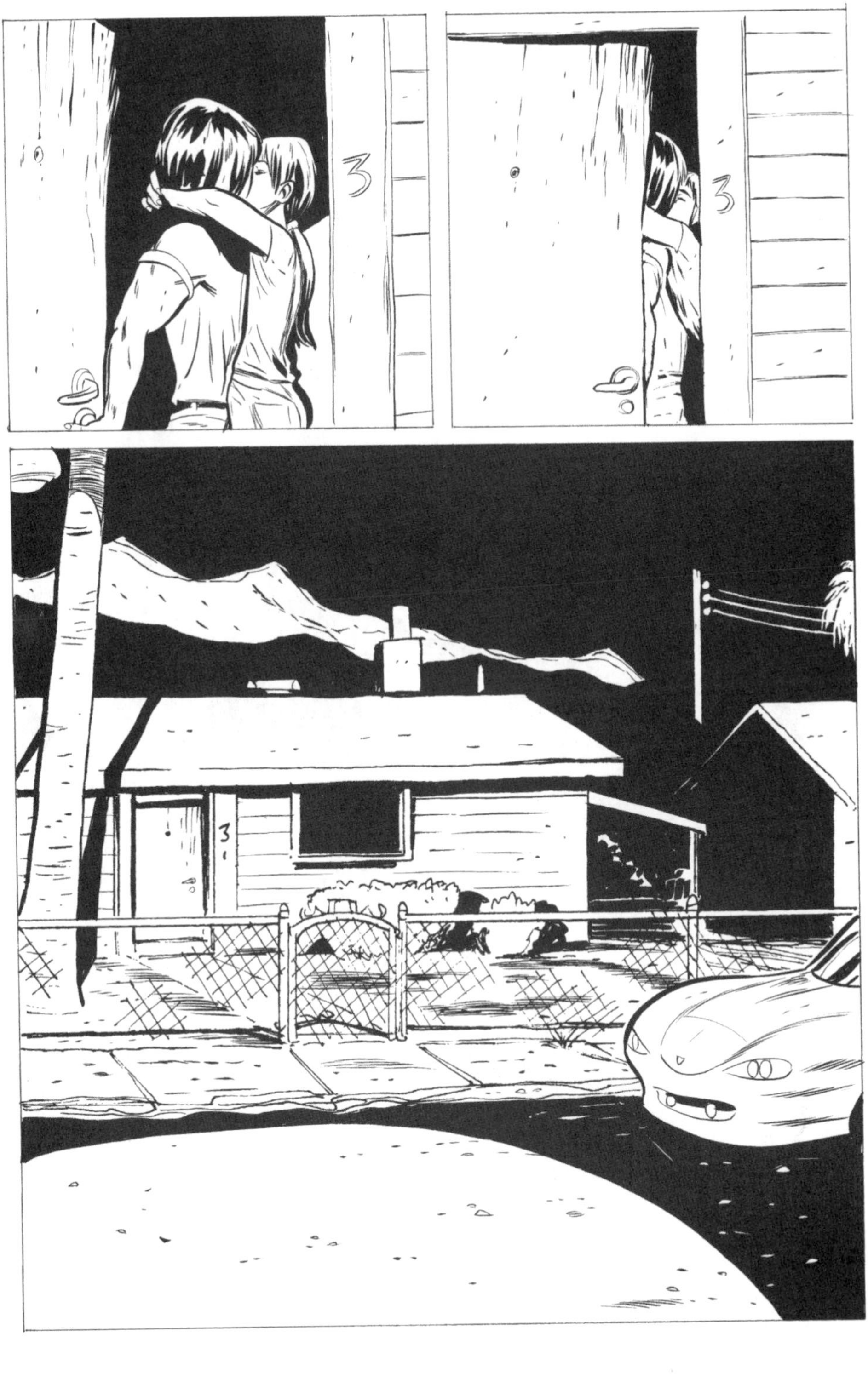

5.
UMA

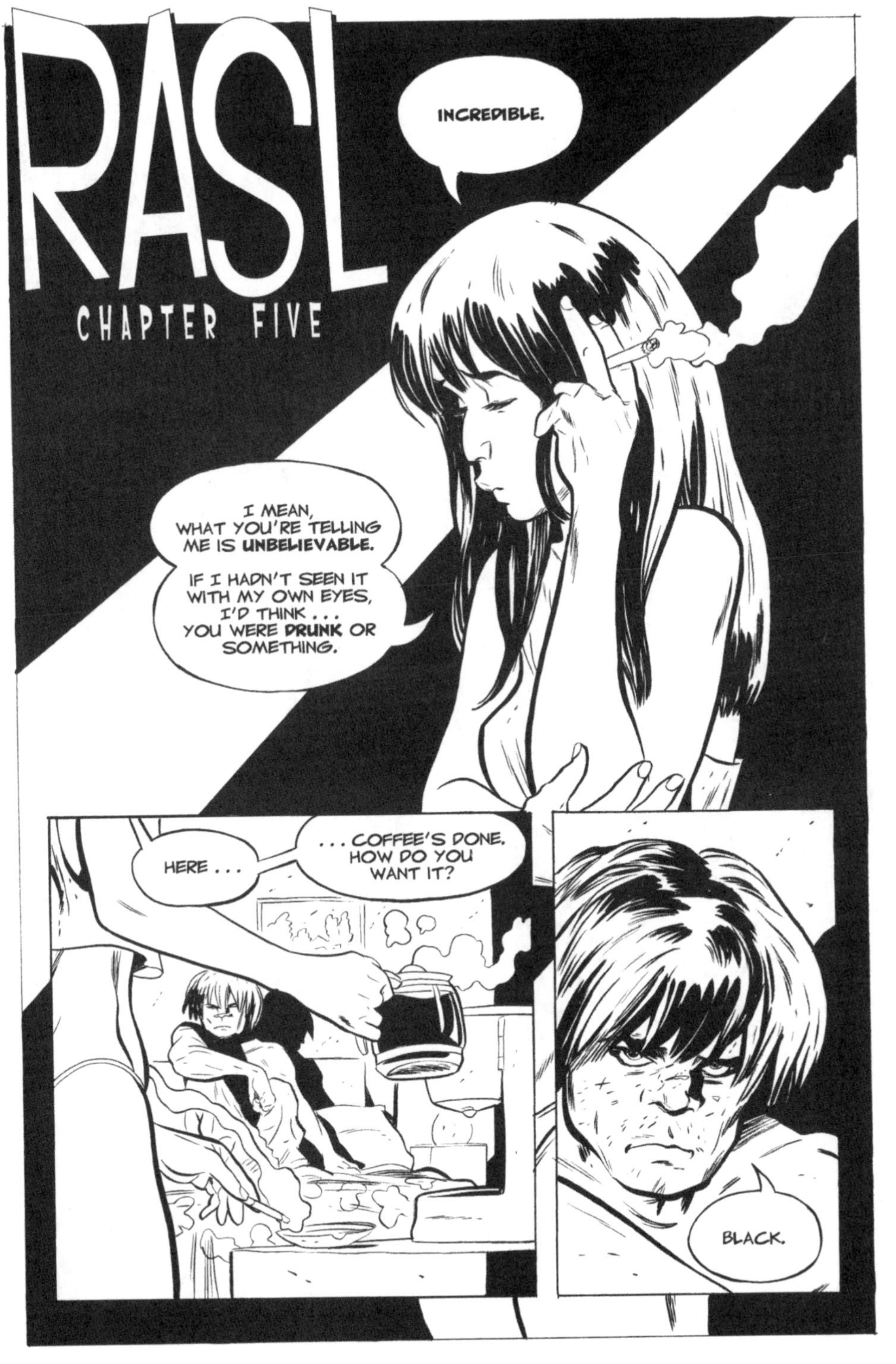
RASL
CHAPTER FIVE
INCREDIBLE.
I MEAN, WHAT YOU'RE TELLING ME IS UNBELIEVABLE.
IF I HADN'T SEEN IT WITH MY OWN EYES, I'D THINK . . . YOU WERE DRUNK OR SOMETHING.
HERE . . .
. . . COFFEE'S DONE. HOW DO YOU WANT IT?
BLACK.

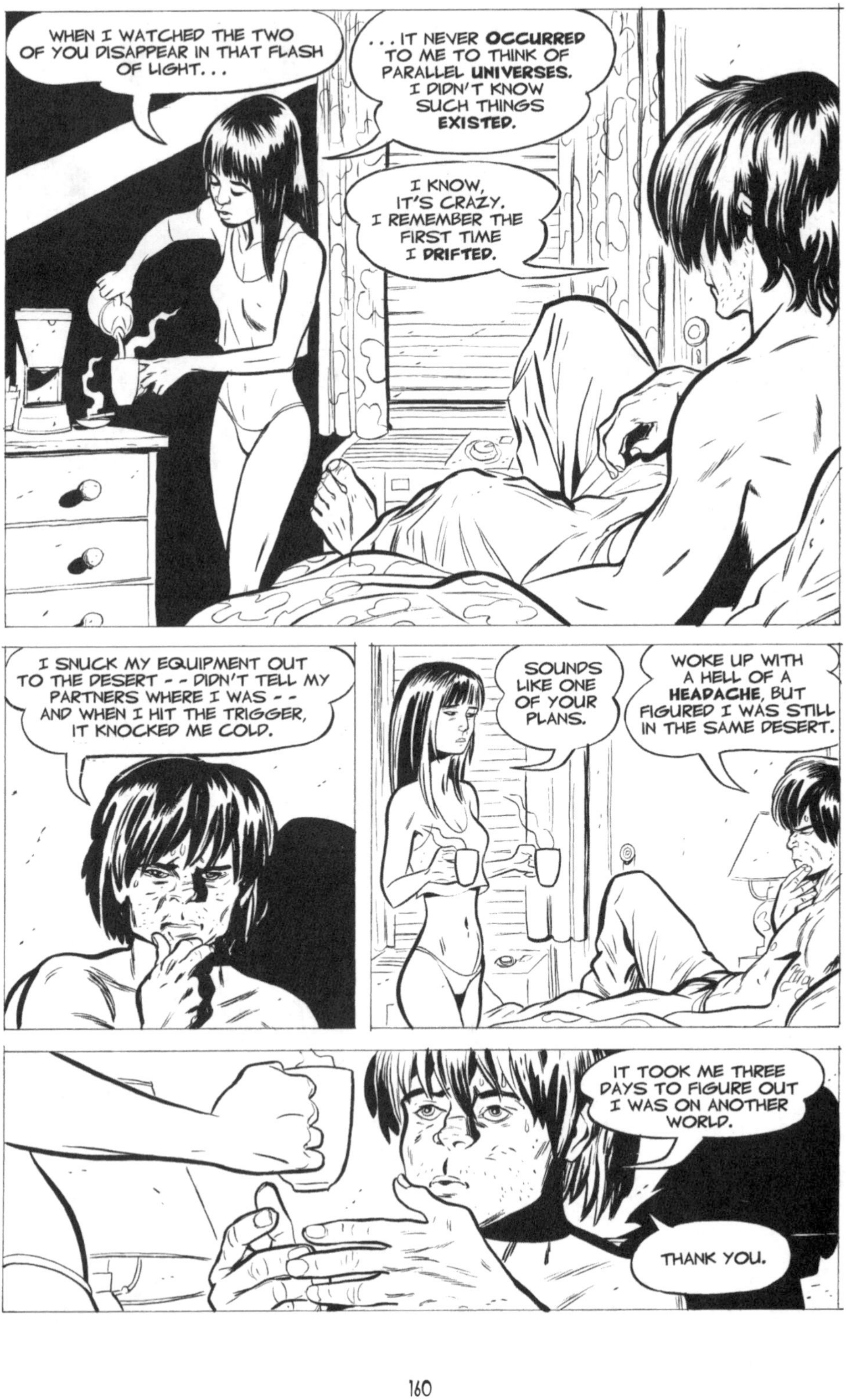
WHEN I WATCHED THE TWO OF YOU DISAPPEAR IN THAT FLASH OF LIGHT...
...IT NEVER **OCCURRED** TO ME TO THINK OF PARALLEL **UNIVERSES.** I DIDN'T KNOW SUCH THINGS **EXISTED.**
I KNOW, IT'S CRAZY. I REMEMBER THE FIRST TIME I **DRIFTED.**
I SNUCK MY EQUIPMENT OUT TO THE DESERT -- DIDN'T TELL MY PARTNERS WHERE I WAS -- AND WHEN I HIT THE TRIGGER, IT KNOCKED ME COLD.
SOUNDS LIKE ONE OF YOUR PLANS.
WOKE UP WITH A HELL OF A **HEADACHE**, BUT FIGURED I WAS STILL IN THE SAME DESERT.
IT TOOK ME THREE DAYS TO FIGURE OUT I WAS ON ANOTHER WORLD.
THANK YOU.

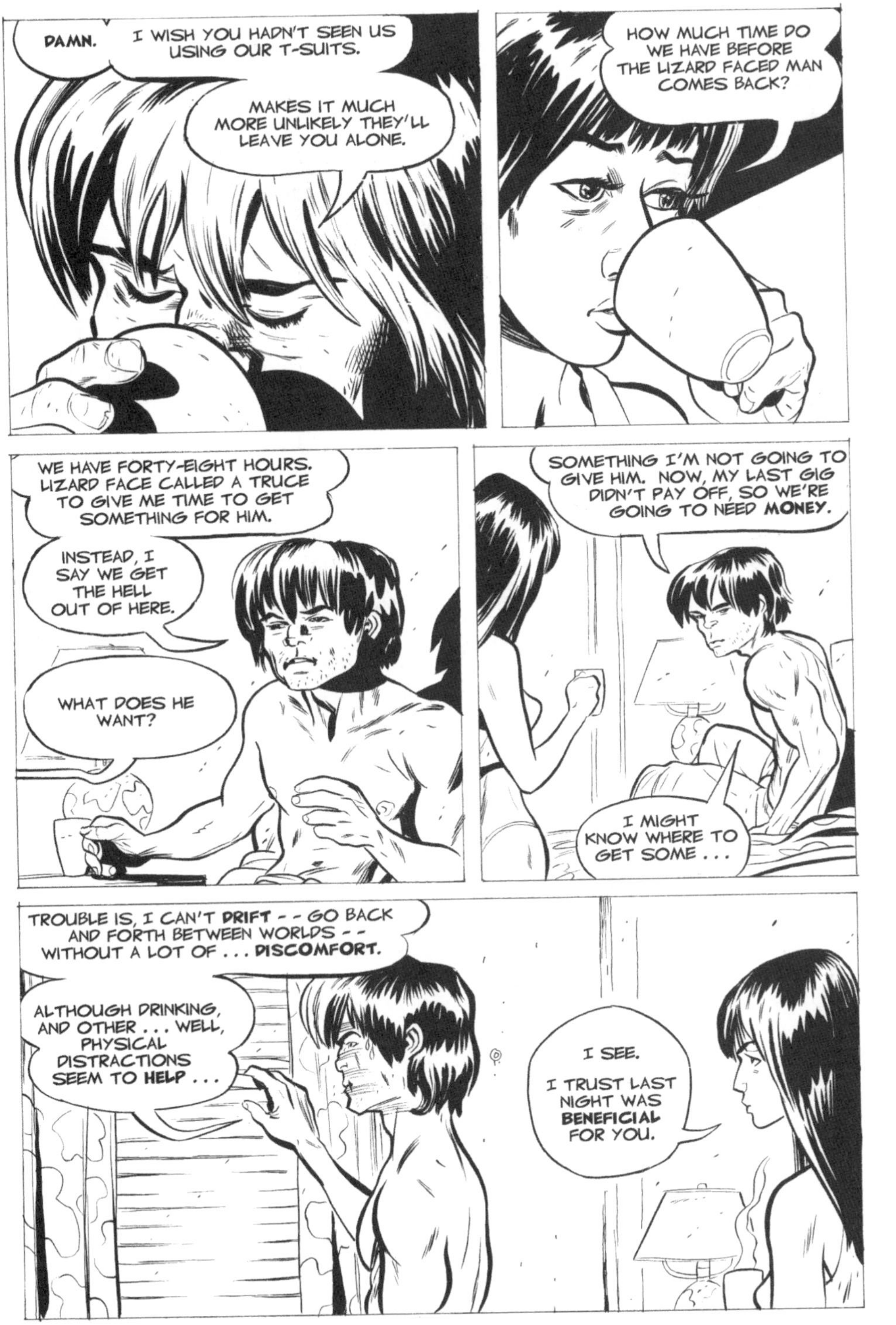
DAMN.
I WISH YOU HADN'T SEEN US USING OUR T-SUITS.
MAKES IT MUCH MORE UNLIKELY THEY'LL LEAVE YOU ALONE.
HOW MUCH TIME DO WE HAVE BEFORE THE LIZARD FACED MAN COMES BACK?
WE HAVE FORTY-EIGHT HOURS. LIZARD FACE CALLED A TRUCE TO GIVE ME TIME TO GET SOMETHING FOR HIM.
INSTEAD, I SAY WE GET THE HELL OUT OF HERE.
WHAT DOES HE WANT?
SOMETHING I'M NOT GOING TO GIVE HIM. NOW, MY LAST GIG DIDN'T PAY OFF, SO WE'RE GOING TO NEED MONEY.
I MIGHT KNOW WHERE TO GET SOME . . .
TROUBLE IS, I CAN'T DRIFT - - GO BACK AND FORTH BETWEEN WORLDS - - WITHOUT A LOT OF . . . DISCOMFORT.
ALTHOUGH DRINKING, AND OTHER . . . WELL, PHYSICAL DISTRACTIONS SEEM TO HELP . . .
I SEE.
I TRUST LAST NIGHT WAS BENEFICIAL FOR YOU.

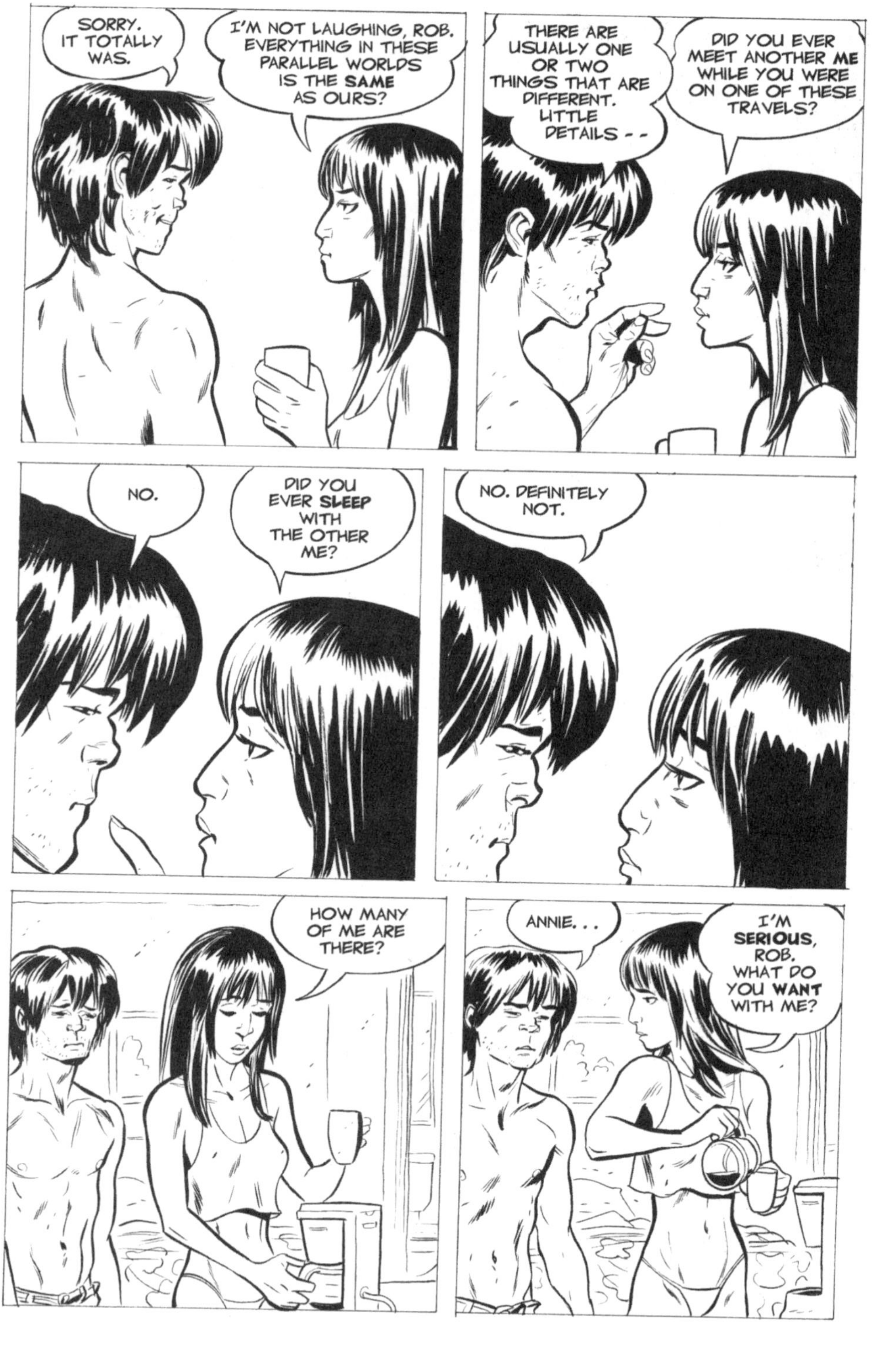
SORRY. IT TOTALLY WAS.
I'M NOT LAUGHING, ROB. EVERYTHING IN THESE PARALLEL WORLDS IS THE SAME AS OURS?
THERE ARE USUALLY ONE OR TWO THINGS THAT ARE DIFFERENT. LITTLE DETAILS - -
DID YOU EVER MEET ANOTHER ME WHILE YOU WERE ON ONE OF THESE TRAVELS?
NO.
DID YOU EVER SLEEP WITH THE OTHER ME?
NO. DEFINITELY NOT.
HOW MANY OF ME ARE THERE?
ANNIE. . .
I'M SERIOUS, ROB. WHAT DO YOU WANT WITH ME?

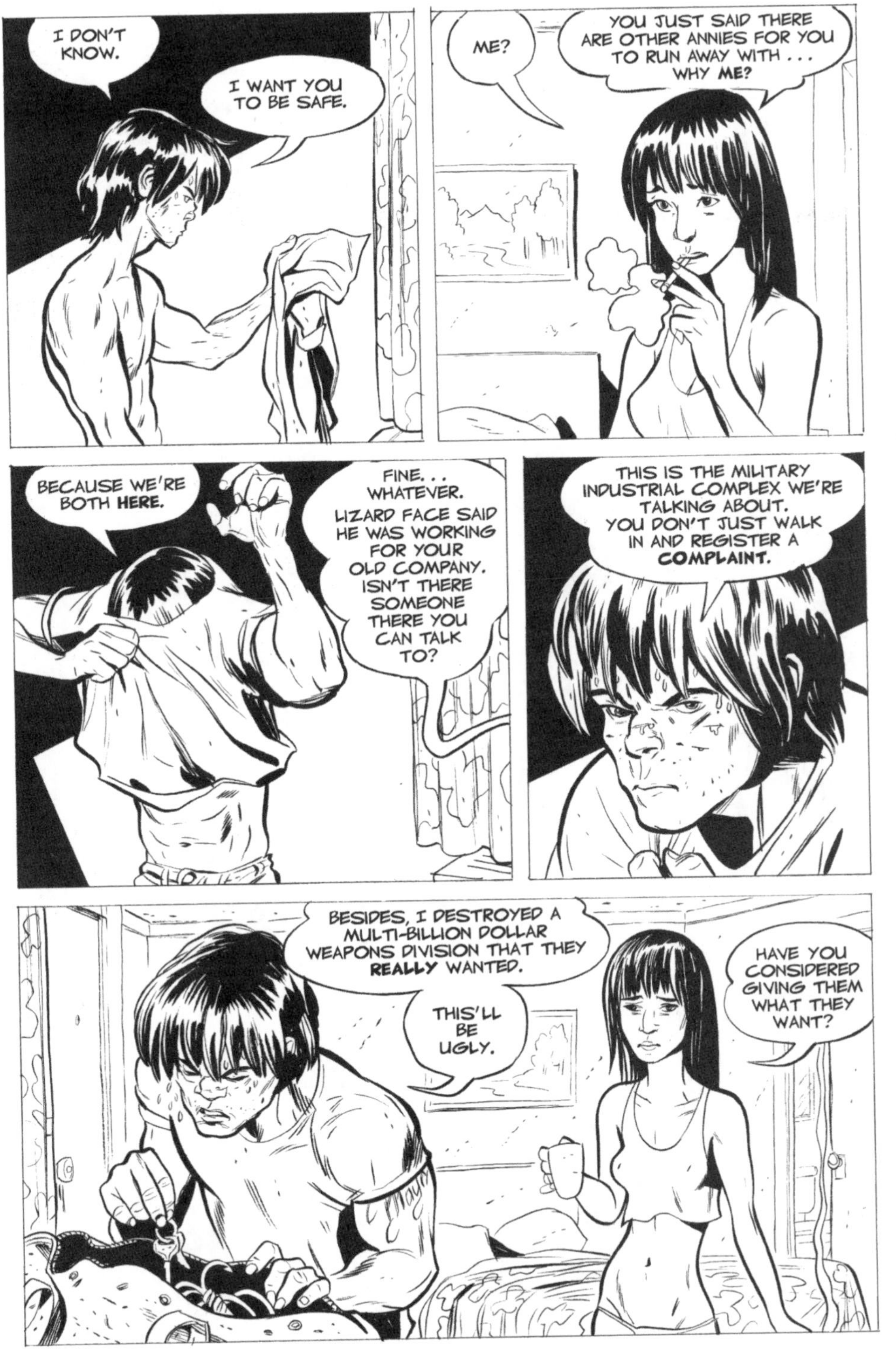
I DON'T KNOW.
I WANT YOU TO BE SAFE.
ME?
YOU JUST SAID THERE ARE OTHER ANNIES FOR YOU TO RUN AWAY WITH . . . WHY **ME?**
BECAUSE WE'RE BOTH **HERE.**
FINE. . . WHATEVER. LIZARD FACE SAID HE WAS WORKING FOR YOUR OLD COMPANY. ISN'T THERE SOMEONE THERE YOU CAN TALK TO?
THIS IS THE MILITARY INDUSTRIAL COMPLEX WE'RE TALKING ABOUT. YOU DON'T JUST WALK IN AND REGISTER A **COMPLAINT.**
BESIDES, I DESTROYED A MULTI-BILLION DOLLAR WEAPONS DIVISION THAT THEY **REALLY** WANTED.
THIS'LL BE UGLY.
HAVE YOU CONSIDERED GIVING THEM WHAT THEY WANT?

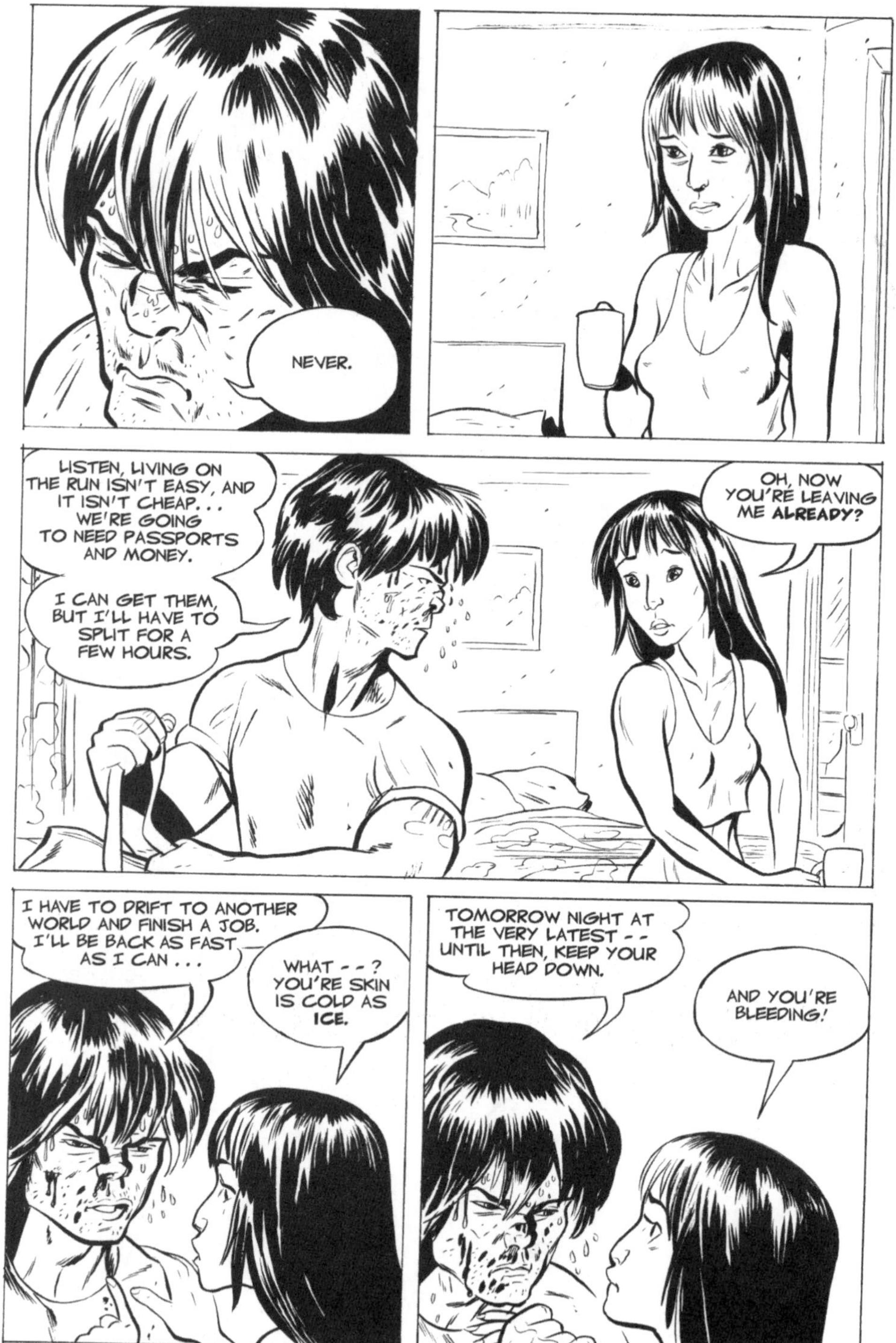
NEVER.
LISTEN, LIVING ON THE RUN ISN'T EASY, AND IT ISN'T CHEAP... WE'RE GOING TO NEED PASSPORTS AND MONEY.
I CAN GET THEM, BUT I'LL HAVE TO SPLIT FOR A FEW HOURS.
OH, NOW YOU'RE LEAVING ME **ALREADY**?
I HAVE TO DRIFT TO ANOTHER WORLD AND FINISH A JOB. I'LL BE BACK AS FAST AS I CAN...
WHAT - - ? YOU'RE SKIN IS COLD AS **ICE**.
TOMORROW NIGHT AT THE VERY LATEST - - UNTIL THEN, KEEP YOUR HEAD DOWN.
AND YOU'RE BLEEDING!

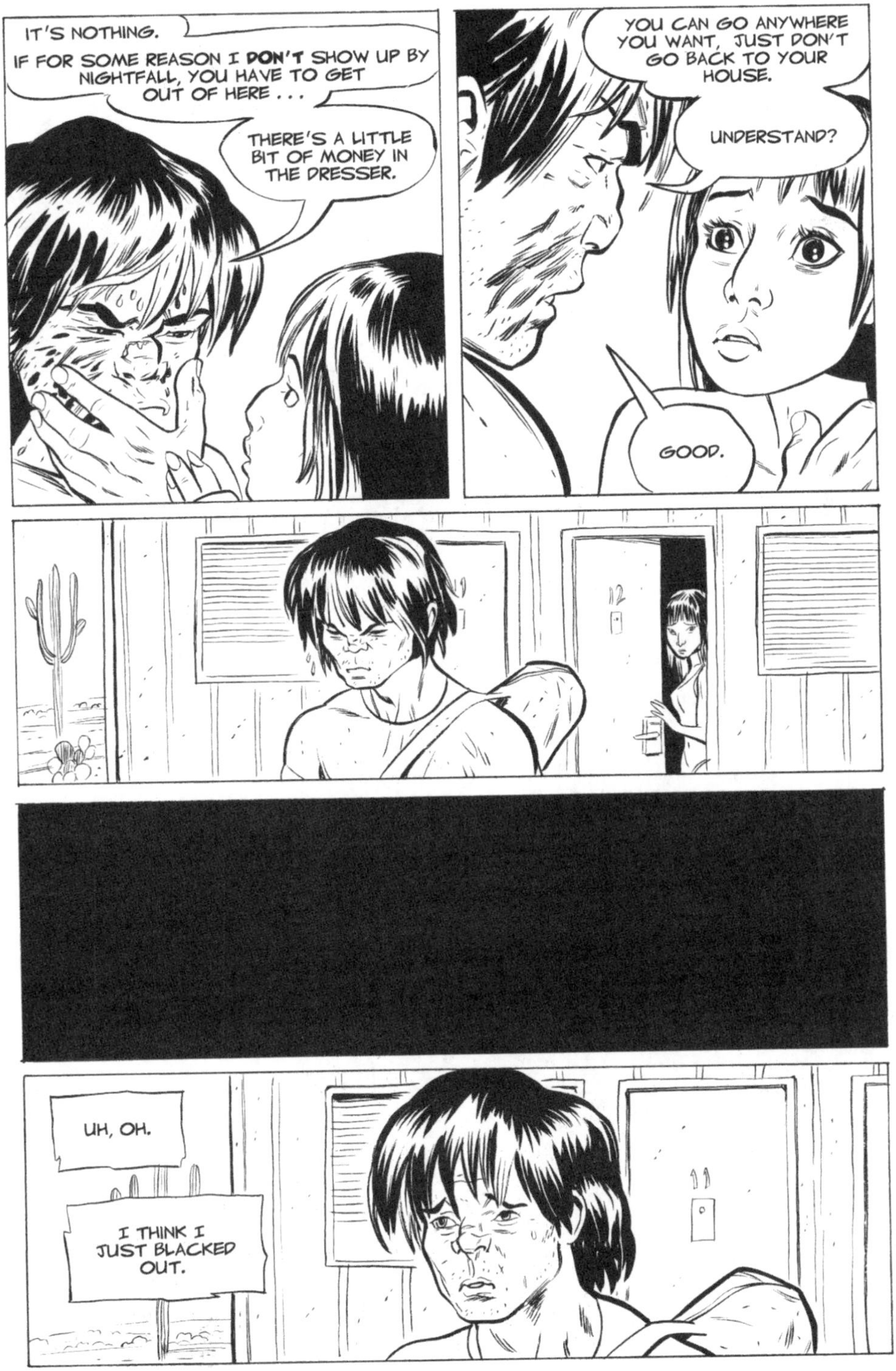
IT'S NOTHING.
IF FOR SOME REASON I **DON'T** SHOW UP BY NIGHTFALL, YOU HAVE TO GET OUT OF HERE . . .
THERE'S A LITTLE BIT OF MONEY IN THE DRESSER.
YOU CAN GO ANYWHERE YOU WANT, JUST DON'T GO BACK TO YOUR HOUSE.
UNDERSTAND?
GOOD.
UH, OH.
I THINK I JUST BLACKED OUT.

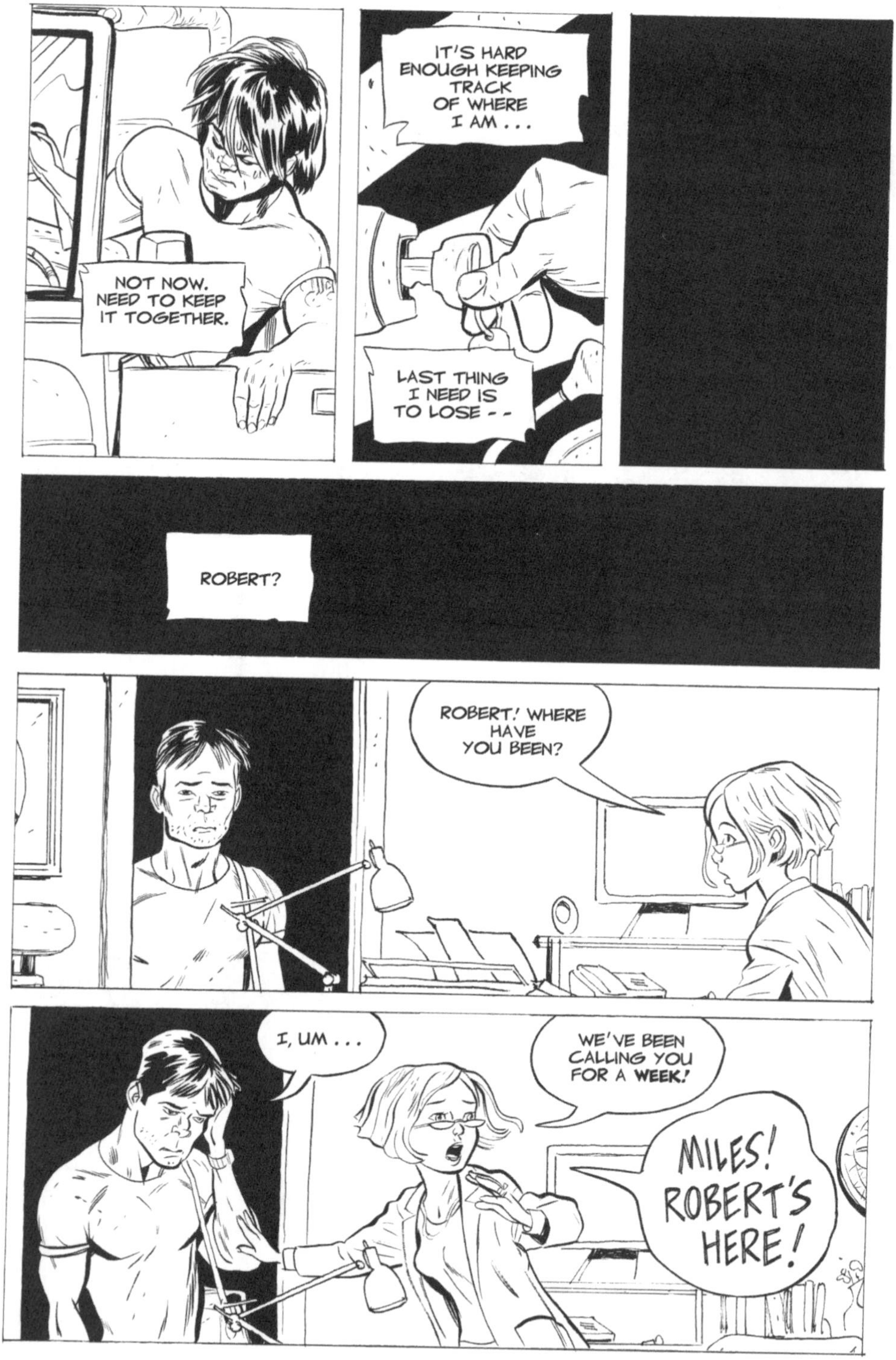
NOT NOW. NEED TO KEEP IT TOGETHER.
IT'S HARD ENOUGH KEEPING TRACK OF WHERE I AM . . .
LAST THING I NEED IS TO LOSE - -
ROBERT?
ROBERT! WHERE HAVE YOU BEEN?
I, UM . . .
WE'VE BEEN CALLING YOU FOR A **WEEK!**
MILES! ROBERT'S HERE!

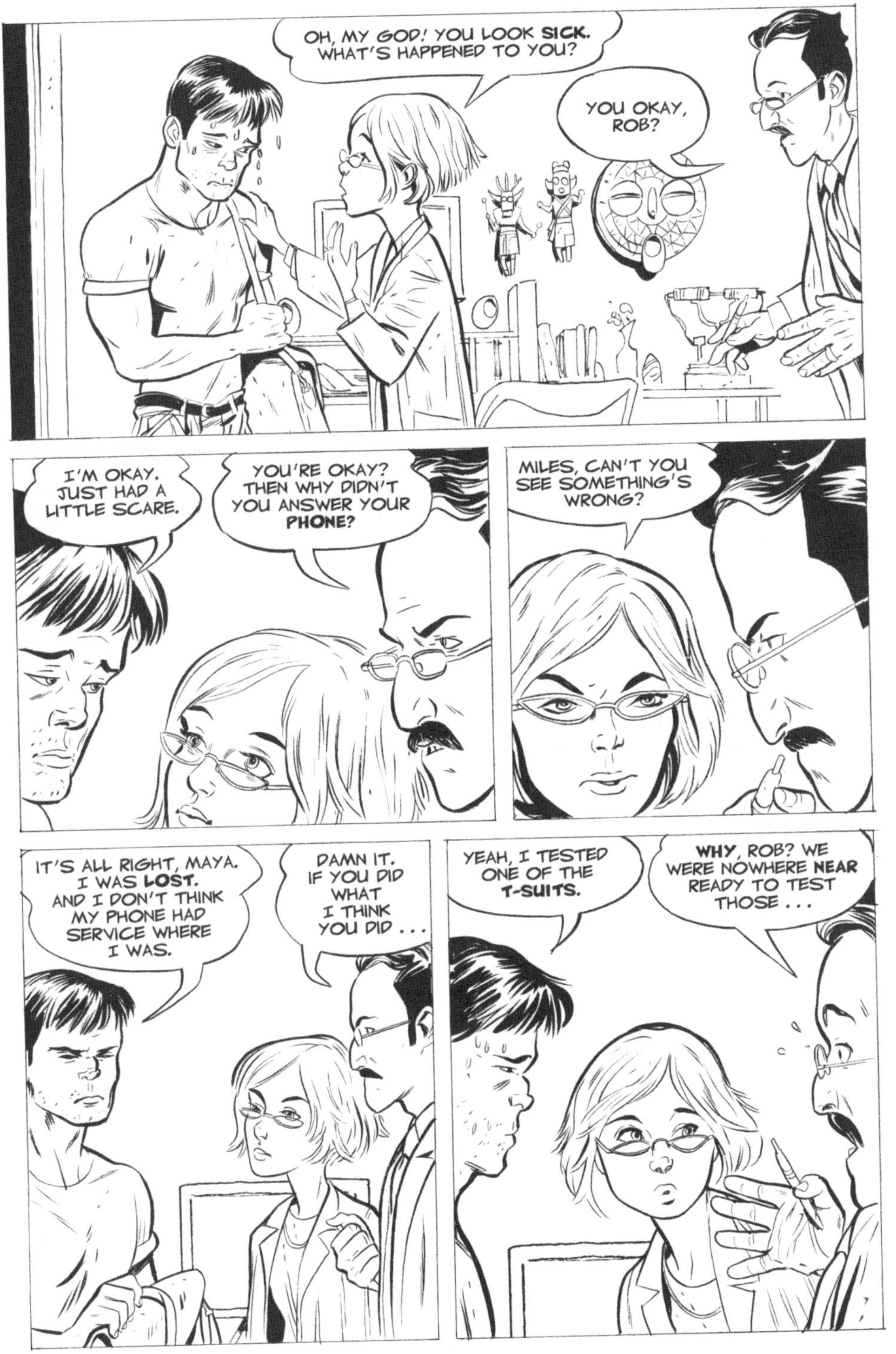
OH, MY GOD! YOU LOOK SICK. WHAT'S HAPPENED TO YOU?
YOU OKAY, ROB?
I'M OKAY. JUST HAD A LITTLE SCARE.
YOU'RE OKAY? THEN WHY DIDN'T YOU ANSWER YOUR PHONE?
MILES, CAN'T YOU SEE SOMETHING'S WRONG?
IT'S ALL RIGHT, MAYA. I WAS LOST. AND I DON'T THINK MY PHONE HAD SERVICE WHERE I WAS.
DAMN IT. IF YOU DID WHAT I THINK YOU DID . . .
YEAH, I TESTED ONE OF THE T-SUITS.
WHY, ROB? WE WERE NOWHERE NEAR READY TO TEST THOSE . . .

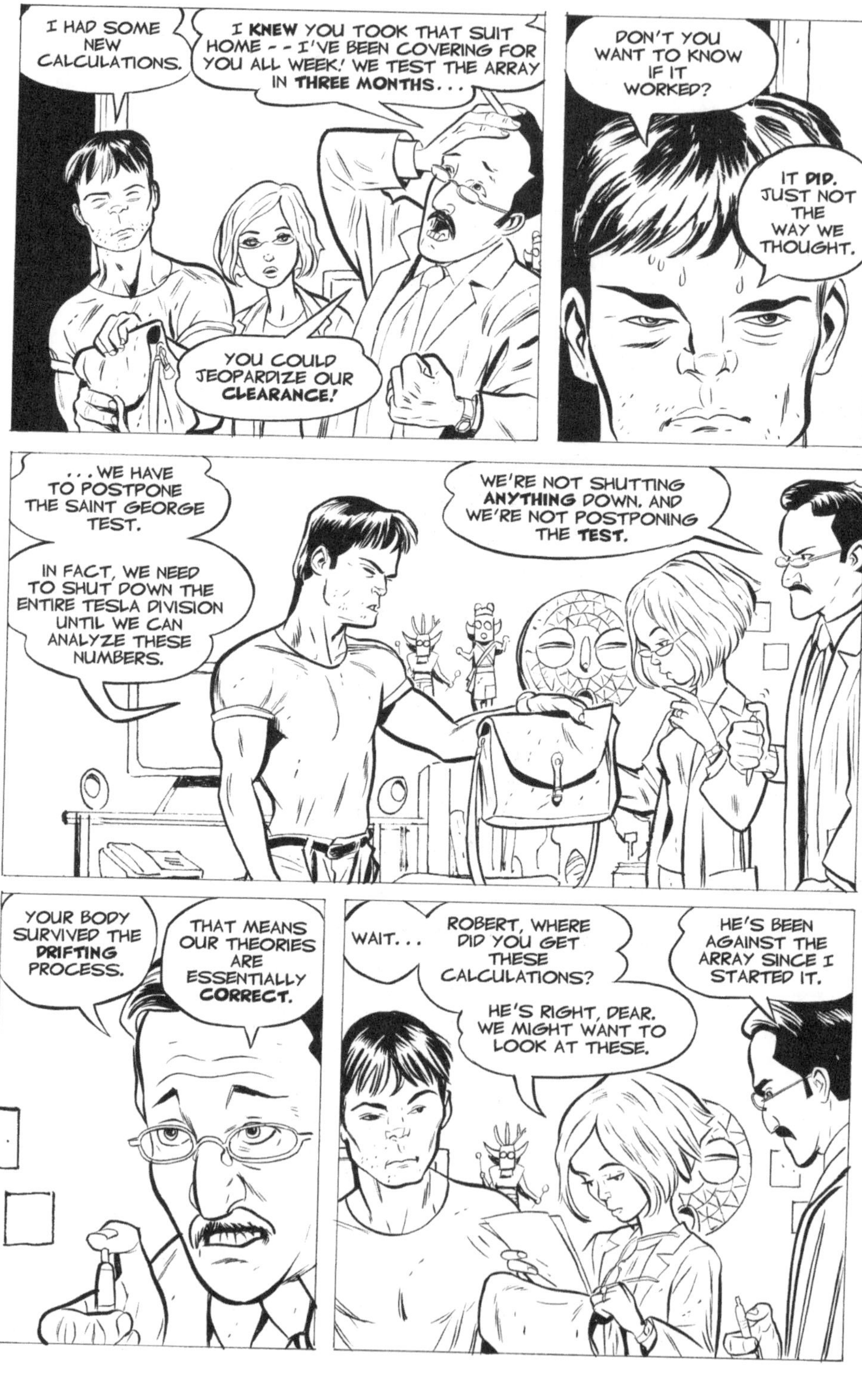
I HAD SOME NEW CALCULATIONS.
I **KNEW** YOU TOOK THAT SUIT HOME - - I'VE BEEN COVERING FOR YOU ALL WEEK! WE TEST THE ARRAY IN **THREE MONTHS**...
YOU COULD JEOPARDIZE OUR **CLEARANCE!**
DON'T YOU WANT TO KNOW IF IT WORKED?
IT **DID.** JUST NOT THE WAY WE THOUGHT.
...WE HAVE TO POSTPONE THE SAINT GEORGE TEST.
IN FACT, WE NEED TO SHUT DOWN THE ENTIRE TESLA DIVISION UNTIL WE CAN ANALYZE THESE NUMBERS.
WE'RE NOT SHUTTING **ANYTHING** DOWN, AND WE'RE NOT POSTPONING THE **TEST.**
YOUR BODY SURVIVED THE **DRIFTING** PROCESS.
THAT MEANS OUR THEORIES ARE ESSENTIALLY **CORRECT.**
WAIT...
ROBERT, WHERE DID YOU GET THESE CALCULATIONS?
HE'S BEEN AGAINST THE ARRAY SINCE I STARTED IT.
HE'S RIGHT, DEAR. WE MIGHT WANT TO LOOK AT THESE.

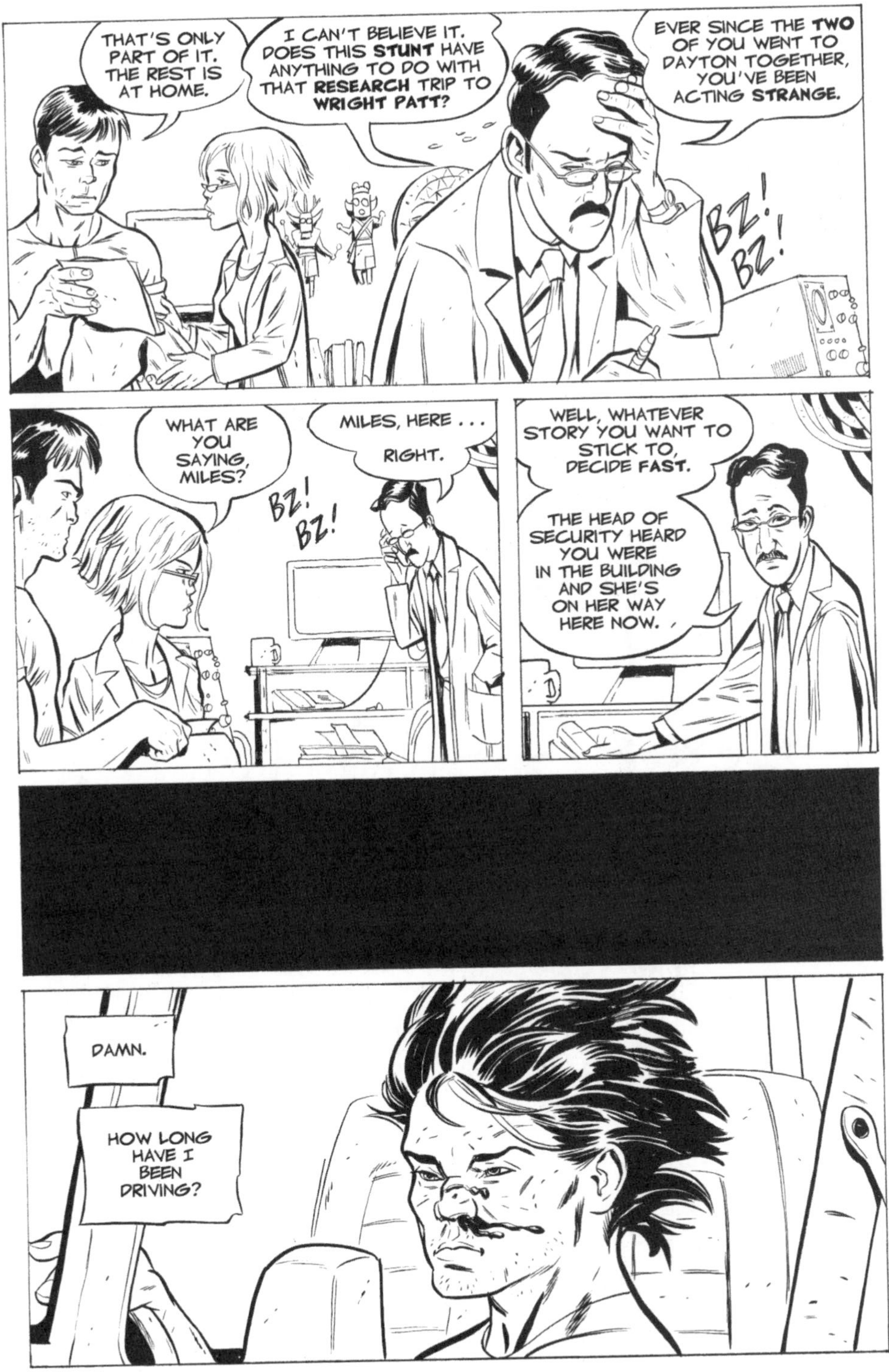
THAT'S ONLY PART OF IT. THE REST IS AT HOME.
I CAN'T BELIEVE IT. DOES THIS **STUNT** HAVE ANYTHING TO DO WITH THAT **RESEARCH** TRIP TO **WRIGHT PATT?**
EVER SINCE THE **TWO** OF YOU WENT TO DAYTON TOGETHER, YOU'VE BEEN ACTING **STRANGE.**
BZ! BZ!
WHAT ARE YOU SAYING, MILES?
BZ! BZ!
MILES, HERE . . .
RIGHT.
WELL, WHATEVER STORY YOU WANT TO STICK TO, DECIDE **FAST.**
THE HEAD OF SECURITY HEARD YOU WERE IN THE BUILDING AND SHE'S ON HER WAY HERE NOW.
DAMN.
HOW LONG HAVE I BEEN DRIVING?

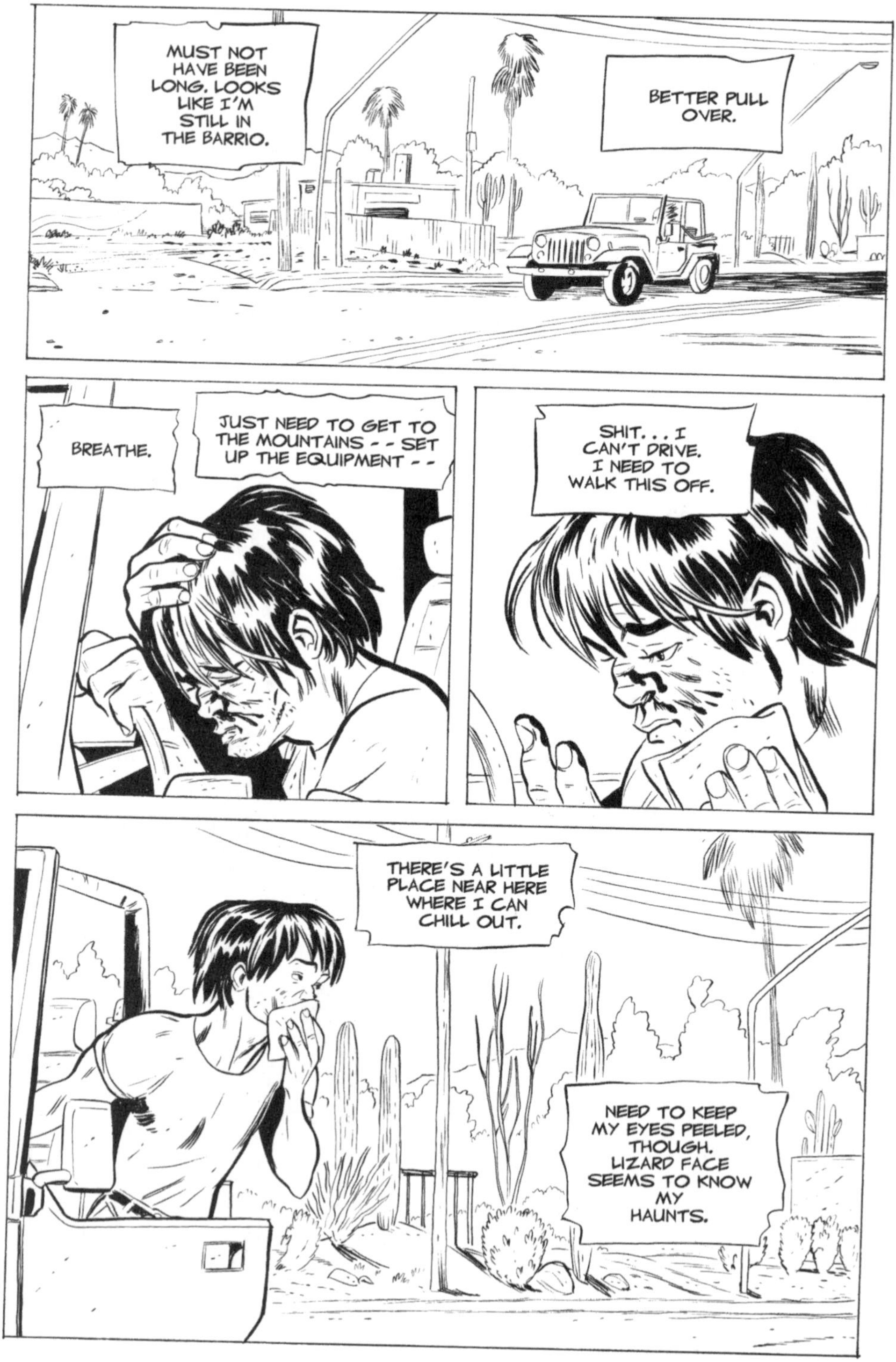
MUST NOT HAVE BEEN LONG. LOOKS LIKE I'M STILL IN THE BARRIO.
BETTER PULL OVER.
BREATHE.
JUST NEED TO GET TO THE MOUNTAINS - - SET UP THE EQUIPMENT - -
SHIT. . . I CAN'T DRIVE. I NEED TO WALK THIS OFF.
THERE'S A LITTLE PLACE NEAR HERE WHERE I CAN CHILL OUT.
NEED TO KEEP MY EYES PEELED, THOUGH. LIZARD FACE SEEMS TO KNOW MY HAUNTS.

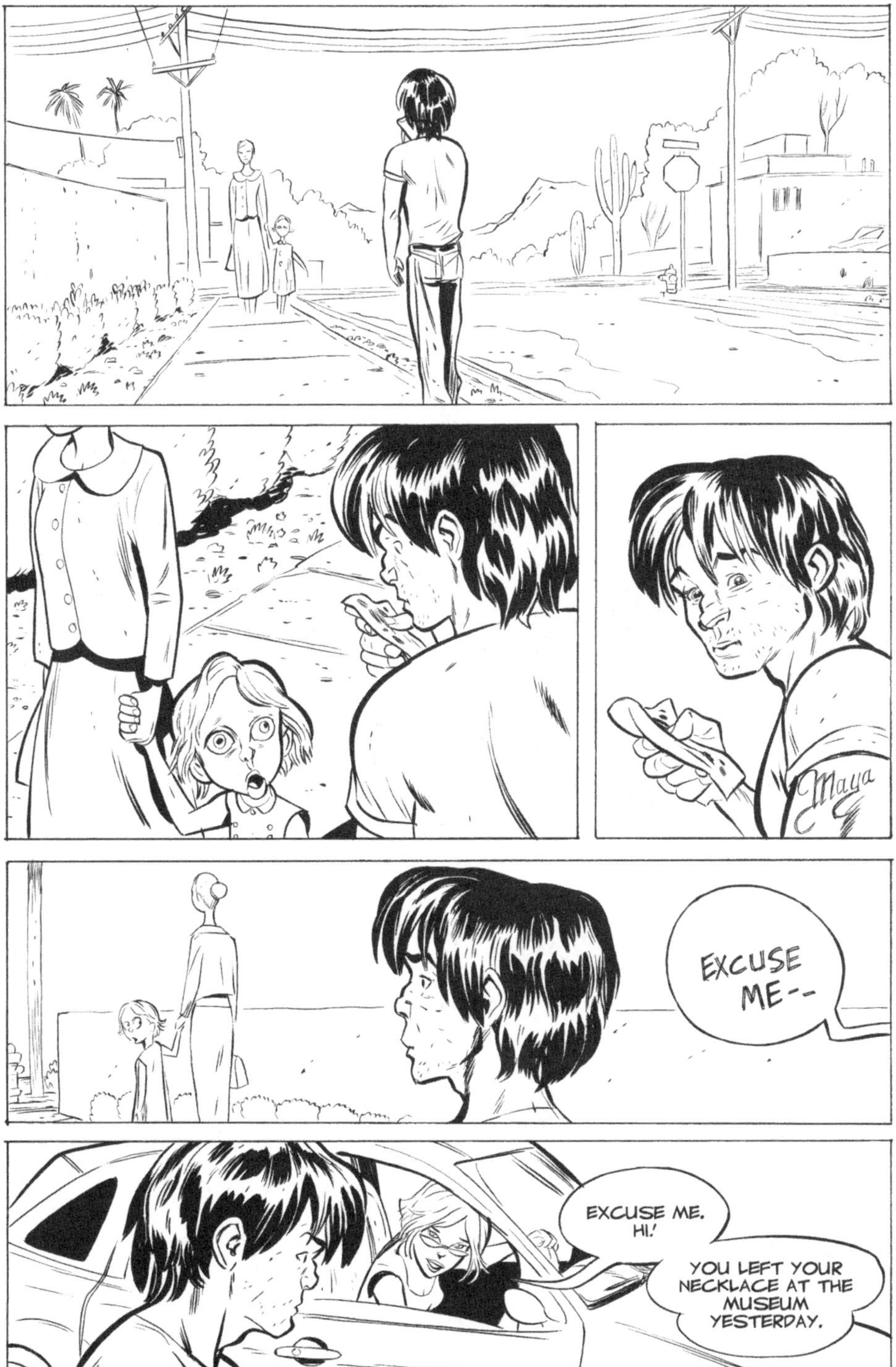
Maya
EXCUSE ME--
EXCUSE ME. HI!
YOU LEFT YOUR NECKLACE AT THE MUSEUM YESTERDAY.

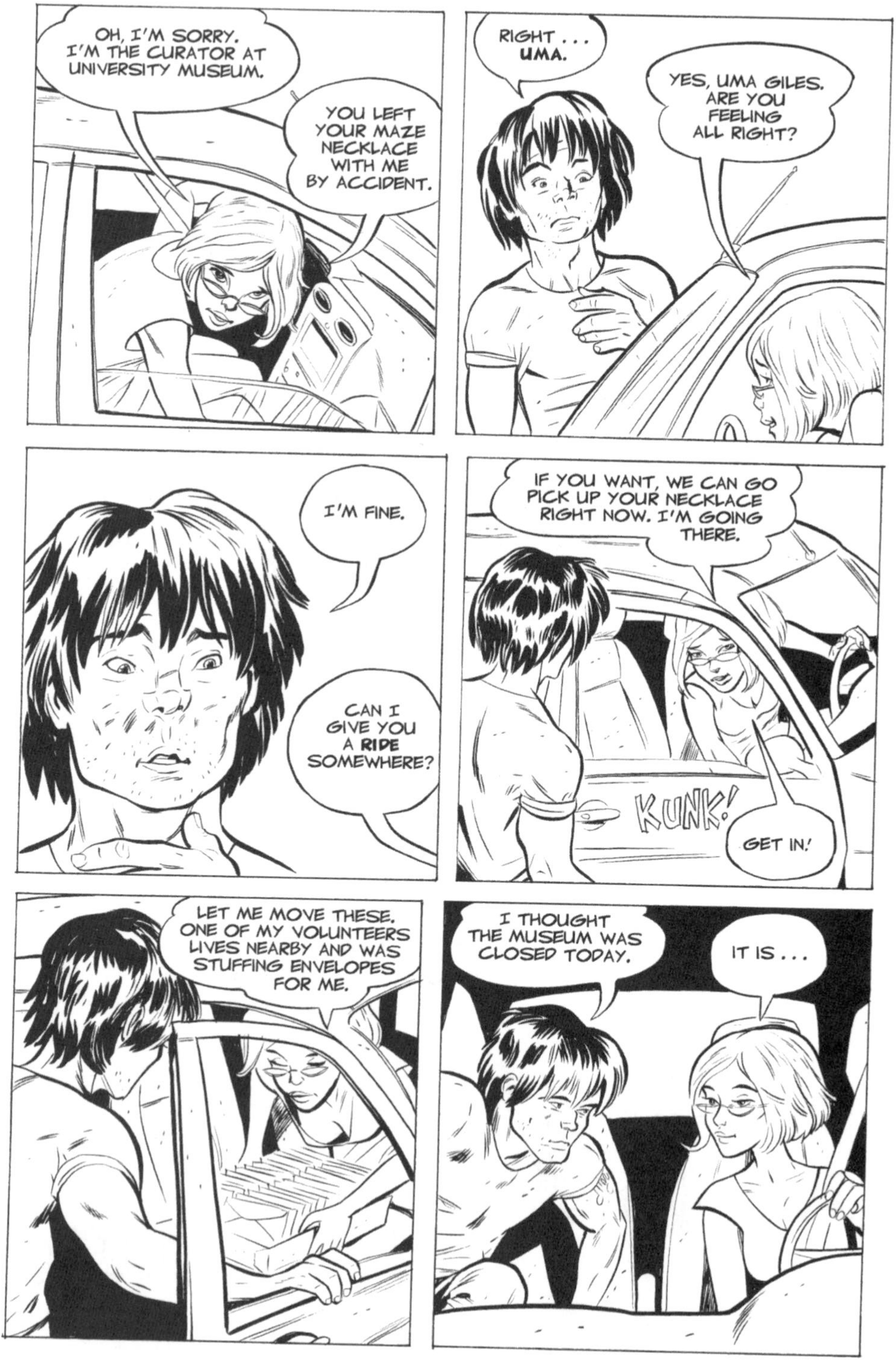
OH, I'M SORRY. I'M THE CURATOR AT UNIVERSITY MUSEUM.
YOU LEFT YOUR MAZE NECKLACE WITH ME BY ACCIDENT.
RIGHT . . . UMA.
YES, UMA GILES. ARE YOU FEELING ALL RIGHT?
I'M FINE.
CAN I GIVE YOU A RIDE SOMEWHERE?
IF YOU WANT, WE CAN GO PICK UP YOUR NECKLACE RIGHT NOW. I'M GOING THERE.
KUNK!
GET IN!
LET ME MOVE THESE. ONE OF MY VOLUNTEERS LIVES NEARBY AND WAS STUFFING ENVELOPES FOR ME.
I THOUGHT THE MUSEUM WAS CLOSED TODAY.
IT IS . . .

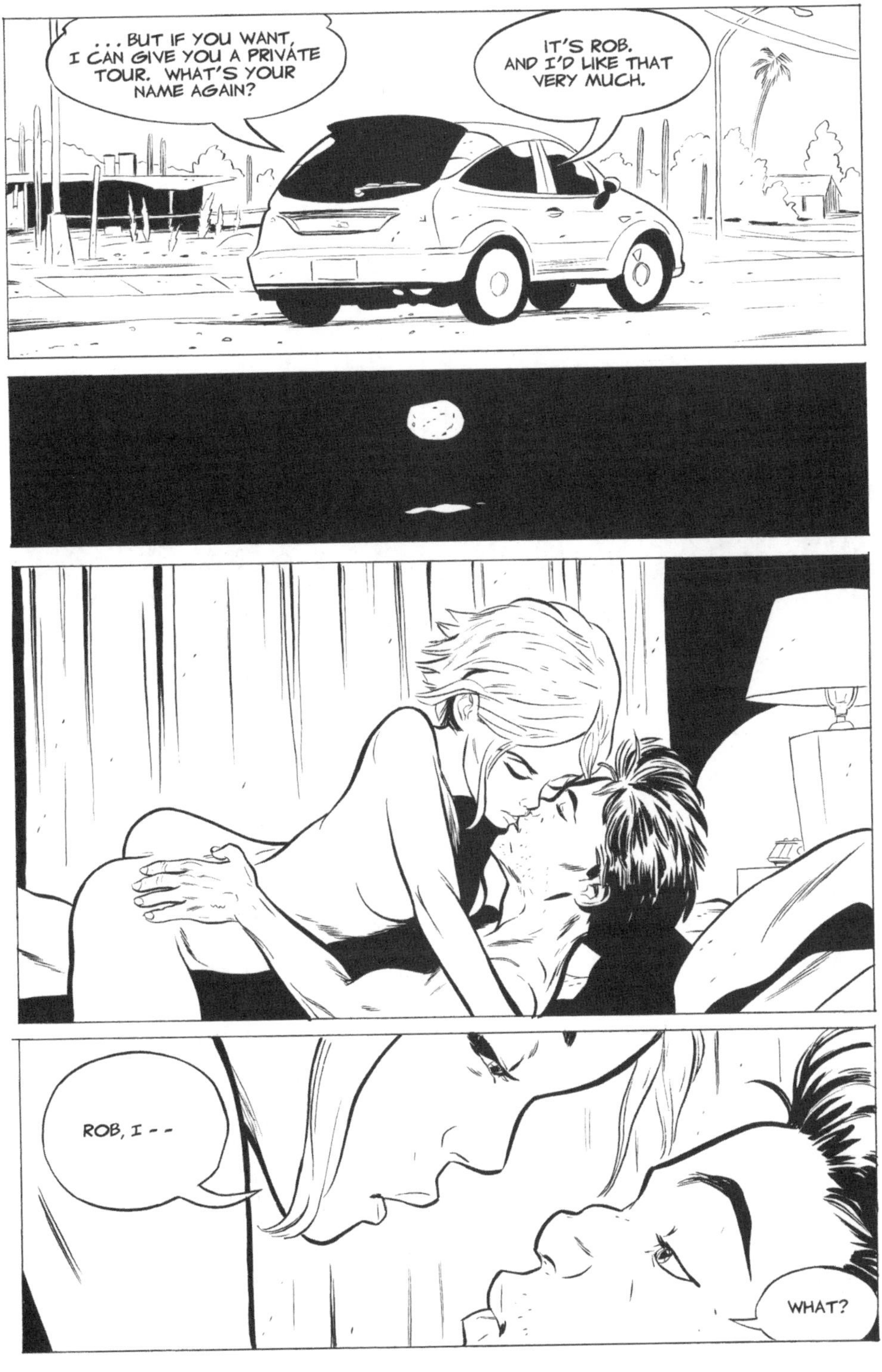
. . . BUT IF YOU WANT, I CAN GIVE YOU A PRIVATE TOUR. WHAT'S YOUR NAME AGAIN?
IT'S ROB. AND I'D LIKE THAT VERY MUCH.
ROB, I - -
WHAT?

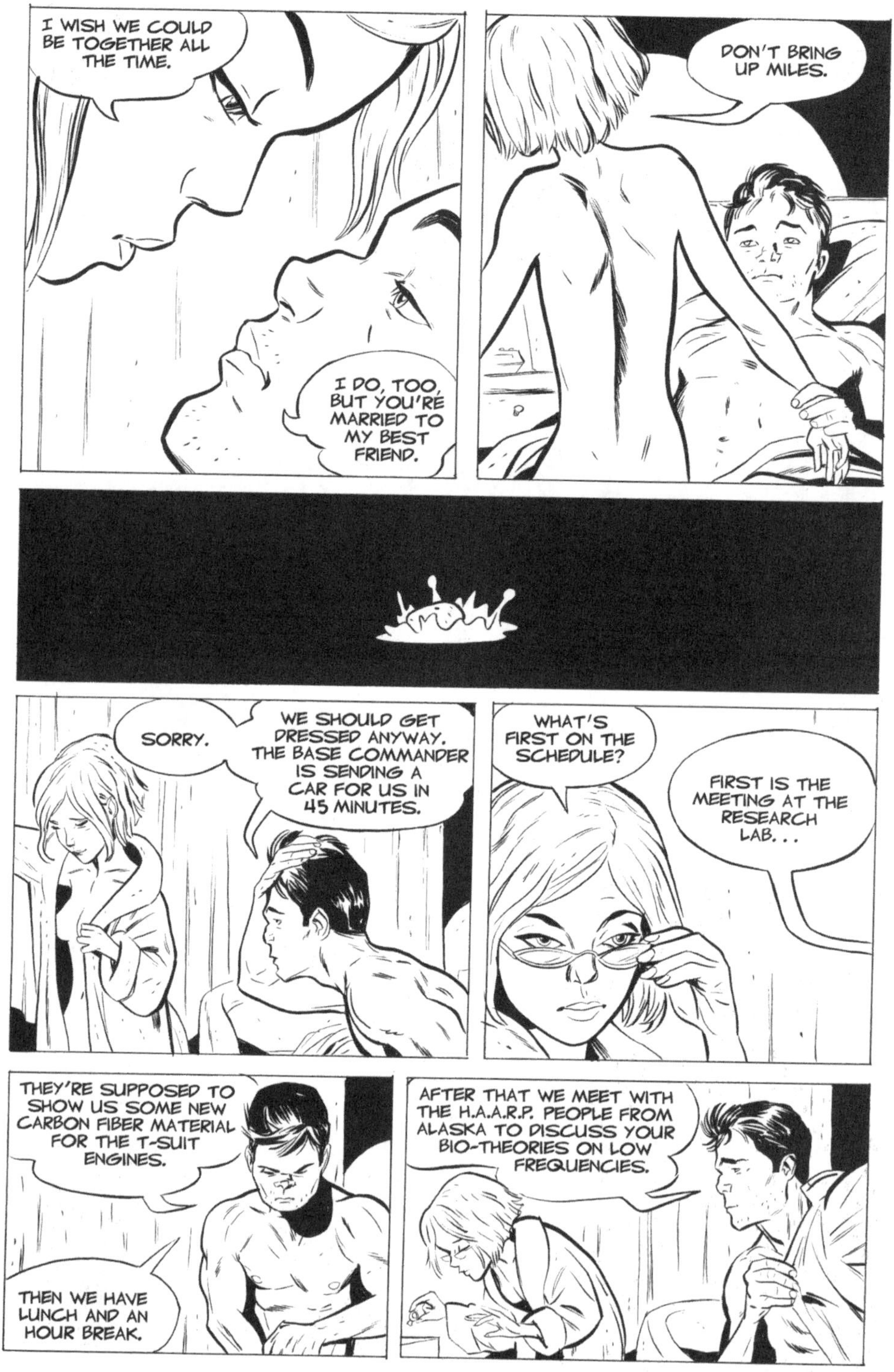
I WISH WE COULD BE TOGETHER ALL THE TIME.
I DO, TOO, BUT YOU'RE MARRIED TO MY BEST FRIEND.
DON'T BRING UP MILES.
SORRY.
WE SHOULD GET DRESSED ANYWAY. THE BASE COMMANDER IS SENDING A CAR FOR US IN 45 MINUTES.
WHAT'S FIRST ON THE SCHEDULE?
FIRST IS THE MEETING AT THE RESEARCH LAB...
THEY'RE SUPPOSED TO SHOW US SOME NEW CARBON FIBER MATERIAL FOR THE T-SUIT ENGINES.
THEN WE HAVE LUNCH AND AN HOUR BREAK.
AFTER THAT WE MEET WITH THE H.A.A.R.P. PEOPLE FROM ALASKA TO DISCUSS YOUR BIO-THEORIES ON LOW FREQUENCIES.

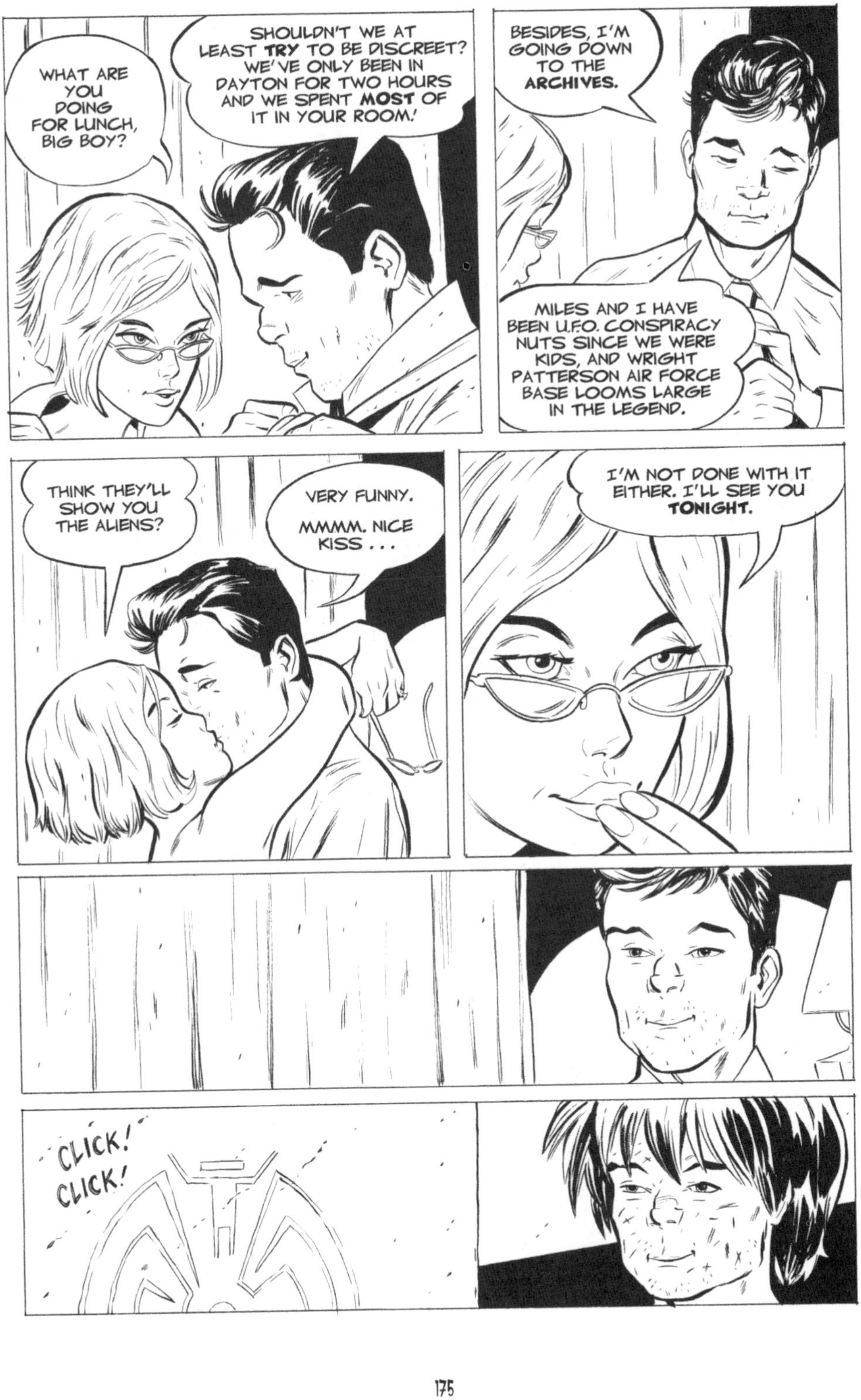
WHAT ARE YOU DOING FOR LUNCH, BIG BOY?
SHOULDN'T WE AT LEAST **TRY** TO BE DISCREET? WE'VE ONLY BEEN IN DAYTON FOR TWO HOURS AND WE SPENT **MOST** OF IT IN YOUR ROOM!
BESIDES, I'M GOING DOWN TO THE **ARCHIVES.**
MILES AND I HAVE BEEN U.F.O. CONSPIRACY NUTS SINCE WE WERE KIDS, AND WRIGHT PATTERSON AIR FORCE BASE LOOMS LARGE IN THE LEGEND.
THINK THEY'LL SHOW YOU THE ALIENS?
VERY FUNNY.
MMMM. NICE KISS . . .
I'M NOT DONE WITH IT EITHER. I'LL SEE YOU **TONIGHT.**
CLICK! CLICK!

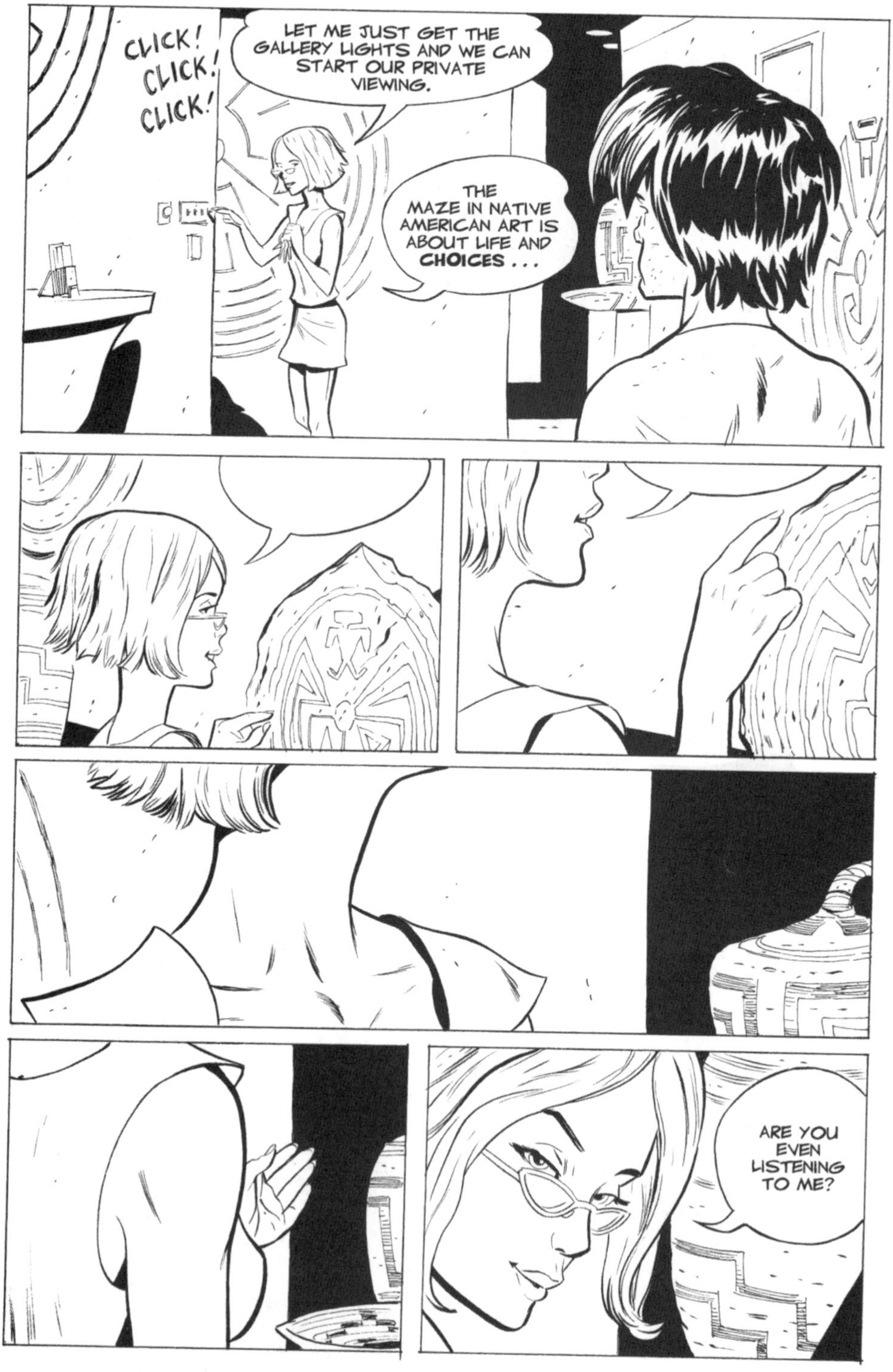
CLICK!
CLICK!
CLICK!
LET ME JUST GET THE GALLERY LIGHTS AND WE CAN START OUR PRIVATE VIEWING.
THE MAZE IN NATIVE AMERICAN ART IS ABOUT LIFE AND CHOICES . . .
ARE YOU EVEN LISTENING TO ME?

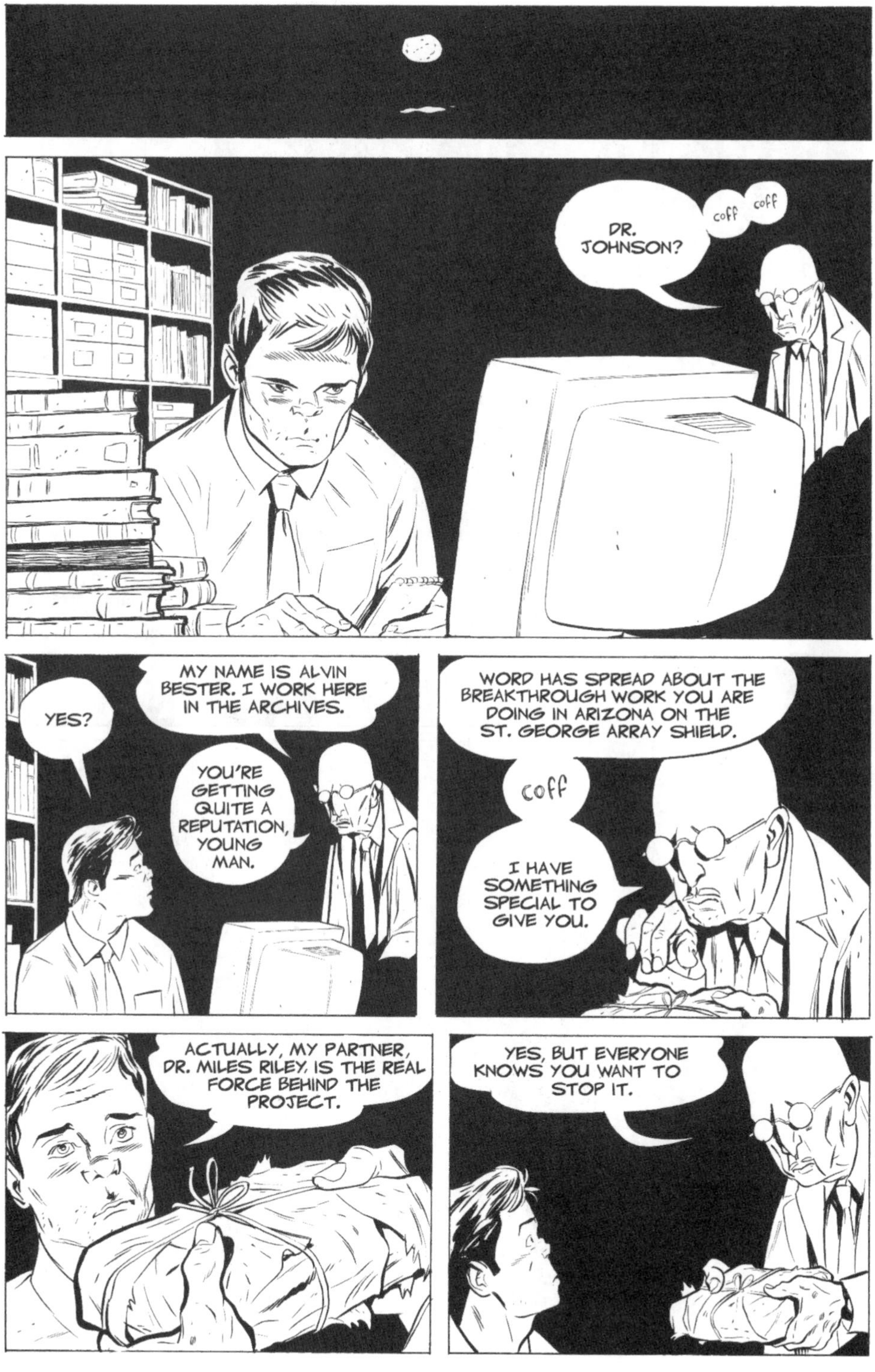
DR. JOHNSON?
coff
coff
YES?
MY NAME IS ALVIN BESTER. I WORK HERE IN THE ARCHIVES.
YOU'RE GETTING QUITE A REPUTATION, YOUNG MAN.
WORD HAS SPREAD ABOUT THE BREAKTHROUGH WORK YOU ARE DOING IN ARIZONA ON THE ST. GEORGE ARRAY SHIELD.
coff
I HAVE SOMETHING SPECIAL TO GIVE YOU.
ACTUALLY, MY PARTNER, DR. MILES RILEY, IS THE REAL FORCE BEHIND THE PROJECT.
YES, BUT EVERYONE KNOWS YOU WANT TO STOP IT.

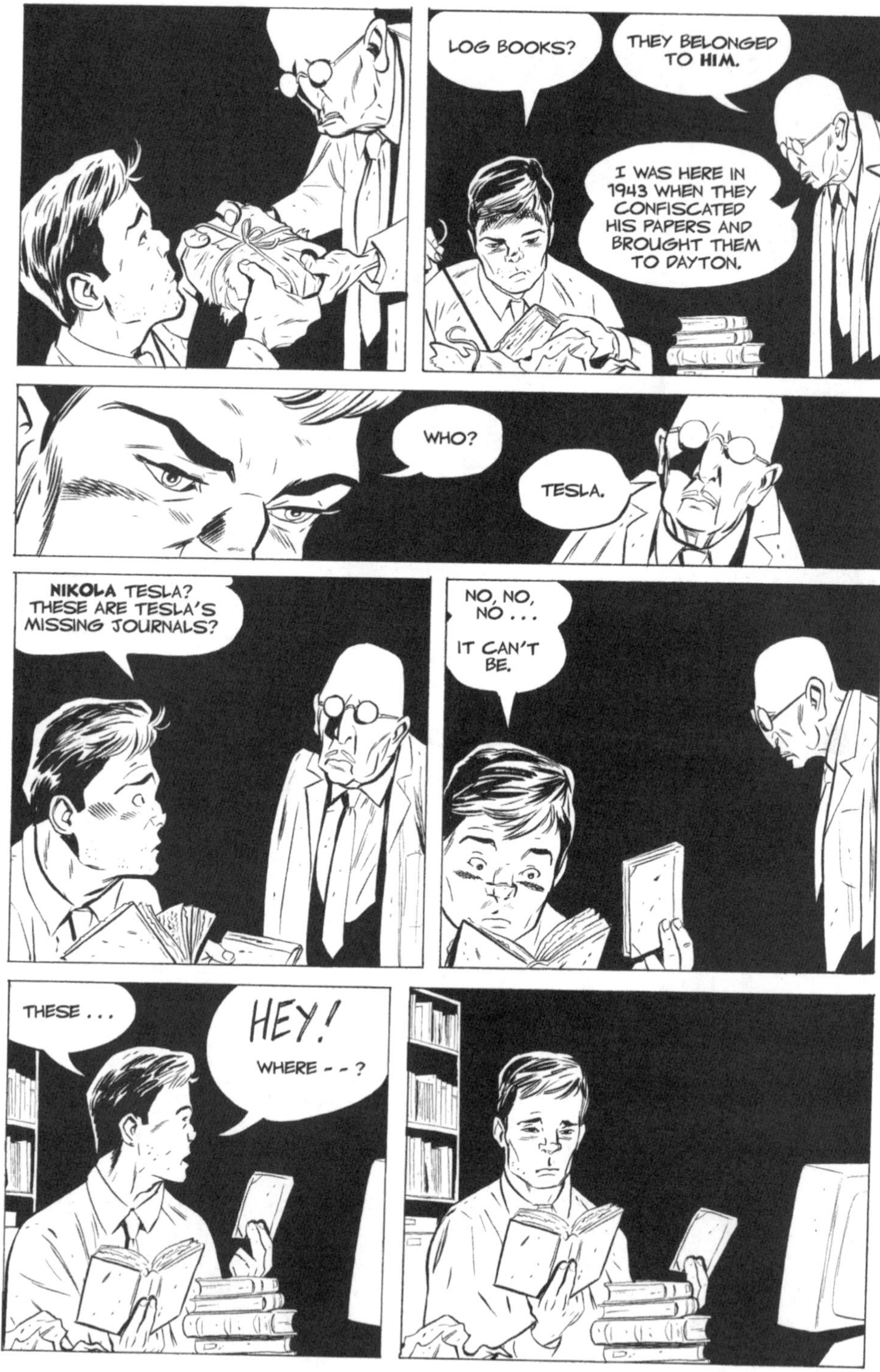
LOG BOOKS?
THEY BELONGED TO **HIM.**
I WAS HERE IN 1943 WHEN THEY CONFISCATED HIS PAPERS AND BROUGHT THEM TO DAYTON.
WHO?
TESLA.
NIKOLA TESLA? THESE ARE TESLA'S MISSING JOURNALS?
NO, NO, NO . . .
IT CAN'T BE.
THESE . . .
HEY!
WHERE - - ?

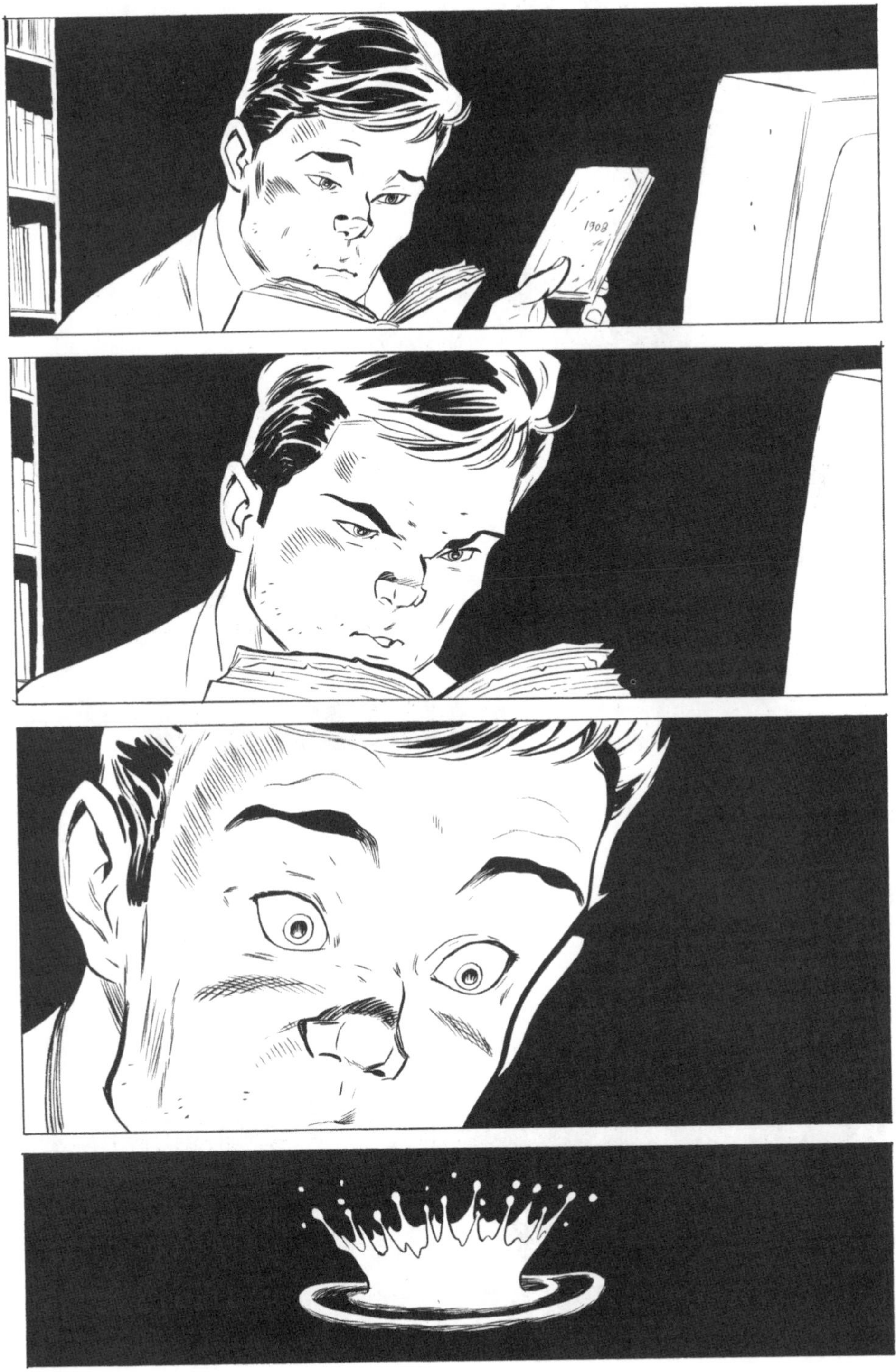
1908

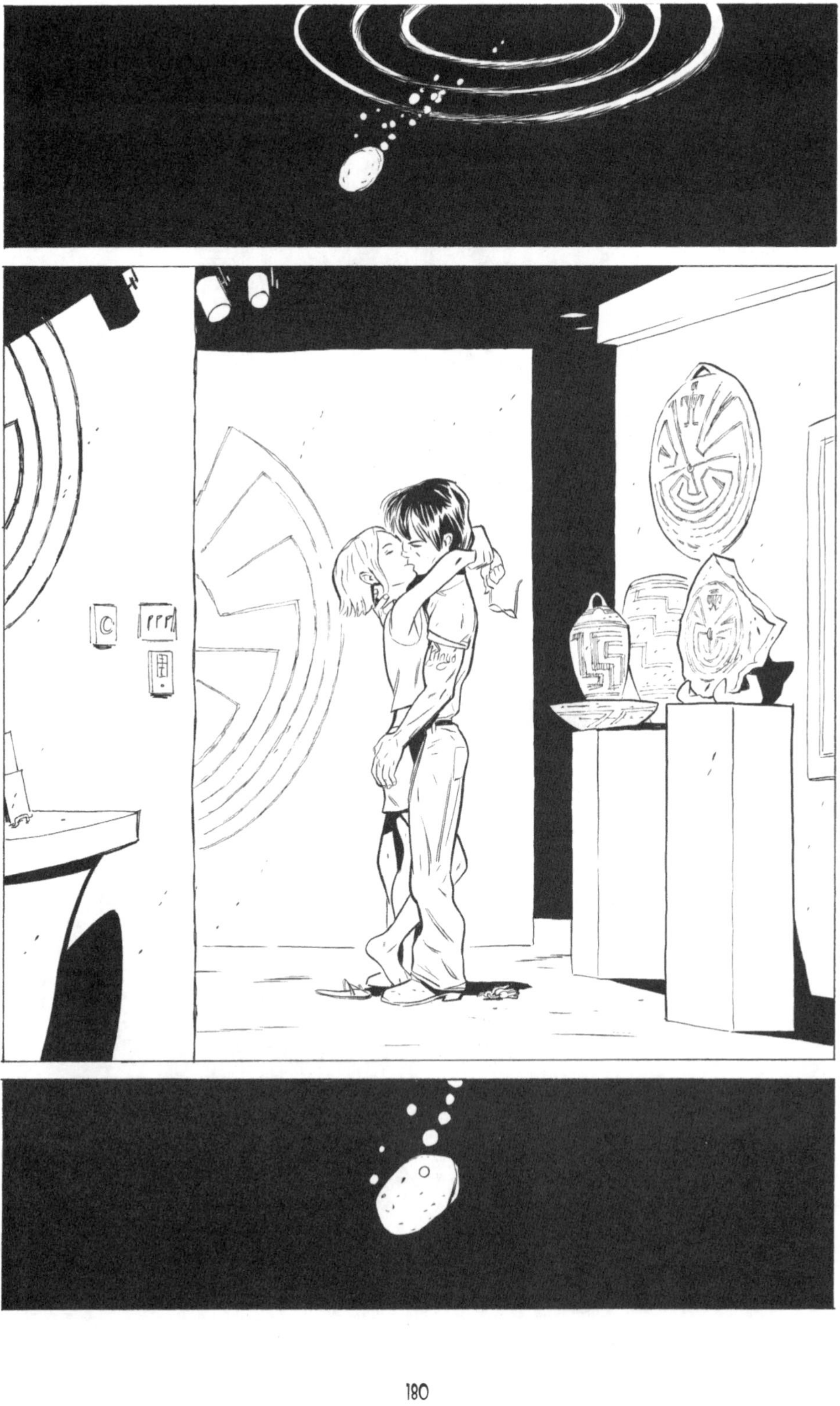

6.
THE MAD SCIENTIST

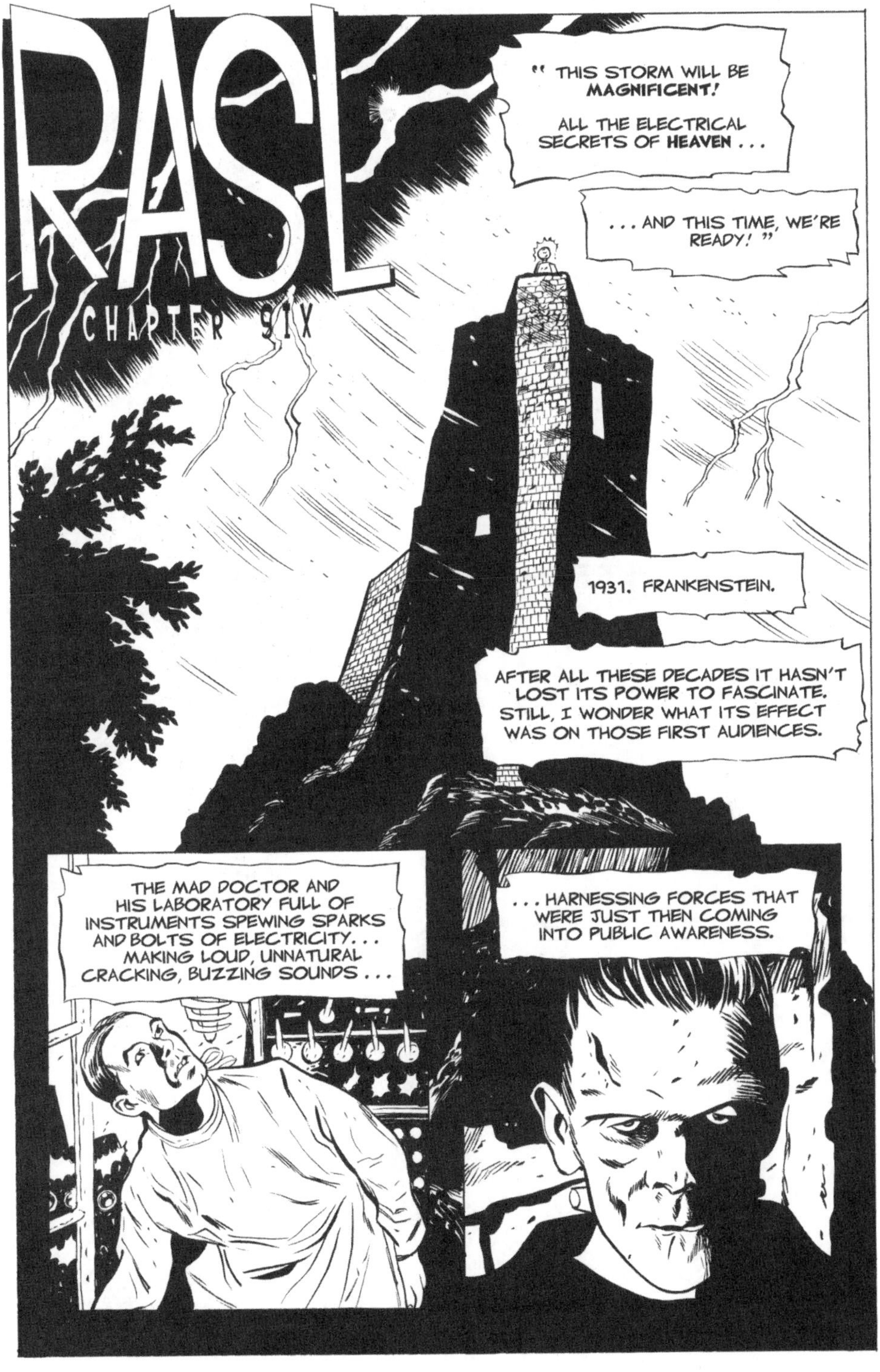
RASL
CHAPTER SIX
" THIS STORM WILL BE **MAGNIFICENT**! ALL THE ELECTRICAL SECRETS OF **HEAVEN** . . .
. . . AND THIS TIME, WE'RE READY! "
1931. FRANKENSTEIN.
AFTER ALL THESE DECADES IT HASN'T LOST ITS POWER TO FASCINATE. STILL, I WONDER WHAT ITS EFFECT WAS ON THOSE FIRST AUDIENCES.
THE MAD DOCTOR AND HIS LABORATORY FULL OF INSTRUMENTS SPEWING SPARKS AND BOLTS OF ELECTRICITY . . . MAKING LOUD, UNNATURAL CRACKING, BUZZING SOUNDS . . .
. . . HARNESSING FORCES THAT WERE JUST THEN COMING INTO PUBLIC AWARENESS.

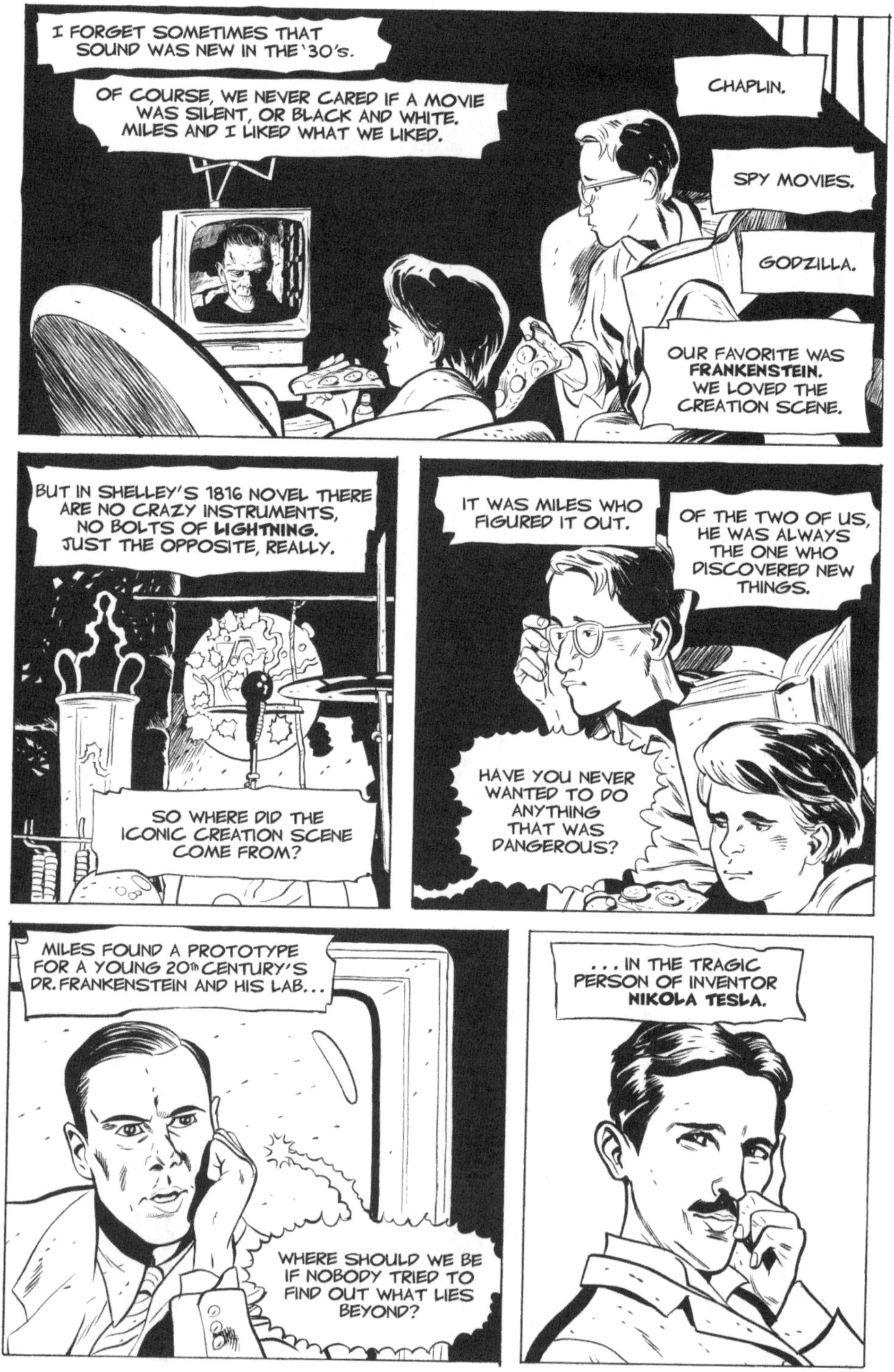

I FORGET SOMETIMES THAT SOUND WAS NEW IN THE '30's.
OF COURSE, WE NEVER CARED IF A MOVIE WAS SILENT, OR BLACK AND WHITE. MILES AND I LIKED WHAT WE LIKED.
CHAPLIN.
SPY MOVIES.
GODZILLA.
OUR FAVORITE WAS FRANKENSTEIN. WE LOVED THE CREATION SCENE.
BUT IN SHELLEY'S 1816 NOVEL THERE ARE NO CRAZY INSTRUMENTS, NO BOLTS OF LIGHTNING. JUST THE OPPOSITE, REALLY.
SO WHERE DID THE ICONIC CREATION SCENE COME FROM?
IT WAS MILES WHO FIGURED IT OUT.
OF THE TWO OF US, HE WAS ALWAYS THE ONE WHO DISCOVERED NEW THINGS.
HAVE YOU NEVER WANTED TO DO ANYTHING THAT WAS DANGEROUS?
MILES FOUND A PROTOTYPE FOR A YOUNG 20th CENTURY'S DR. FRANKENSTEIN AND HIS LAB...
WHERE SHOULD WE BE IF NOBODY TRIED TO FIND OUT WHAT LIES BEYOND?
...IN THE TRAGIC PERSON OF INVENTOR NIKOLA TESLA.

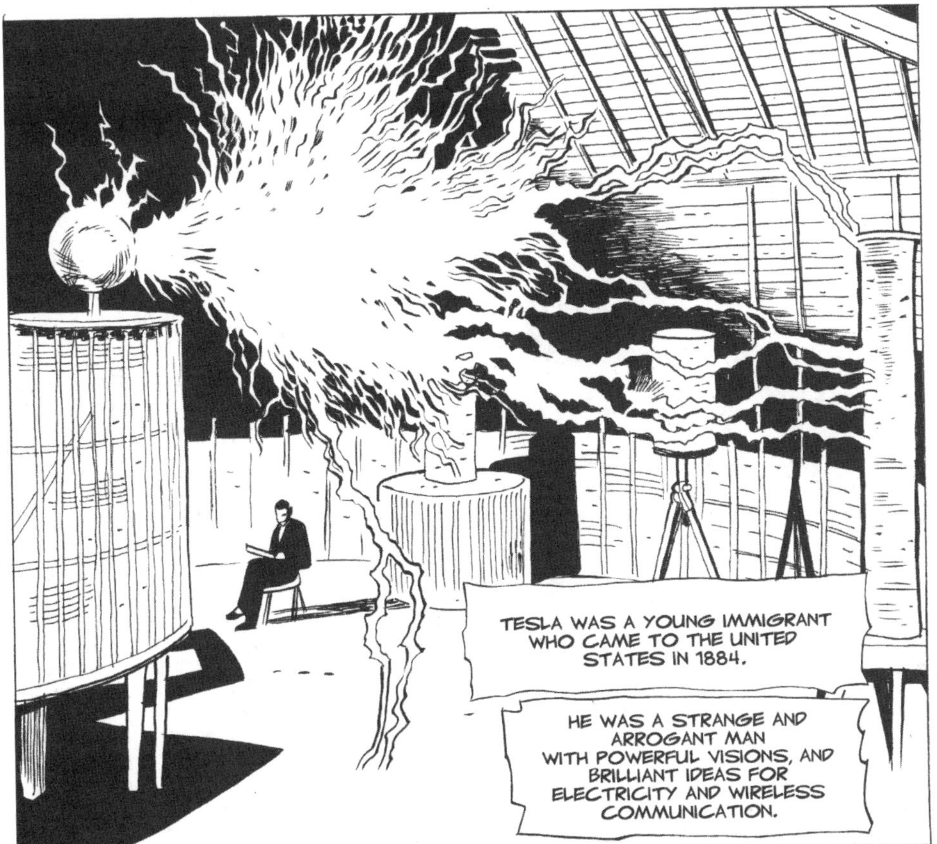
TESLA WAS A YOUNG IMMIGRANT WHO CAME TO THE UNITED STATES IN 1884.
HE WAS A STRANGE AND ARROGANT MAN WITH POWERFUL VISIONS, AND BRILLIANT IDEAS FOR ELECTRICITY AND WIRELESS COMMUNICATION.

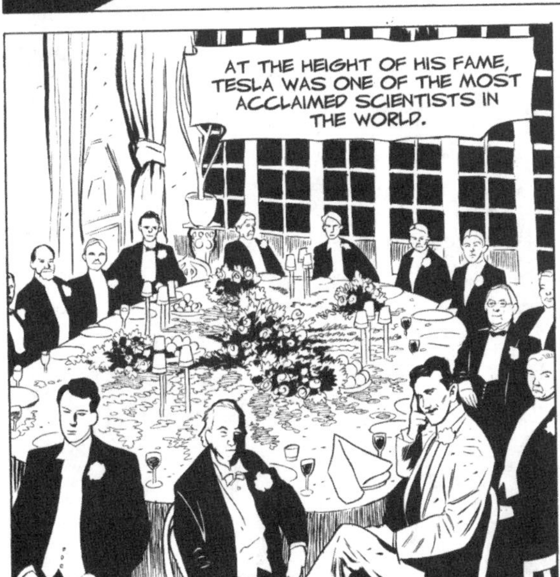
AT THE HEIGHT OF HIS FAME, TESLA WAS ONE OF THE MOST ACCLAIMED SCIENTISTS IN THE WORLD.

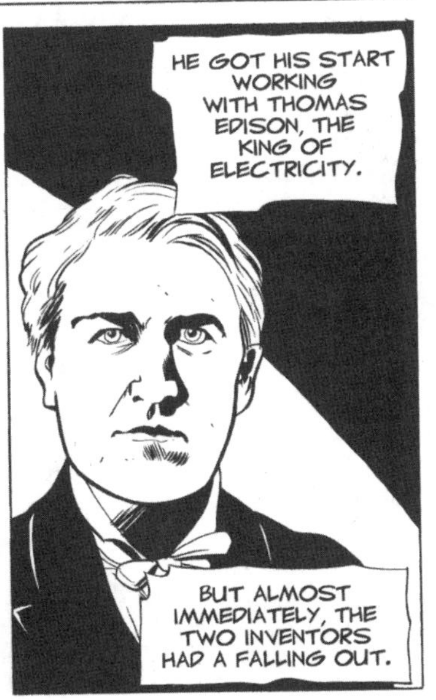
HE GOT HIS START WORKING WITH THOMAS EDISON, THE KING OF ELECTRICITY.
BUT ALMOST IMMEDIATELY, THE TWO INVENTORS HAD A FALLING OUT.

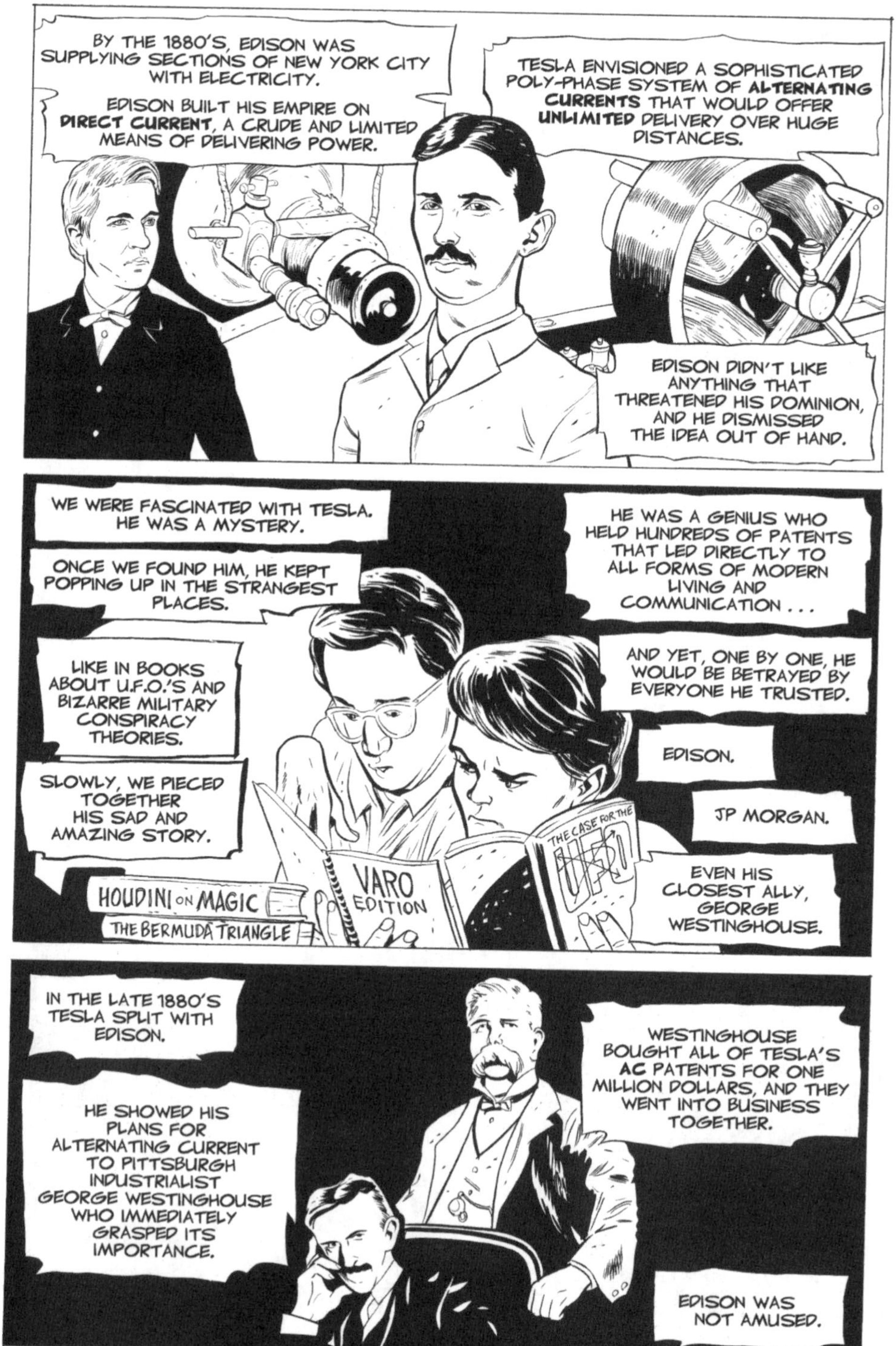
BY THE 1880'S, EDISON WAS SUPPLYING SECTIONS OF NEW YORK CITY WITH ELECTRICITY.
EDISON BUILT HIS EMPIRE ON **DIRECT CURRENT**, A CRUDE AND LIMITED MEANS OF DELIVERING POWER.
TESLA ENVISIONED A SOPHISTICATED POLY-PHASE SYSTEM OF **ALTERNATING CURRENTS** THAT WOULD OFFER **UNLIMITED** DELIVERY OVER HUGE DISTANCES.
EDISON DIDN'T LIKE ANYTHING THAT THREATENED HIS DOMINION, AND HE DISMISSED THE IDEA OUT OF HAND.
WE WERE FASCINATED WITH TESLA. HE WAS A MYSTERY.
ONCE WE FOUND HIM, HE KEPT POPPING UP IN THE STRANGEST PLACES.
LIKE IN BOOKS ABOUT U.F.O.'S AND BIZARRE MILITARY CONSPIRACY THEORIES.
SLOWLY, WE PIECED TOGETHER HIS SAD AND AMAZING STORY.
HOUDINI ON MAGIC
THE BERMUDA TRIANGLE
VARO EDITION
THE CASE FOR THE UFO
HE WAS A GENIUS WHO HELD HUNDREDS OF PATENTS THAT LED DIRECTLY TO ALL FORMS OF MODERN LIVING AND COMMUNICATION . . .
AND YET, ONE BY ONE, HE WOULD BE BETRAYED BY EVERYONE HE TRUSTED.
EDISON.
JP MORGAN.
EVEN HIS CLOSEST ALLY, GEORGE WESTINGHOUSE.
IN THE LATE 1880'S TESLA SPLIT WITH EDISON.
HE SHOWED HIS PLANS FOR ALTERNATING CURRENT TO PITTSBURGH INDUSTRIALIST GEORGE WESTINGHOUSE WHO IMMEDIATELY GRASPED ITS IMPORTANCE.
WESTINGHOUSE BOUGHT ALL OF TESLA'S **AC** PATENTS FOR ONE MILLION DOLLARS, AND THEY WENT INTO BUSINESS TOGETHER.
EDISON WAS NOT AMUSED.

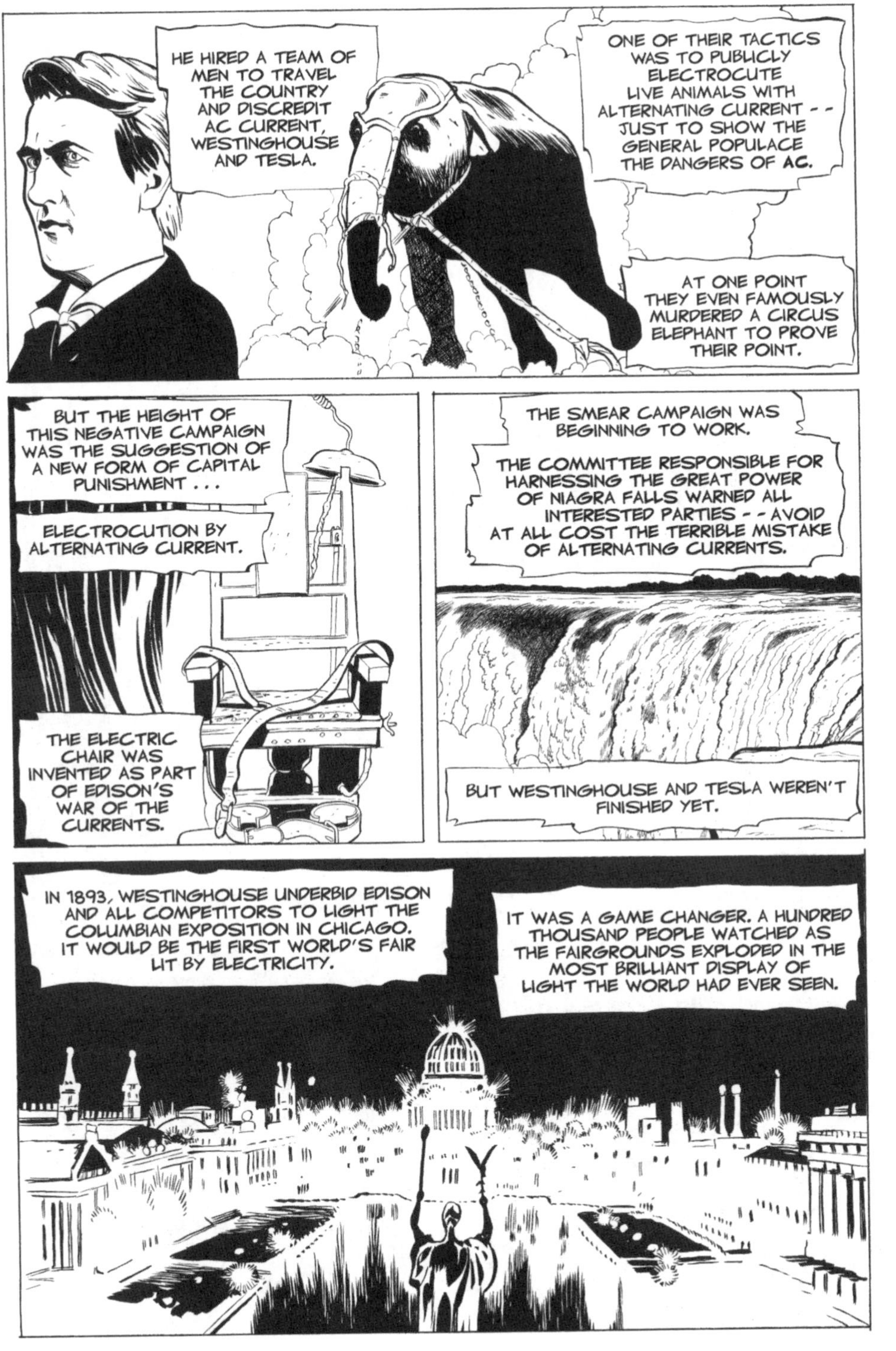
HE HIRED A TEAM OF MEN TO TRAVEL THE COUNTRY AND DISCREDIT AC CURRENT, WESTINGHOUSE AND TESLA.
ONE OF THEIR TACTICS WAS TO PUBLICLY ELECTROCUTE LIVE ANIMALS WITH ALTERNATING CURRENT - - JUST TO SHOW THE GENERAL POPULACE THE DANGERS OF AC.
AT ONE POINT THEY EVEN FAMOUSLY MURDERED A CIRCUS ELEPHANT TO PROVE THEIR POINT.
BUT THE HEIGHT OF THIS NEGATIVE CAMPAIGN WAS THE SUGGESTION OF A NEW FORM OF CAPITAL PUNISHMENT . . .
ELECTROCUTION BY ALTERNATING CURRENT.
THE ELECTRIC CHAIR WAS INVENTED AS PART OF EDISON'S WAR OF THE CURRENTS.
THE SMEAR CAMPAIGN WAS BEGINNING TO WORK.
THE COMMITTEE RESPONSIBLE FOR HARNESSING THE GREAT POWER OF NIAGRA FALLS WARNED ALL INTERESTED PARTIES - - AVOID AT ALL COST THE TERRIBLE MISTAKE OF ALTERNATING CURRENTS.
BUT WESTINGHOUSE AND TESLA WEREN'T FINISHED YET.
IN 1893, WESTINGHOUSE UNDERBID EDISON AND ALL COMPETITORS TO LIGHT THE COLUMBIAN EXPOSITION IN CHICAGO. IT WOULD BE THE FIRST WORLD'S FAIR LIT BY ELECTRICITY.
IT WAS A GAME CHANGER. A HUNDRED THOUSAND PEOPLE WATCHED AS THE FAIRGROUNDS EXPLODED IN THE MOST BRILLIANT DISPLAY OF LIGHT THE WORLD HAD EVER SEEN.

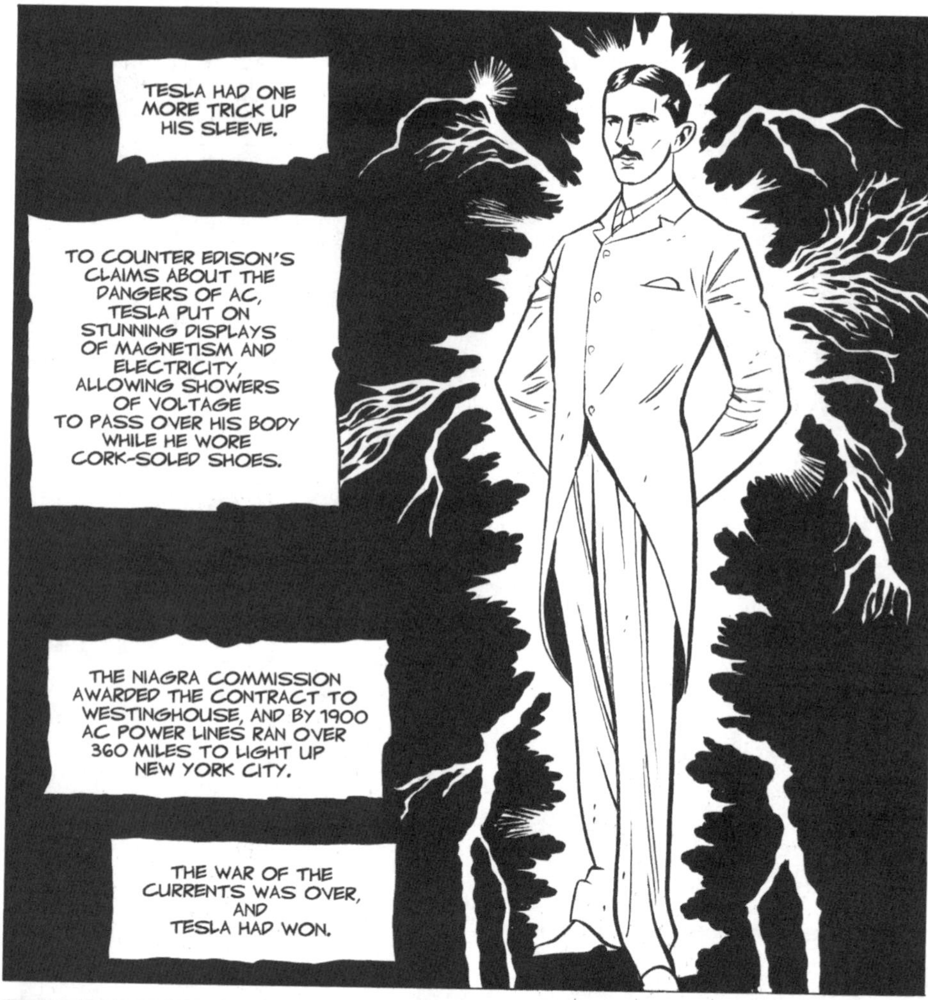
TESLA HAD ONE MORE TRICK UP HIS SLEEVE.
TO COUNTER EDISON'S CLAIMS ABOUT THE DANGERS OF AC, TESLA PUT ON STUNNING DISPLAYS OF MAGNETISM AND ELECTRICITY, ALLOWING SHOWERS OF VOLTAGE TO PASS OVER HIS BODY WHILE HE WORE CORK-SOLED SHOES.
THE NIAGRA COMMISSION AWARDED THE CONTRACT TO WESTINGHOUSE, AND BY 1900 AC POWER LINES RAN OVER 360 MILES TO LIGHT UP NEW YORK CITY.
THE WAR OF THE CURRENTS WAS OVER, AND TESLA HAD WON.
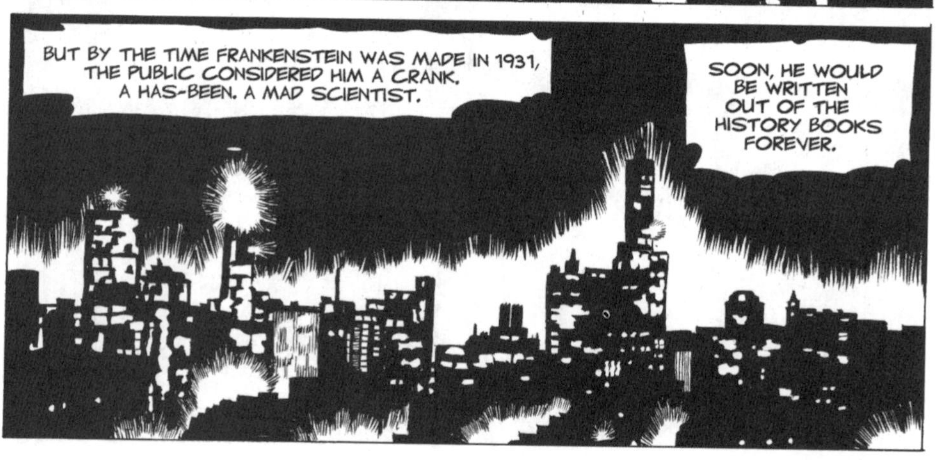
BUT BY THE TIME FRANKENSTEIN WAS MADE IN 1931, THE PUBLIC CONSIDERED HIM A CRANK. A HAS-BEEN. A MAD SCIENTIST.
SOON, HE WOULD BE WRITTEN OUT OF THE HISTORY BOOKS FOREVER.

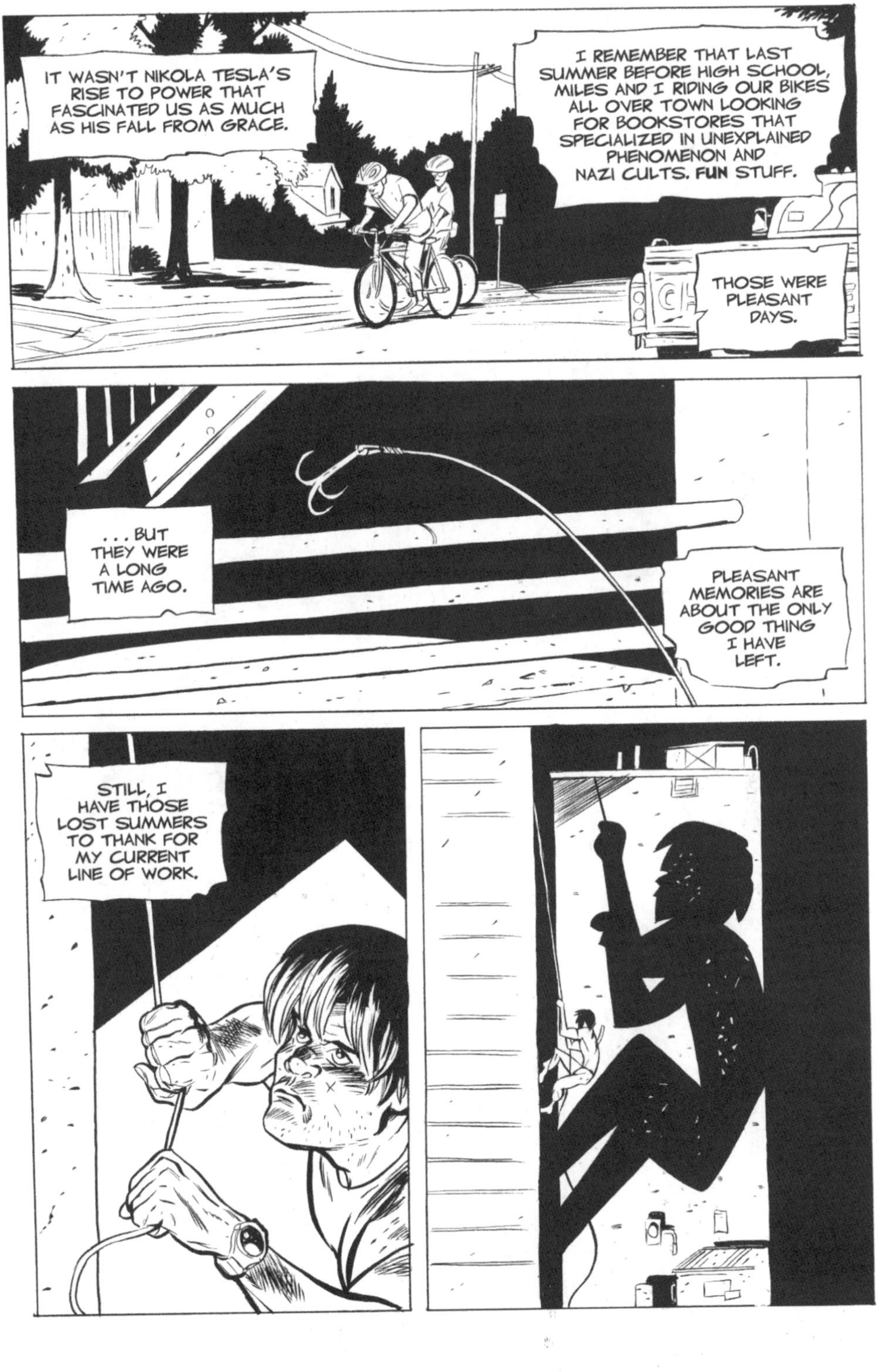
IT WASN'T NIKOLA TESLA'S RISE TO POWER THAT FASCINATED US AS MUCH AS HIS FALL FROM GRACE.
I REMEMBER THAT LAST SUMMER BEFORE HIGH SCHOOL, MILES AND I RIDING OUR BIKES ALL OVER TOWN LOOKING FOR BOOKSTORES THAT SPECIALIZED IN UNEXPLAINED PHENOMENON AND NAZI CULTS. FUN STUFF.
THOSE WERE PLEASANT DAYS.
...BUT THEY WERE A LONG TIME AGO.
PLEASANT MEMORIES ARE ABOUT THE ONLY GOOD THING I HAVE LEFT.
STILL, I HAVE THOSE LOST SUMMERS TO THANK FOR MY CURRENT LINE OF WORK.

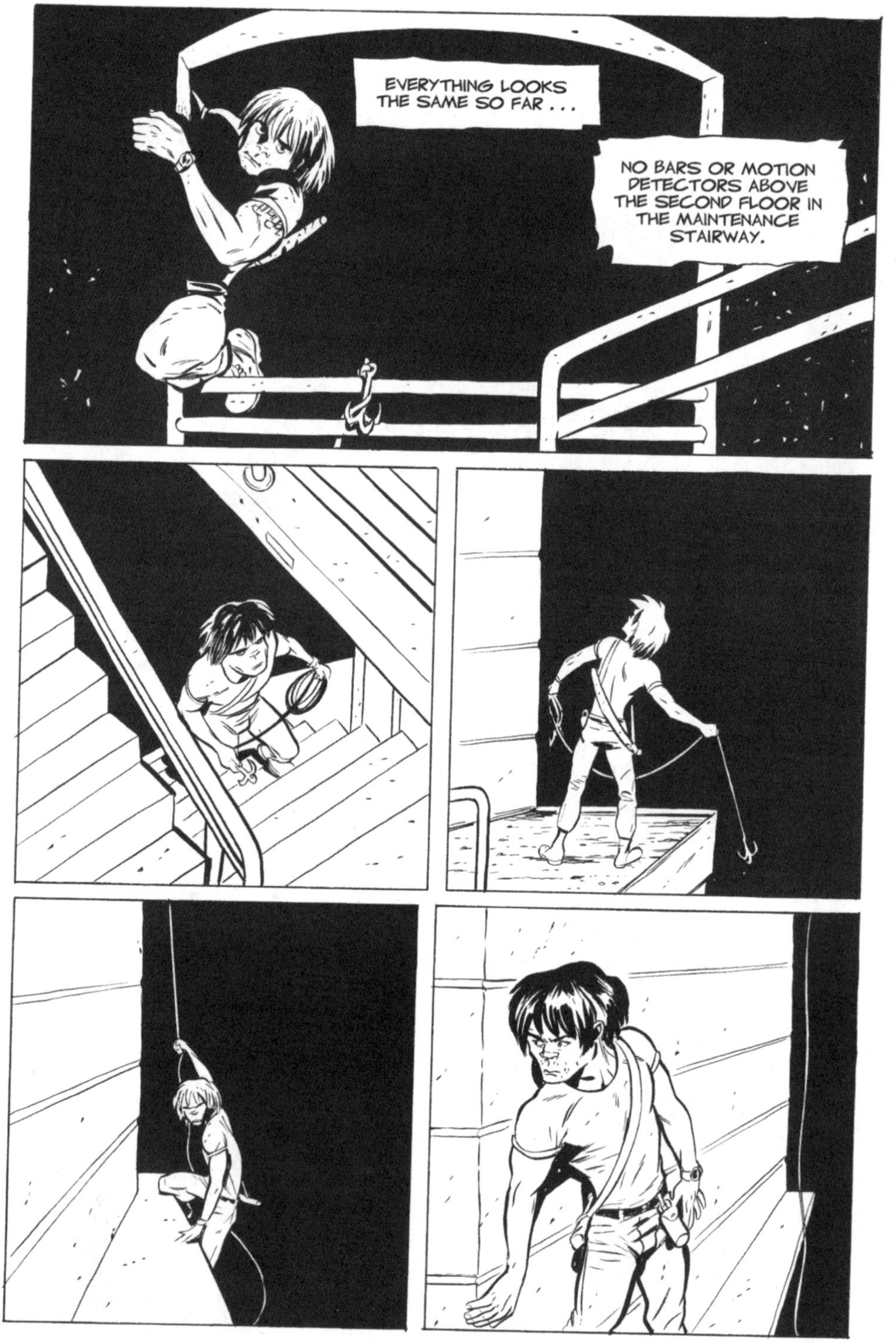
EVERYTHING LOOKS THE SAME SO FAR . . .
NO BARS OR MOTION DETECTORS ABOVE THE SECOND FLOOR IN THE MAINTENANCE STAIRWAY.

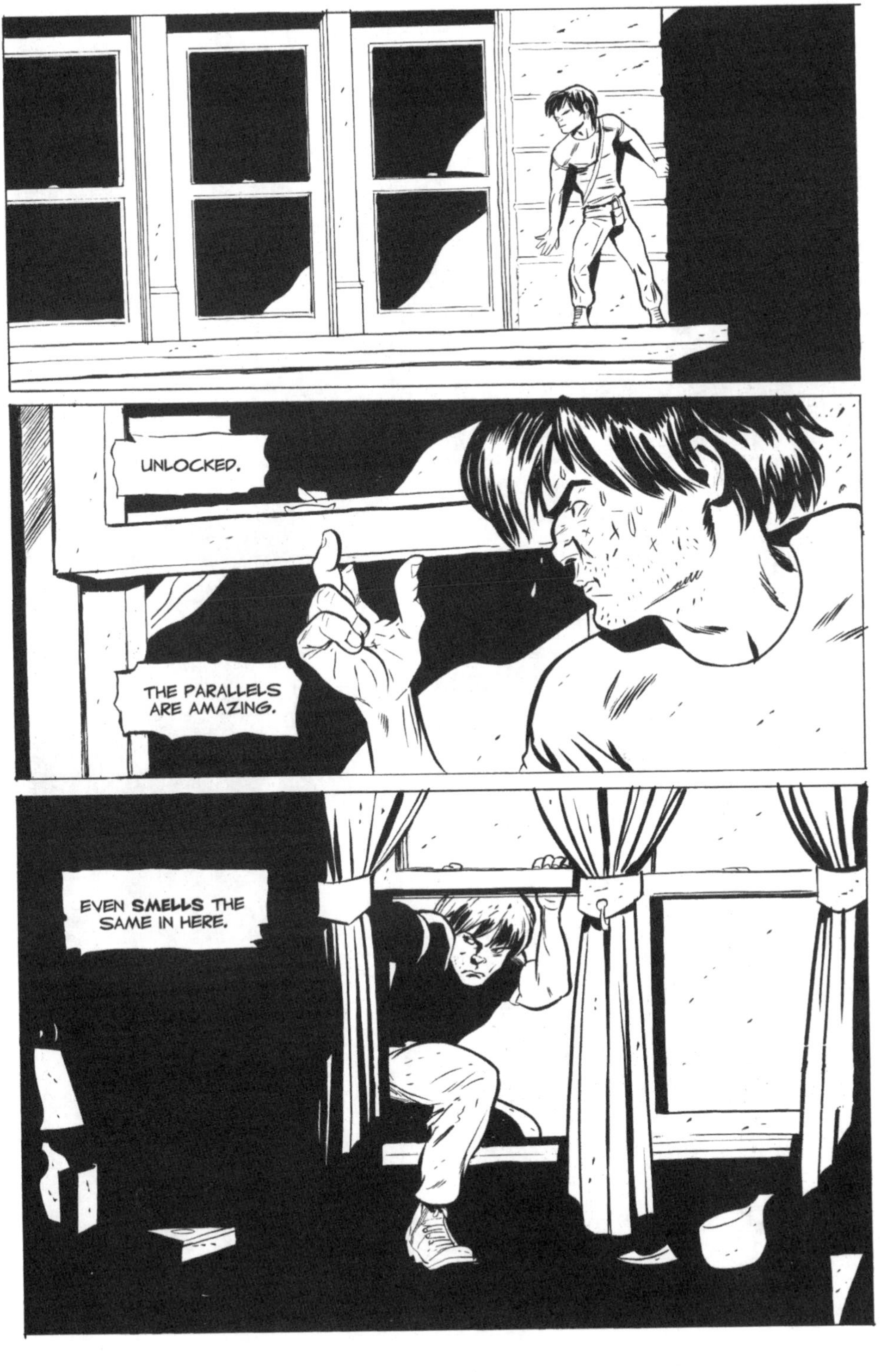
UNLOCKED.
THE PARALLELS ARE AMAZING.
EVEN SMELLS THE SAME IN HERE.

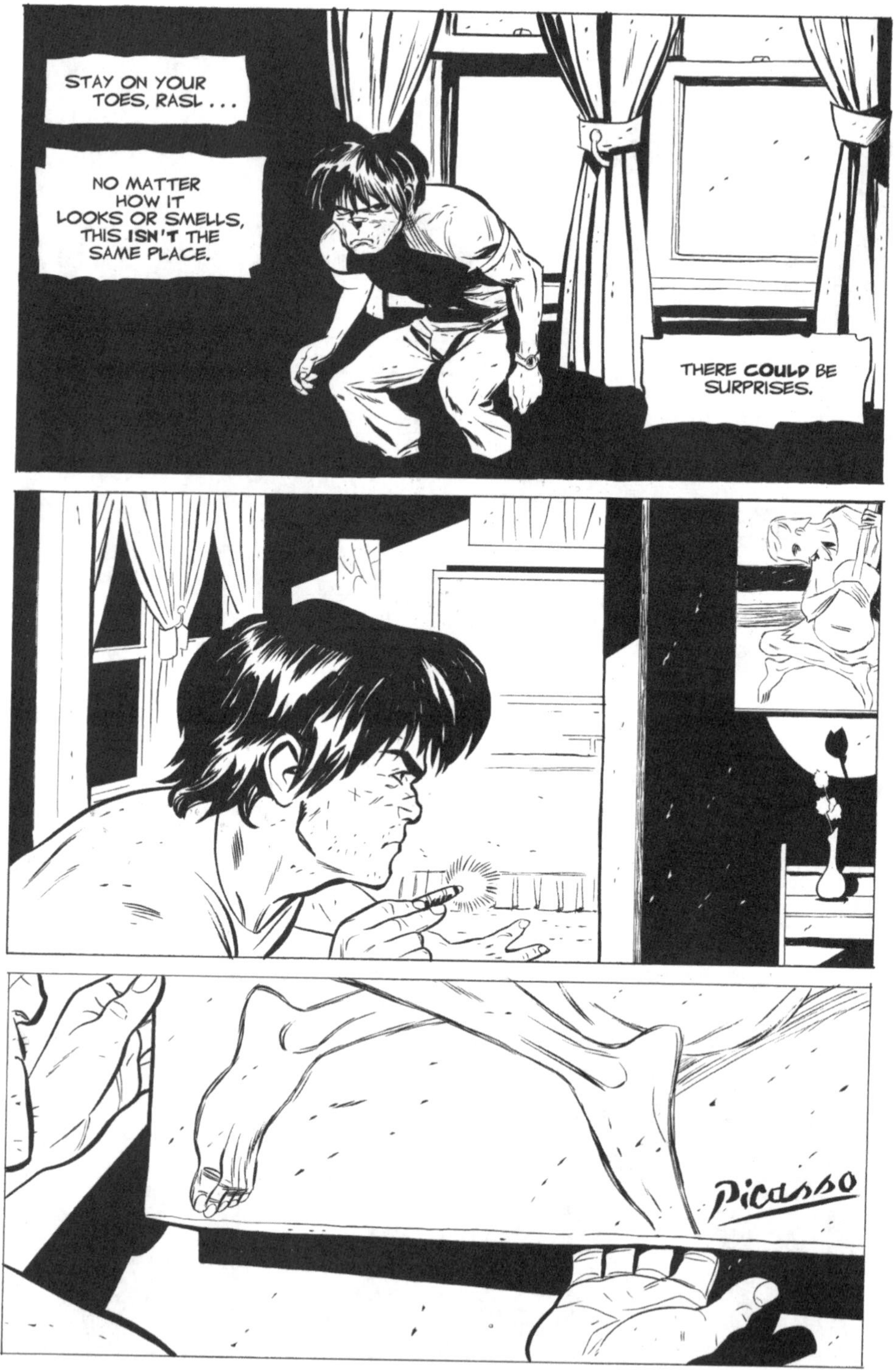

STAY ON YOUR TOES, RASL . . .
NO MATTER HOW IT LOOKS OR SMELLS, THIS ISN'T THE SAME PLACE.
THERE COULD BE SURPRISES.
Picasso

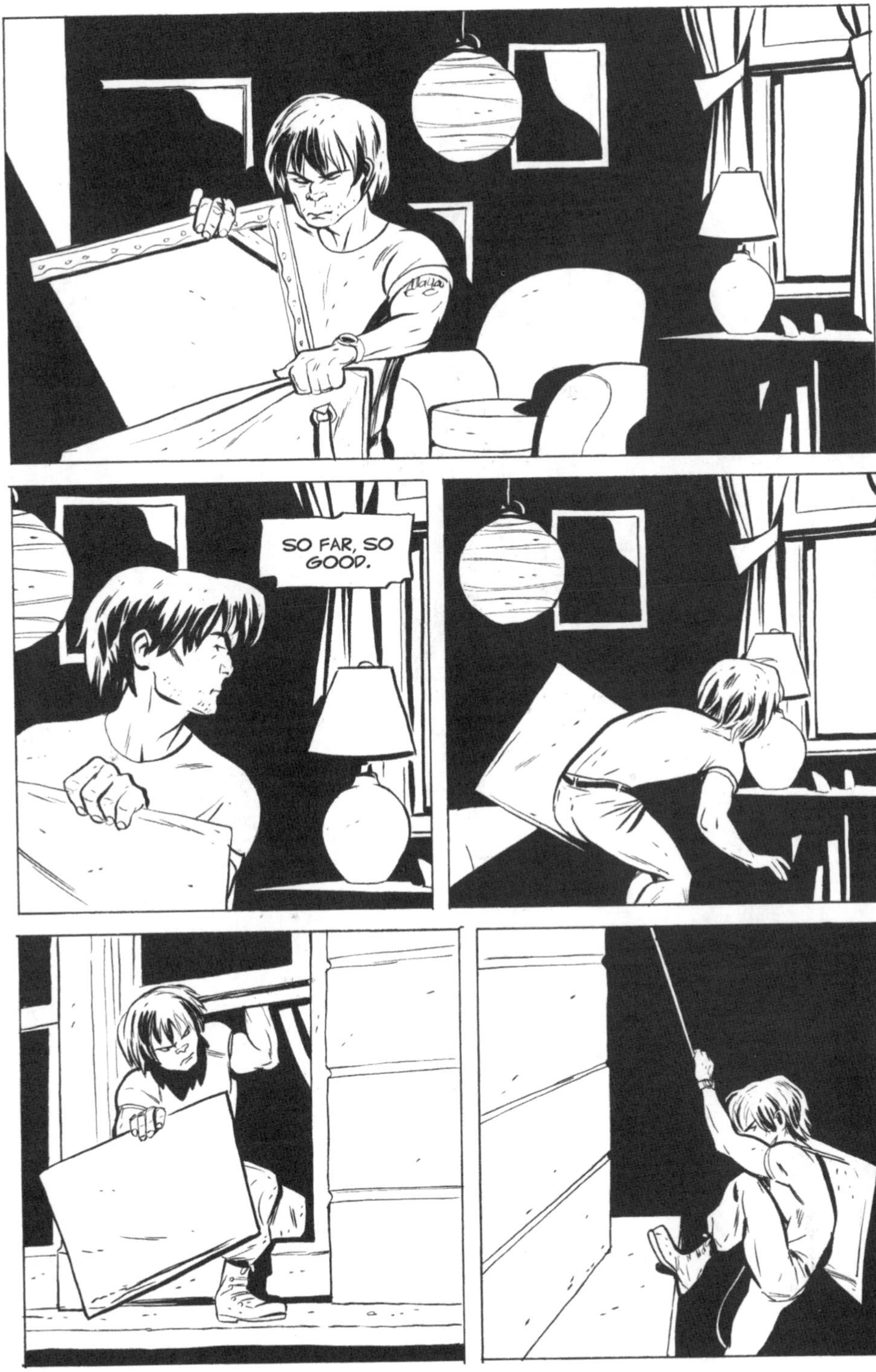
SO FAR, SO GOOD.

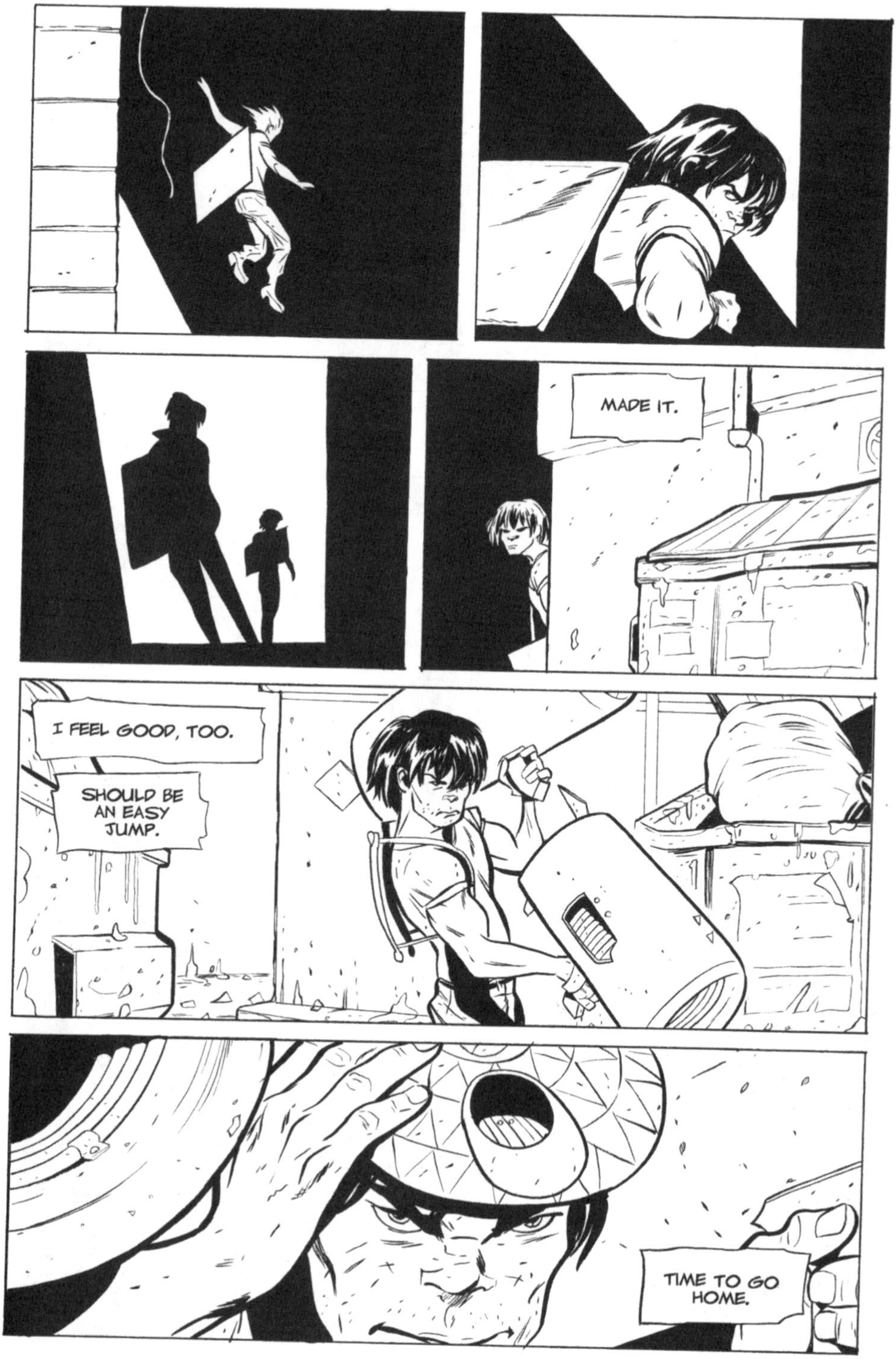
MADE IT.
I FEEL GOOD, TOO.
SHOULD BE AN EASY JUMP.
TIME TO GO HOME.

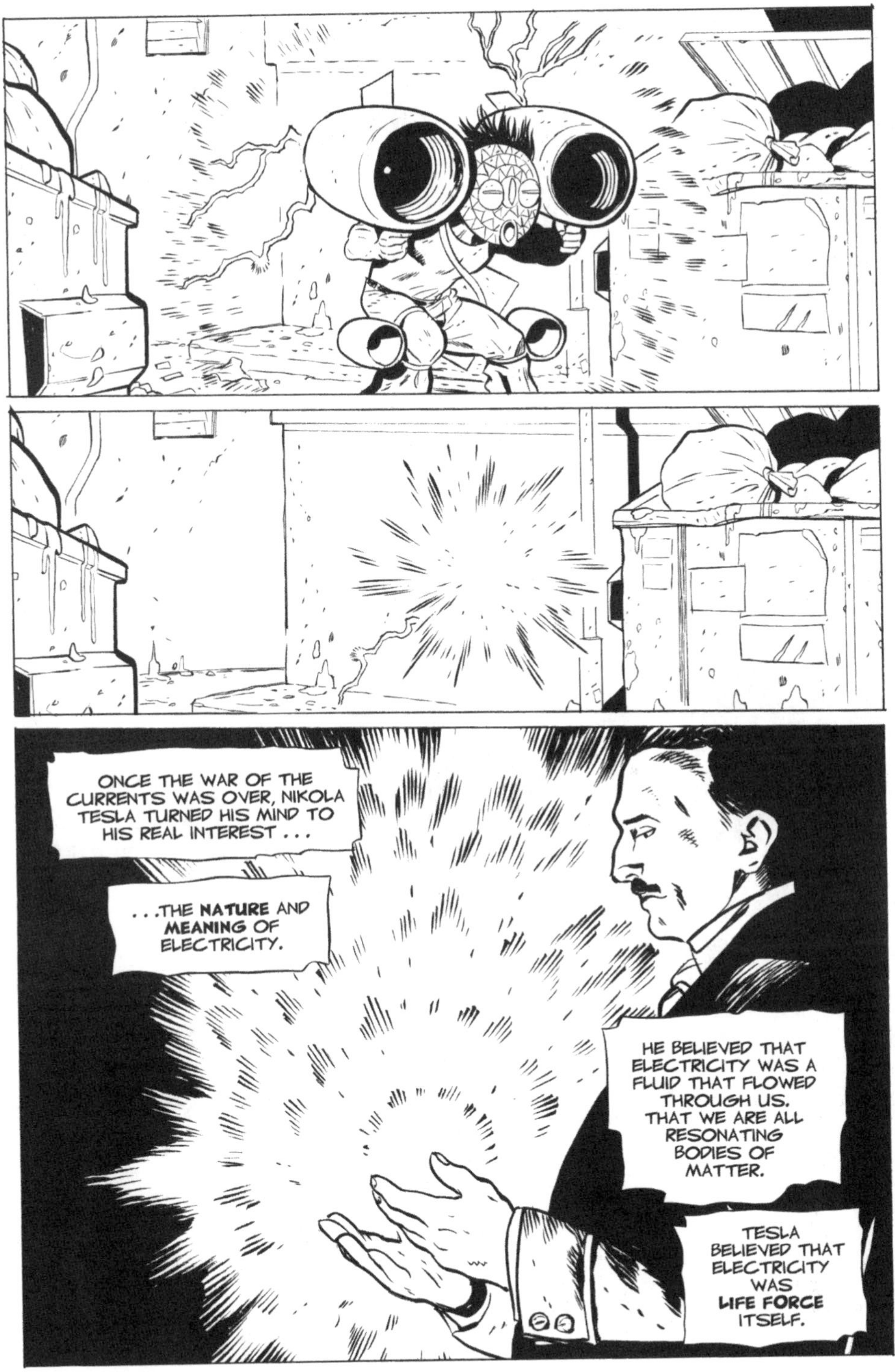
ONCE THE WAR OF THE CURRENTS WAS OVER, NIKOLA TESLA TURNED HIS MIND TO HIS REAL INTEREST . . .
. . .THE **NATURE** AND **MEANING** OF ELECTRICITY.
HE BELIEVED THAT ELECTRICITY WAS A FLUID THAT FLOWED THROUGH US. THAT WE ARE ALL RESONATING BODIES OF MATTER.
TESLA BELIEVED THAT ELECTRICITY WAS **LIFE FORCE** ITSELF.

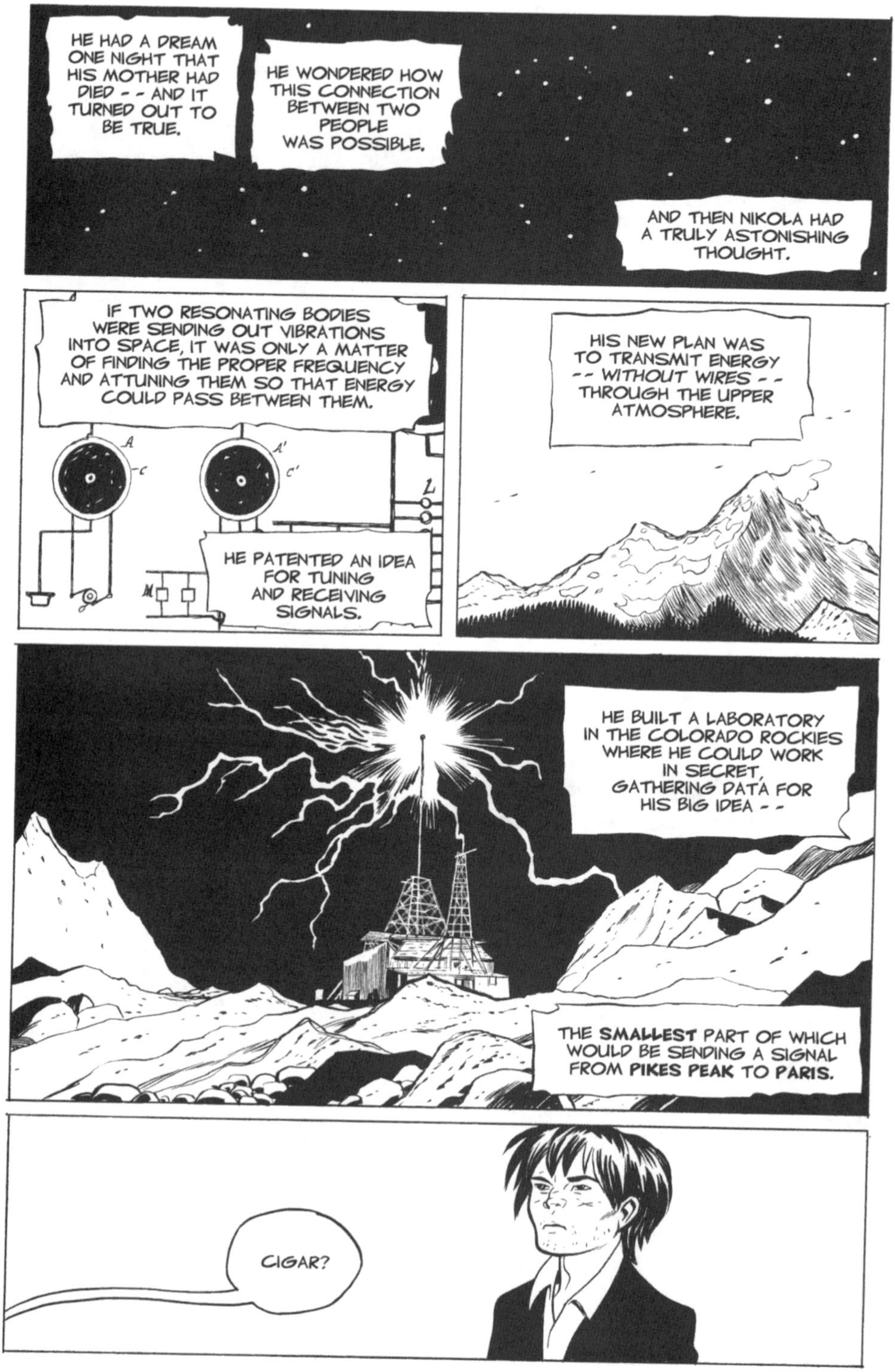
HE HAD A DREAM ONE NIGHT THAT HIS MOTHER HAD DIED - - AND IT TURNED OUT TO BE TRUE.
HE WONDERED HOW THIS CONNECTION BETWEEN TWO PEOPLE WAS POSSIBLE.
AND THEN NIKOLA HAD A TRULY ASTONISHING THOUGHT.
IF TWO RESONATING BODIES WERE SENDING OUT VIBRATIONS INTO SPACE, IT WAS ONLY A MATTER OF FINDING THE PROPER FREQUENCY AND ATTUNING THEM SO THAT ENERGY COULD PASS BETWEEN THEM.
HE PATENTED AN IDEA FOR TUNING AND RECEIVING SIGNALS.
HIS NEW PLAN WAS TO TRANSMIT ENERGY - - WITHOUT WIRES - - THROUGH THE UPPER ATMOSPHERE.
HE BUILT A LABORATORY IN THE COLORADO ROCKIES WHERE HE COULD WORK IN SECRET, GATHERING DATA FOR HIS BIG IDEA - -
THE SMALLEST PART OF WHICH WOULD BE SENDING A SIGNAL FROM PIKES PEAK TO PARIS.
CIGAR?

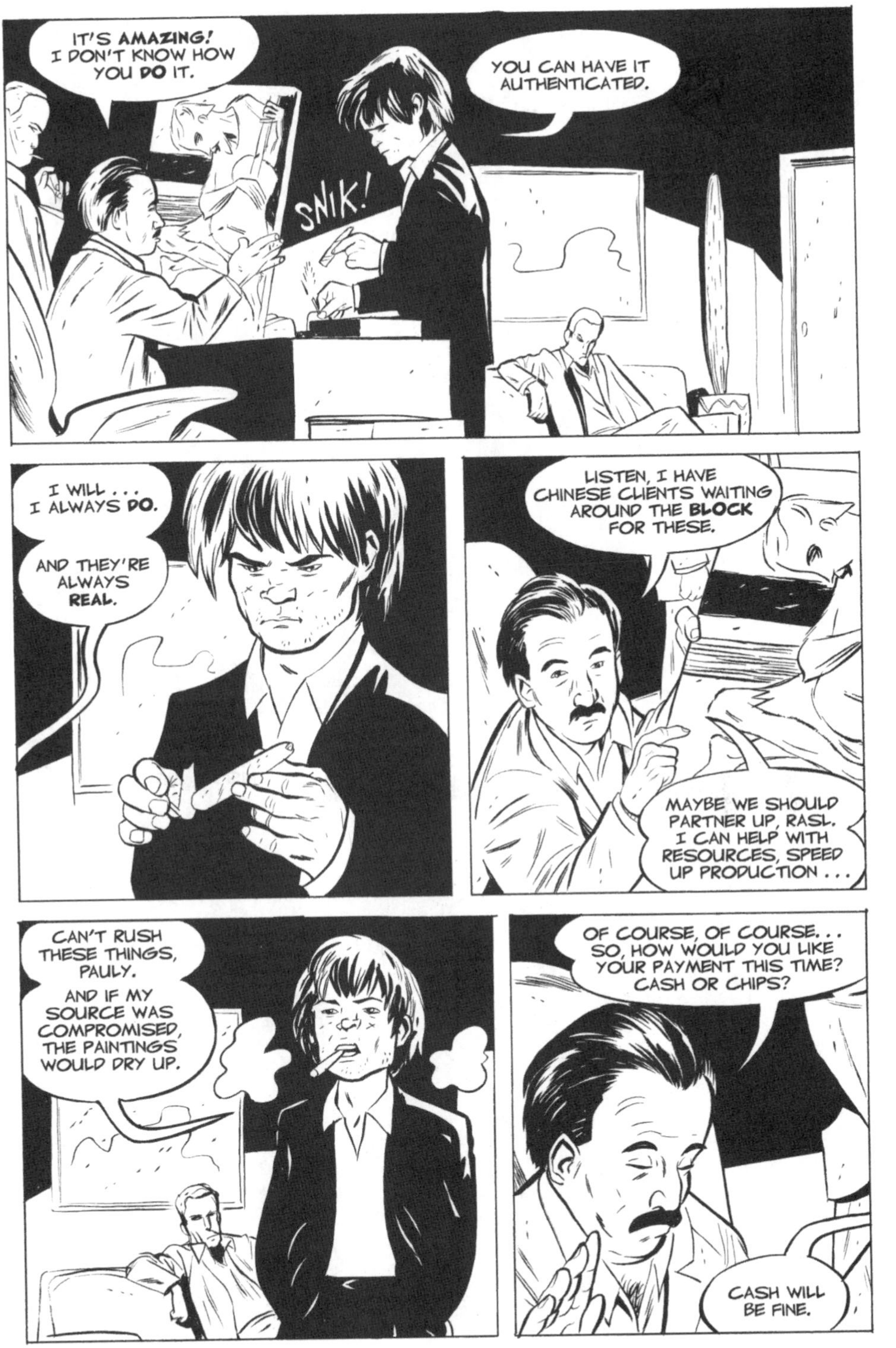
IT'S AMAZING! I DON'T KNOW HOW YOU DO IT.
YOU CAN HAVE IT AUTHENTICATED.
SNIK!
I WILL . . . I ALWAYS DO.
AND THEY'RE ALWAYS REAL.
LISTEN, I HAVE CHINESE CLIENTS WAITING AROUND THE BLOCK FOR THESE.
MAYBE WE SHOULD PARTNER UP, RASL. I CAN HELP WITH RESOURCES, SPEED UP PRODUCTION . . .
CAN'T RUSH THESE THINGS, PAULY.
AND IF MY SOURCE WAS COMPROMISED, THE PAINTINGS WOULD DRY UP.
OF COURSE, OF COURSE. . . SO, HOW WOULD YOU LIKE YOUR PAYMENT THIS TIME? CASH OR CHIPS?
CASH WILL BE FINE.

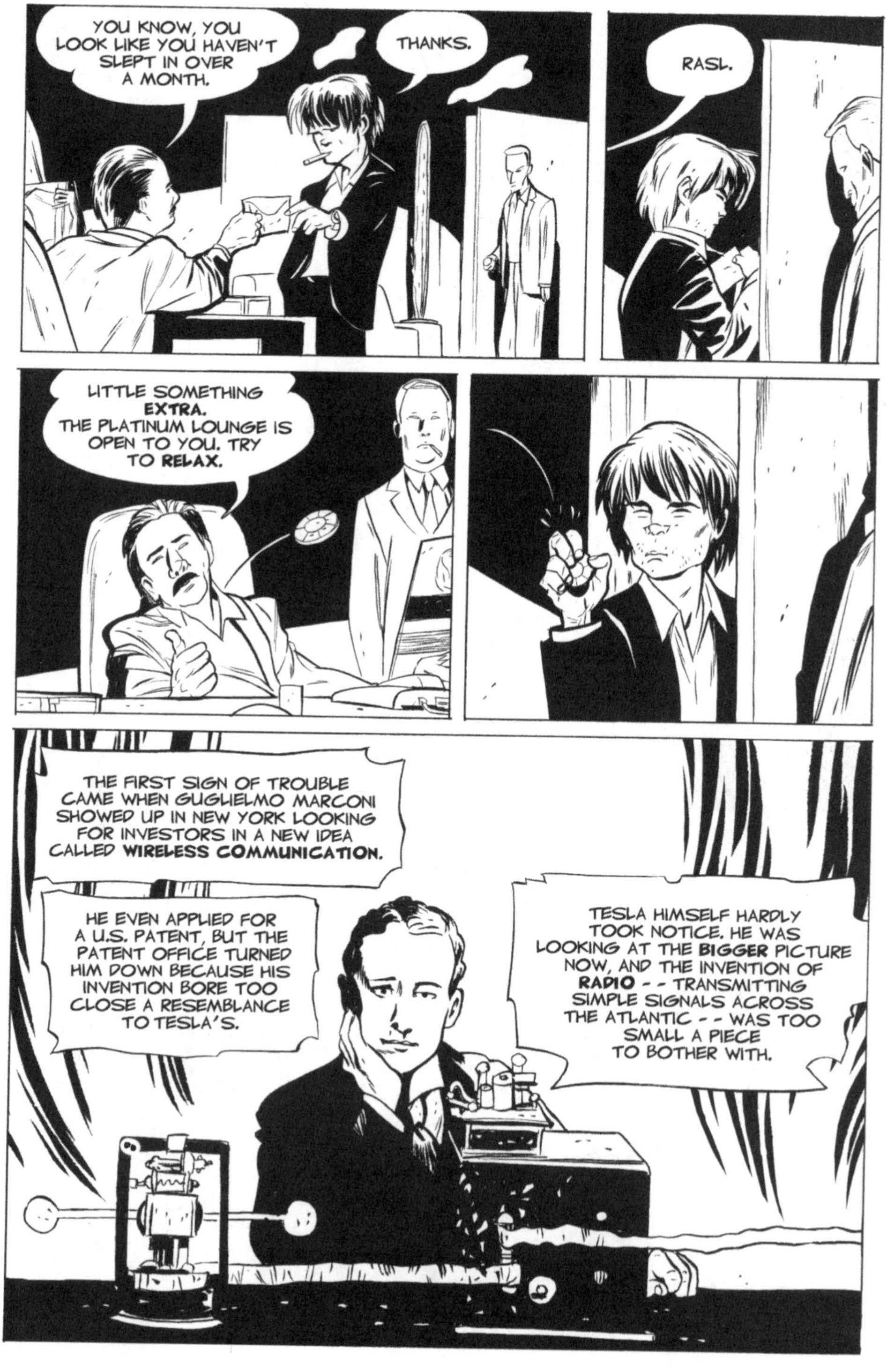
YOU KNOW, YOU LOOK LIKE YOU HAVEN'T SLEPT IN OVER A MONTH.
THANKS.
RASL.
LITTLE SOMETHING EXTRA. THE PLATINUM LOUNGE IS OPEN TO YOU. TRY TO RELAX.
THE FIRST SIGN OF TROUBLE CAME WHEN GUGLIELMO MARCONI SHOWED UP IN NEW YORK LOOKING FOR INVESTORS IN A NEW IDEA CALLED WIRELESS COMMUNICATION.
HE EVEN APPLIED FOR A U.S. PATENT, BUT THE PATENT OFFICE TURNED HIM DOWN BECAUSE HIS INVENTION BORE TOO CLOSE A RESEMBLANCE TO TESLA'S.
TESLA HIMSELF HARDLY TOOK NOTICE. HE WAS LOOKING AT THE BIGGER PICTURE NOW, AND THE INVENTION OF RADIO - - TRANSMITTING SIMPLE SIGNALS ACROSS THE ATLANTIC - - WAS TOO SMALL A PIECE TO BOTHER WITH.

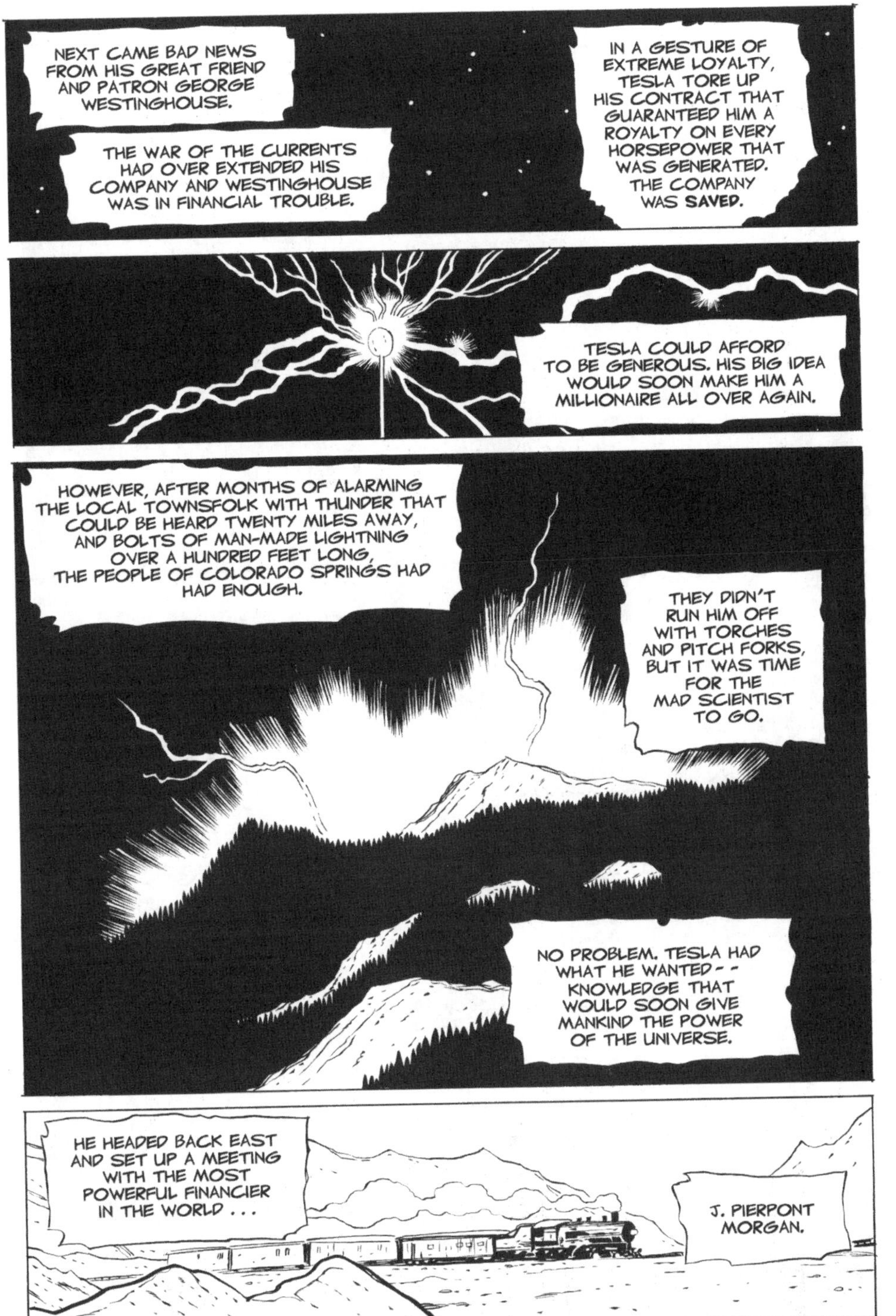
NEXT CAME BAD NEWS FROM HIS GREAT FRIEND AND PATRON GEORGE WESTINGHOUSE.
THE WAR OF THE CURRENTS HAD OVER EXTENDED HIS COMPANY AND WESTINGHOUSE WAS IN FINANCIAL TROUBLE.
IN A GESTURE OF EXTREME LOYALTY, TESLA TORE UP HIS CONTRACT THAT GUARANTEED HIM A ROYALTY ON EVERY HORSEPOWER THAT WAS GENERATED. THE COMPANY WAS **SAVED**.
TESLA COULD AFFORD TO BE GENEROUS. HIS BIG IDEA WOULD SOON MAKE HIM A MILLIONAIRE ALL OVER AGAIN.
HOWEVER, AFTER MONTHS OF ALARMING THE LOCAL TOWNSFOLK WITH THUNDER THAT COULD BE HEARD TWENTY MILES AWAY, AND BOLTS OF MAN-MADE LIGHTNING OVER A HUNDRED FEET LONG, THE PEOPLE OF COLORADO SPRINGS HAD HAD ENOUGH.
THEY DIDN'T RUN HIM OFF WITH TORCHES AND PITCH FORKS, BUT IT WAS TIME FOR THE MAD SCIENTIST TO GO.
NO PROBLEM. TESLA HAD WHAT HE WANTED- - KNOWLEDGE THAT WOULD SOON GIVE MANKIND THE POWER OF THE UNIVERSE.
HE HEADED BACK EAST AND SET UP A MEETING WITH THE MOST POWERFUL FINANCIER IN THE WORLD . . .
J. PIERPONT MORGAN.

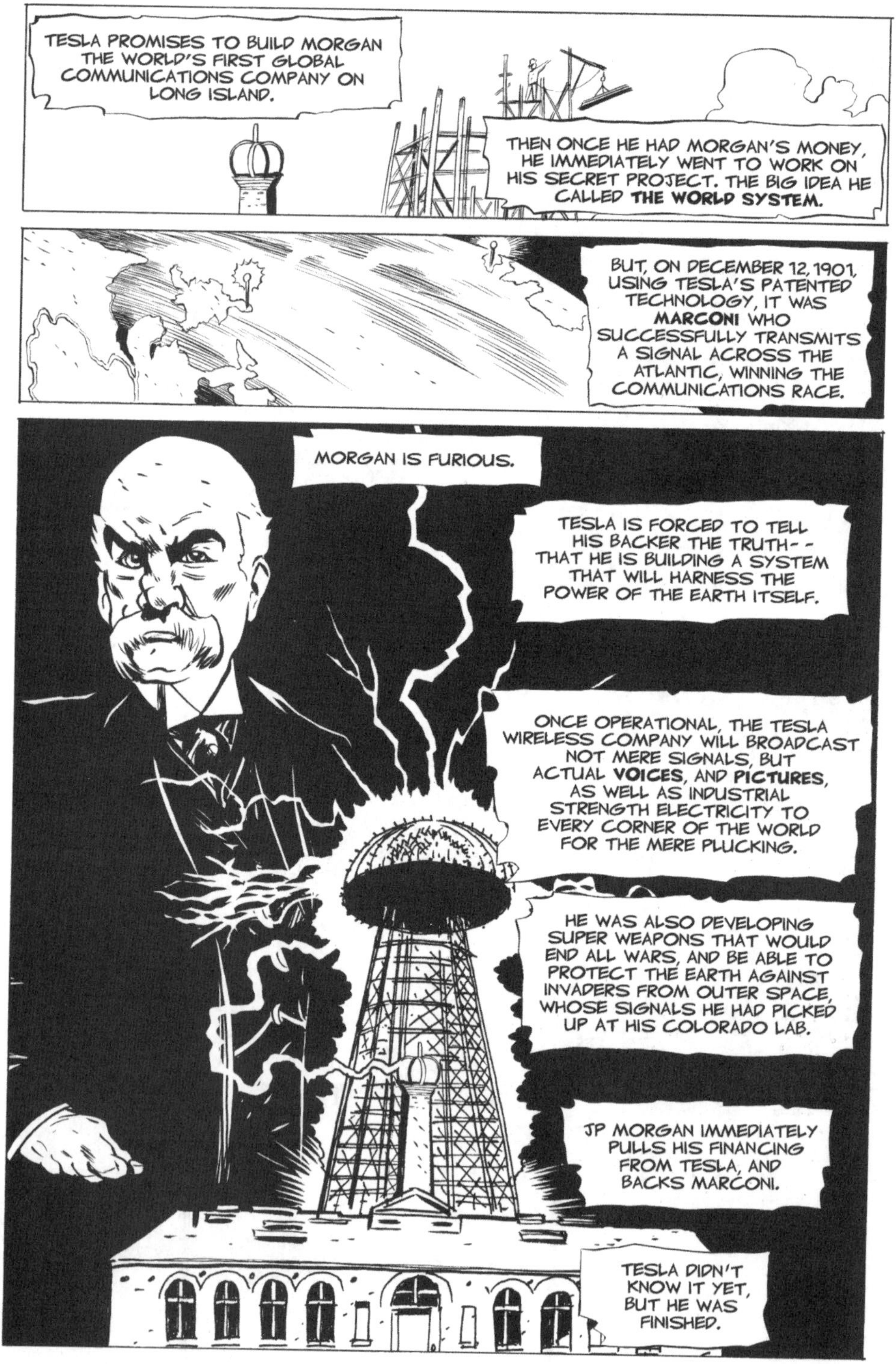
TESLA PROMISES TO BUILD MORGAN THE WORLD'S FIRST GLOBAL COMMUNICATIONS COMPANY ON LONG ISLAND.
THEN ONCE HE HAD MORGAN'S MONEY, HE IMMEDIATELY WENT TO WORK ON HIS SECRET PROJECT. THE BIG IDEA HE CALLED **THE WORLD SYSTEM.**
BUT, ON DECEMBER 12, 1901, USING TESLA'S PATENTED TECHNOLOGY, IT WAS **MARCONI** WHO SUCCESSFULLY TRANSMITS A SIGNAL ACROSS THE ATLANTIC, WINNING THE COMMUNICATIONS RACE.
MORGAN IS FURIOUS.
TESLA IS FORCED TO TELL HIS BACKER THE TRUTH-- THAT HE IS BUILDING A SYSTEM THAT WILL HARNESS THE POWER OF THE EARTH ITSELF.
ONCE OPERATIONAL, THE TESLA WIRELESS COMPANY WILL BROADCAST NOT MERE SIGNALS, BUT ACTUAL **VOICES**, AND **PICTURES**, AS WELL AS INDUSTRIAL STRENGTH ELECTRICITY TO EVERY CORNER OF THE WORLD FOR THE MERE PLUCKING.
HE WAS ALSO DEVELOPING SUPER WEAPONS THAT WOULD END ALL WARS, AND BE ABLE TO PROTECT THE EARTH AGAINST INVADERS FROM OUTER SPACE, WHOSE SIGNALS HE HAD PICKED UP AT HIS COLORADO LAB.
JP MORGAN IMMEDIATELY PULLS HIS FINANCING FROM TESLA, AND BACKS MARCONI.
TESLA DIDN'T KNOW IT YET, BUT HE WAS FINISHED.

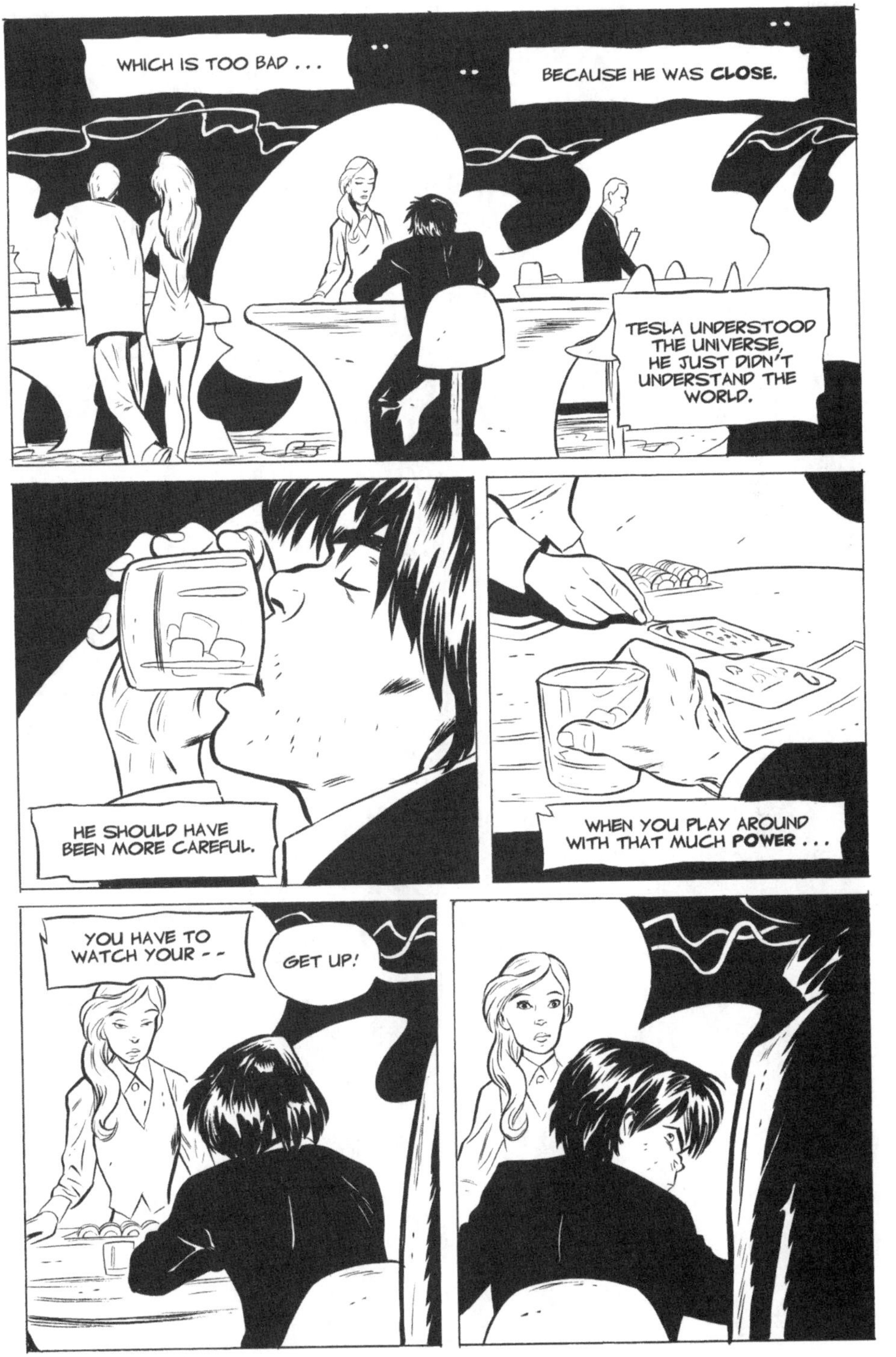
WHICH IS TOO BAD . . .
BECAUSE HE WAS CLOSE.
TESLA UNDERSTOOD THE UNIVERSE, HE JUST DIDN'T UNDERSTAND THE WORLD.
HE SHOULD HAVE BEEN MORE CAREFUL.
WHEN YOU PLAY AROUND WITH THAT MUCH POWER . . .
YOU HAVE TO WATCH YOUR - -
GET UP!

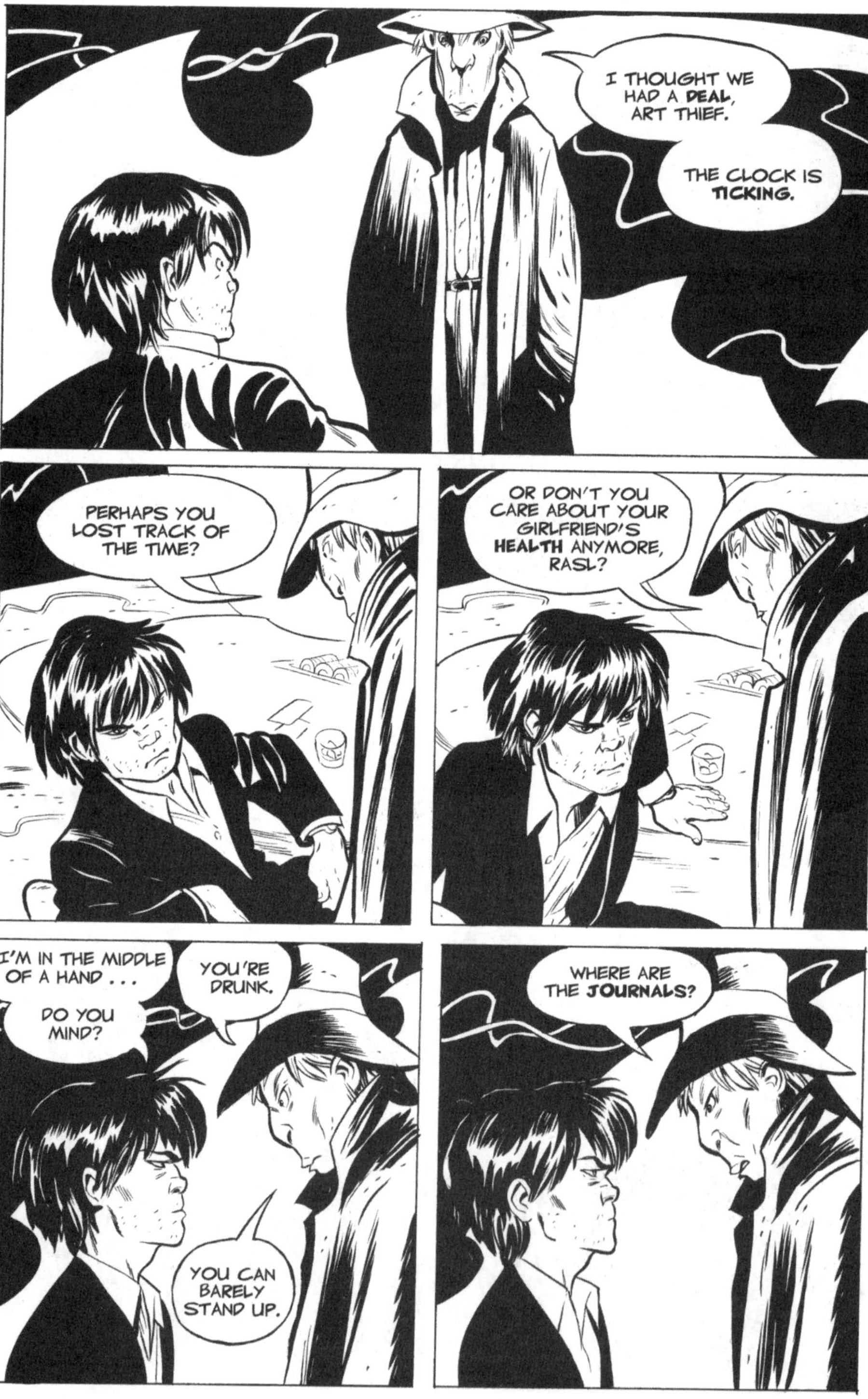
I THOUGHT WE HAD A **DEAL**, ART THIEF.
THE CLOCK IS **TICKING**.
PERHAPS YOU LOST TRACK OF THE TIME?
OR DON'T YOU CARE ABOUT YOUR GIRLFRIEND'S **HEALTH** ANYMORE, RASL?
I'M IN THE MIDDLE OF A HAND . . .
DO YOU MIND?
YOU'RE DRUNK.
YOU CAN BARELY STAND UP.
WHERE ARE THE **JOURNALS**?

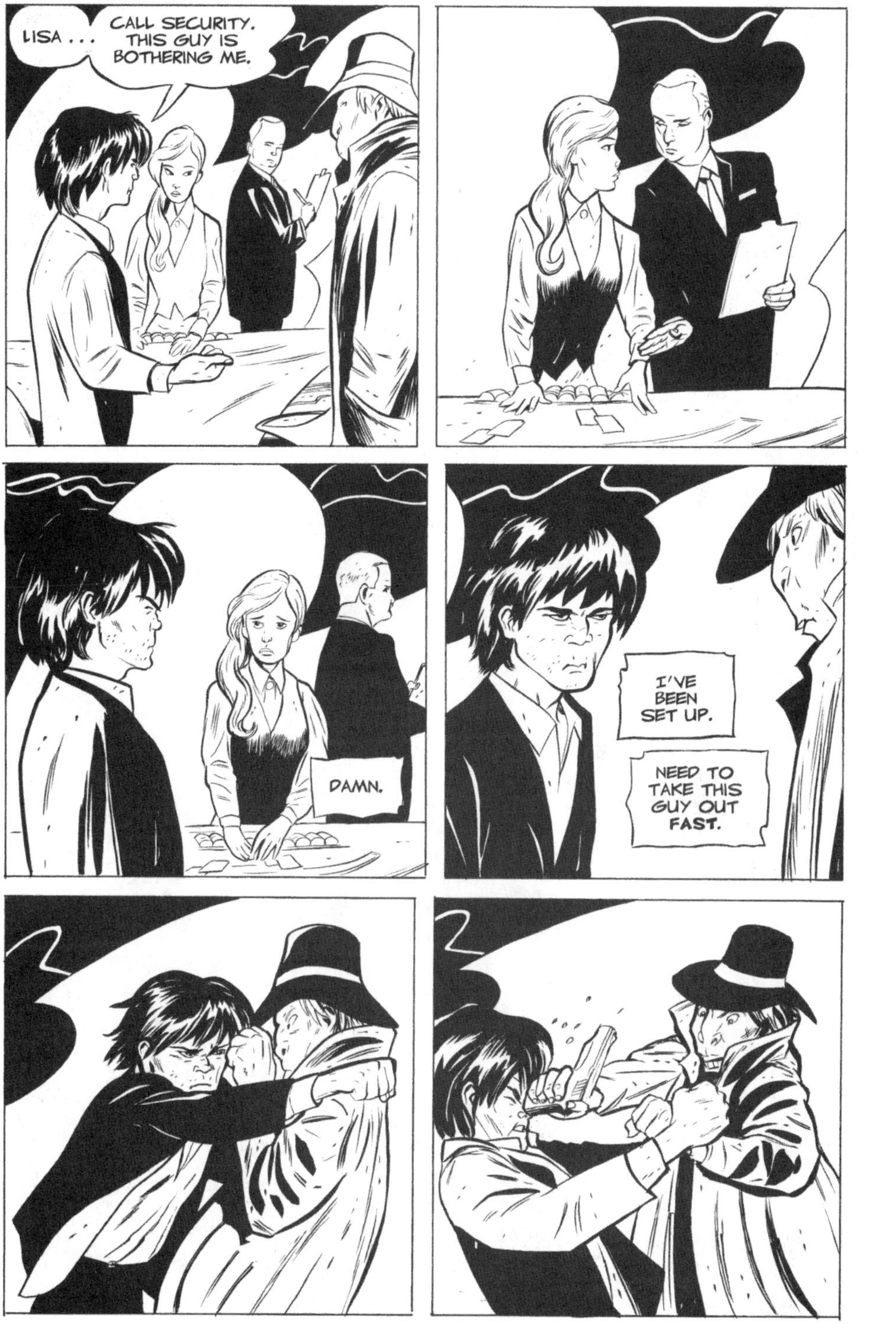
LISA . . .
CALL SECURITY. THIS GUY IS BOTHERING ME.
DAMN.
I'VE BEEN SET UP.
NEED TO TAKE THIS GUY OUT FAST.

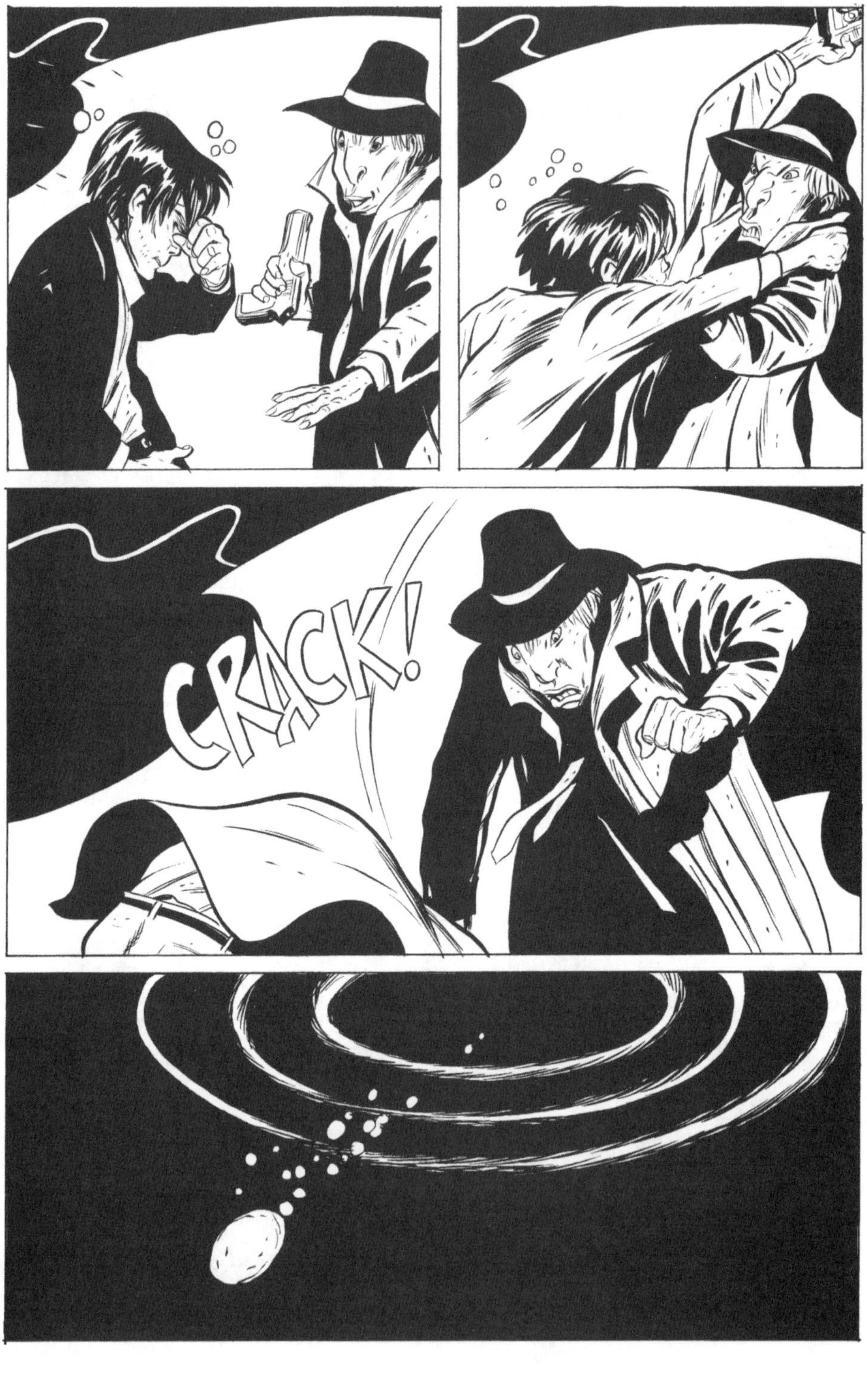
CRACK!

7.
Brighter Than The Sun

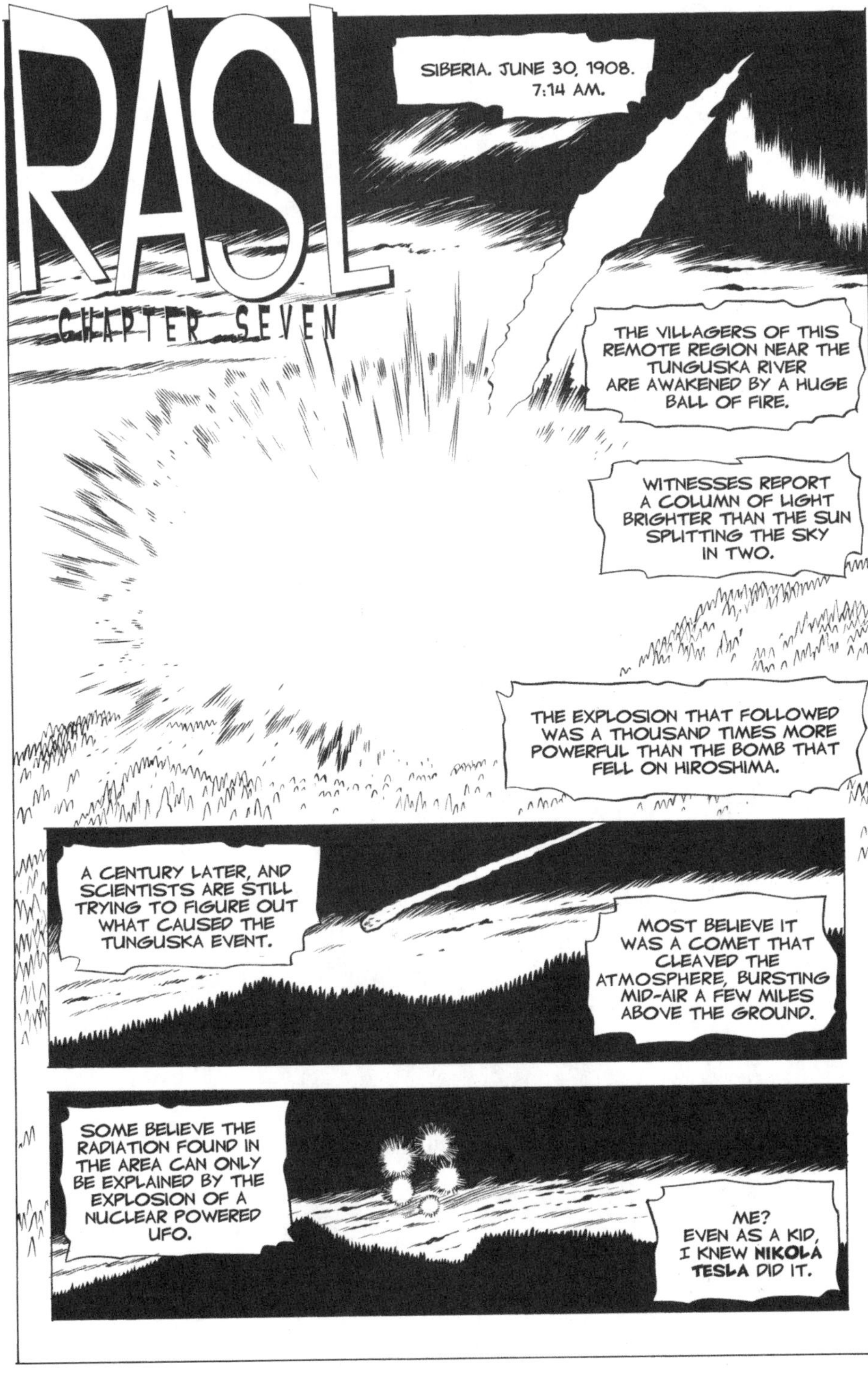
RASL
CHAPTER SEVEN
SIBERIA. JUNE 30, 1908. 7:14 AM.
THE VILLAGERS OF THIS REMOTE REGION NEAR THE TUNGUSKA RIVER ARE AWAKENED BY A HUGE BALL OF FIRE.
WITNESSES REPORT A COLUMN OF LIGHT BRIGHTER THAN THE SUN SPLITTING THE SKY IN TWO.
THE EXPLOSION THAT FOLLOWED WAS A THOUSAND TIMES MORE POWERFUL THAN THE BOMB THAT FELL ON HIROSHIMA.
A CENTURY LATER, AND SCIENTISTS ARE STILL TRYING TO FIGURE OUT WHAT CAUSED THE TUNGUSKA EVENT.
MOST BELIEVE IT WAS A COMET THAT CLEAVED THE ATMOSPHERE, BURSTING MID-AIR A FEW MILES ABOVE THE GROUND.
SOME BELIEVE THE RADIATION FOUND IN THE AREA CAN ONLY BE EXPLAINED BY THE EXPLOSION OF A NUCLEAR POWERED UFO.
ME? EVEN AS A KID, I KNEW NIKOLA TESLA DID IT.

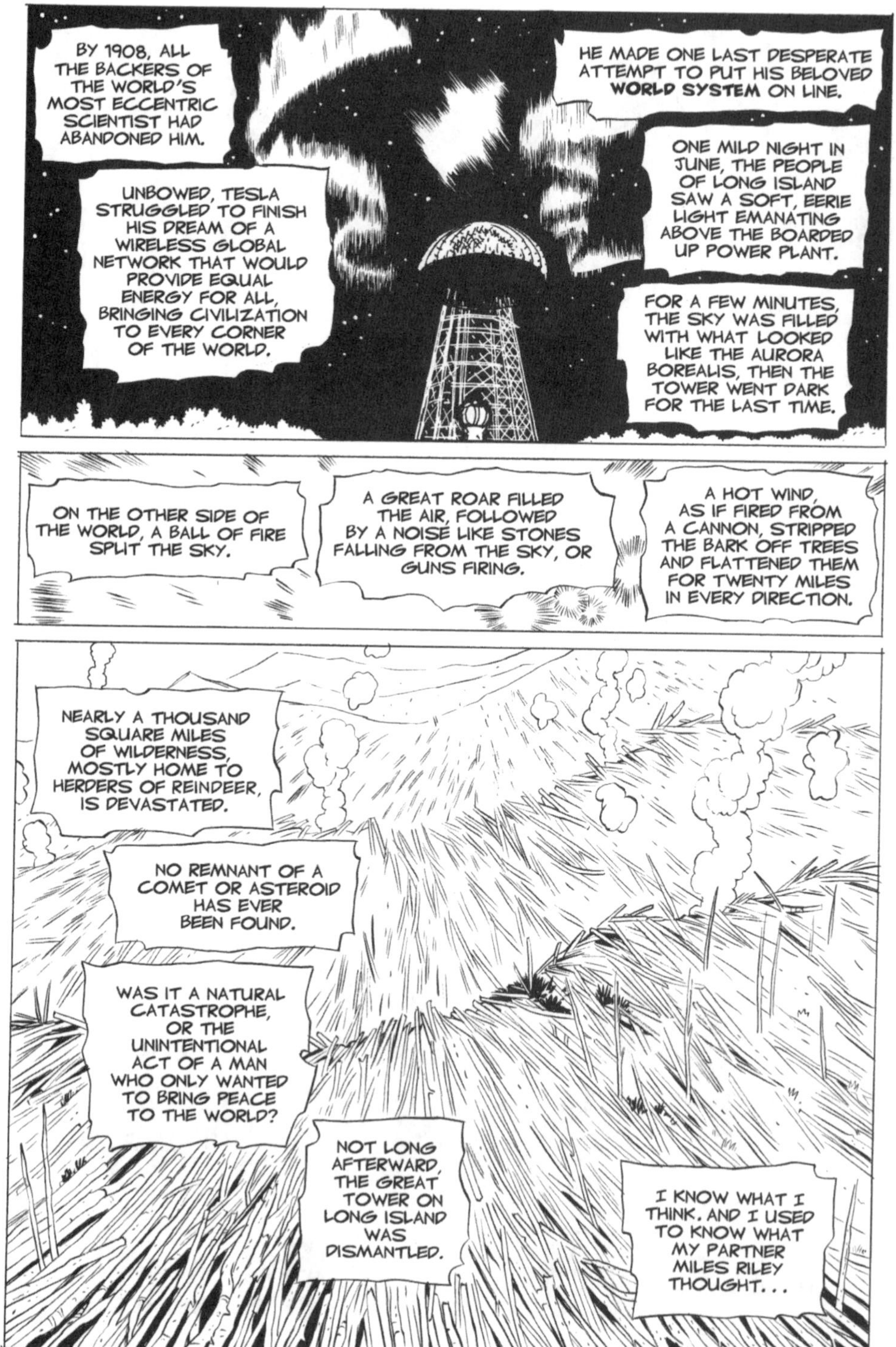
BY 1908, ALL THE BACKERS OF THE WORLD'S MOST ECCENTRIC SCIENTIST HAD ABANDONED HIM.
UNBOWED, TESLA STRUGGLED TO FINISH HIS DREAM OF A WIRELESS GLOBAL NETWORK THAT WOULD PROVIDE EQUAL ENERGY FOR ALL, BRINGING CIVILIZATION TO EVERY CORNER OF THE WORLD.
HE MADE ONE LAST DESPERATE ATTEMPT TO PUT HIS BELOVED **WORLD SYSTEM** ON LINE.
ONE MILD NIGHT IN JUNE, THE PEOPLE OF LONG ISLAND SAW A SOFT, EERIE LIGHT EMANATING ABOVE THE BOARDED UP POWER PLANT.
FOR A FEW MINUTES, THE SKY WAS FILLED WITH WHAT LOOKED LIKE THE AURORA BOREALIS, THEN THE TOWER WENT DARK FOR THE LAST TIME.
ON THE OTHER SIDE OF THE WORLD, A BALL OF FIRE SPLIT THE SKY.
A GREAT ROAR FILLED THE AIR, FOLLOWED BY A NOISE LIKE STONES FALLING FROM THE SKY, OR GUNS FIRING.
A HOT WIND, AS IF FIRED FROM A CANNON, STRIPPED THE BARK OFF TREES AND FLATTENED THEM FOR TWENTY MILES IN EVERY DIRECTION.
NEARLY A THOUSAND SQUARE MILES OF WILDERNESS, MOSTLY HOME TO HERDERS OF REINDEER, IS DEVASTATED.
NO REMNANT OF A COMET OR ASTEROID HAS EVER BEEN FOUND.
WAS IT A NATURAL CATASTROPHE, OR THE UNINTENTIONAL ACT OF A MAN WHO ONLY WANTED TO BRING PEACE TO THE WORLD?
NOT LONG AFTERWARD, THE GREAT TOWER ON LONG ISLAND WAS DISMANTLED.
I KNOW WHAT I THINK. AND I USED TO KNOW WHAT MY PARTNER MILES RILEY THOUGHT...

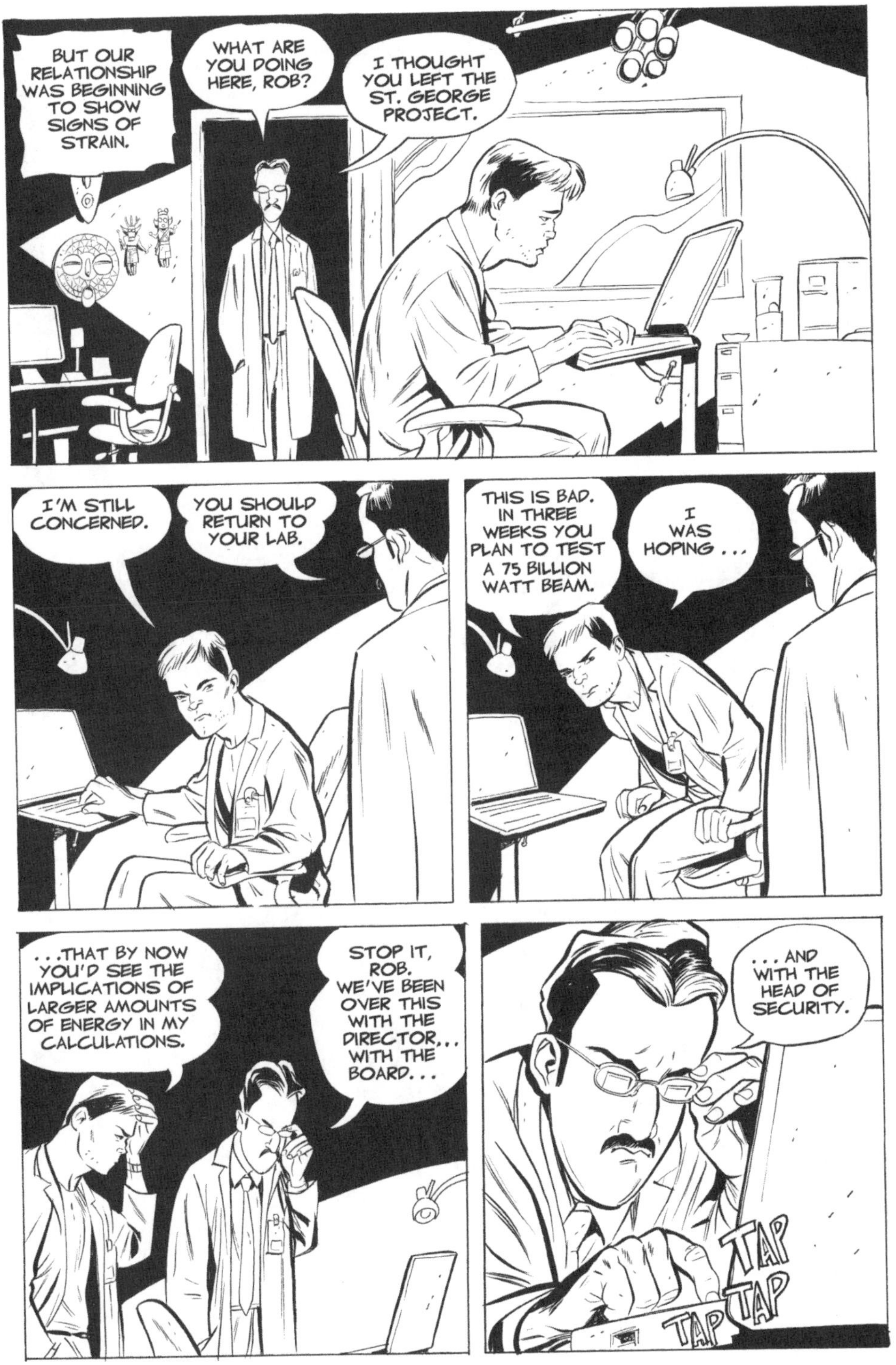
BUT OUR RELATIONSHIP WAS BEGINNING TO SHOW SIGNS OF STRAIN.
WHAT ARE YOU DOING HERE, ROB?
I THOUGHT YOU LEFT THE ST. GEORGE PROJECT.
I'M STILL CONCERNED.
YOU SHOULD RETURN TO YOUR LAB.
THIS IS BAD. IN THREE WEEKS YOU PLAN TO TEST A 75 BILLION WATT BEAM.
I WAS HOPING . . .
. . .THAT BY NOW YOU'D SEE THE IMPLICATIONS OF LARGER AMOUNTS OF ENERGY IN MY CALCULATIONS.
STOP IT, ROB. WE'VE BEEN OVER THIS WITH THE DIRECTOR,... WITH THE BOARD...
. . . AND WITH THE HEAD OF SECURITY.
TAP TAP TAP

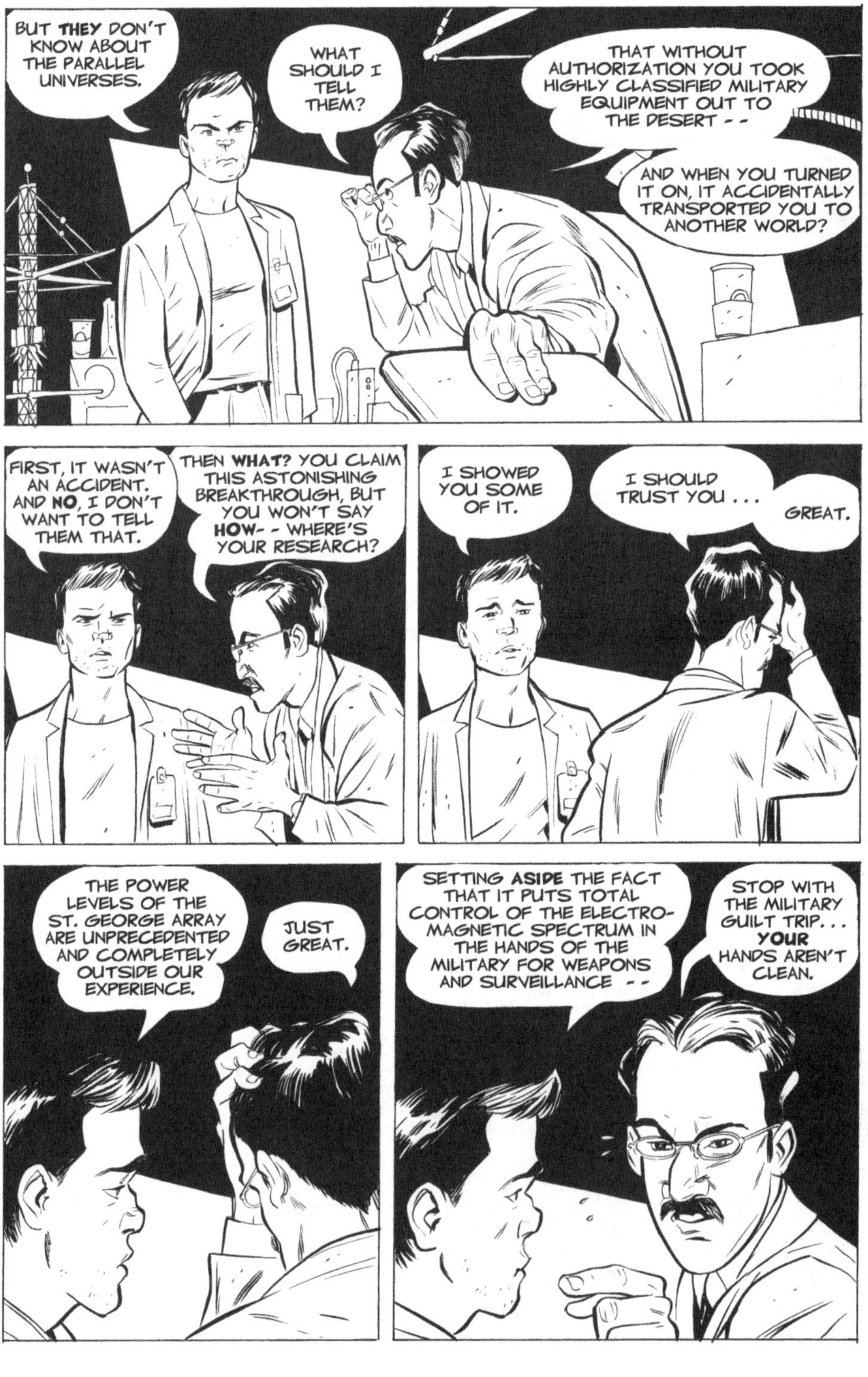

BUT THEY DON'T KNOW ABOUT THE PARALLEL UNIVERSES.
WHAT SHOULD I TELL THEM?
THAT WITHOUT AUTHORIZATION YOU TOOK HIGHLY CLASSIFIED MILITARY EQUIPMENT OUT TO THE DESERT - -
AND WHEN YOU TURNED IT ON, IT ACCIDENTALLY TRANSPORTED YOU TO ANOTHER WORLD?
FIRST, IT WASN'T AN ACCIDENT. AND NO, I DON'T WANT TO TELL THEM THAT.
THEN WHAT? YOU CLAIM THIS ASTONISHING BREAKTHROUGH, BUT YOU WON'T SAY HOW- - WHERE'S YOUR RESEARCH?
I SHOWED YOU SOME OF IT.
I SHOULD TRUST YOU . . .
GREAT.
THE POWER LEVELS OF THE ST. GEORGE ARRAY ARE UNPRECEDENTED AND COMPLETELY OUTSIDE OUR EXPERIENCE.
JUST GREAT.
SETTING ASIDE THE FACT THAT IT PUTS TOTAL CONTROL OF THE ELECTRO-MAGNETIC SPECTRUM IN THE HANDS OF THE MILITARY FOR WEAPONS AND SURVEILLANCE - -
STOP WITH THE MILITARY GUILT TRIP... YOUR HANDS AREN'T CLEAN.

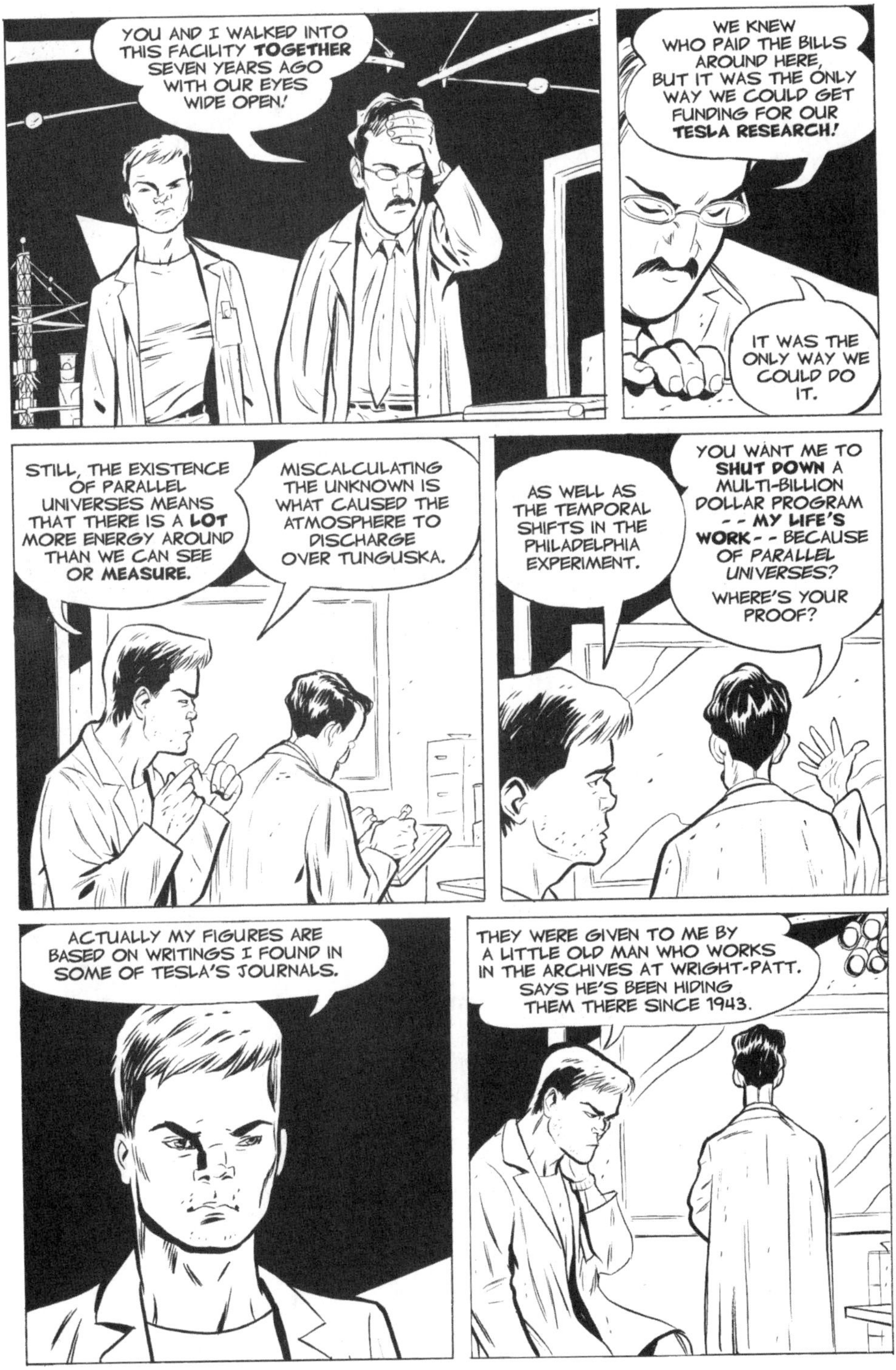
YOU AND I WALKED INTO THIS FACILITY **TOGETHER** SEVEN YEARS AGO WITH OUR EYES WIDE OPEN!
WE KNEW WHO PAID THE BILLS AROUND HERE, BUT IT WAS THE ONLY WAY WE COULD GET FUNDING FOR OUR **TESLA RESEARCH!**
IT WAS THE ONLY WAY WE COULD DO IT.
STILL, THE EXISTENCE OF PARALLEL UNIVERSES MEANS THAT THERE IS A **LOT** MORE ENERGY AROUND THAN WE CAN SEE OR **MEASURE.**
MISCALCULATING THE UNKNOWN IS WHAT CAUSED THE ATMOSPHERE TO DISCHARGE OVER TUNGUSKA.
AS WELL AS THE TEMPORAL SHIFTS IN THE PHILADELPHIA EXPERIMENT.
YOU WANT ME TO **SHUT DOWN** A MULTI-BILLION DOLLAR PROGRAM -- **MY LIFE'S WORK**-- BECAUSE OF *PARALLEL UNIVERSES?*
WHERE'S YOUR PROOF?
ACTUALLY MY FIGURES ARE BASED ON WRITINGS I FOUND IN SOME OF TESLA'S JOURNALS.
THEY WERE GIVEN TO ME BY A LITTLE OLD MAN WHO WORKS IN THE ARCHIVES AT WRIGHT-PATT. SAYS HE'S BEEN HIDING THEM THERE SINCE 1943.

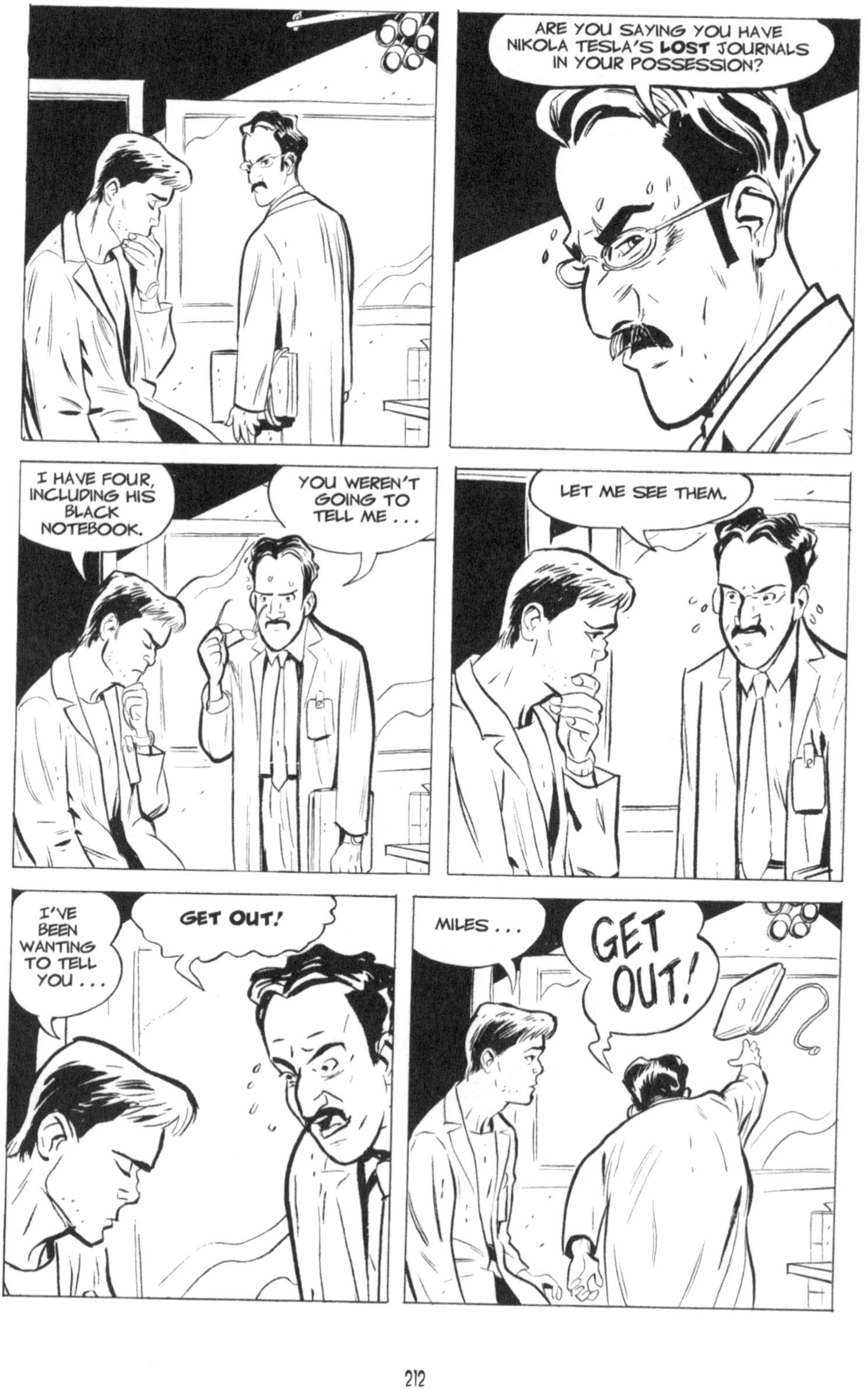
ARE YOU SAYING YOU HAVE NIKOLA TESLA'S LOST JOURNALS IN YOUR POSSESSION?
I HAVE FOUR, INCLUDING HIS BLACK NOTEBOOK.
YOU WEREN'T GOING TO TELL ME . . .
LET ME SEE THEM.
I'VE BEEN WANTING TO TELL YOU . . .
GET OUT!
MILES . . .
GET OUT!

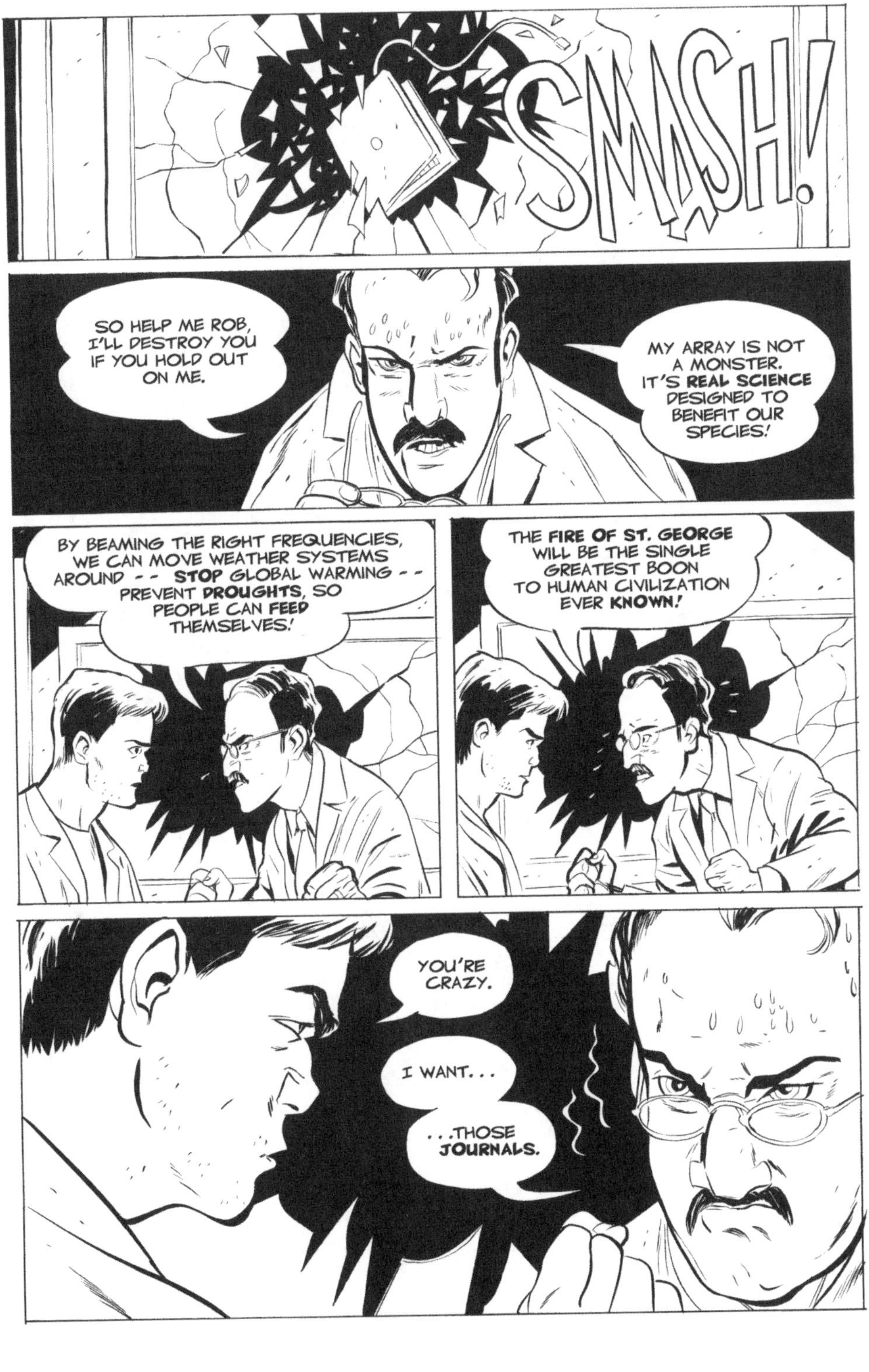
SMASH!
SO HELP ME ROB, I'LL DESTROY YOU IF YOU HOLD OUT ON ME.
MY ARRAY IS NOT A MONSTER. IT'S REAL SCIENCE DESIGNED TO BENEFIT OUR SPECIES!
BY BEAMING THE RIGHT FREQUENCIES, WE CAN MOVE WEATHER SYSTEMS AROUND -- STOP GLOBAL WARMING -- PREVENT DROUGHTS, SO PEOPLE CAN FEED THEMSELVES!
THE FIRE OF ST. GEORGE WILL BE THE SINGLE GREATEST BOON TO HUMAN CIVILIZATION EVER KNOWN!
YOU'RE CRAZY.
I WANT...
...THOSE JOURNALS.

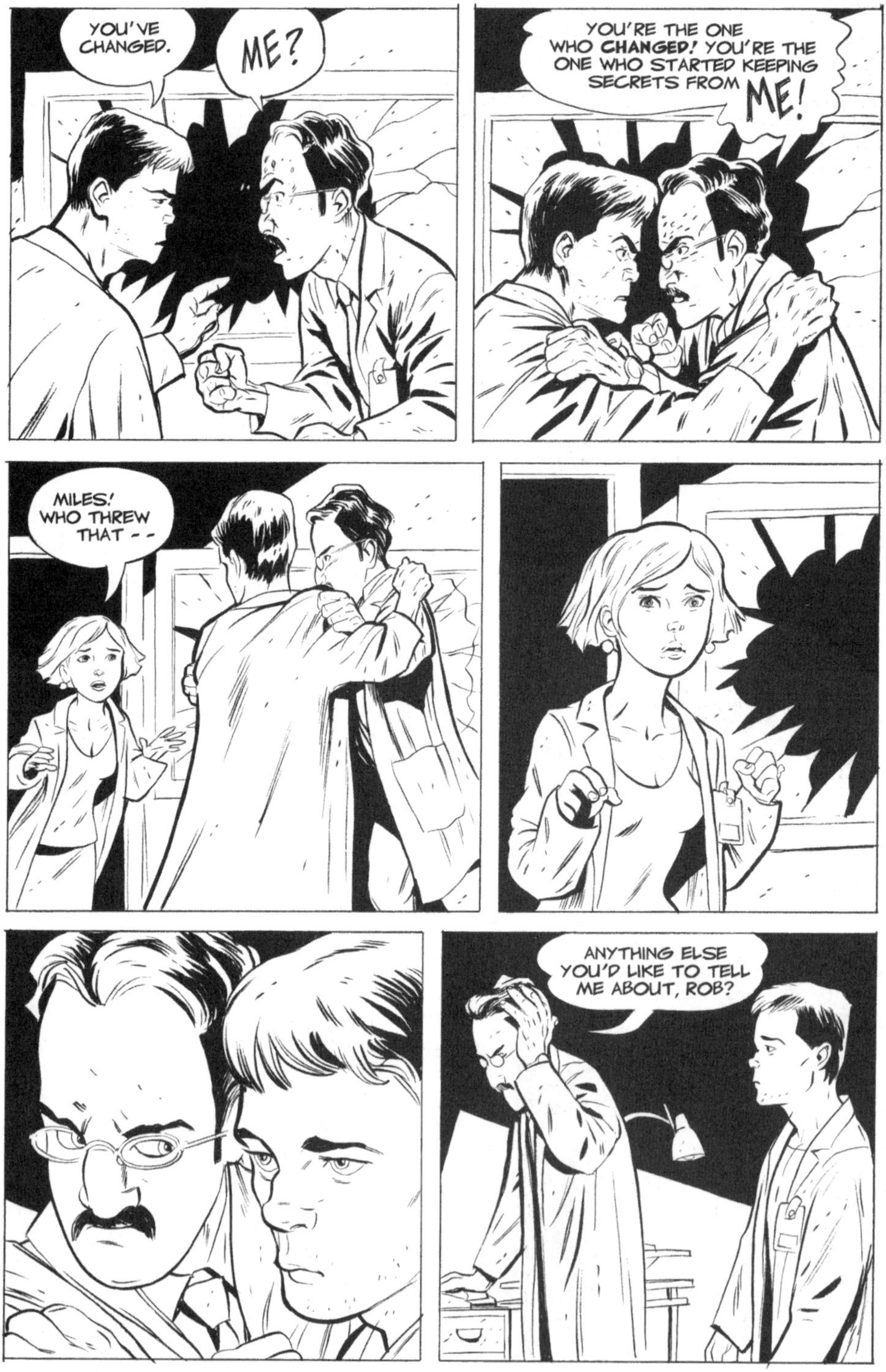

YOU'VE CHANGED.
ME?
YOU'RE THE ONE WHO **CHANGED!** YOU'RE THE ONE WHO STARTED KEEPING SECRETS FROM ME!
MILES! WHO THREW THAT --
ANYTHING ELSE YOU'D LIKE TO TELL ME ABOUT, ROB?

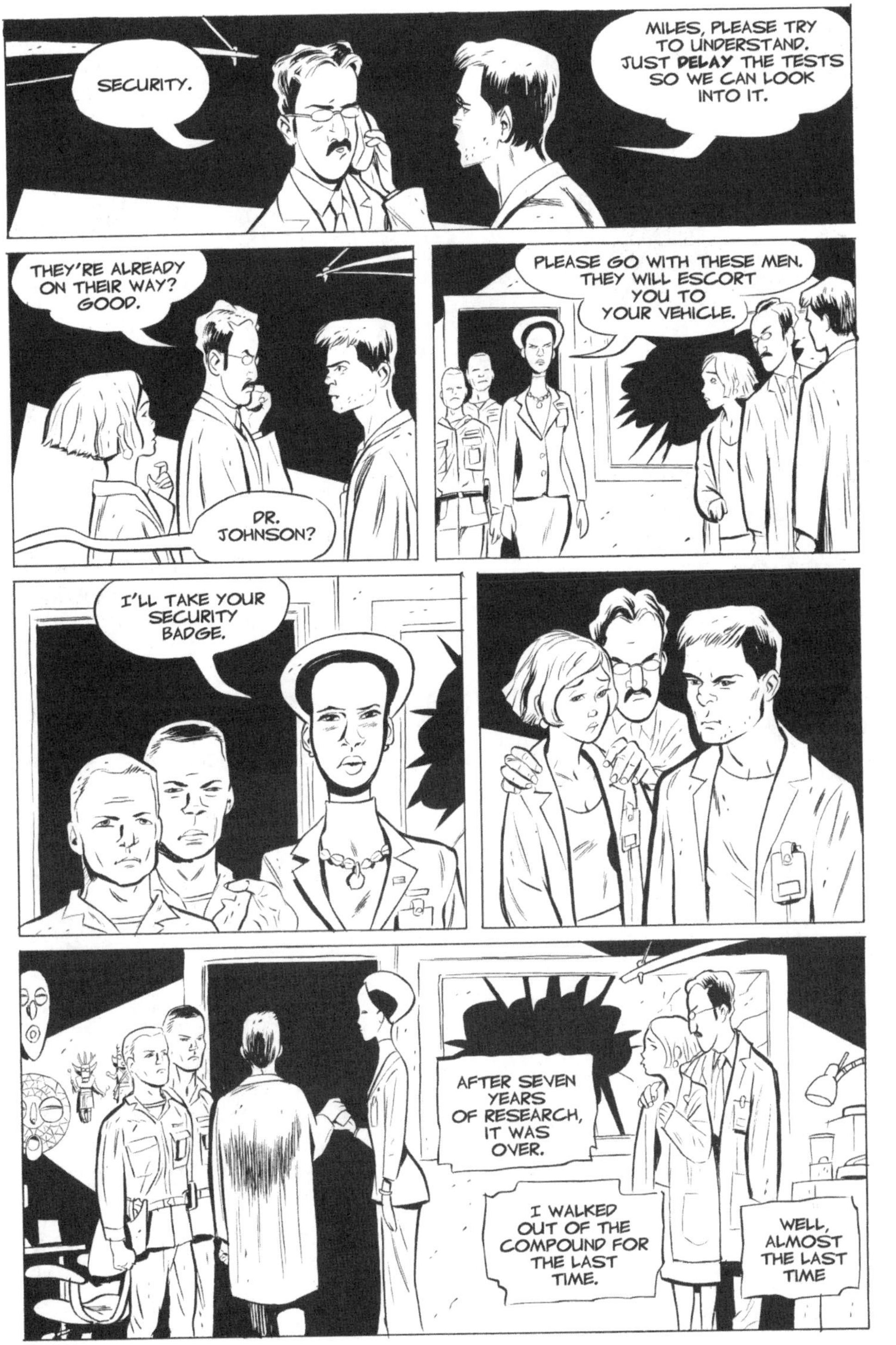
SECURITY.
MILES, PLEASE TRY TO UNDERSTAND. JUST **DELAY** THE TESTS SO WE CAN LOOK INTO IT.
THEY'RE ALREADY ON THEIR WAY? GOOD.
DR. JOHNSON?
PLEASE GO WITH THESE MEN. THEY WILL ESCORT YOU TO YOUR VEHICLE.
I'LL TAKE YOUR SECURITY BADGE.
AFTER SEVEN YEARS OF RESEARCH, IT WAS OVER.
I WALKED OUT OF THE COMPOUND FOR THE LAST TIME.
WELL, ALMOST THE LAST TIME

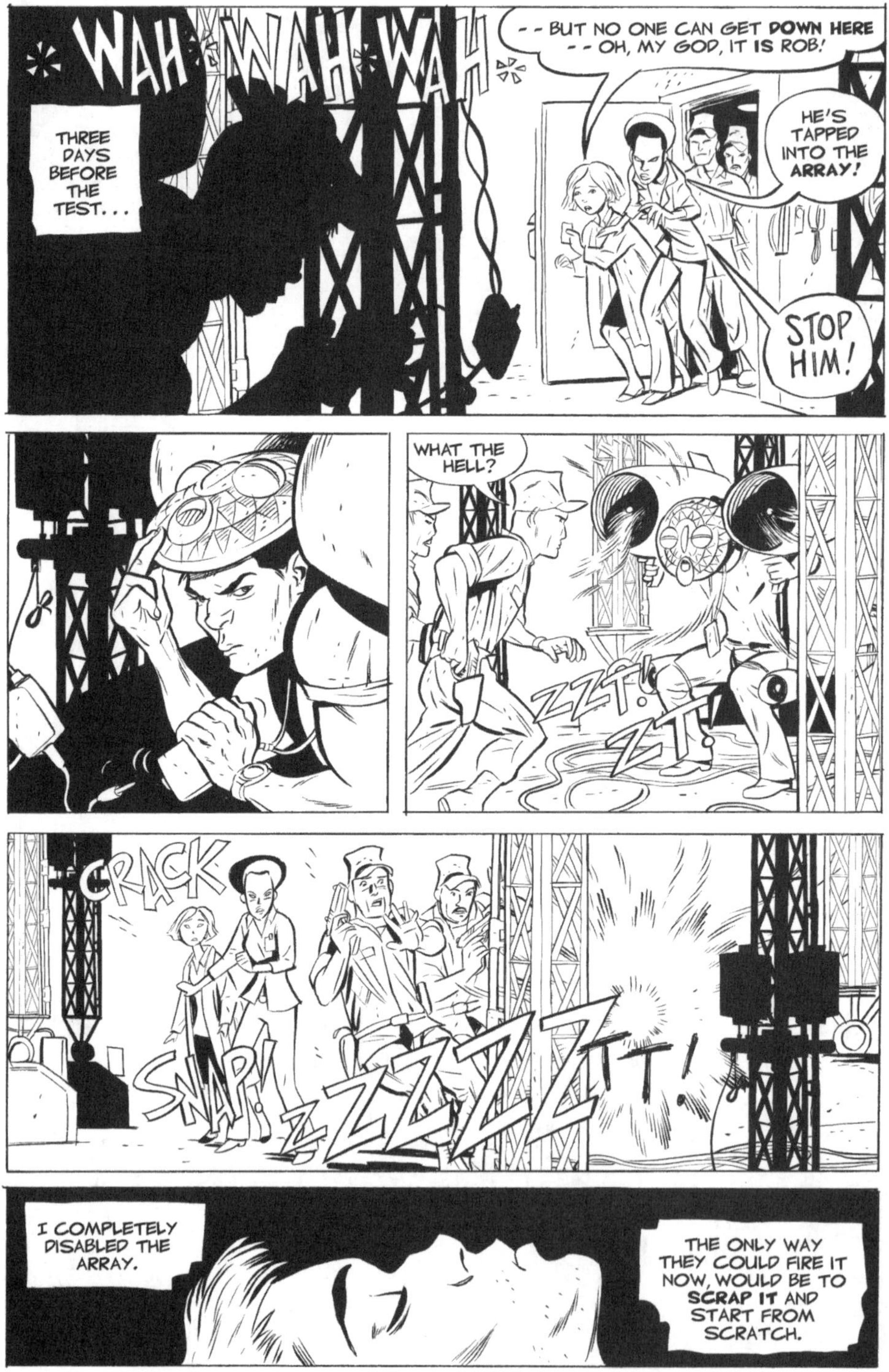
WAH WAH WAH WAH
THREE DAYS BEFORE THE TEST...
-- BUT NO ONE CAN GET DOWN HERE -- OH, MY GOD, IT IS ROB!
HE'S TAPPED INTO THE ARRAY!
STOP HIM!
WHAT THE HELL?
ZZZT! ZT!
CRACK
SNAP!
ZZZZZZTTT!
I COMPLETELY DISABLED THE ARRAY.
THE ONLY WAY THEY COULD FIRE IT NOW, WOULD BE TO SCRAP IT AND START FROM SCRATCH.

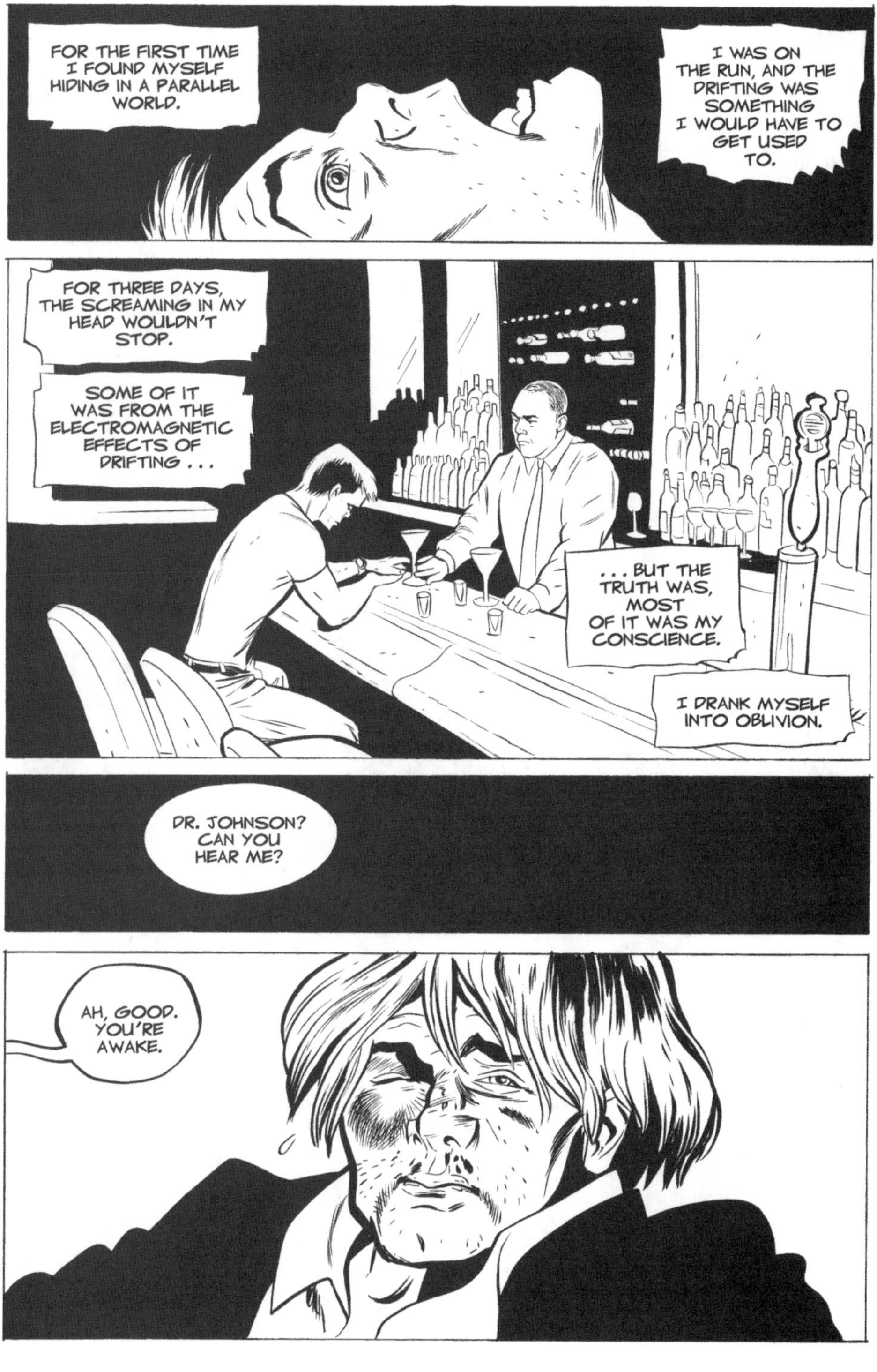
FOR THE FIRST TIME I FOUND MYSELF HIDING IN A PARALLEL WORLD.
I WAS ON THE RUN, AND THE DRIFTING WAS SOMETHING I WOULD HAVE TO GET USED TO.
FOR THREE DAYS, THE SCREAMING IN MY HEAD WOULDN'T STOP.
SOME OF IT WAS FROM THE ELECTROMAGNETIC EFFECTS OF DRIFTING . . .
. . . BUT THE TRUTH WAS, MOST OF IT WAS MY CONSCIENCE.
I DRANK MYSELF INTO OBLIVION.
DR. JOHNSON? CAN YOU HEAR ME?
AH, GOOD. YOU'RE AWAKE.

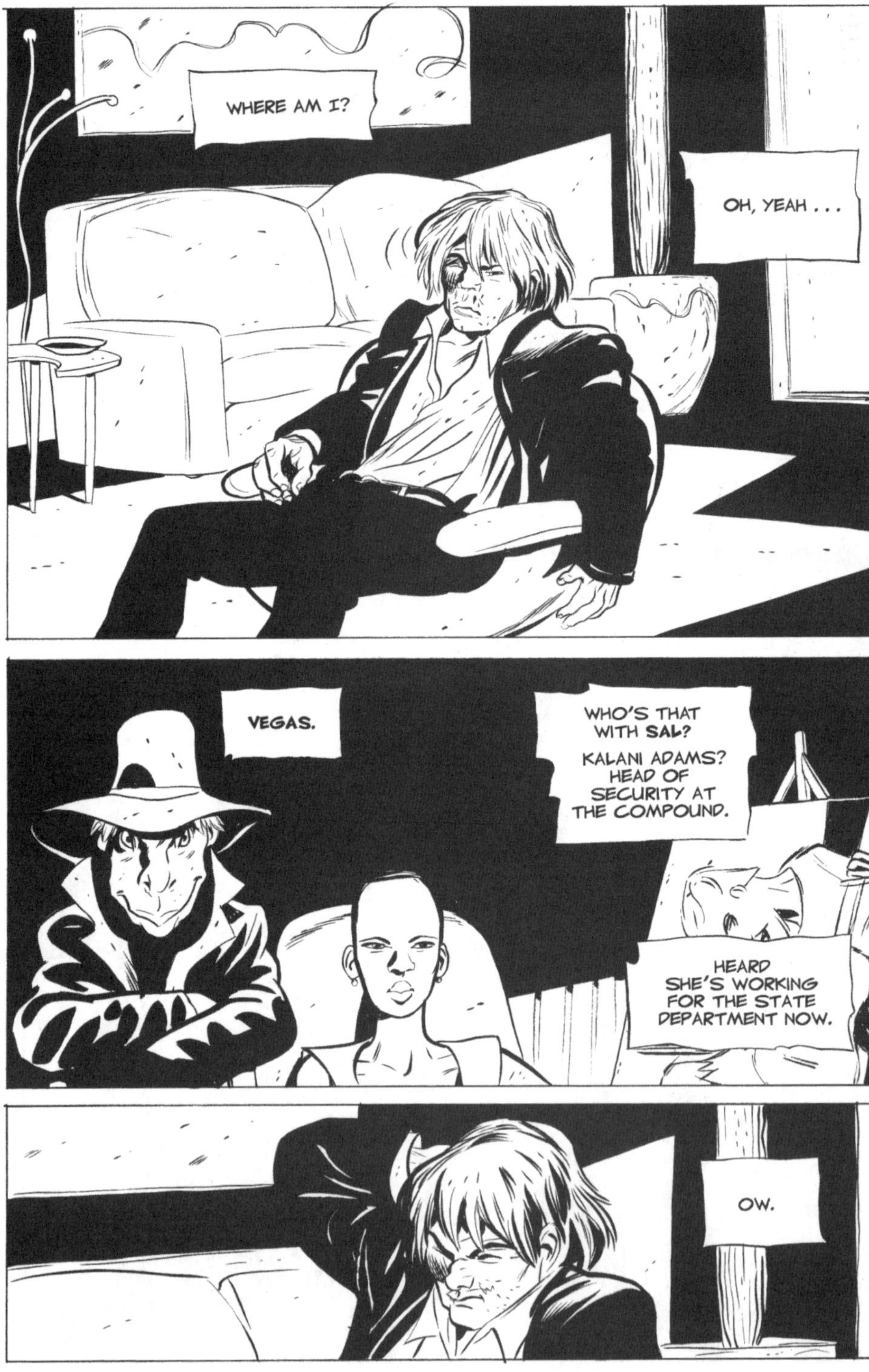
WHERE AM I?
OH, YEAH . . .
VEGAS.
WHO'S THAT WITH SAL?
KALANI ADAMS? HEAD OF SECURITY AT THE COMPOUND.
HEARD SHE'S WORKING FOR THE STATE DEPARTMENT NOW.
OW.

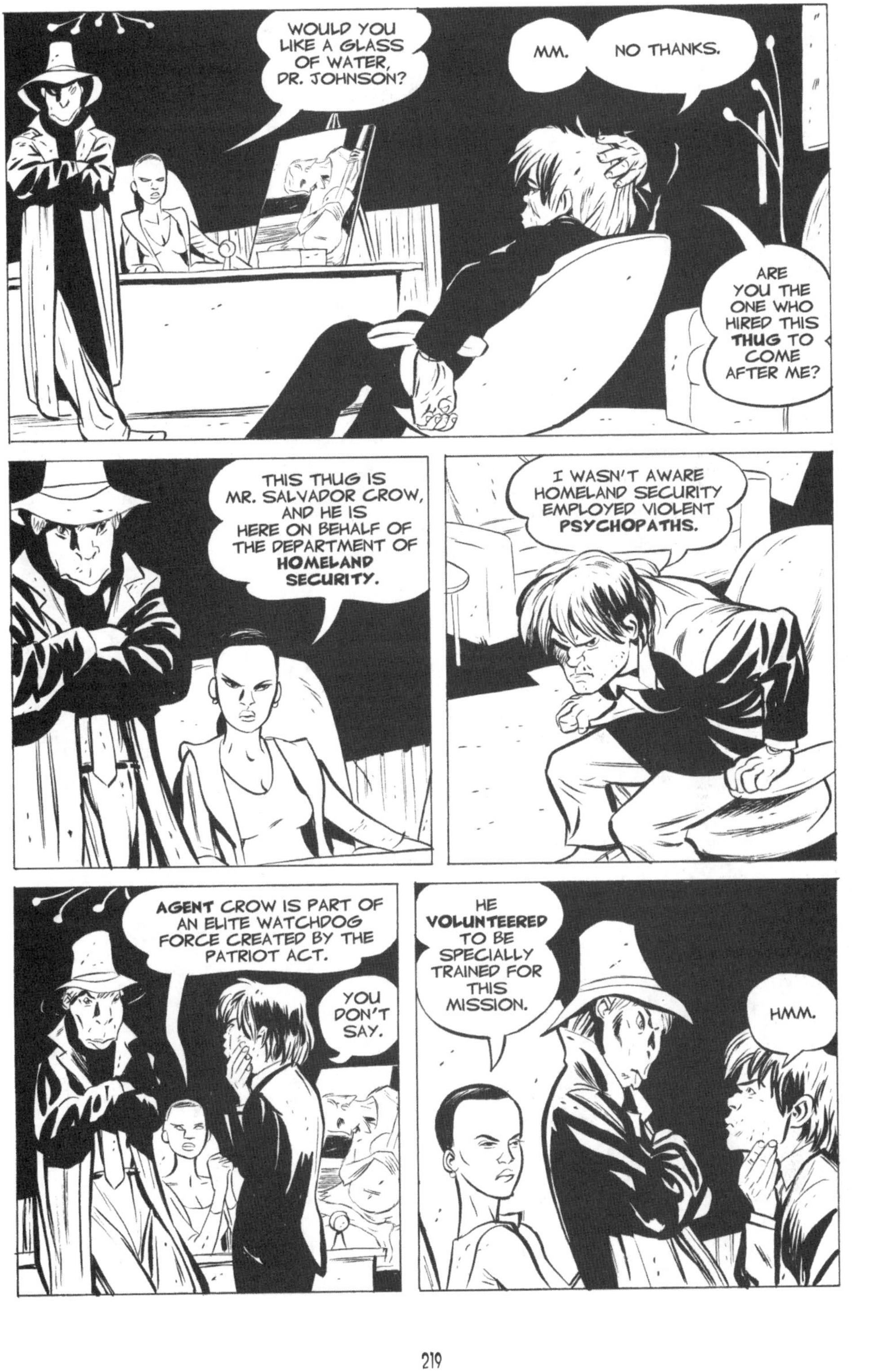
WOULD YOU LIKE A GLASS OF WATER, DR. JOHNSON?
MM.
NO THANKS.
ARE YOU THE ONE WHO HIRED THIS THUG TO COME AFTER ME?
THIS THUG IS MR. SALVADOR CROW, AND HE IS HERE ON BEHALF OF THE DEPARTMENT OF HOMELAND SECURITY.
I WASN'T AWARE HOMELAND SECURITY EMPLOYED VIOLENT PSYCHOPATHS.
AGENT CROW IS PART OF AN ELITE WATCHDOG FORCE CREATED BY THE PATRIOT ACT.
YOU DON'T SAY.
HE VOLUNTEERED TO BE SPECIALLY TRAINED FOR THIS MISSION.
HMM.

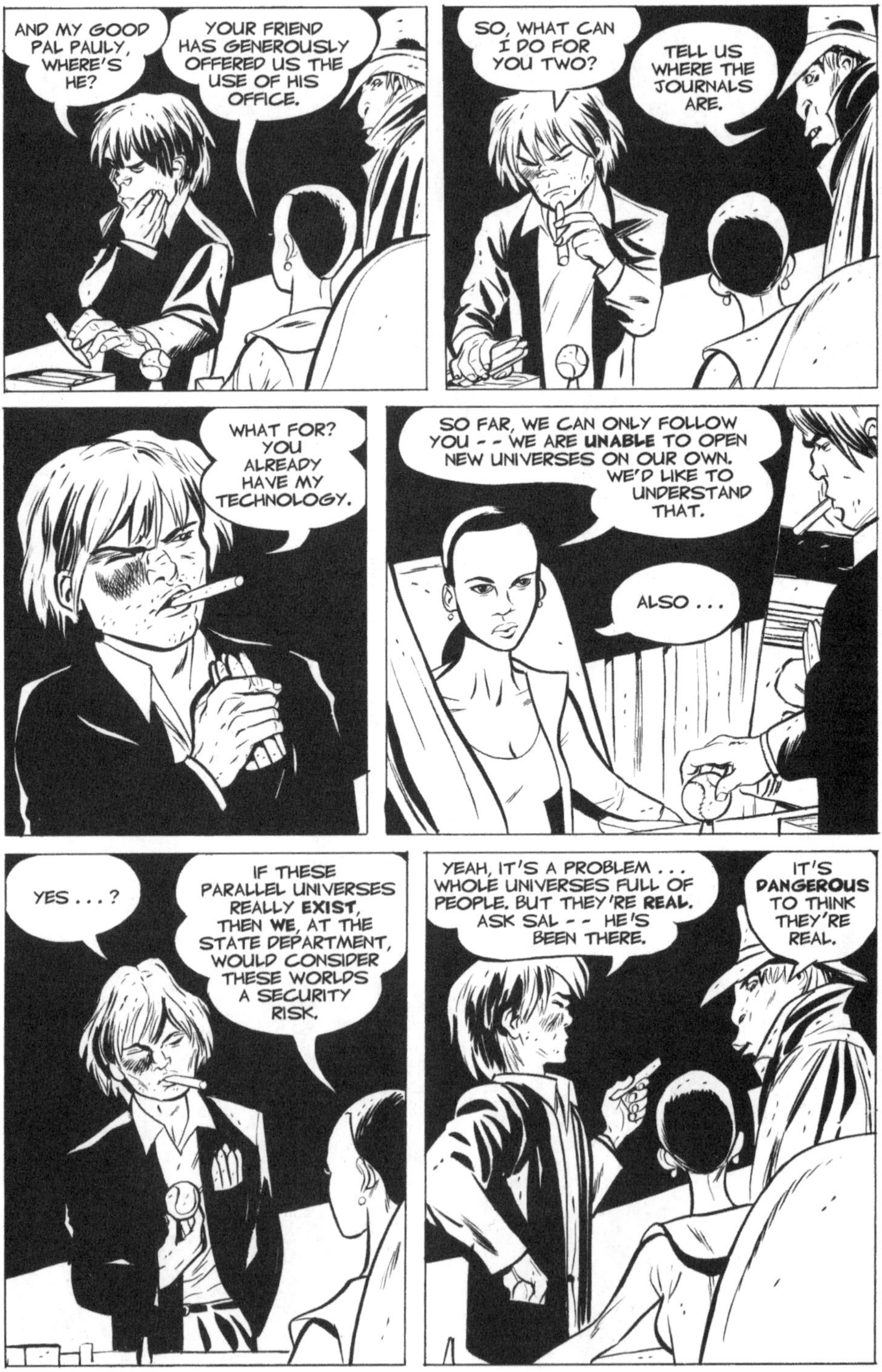
AND MY GOOD PAL PAULY, WHERE'S HE?
YOUR FRIEND HAS GENEROUSLY OFFERED US THE USE OF HIS OFFICE.
SO, WHAT CAN I DO FOR YOU TWO?
TELL US WHERE THE JOURNALS ARE.
WHAT FOR? YOU ALREADY HAVE MY TECHNOLOGY.
SO FAR, WE CAN ONLY FOLLOW YOU - - WE ARE UNABLE TO OPEN NEW UNIVERSES ON OUR OWN. WE'D LIKE TO UNDERSTAND THAT.
ALSO . . .
YES . . . ?
IF THESE PARALLEL UNIVERSES REALLY EXIST, THEN WE, AT THE STATE DEPARTMENT, WOULD CONSIDER THESE WORLDS A SECURITY RISK.
YEAH, IT'S A PROBLEM . . . WHOLE UNIVERSES FULL OF PEOPLE. BUT THEY'RE REAL. ASK SAL - - HE'S BEEN THERE.
IT'S DANGEROUS TO THINK THEY'RE REAL.

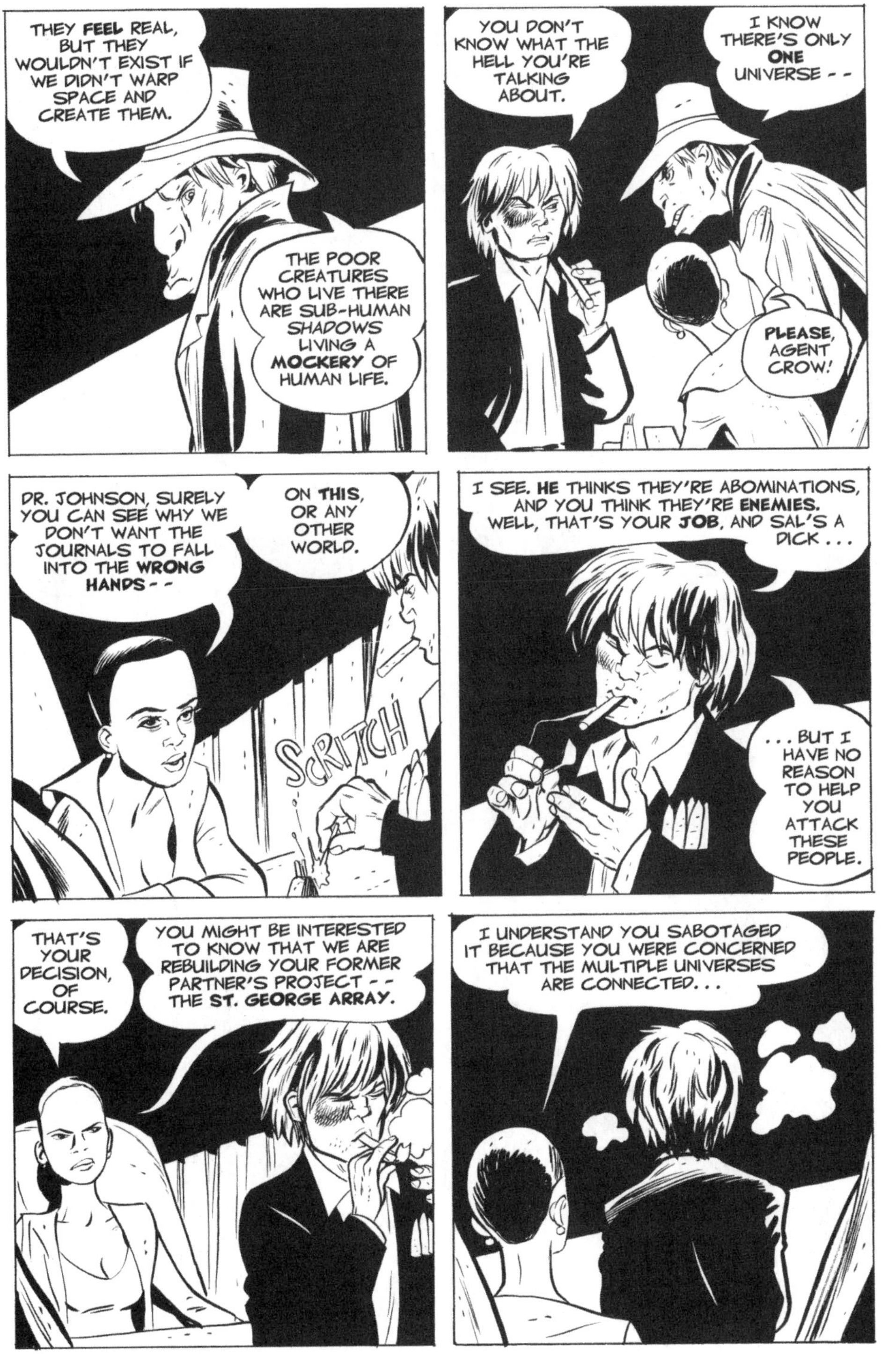

THEY FEEL REAL, BUT THEY WOULDN'T EXIST IF WE DIDN'T WARP SPACE AND CREATE THEM.
THE POOR CREATURES WHO LIVE THERE ARE SUB-HUMAN SHADOWS LIVING A MOCKERY OF HUMAN LIFE.
YOU DON'T KNOW WHAT THE HELL YOU'RE TALKING ABOUT.
I KNOW THERE'S ONLY ONE UNIVERSE - -
PLEASE, AGENT CROW!
DR. JOHNSON, SURELY YOU CAN SEE WHY WE DON'T WANT THE JOURNALS TO FALL INTO THE WRONG HANDS - -
ON THIS, OR ANY OTHER WORLD.
SCRITCH
I SEE. HE THINKS THEY'RE ABOMINATIONS, AND YOU THINK THEY'RE ENEMIES. WELL, THAT'S YOUR JOB, AND SAL'S A DICK . . .
. . . BUT I HAVE NO REASON TO HELP YOU ATTACK THESE PEOPLE.
THAT'S YOUR DECISION, OF COURSE.
YOU MIGHT BE INTERESTED TO KNOW THAT WE ARE REBUILDING YOUR FORMER PARTNER'S PROJECT - - THE ST. GEORGE ARRAY.
I UNDERSTAND YOU SABOTAGED IT BECAUSE YOU WERE CONCERNED THAT THE MULTIPLE UNIVERSES ARE CONNECTED . . .

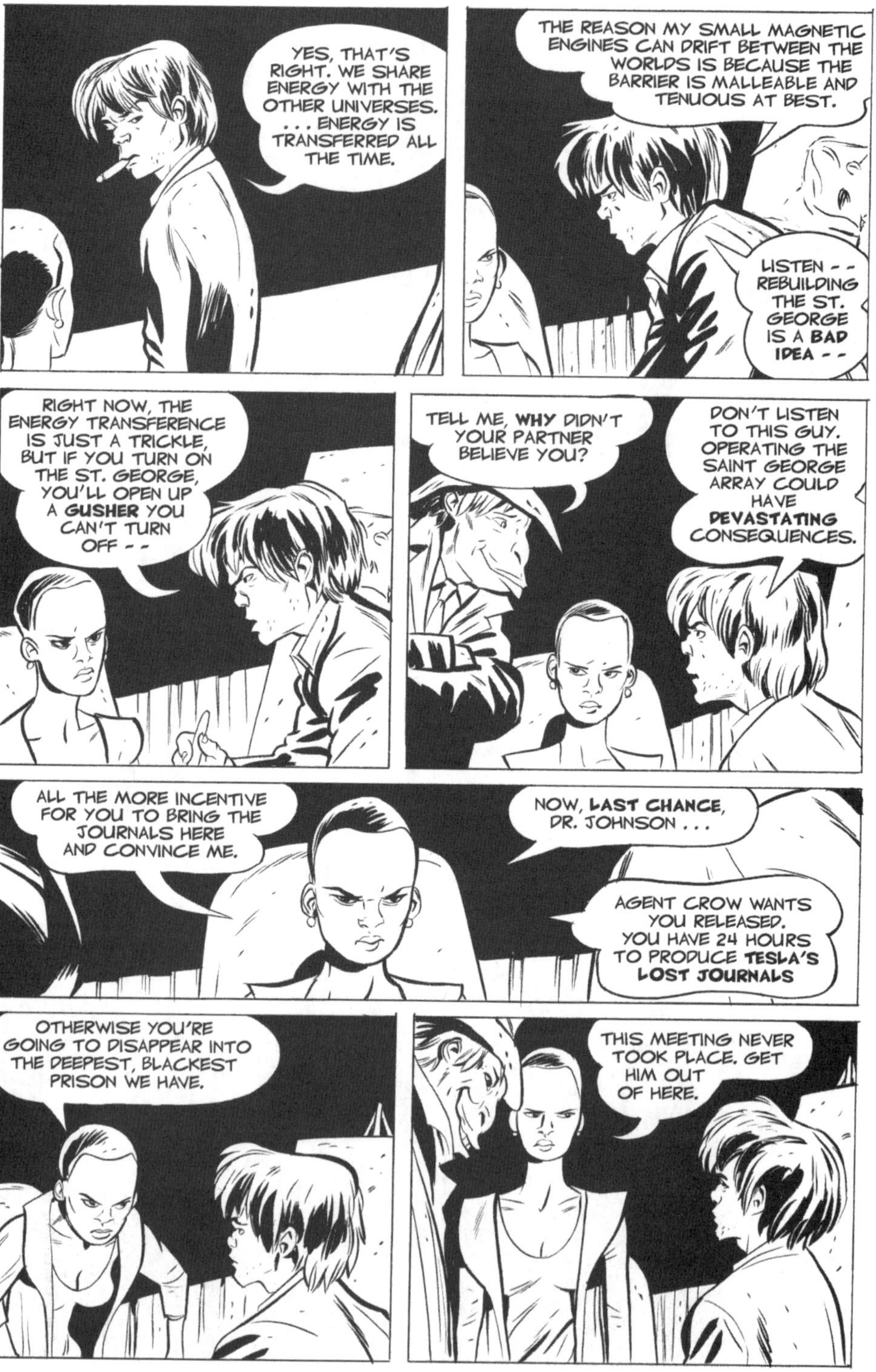
YES, THAT'S RIGHT. WE SHARE ENERGY WITH THE OTHER UNIVERSES. . . . ENERGY IS TRANSFERRED ALL THE TIME.
THE REASON MY SMALL MAGNETIC ENGINES CAN DRIFT BETWEEN THE WORLDS IS BECAUSE THE BARRIER IS MALLEABLE AND TENUOUS AT BEST.
LISTEN - - REBUILDING THE ST. GEORGE IS A BAD IDEA - -
RIGHT NOW, THE ENERGY TRANSFERENCE IS JUST A TRICKLE, BUT IF YOU TURN ON THE ST. GEORGE, YOU'LL OPEN UP A GUSHER YOU CAN'T TURN OFF - -
TELL ME, WHY DIDN'T YOUR PARTNER BELIEVE YOU?
DON'T LISTEN TO THIS GUY. OPERATING THE SAINT GEORGE ARRAY COULD HAVE DEVASTATING CONSEQUENCES.
ALL THE MORE INCENTIVE FOR YOU TO BRING THE JOURNALS HERE AND CONVINCE ME.
NOW, LAST CHANCE, DR. JOHNSON . . .
AGENT CROW WANTS YOU RELEASED. YOU HAVE 24 HOURS TO PRODUCE TESLA'S LOST JOURNALS
OTHERWISE YOU'RE GOING TO DISAPPEAR INTO THE DEEPEST, BLACKEST PRISON WE HAVE.
THIS MEETING NEVER TOOK PLACE. GET HIM OUT OF HERE.

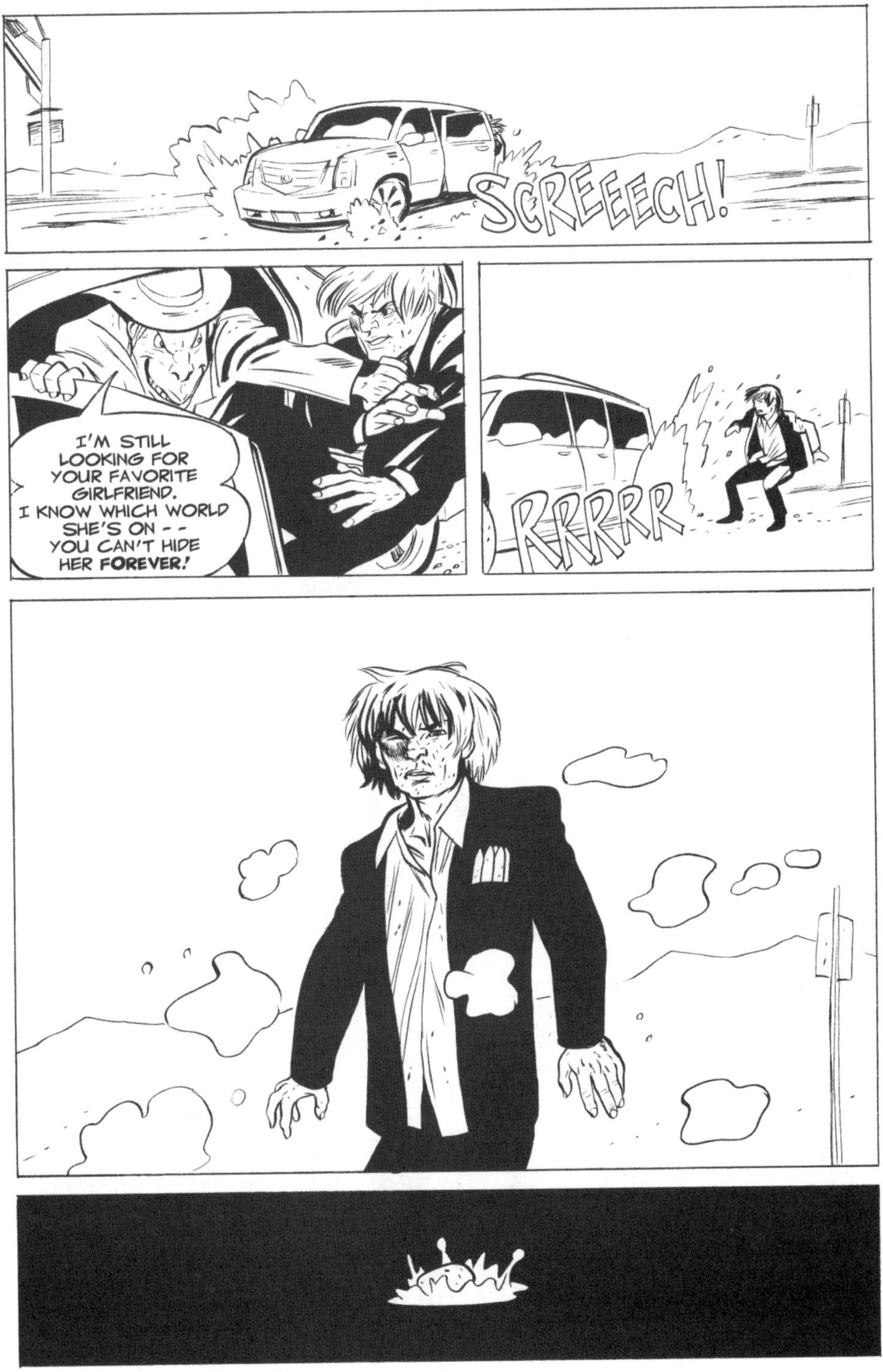
SCREEECH!
I'M STILL LOOKING FOR YOUR FAVORITE GIRLFRIEND. I KNOW WHICH WORLD SHE'S ON - - YOU CAN'T HIDE HER **FOREVER**!
RRRRR

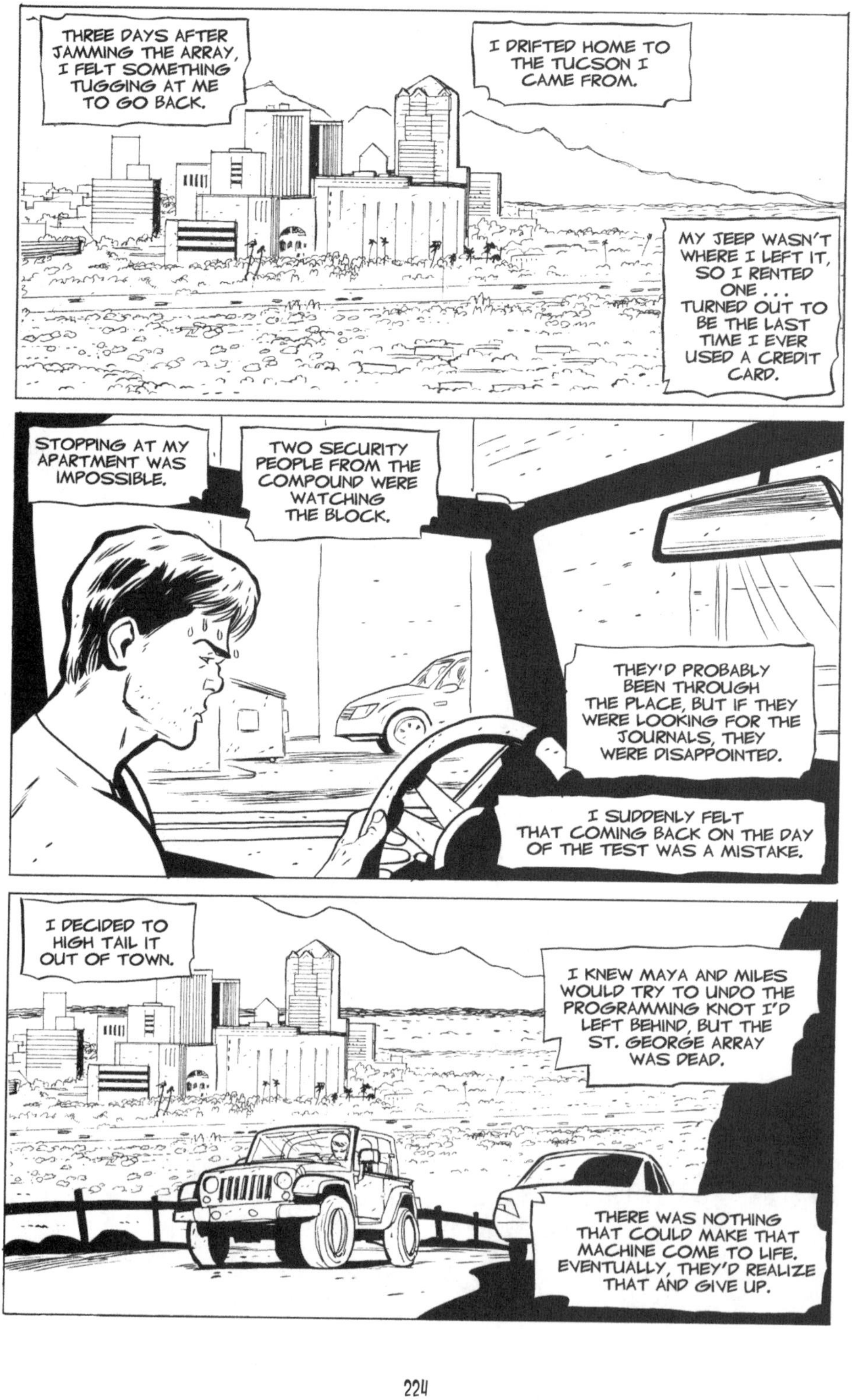
THREE DAYS AFTER JAMMING THE ARRAY, I FELT SOMETHING TUGGING AT ME TO GO BACK.
I DRIFTED HOME TO THE TUCSON I CAME FROM.
MY JEEP WASN'T WHERE I LEFT IT, SO I RENTED ONE . . . TURNED OUT TO BE THE LAST TIME I EVER USED A CREDIT CARD.
STOPPING AT MY APARTMENT WAS IMPOSSIBLE.
TWO SECURITY PEOPLE FROM THE COMPOUND WERE WATCHING THE BLOCK.
THEY'D PROBABLY BEEN THROUGH THE PLACE, BUT IF THEY WERE LOOKING FOR THE JOURNALS, THEY WERE DISAPPOINTED.
I SUDDENLY FELT THAT COMING BACK ON THE DAY OF THE TEST WAS A MISTAKE.
I DECIDED TO HIGH TAIL IT OUT OF TOWN.
I KNEW MAYA AND MILES WOULD TRY TO UNDO THE PROGRAMMING KNOT I'D LEFT BEHIND, BUT THE ST. GEORGE ARRAY WAS DEAD.
THERE WAS NOTHING THAT COULD MAKE THAT MACHINE COME TO LIFE. EVENTUALLY, THEY'D REALIZE THAT AND GIVE UP.

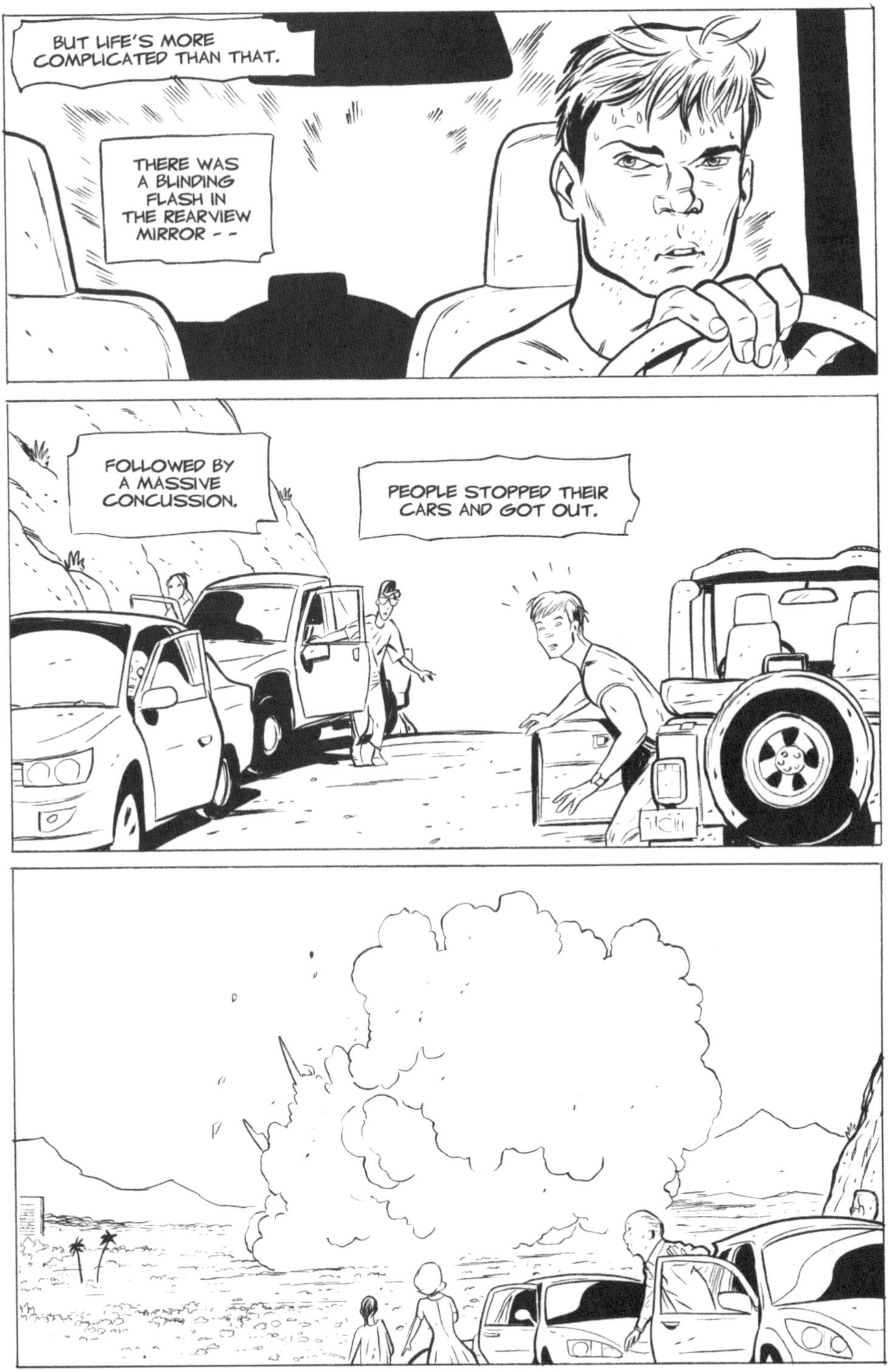
BUT LIFE'S MORE COMPLICATED THAN THAT.
THERE WAS A BLINDING FLASH IN THE REARVIEW MIRROR - -
FOLLOWED BY A MASSIVE CONCUSSION.
PEOPLE STOPPED THEIR CARS AND GOT OUT.

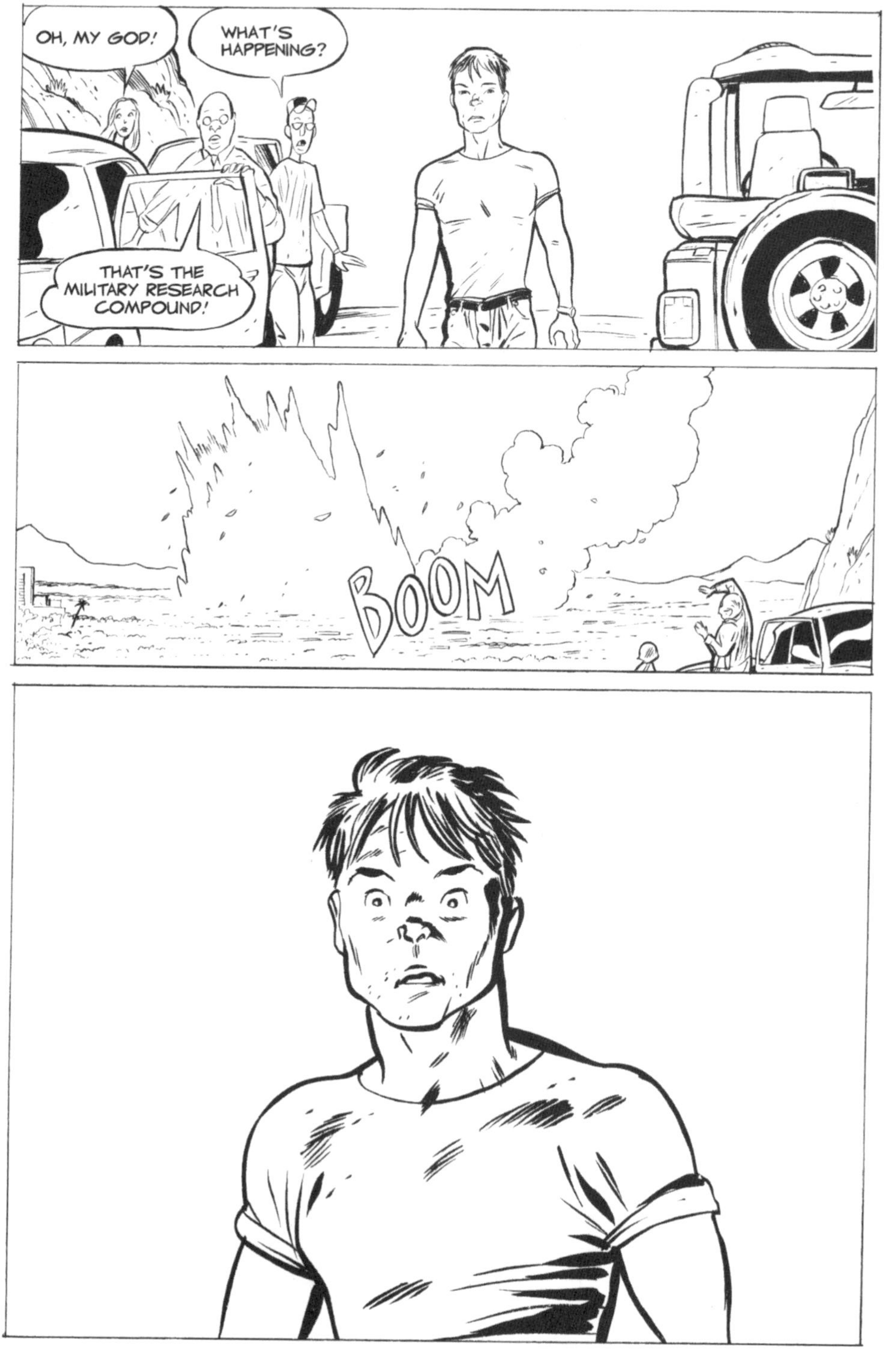
OH, MY GOD!
WHAT'S HAPPENING?
THAT'S THE MILITARY RESEARCH COMPOUND!
BOOM

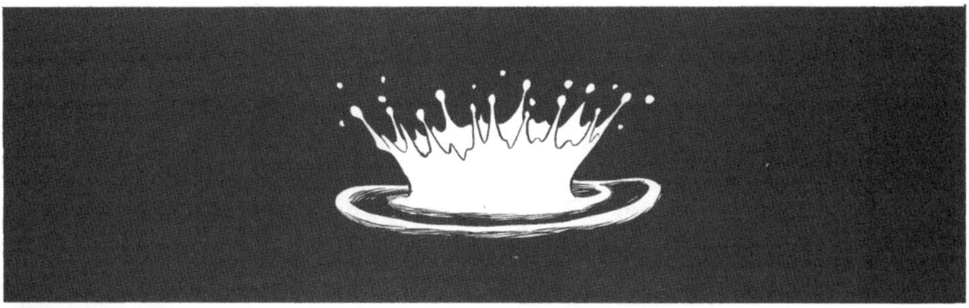

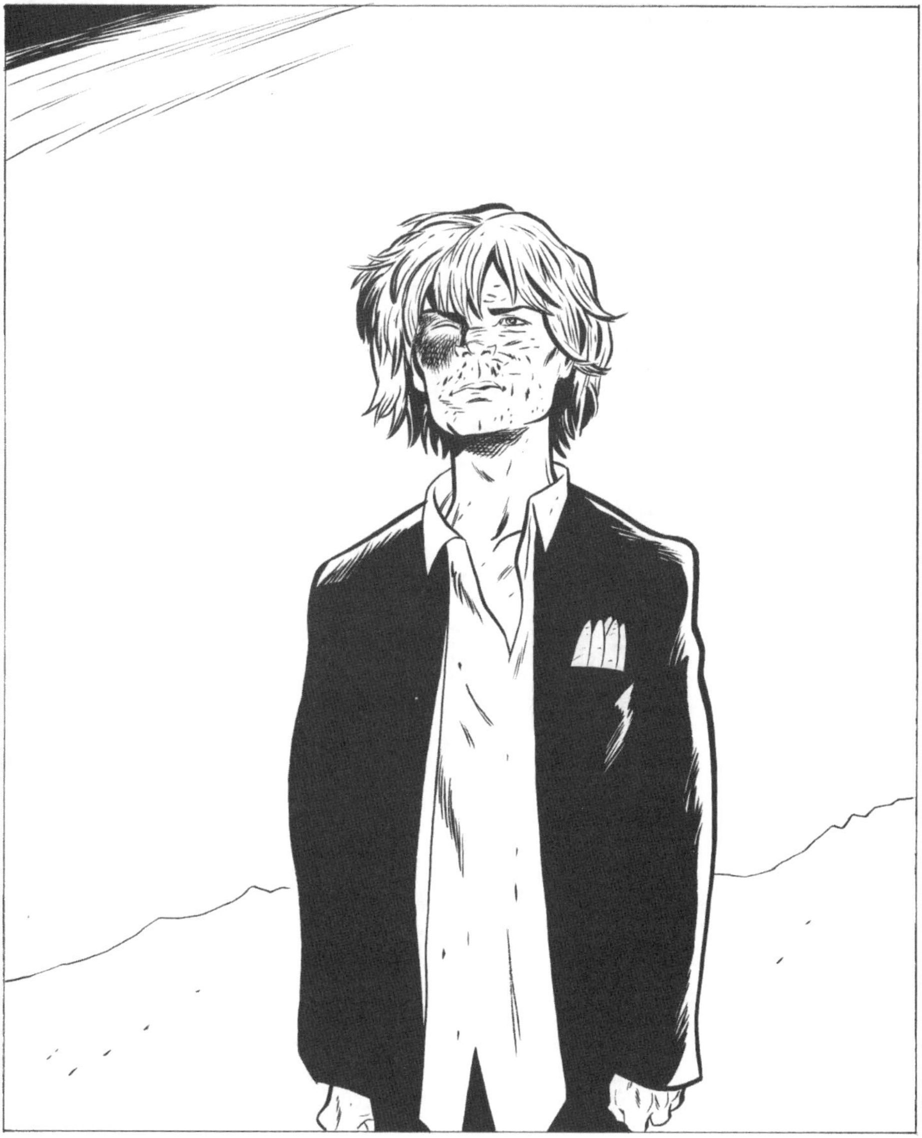

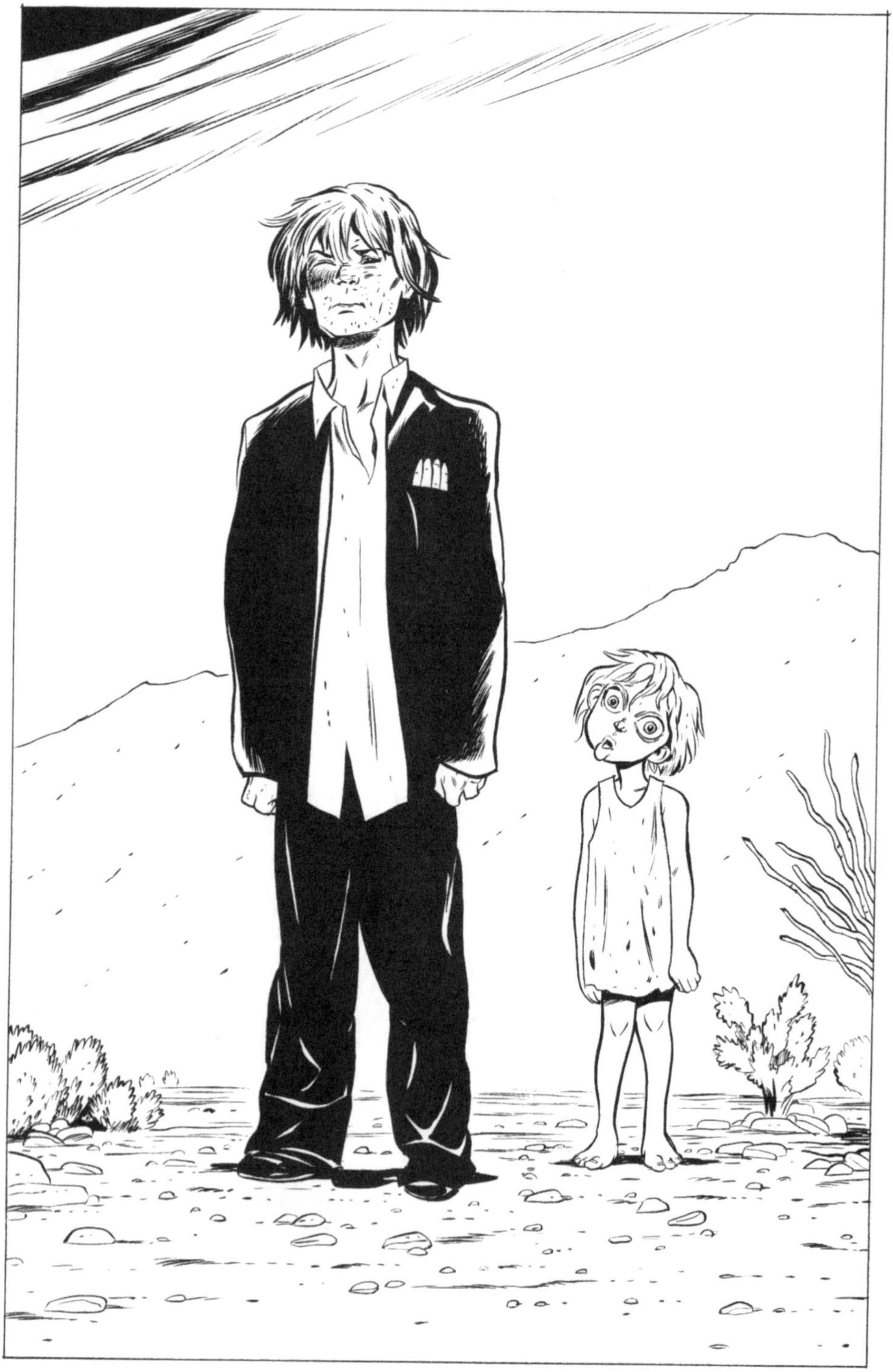

TO BE CONTINUED IN
RASL POCKET BOOK 2

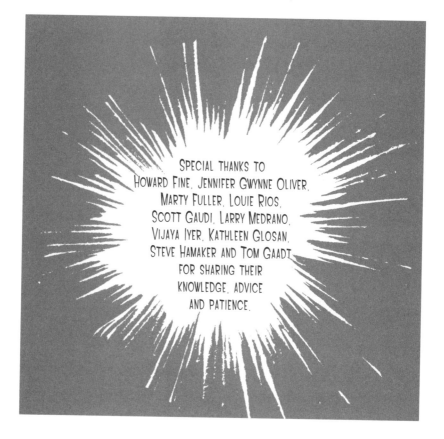

SPECIAL THANKS TO
HOWARD FINE, JENNIFER GWYNNE OLIVER,
MARTY FULLER, LOUIE RIOS,
SCOTT GAUDI, LARRY MEDRANO,
VIJAYA IYER, KATHLEEN GLOSAN,
STEVE HAMAKER AND TOM GAADT
FOR SHARING THEIR
KNOWLEDGE, ADVICE
AND PATIENCE.

A Brief Bibliography

Books:

Fabric of the Cosmos
by Brian Greene
(Vintage)

Parallel Worlds
by Michio Kaku
(Anchor Books)

Secrets of the Unified Field
by Joseph P. Farrell
(Adventures Unlimited Press)

Paths of Life
edited by Sheridan & Parezo (University of
Arizona Press)

The Philadelphia Experiment
by Moore & Berlitz
(Fawcett)

DVDs:

Tesla: Master of Lightning
(PBS Home Videos)

Nova: The Elegant Universe
(WGBH Boston Video)

Cosmos by Carl Sagan
(Cosmos Studios)

*Holes in Heaven? H.A.A.R.P. and Advances in
Tesla Technology*
(NSI)

Frankenstein
directed by James Whale
(Universal Studio)

Google:

Key words: Tesla, H.A.A.R.P., Philadelphia
Experiment, Tunguska. Enter any combina-
tion of these words and hold on to your hat!

ABOUT THE AUTHOR:

A co-founder of the 90's Self-Publishing Movement, and an early adopter of the graphic novel format, Jeff Smith is best known as the writer and artist of *BONE*, an award winning adventure about three cartoon cousins lost in a world of myth and ancient mysteries. In 2008, Smith was the subject of a documentary called *The Cartoonist: Jeff Smith, BONE, and the Changing Face of Comics*.

Besides *BONE* and *RASL*, his other books include *Shazam: The Monster Society of Evil*, and *Little Mouse Gets Ready*!